COOKING
WITH THE
NEW
AMERICAN
CHEFS

Anne Cullen tormey
alliance 1985
8 october

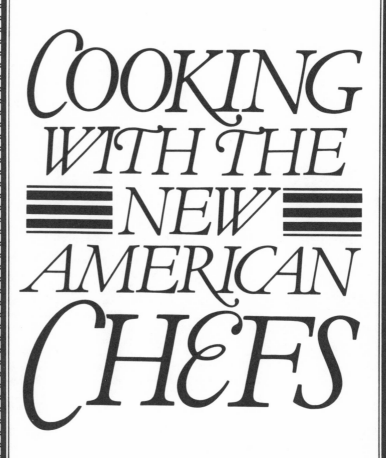

COOKING WITH THE NEW AMERICAN CHEFS

ELLEN BROWN

A Harper Colophon Book

1817

HARPER & ROW, PUBLISHERS, NEW YORK

CAMBRIDGE, PHILADELPHIA, SAN FRANCISCO, LONDON
MEXICO CITY, SÃO PAULO, SYDNEY

Photo credits: John Barr, pages 30, 72, 76, 104; G. Andrew Boyd, 66; Jim Dennis, 94; Paul Fetters, 24; Rick Friedman, 38; Jeanne Marklin, 50; Doug Menuez, 42; Kenny Wasserman, 16. All other photographs are reprinted courtesy of individual chefs.

Grateful acknowledgment is made for permission to reprint the recipes for Jalapeño Cheese Bread, Chicken and Seafood Jambalaya, Sweet-Potato Pecan Pie, Red Beans and Rice with Ham Hocks and Andouille Smoked Sausage, Duck Etouffée, Seafood Filé Gumbo and Blackened Redfish from *Chef Paul Prudhomme's Louisiana Kitchen* by Paul Prudhomme. Copyright © 1984 by Paul Prudomme. Reprinted by permission of William Morrow & Company, Inc.

Anne Greer sorbet recipes are reprinted by permission of Cuisinart Cooking Club.

The recipes on the following pages are copyright by Barbara Tropp: 151, 152, 156, 171, 237, 268, 284, 294, 299, 314, 315.

FIRST EDITION

Design by Joel Avirom

Library of Congress Cataloging in Publication Data

Brown, Ellen.
   Cooking with the new American chefs.

   Includes index.
   1. Cookery, American.   2. Cooks—United States.
I. Title.
TX715.B491453 1985   641.5   84–48141
ISBN 0–06–015373–3   85 86 87 88 89 10 9 8 7 6 5 4 3 2 1
ISBN 0–06–091237–5 (pbk.)   85 86 87 88 89 10 9 8 7 6 5 4 3 2 1

ACKNOWLEDGMENTS

To the chefs, for sharing themselves and their creativity so generously; without their cooperation this book would have been impossible. Thanks especially to Barbara Tropp and Anne Greer for their personal friendship.

To David Vaughan, my wine consultant, for allowing me to tap his great talents and knowledge of pairing wine and food.

To Leonida Weintraub and Donna Gould, my agents, who had faith in my idea and without whose efforts the idea might never have found a publisher.

To Ann Bramson, my editor, for her constant encouragement and enthusiasm, and her willingness to provide guidance while allowing me the flexibility to tell the chefs' stories in my own way.

To Meredith Armstrong, the best bread tester and friend a person could be lucky enough to have.

To Carol Cutler, Jan Fox, Connie Kurz, John Mariani, Joan Nathan, Diane Worthington, and Lisa Yockelson, my colleagues in the food world, for their expertise and advice on how to write a good cookbook.

To Peggy Loar, Katherine Morrison, Lucy Scardino Ainslie, Jack Lichtenstein, Nancy Unger, Kip Forbes, Nancy Malitz, Lyn Farmer, Michael Ainslie, Dianne Spencer, Bunny Polmer, and many other friends for their support, encouragement, and attendance at what seemed like an endless string of testing dinners.

To Lorraine Hamblin, for her participation in this project from the beginning and putting up with the typing deadlines set for her.

To the management of *USA Today,* my former employer, for their cooperation, and for sparking the idea through various chefs interviewed on assignment.

To Sam Cat the Magnificent and George Washington Park Cat, my constant companions, who kept me company every minute and ate all the mistakes.

AUTHOR UPDATE: Between the time these interviews were conducted and publication of this book the following changes have occurred: Mark Miller has sold his interest in the Fourth Street Grill and is living in Sante Fe, New Mexico; Amy Ferguson has left Charley's 517 and is a chef in Kona, Hawaii; and owing to financial difficulties, China Moon is not open to the public.

(202)
965-2300

PART II

THE RECIPES

PART I

THE CHEFS

America severed political ties with England more than two hundred years ago. Yet it was only after World War II that we began to emerge from a chronic case of cultural and culinary inferiority.

In the arts, the likes of Jackson Pollock and Willem de Kooning created Abstract Expressionism as the postwar style, and soon New York eclipsed Paris as the world's art center. No one quibbled if the artists were foreign-born; they were credited as American artists.

We began to appreciate artists whose styles were indebted to European movements, but whose imagery was as homegrown as Kansas corn. Following the violence of the Abstract Expressionists was the light-hearted cockiness of Pop Art, glorifying the everyday objects of American society, such as Andy Warhol's Campbell's soup cans and the comic-strip romances of Roy Lichtenstein.

But it took American cuisine thirty years longer to come of age—in part because its intellectual base was soufflé light. American cooking consisted of regional fare verbally transmitted, with the most basic recipes recorded for the novice.

Food was viewed as the fuel to power our bodies. And the American spirit of independence likened an appreciation of fine food to a sense of European snobbery antithetical to the pioneer spirit. Little did we ever think that today fast-food chains would be serving croissant sandwiches, and quiche fillings would be next to the chocolate milk at the supermarkets.

From the White House with its state dinners to the salons of the New York Four Hundred, to the mansions of Nob Hill, haute cuisine implied a slavish re-creation of Escoffier's dicta. It was the style that rich Americans assumed, and rightly so, was being served at similar tables in Paris. The American culinary heritage, from Rhode Island johnnycakes to New Mexican posole, was maintained for the family, but rarely for guests.

As World War II made the U.S. the refuge for artists, so the return of the soldiers fundamentally changed the course of American cuisine. Soldiers who fought for the beachheads at Anzio also discovered Neapolitan pizza, and soon an enterprising Ike Sowell opened the first pizzeria—Pizzeria Uno in Chicago. Similarly, the soldiers who served in the Orient returned with a craving for Oriental foods.

During the 1950s and '60s, gastronomic gurus such as M. F. K. Fisher, Craig Claiborne, Julia Child, and the late James Beard gave cooking a sense of dignity and adventure.

Fisher explored the sensuality of cooking, down to the most seemingly commonplace bowl of mashed potatoes. Beard's recipes were imbued with love for ingredients and theatrical flair in their use. Claiborne drew upon his position in the cultural and ethnic center, and from the chefs manning New York's kitchens, to add international flavor to the food pages of the *New York Times*. And Child, who says all she did was "take the la-de-dah out of sauces," appealed to the growing number of college-educated cooks—admittedly mostly women when *Mastering the Art of French Cooking,* Volume 1, appeared in 1962. Her greater influence was in demystifying cooking before an estimated three million viewers on television. She elevated cooking to an intellectual pastime worthy of effort and attention.

Through Beard's and Fisher's writings, through Child's books and TV series, through Claiborne's columns, an awareness arose of the pleasure of food. And our appreciation of food's sensual potential dovetailed in the 1960s with our growing awareness of human sensuality. "The *Joy of Cooking* went hand in hand with the *Joy of Sex,"* said Betty Fussell, author of *Masters of American Cooking.*

But the cuisine most revered remained French. When Child was removing the "la-de-dah," she was still talking about French sauces and their mastery. French was still revered, in our restaurants and our kitchens. The great American restaurants had menus written in French, maître d's with French accents, and wine lists listing nothing but French châteaux.

On the fringes were the "continental" restaurants, about which food writer Calvin Trillin once quipped, "The continent in question must be Antarctica since all the food was frozen."

American cooking was relegated to being an offshoot of tourism. We ate tacos in Tucson, crab cakes in Baltimore, oyster stew in Boston, gumbo in New Orleans, and grits in Charleston. Discovering regional American foods became part of the traveler's adventure.

But all of this has changed. An American cuisine, cooked primarily by the new breed of American-born and college-educated chefs, has taken root as deeply as a Vermont maple. The chefs, primarily under forty, are responding to a climate of educated palates, cleared by the generation before them. They are being applauded by an audience indulged by "fancy French food"; weaned on quiches, Brie, and

Chablis; and willing to progress beyond them.

The new American chefs draw from their imaginations to create personal styles. Some bring to cooking philosophies developed in unrelated academic areas such as Chinese philosophy and electrical engineering. Others are classically trained in the time-honored French traditions, and believe that, as in jazz or the visual arts, the classics must be mastered before improvisation can begin.

California is the American Garden of Eden as well as the source of the finest fruits of the vine, and it is not surprising that most of the culinary ferment is taking place in that state. There is an abundance of the freshest and most varied ingredients, and a clientele for those foodstuffs. But, while the concentration of culinary pioneers might be higher in California, those chefs have counterparts in every region of the country.

More than three hundred food writers, chefs, and restaurateurs gathered in New Orleans in 1983 to battle over the definition of what American cuisine was and who its authentic practitioners were. No consensus was reached, with James Villas of *Town and Country* magazine damning those chefs experimenting with American products using nouvelle French techniques, and Betsy Balsley, food editor of the Los Angeles *Times*, defending the school of "maverick chefs."

By the time the Symposium on American Cuisine met in Boston the following year, the emphasis had shifted from a definition to an exploration of the American larder, which is the greatest in the world. But the recognition of that abundance had been blurred by the same sense of inferiority.

John Mariani in his keynote address at the 1984 Symposium, listed the products exported to the rest of the world from our shores. "The Italians would not be doing tomato sauce if we hadn't sent them the tomato in the Eighteenth century, and there would be no chili peppers in Szechuan food if they were not grown in this hemisphere first," said Mariani.

The new American chefs have no sense of inferiority. When they draw from the American cookery of the past, it is because it is a component of their philosophies. There are some who have based their styles on the American tradition, such as Lawrence Forgione in New York, Anne Greer in Dallas, and Bradley Ogden in San Francisco. But others of equal ability and creativity are more personal in their approach, and base their cuisines on foreign elements in their backgrounds or on their penchants for exotic flavors. Barbara Tropp's permutations on Chinese food for China Moon stem from her deep love and reverence for the culture, while the Oriental influences on Jackie Etcheber are based on her upbringing in Hong Kong.

While it may be impossible to define American cuisine, it is quite easy to describe new American chefs: They are cooking creatively with a personal style. They are concocting dishes nightly bearing personal signatures as large as John Hancock's on the Declaration of Independence. And they are shaping the next chapter in the history of American food. ∎

MARCEL DESAULNIERS

■ The Trellis ■

W

illiamsburg, in the Tidewater area of coastal Virginia, was brought back to life by its restoration to colonial grandeur. Part of the re-creation—beyond blacksmith's shops and the venerable House of Burgesses—was also re-creating colonial fare for the Colonial Williamsburg Foundation's inns and taverns. Game pies and Brunswick stews reigned supreme in the community so important to American history until Marcel Desaulniers began providing an alternative when The Trellis opened in 1980.

Visitors now have the option of eating their country ham, a colonial staple, with coffee-laced red-eye gravy, or as a julienne along with sautéed lump backfin crabmeat from the nearby Chesapeake Bay on scallion tagliatelle garnished with toasted almonds. Instead of Surry sausage served alongside scrambled eggs, Desaulniers's patrons can enjoy the regional specialty with roasted red peppers and jalapeño fettuccine.

"In a town like Williamsburg, my challenge is to be creative for my own sense of self, but at a reasonable cost, and pastas are a way I can do both."

The sense of realism underpinning creativity is one of Desaulniers's hallmarks as a chef, and one that has made him look to the ingredients of Virginia for their proximity as well as the individuality they add to his food.

Becoming a chef was the way Desaulniers, now thirty-nine, could be assured of having good food in his family. Born and raised in Woonsocket, R.I., he is from a French-Canadian background. "I spoke only French until I was in school, and my mother was a horrible cook.

"When I was in high school a friend's father was general manager of one of the mills that employed most of the town, and he had friends who were chefs in New York. I would eat things at his house like rabbit and wild game, and after eating chop suey and hard hamburgers all my life it was a great awakening. My taste buds were turned on for the first time, and I learned the difference between eating and dining. I remember the men lighting different brandies to see the proof."

He remembers telling his

mother about the meals, and her lack of interest in duplicating them. "My father was dead and my dear mother was raising six children on her own, and she hardly had time or energy left for good food, so I decided I'd learn to be the chef of the family."

After jobs in various Rhode Island restaurants, Desaulniers was sponsored for the Culinary Institute of America, still in New Haven, Connecticut, on the campus of Yale between the forestry and divinity schools. "We had archaic kitchens, and the chefs were there almost as a vacation rather than because they were devoted to teaching, and when I graduated in 1965 it hardly opened any big doors for me. The CIA has come a long way since those days."

Desaulniers moved to New York, and after jobs in the executive dining room of the Irving Trust Company on Wall Street and at the Colony Club, an exclusive women's club on Park Avenue, he was drafted into the Marines and served in Vietnam.

"Starting out to be a chef in New York in those days, even if you had a French last name, was rough. No one would consider you for anything but a cook on the line."

After returning from the service in 1968, he became saucier at the Pierre Hotel, then was lured to the bucolic life of Virginia to do off-premises catering for the Colonial Williamsburg Foundation in 1970. "I had been so busy trying to survive in New York that I really never thought through my own philosophy as a chef, and I started doing a lot of reading and studying once I moved down here."

He left the kitchen entirely in 1974 to go into the food-brokerage business, and while he missed cooking, the travel involved gave him the opportunity to internalize a number of concepts about food he had been dabbling with.

"I visited California and saw the freshness and innovation going on there, and it was different from everything in the East, which was still so hung up on French food. I decided if that was the sort of cooking I could be doing, I'd go back on the firing line."

He teamed up with John Curtis, who runs an antique bookstore in Merchant's Square, and Tom Powers, a local wine merchant, and opened The Trellis. The flamestitch banquettes and peach linens are more reminiscent of a California restaurant than the antique appearance of most Williamsburg taverns. So is the aroma from the mesquite-charcoal grill.

The Trellis changes its menu with the seasons, and lunch and dinner are more like the meals of two different restaurants than expansions of the same concept. "This is basically a tourist town, and they don't want to spend a lot of time over lunch, so it's basically sophisticated fast food, with some grilled specialties, quiches, and salads."

But dinner is a different matter. Appetizers can include anything from braised tenderloin of beef with black beans, tomatoes, and jalapeño peppers served in miniature homemade hollowed-out brioches, to sautéed Chesapeake soft-shell crabs with Louisiana crawfish, to chilled salmon and fresh shiitake mushroom pâté with avocado cream sauce.

While Desaulniers draws from Virginia ingredients—both traditional ones such as Surry sausage, Urbana ducks, Smithfield hams, and the many species of fish from Chesapeake Bay—he does not consider the food at The Trellis an updating of

Virginia fare. "What I am doing is applying the principles of California cooking and lightness to the ingredients we have here, but I don't limit myself to those ingredients. I am interested in all regions of American cooking, especially the Southwest. I love black beans, and have used them in everything from salads and stews to pastas."

In addition to the foods that were around in colonial days, he is intrigued by the fresh shiitake mushrooms and cheeses being produced in the state. "One of the problems we face not being near a large metropolitan area is ingredients, and even with air shipments to Richmond, if I can find things grown locally they will be fresher."

The Trellis makes quick breads—from apricot almond to scallion soda bread—daily, and churns all its own ice creams and sorbets. One sorbet, made from beer, was developed for a tasting dinner to follow the tenderloin with black beans, and proved so popular it has become a standard intermezzo. And Desaulniers's imagination is also imprinted on the ice creams. Drawing from the colonial heritage, he makes pumpkin caramel ice cream that is like a frozen pumpkin pie, but much more intensely flavored.

In addition, Desaulniers's staff put up a number of different chutneys and preserves, including native damson plums and apricot with raisins, which he serves with simple grilled meats. In the summer, they pickle cherries to accompany pâtés.

"There are a number of delicious fruits native to this part of the country, and a lot of them were planted by Thomas Jefferson in Charlottesville, and then moved to this part of the state."

Although Desaulniers has one foot in the traditional rolling hills of Virginia and the other in the avant-garde kitchens of California, he unites the seemingly disparate styles with his concern for the diner: "I want food to be interesting but not so bizarre that dishes won't give people a good eating experience. What I'm interested in is maintaining high quality with consistency. I tell the staff that I want them to pretend that Julia Child or James Beard is in the dining room every night, and that's who they're cooking for." ∎

RECIPES FROM MARCEL DESAULNIERS

JACKIE ETCHEBER

■ *Jackie's* ■

J ackie Etcheber looks too frail to be lifting a ten-gallon stockpot almost her height off the stove of her restaurant. She's just five feet tall, and has the delicate features of a porcelain doll a tourist might bring home from her native Hong Kong.

But the recipe for the success of Jackie's, the dream come true for this thirty-one-year-old, who arrived in this country at the age of seventeen with $1,000 to her name, is based on her tough fiber. Start with equal parts of talent, intelligence, and energy. Blend with the skill of the chefs from whom she learned cooking. Add a dash of romance, perhaps some luck, for jobs came open at opportune times. The end result is Jackie's, her forty-five-seat restaurant behind a green-and-white-striped awning in Chicago's Lincoln Park West neighborhood.

Her menu reflects her Oriental background and her Western training at the hands of master chef Jean Banchet at La Mer in Chicago. She started at the salad station, and then convinced Banchet she could handle a spot on the cooking line as well. "I learn fast. You only have to tell me something once. And I told Banchet from the beginning that I wanted my own restaurant; I was not there to work for him forever."

And she learned so quickly, and so well, that within six months after Jackie's opened, in September 1982, it was lauded in *Chicago* magazine as one of the new highlights of a city that prides itself on elegant dining options.

Etcheber's original goal was not to be a chef but to be a hotel manager in Hong Kong. "A teacher in high school suggested that as a career since Hong Kong is such a popular spot for tourism. Since we were raised bilingual, she suggested I come to this country to learn.

"My father thought I should be a secretary if I wanted to work, and then get married and have children. And my mother just thought I was crazy. So I asked my father for $1,000, since I heard I could work as a waitress during the summer to support myself after the first year."

She first enrolled in Ottumwa Heights College, a junior college in Iowa attended by a friend from home. And then she was accepted in the hotel-management program at the University of Houston, entering in 1973.

She began as an assistant manager for a small restaurant in Chicago's Ritz-Carlton in 1976, and then switched to restaurant management at the nearby Park Hyatt after one year. "The Hyatt was the up and coming hotel, and when the steward quit, I asked to be transferred to the kitchen. The food and beverage director and the general manager thought I was crazy. It was a job nobody wanted—to work with a bunch of dirty pans in a hot kitchen. But after six months I proved a woman could do the job."

While at the Ritz-Carlton, Jackie Shen met Pierre Etcheber, the handsome French-born

wine steward at her restaurant; they were married in 1981.

A first step to acquiring her own restaurant was taking the $4,000 she had saved to buy a seventeen-seat snack shop. "It was a taco place in a very conservative neighborhood, and everything I needed was there—a grill, an exhaust fan, a counter. I thought I'd take a chance, and if I lost I could always go back to the Hyatt. I called it Uncle Pete's Snack Shop, since I thought a family-oriented name would work. There was no payroll, and my break-even point was $60 a day."

But Etcheber was soon doing five times that amount. She developed a technique for handling customers that she now follows at Jackie's. She personally takes all reservations so she knows who is in the dining room and can greet them during momentary lulls in the kitchen.

"I am very good with names and faces, and what people like and don't like. People know if you're paying attention to them, and they like attention if they go to a restaurant to eat, no matter what sort of restaurant it is. After a few times, I knew someone liked an egg-salad sandwich for lunch, or extra cream in their coffee. That built the business."

After owning Uncle Pete's for eighteen months, she sold it for $20,000 in 1981, and Pierre invested the money. She then went to work at La Mer.

"I was doing two jobs after a few months, and I'd also watch what the pastry chef was doing every moment I could and I'd go home at night and practice pastry making on my own."

After a year at La Mer, she quit because her hot temper matched that of the chef. "We almost murdered each other a few times, and when I quit I didn't have a job. But I heard that week that Le Ciel Bleu needed a cook on the line."

In the less than two years since the sale of her snack shop, Pierre had parlayed her working capital to $60,000, $35,000 of which was pledged to the contractor for renovations of a bar, then called Oscar, on North Lincoln Avenue.

Diners are greeted by a panel of etched glass depicting lotus flowers, echoed by a similar pattern above the bar. The walls are a pale gray, and a mirrored wall at the far end of the room visually expands the narrow storefront space.

She talks as rapidly as she works, and expects her staff to share her drive and hours. She arrives at Jackie's at 6 A.M. to supervise the kitchen cleaning, orders for the day, cooks lunch, and then immediately launches into dinner, ending her day around midnight.

But she says, "It's different when you're doing what you want to do, and it's your own. I know I'm not the easiest person to work for because I expect everyone to work as hard as I do."

And what is also decidedly her own is the style of food at Jackie's. The silky chicken-liver pâté is classically French, while her poached salmon with vermicelli in a white wine chive sauce is more than a casual nod to nouvelle cuisine. The fillet of whitefish is baked with water chestnuts, bamboo shoots, baby corn, and ginger; and the rainbow trout stuffed with a julienne of turnips and carrots and mushroom purée is sauced with Chinese rose wine in addition to the saffron cream sauce. Then one evening there is a boned breast of pheasant as a special. The succulent meat is rolled around a stuffing of sweetbread purée, spinach, and pistachio nuts, and the sliced medallions are placed on a morel and chanterelle sauce.

If Jackie's needs definition, the bent is toward seafood, which is prepared in basically a French fashion with Chinese influences and artful presentation, and never to be overlooked is her own imagination.

"I love doing fish, and place most of my time on the nightly specials since I can get bored doing the same dishes too often. I throw in Oriental ingredients and love making discoveries in Chinese grocery stores. But I don't follow the methods of Chinese chefs."

A julienne of snow peas is one of her favorite garnishes, and sesame seeds and oil, ginger, green onions, and bok choy find their way into many dishes. "My only rule for cooking is never walk away from a piece of fish when it's cooking. Dishes like whitefish and scallops of salmon should not cook for more than a minute or they will dry out."

She relies on her seafood purveyor to alert her to any potential specials. A nightly option is a hot seafood salad, which typifies her style. One evening, plump mussels were surrounding a leaf of radicchio filled with a warm noodle mixture and topped with dollops of warm goat cheese and golden caviar.

Desserts also vary, and combine the Chinese preference for fresh fruit with the richness of a crème pâtisserie. "I love fruit tarts, and I love the way the fruit looks arranged on top." On a given evening she usually offers diners three or four options on a silver tray. They may include apricot, blueberry, and peach tarts, to be complemented by richer choices such as a walnut rum tart and double chocolate cake.

The wine list for Jackie's was chosen by Pierre, and, like the menu items, it is reasonably priced. "I've been conscious of saving money since I came to this country, but I'll never cut corners on ingredients. But I'm very aware of waste, and do many jobs myself so I can save money."

She thinks her clientele appreciates her food, and does not worry if the dining room has fifty people in the course of an evening rather than one hundred.

"After we were so well reviewed, it was suddenly mobbed. But I can feel from customers if they're in to have a good time and enjoy the food, or if their attitude is to challenge me and see if I'm really as good as they say I am. There's a whole different look on their faces and in the way they say hello to me. And I do care. Jackie's is what I have wanted for a long time." ∎

RECIPES FROM JACKIE ETCHEBER

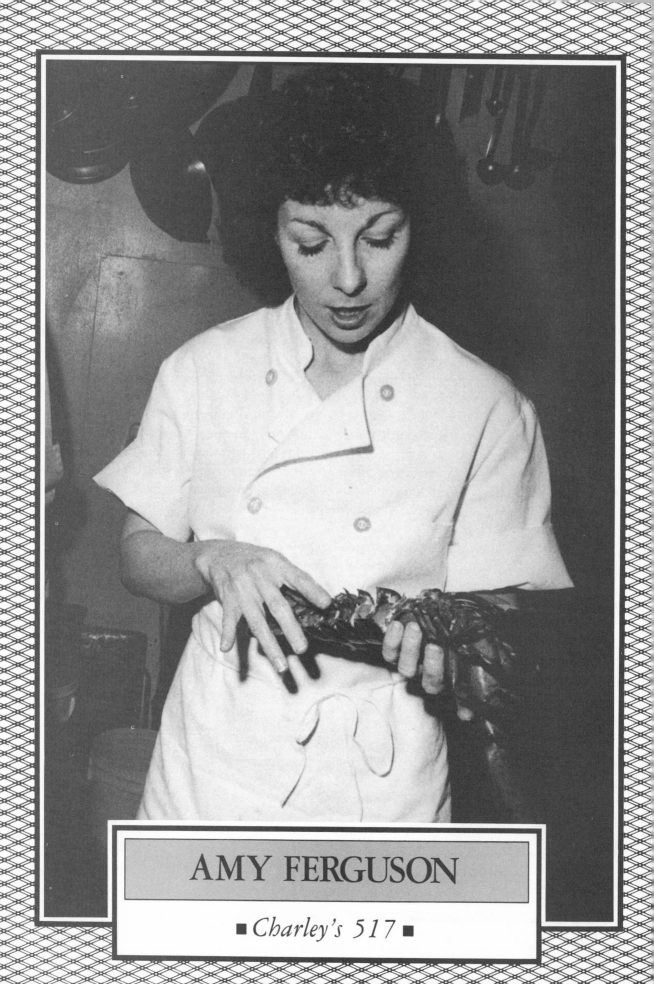

AMY FERGUSON

■ *Charley's 517* ■

W

hile other eleven-year-old girls in Houston were reading Nancy Drew mystery stories and watching the *Donna Reed Show* on television, Amy Ferguson was teaching herself to cook from the *Larousse Gastronomique* and was devoted to Julia Child and the *Galloping Gourmet.* She drew looks of incredulity (since they'd barely heard of Paris) from her grade-school class when she said her goal was to become a Cordon Bleu chef.

Ferguson is now at twenty-nine the executive chef at Charley's 517, the showplace of the General Leisure Corporation's chain of Texas restaurants.

One aspect of her cooking has not changed in eighteen years—the emotional satisfaction she derives from it. "My strongest instinct is one of liking to cater to people, and I learned at an early age that my food pleased people. I find food is visually and physically satisfying. I love the textures, colors, and smells of it; it's the same reason that I'm wild about flowers and used to work the graveyard shift at a twenty-four-hour florist.

"But the real payoff for me was doing something special for family and friends."

When she was fourteen, she catered her parents' twenty-fifth wedding anniversary, with a cold salmon mousse, cream puffs, and breads she had baked. "I knew all I wanted to do was be a cook, and I had seen Humphrey Bogart in *Sabrina.* I was such a dreamer and a romantic that I thought that was what it was all about."

Armed with instinct if not knowledge, Ferguson went to Paris at age fifteen, to study at the Cordon Bleu as well as the Sorbonne and the American College. "I kept wanting to learn more and more, so I'd sneak into bake shops and charcuteries. I still love to butcher meat, and the structure of the French kitchens influenced my thinking for how my kitchen runs today.

"Everyone in the French kitchen took orders from the chef. There was no room for

personal interpretation, or women for that matter. The majority of my staff are women, and I want to allow people their own creative flow, within reason. So many chefs of either sex cannot let go."

Ferguson says she would never turn down a good cook of either sex, but likes the fluidity of a female-oriented kitchen. "I can't stand it when it's slow. I dance around like a ballerina and kick people off the line so I can keep working and moving." And that's just the sort of energy that propelled her to her present position.

She returned to Houston in 1975 and, by becoming a vegetarian, she shed the sixty pounds she had gained in Paris and began teaching cooking at the University of Houston and Gourmet World, the city's foremost cooking school and the one Ferguson had attended as a teenager. "It was a thrill for me to be asked to teach there, because Neva Paul, from whom I learned, was the city's best-known teacher, and when she died they asked me to take over her classes."

But teaching was too sedentary, and Ferguson had never lost the dream that led her to Paris—her own kitchen. She landed a job at Che by "picking the most prestigious restaurant in the city and literally chasing the chef, Tom Emerick, around the city for two weeks from meat market to bakery until I convinced him to hire me. I had no restaurant experience, and he'd never worked with a woman before."

In the two years before she took over as executive chef at age twenty-two, Ferguson learned the business, and then she began carving out her own culinary style. A carryover from her Che period is a fondness for dual, complementary sauces with dishes. She tops loin of lamb with a béarnaise enriched with glace de viande, but underneath it is a wine-reduction sauce, and she'll use a red-wine reduction with salmon topped with hollandaise. "I think I started doing dual sauces because I worry about not being creative enough. I'm very critical of myself, and think of all I have to learn."

Regardless of her self-doubts, her reputation and Che's two-star rating her first year as chef made her appealing to J. William Sharman, Jr., president of General Leisure. After converting a club and pool hall called Western Off the Square into Charley's, an elegant French restaurant, he started courting Ferguson in 1981.

The restaurant's decor is an elegant mix, with French Impressionist and contemporary paintings suspended in front of mirrors behind bottle-green leather banquettes. The lounge area is decorated with framed collections of old performing-arts programs, and vases of orchids top the grand piano separating the lounge from the ninety-seat dining room, further set off by an antique Chinese Coromandel screen.

There's nothing about the setting that implies it's in Houston except the names on the theater programs. What has made the restaurant part of its location is Ferguson's reliance on the game and garnishes indigenous to the region.

"During the years I was a vegetarian, I became acutely aware of the importance of freshness, and I started looking at what was best and freshest without having to fly it in. I'm a Texan; I was hunting at an early age and my father taught me to smoke meats when I was a child. But Texans were ashamed of our food, and thought the only good food was French. I should know, since I felt that way, too. But it's now considered acceptable to use local products and mix them with a French influence. I'll serve frogs' legs dipped in a Southern fritter batter or put a classic Norman dish like veal and Calvados next to a mixed grill of Texas game on my menu, or put a fresh cilantro sauce on John Dory."

Her menu stresses game, but it is handled with sensitivity to the individual flavors. "I like to cook over a fire of mesquite, pecan, hickory, and grapevines in a smoking pit in back of the restaurant, but I've found grapevine is too strong for domestic rabbit, so I do rabbit first before adding vines to the fire, then I'll smoke the black buck and axis venison after they have been marinated in different marinades, and place herbs on the fire for the last few minutes."

What she achieves is the perfect embellishment of each meat, and then she takes her sense of French refinement to the garnishes. She makes spiced cantaloupe to serve with game dishes, and contrasts the sweet and sour flavor with light fried corncakes and a vegetable mélange of corn, red and green bell peppers, and a touch of jalapeño.

But not all dishes at Charley's follow this newly emerging side of Ferguson's talents. There are still many dishes rooted in classic French that she is personalizing. Her quenelles are light enough to make Escoffier proud, but she makes them with smoked salmon and scallops, and tops them with a julienne of red and yellow peppers and a fresh dill sauce. Her slices of sautéed foie gras are sauced with a French-inspired mushroom ragout, but the mushrooms are all American wild mushrooms.

Her salad dressings are still vinaigrettes, but she'll use tequila and lime or hazelnuts and sherry vinegar as flavorings.

The presentation of her dishes follows suit; they are arranged but not formal. "I'm down to earth, and not a frou-frou cook. I want the garnishes on plates to have a purpose." The long thin strips of sautéed salsify on the buttery slices of foie gras are an example.

Desserts are the course still owing the most allegiance to French cooking. Her charlotte is fused with fresh mint, inlaid with strawberries, and covered with a raspberry sauce, and her flourless chocolate soufflé is light but still intensely flavored with chocolate.

"My food may be changing but my attitude is the same as when I was a little girl. There's a spirit of loving and giving in cookery that makes me feel fulfilled as a person at the end of an evening at the stove." ∎

RECIPES FROM AMY FERGUSON

LAWRENCE FORGIONE

■ An American Place ■

No restaurant could be as appropriately named as the one behind a black awning on Lexington Avenue in New York: An American Place. It describes both the conceptions of the dishes and the ingredients comprising them.

The restaurant, owned by chef Lawrence Forgione, uses no imported foods. And Forgione is the first to admit that the dishes he creates could not have been listed on his menu a decade ago, since the raw ingredients were not domestically obtainable. Encouraging the production of everything from smoked shrimp to fresh foie gras has been as important to Forgione as developing his own style of cooking, one based on historic American foods lightened and updated to suit the palates of today.

"The key to the future of American cooking is to get the ingredients. I remember reading that Ferdinand Point once said of La Pyramide that you can't have great food without great ingredients. And I decided that no American-food restaurant could be of world-class caliber until the ingredients were at that level."

But Forgione needed the distance of the Atlantic Ocean to come to these conclusions. While he now draws inspiration from nineteenth-century American cookbooks, his first mentors were French, and his presentations are based on his nouvelle training.

Forgione respects the honesty and integrity of American food, and does not believe that unattractive presentation goes hand-in-hand with simple concepts. Even an oven-roasted potato is sliced and slightly shingled when it appears on a plate. He greets criticism of his elegance with anger. "Critics who don't understand that food—no matter where it's drawn from—must appeal to the eyes

An American Place

969 LEXINGTON AVENUE
NEW YORK, NEW YORK 10021
(212) 517-7660

before it hits the stomach are missing a basic point of cooking. They will criticize my pâté as 'too fussy' and review one from a nearby French restaurant and praise the elegance of a similar presentation."

Forgione, a thirty-two-year-old Long Island native, entered the kitchen as a short-term necessity rather than a long-term goal. He was a physical-education major at a college in West Virginia, and had to skip a semester after contracting pneumonia. A cousin owned a catering firm in Brooklyn, and Forgione started in the business by "picking through parsley, and doing all the things an eighteen-year-old with no experience would do."

He soon became hooked on working with food, and stayed with the firm for one year, after which he went to work at the posh Breakers Hotel in Palm Beach, Florida.

"I realized food appealed to my senses and it was exciting to see all this action going on in the kitchen."

Without hesitation, he enrolled in the Culinary Institute in Hyde Park, and graduated in 1974. His goal was to work at one of New York's fine French restaurants, so he sought additional training at the source for the style.

"As a young American interested in cooking you couldn't get a job in a French kitchen. The French government had closed the doors, since all the foreigners were willing to work for nothing, and the kitchens had become flooded with Japanese by that time."

He secured a job at London's Connaught Hotel, working for Michel Bourdin, who had been sous chef at Maxim's. "I was there for more than two years, and each day I would see wonderful new foods we didn't have here—the seafood from France, chanterelles and black chanterelles, tiny haricots verts. It started to dawn on me, how come they have everything and we have nothing? Why don't we have chanterelles in the U.S.? We have trees, don't we?"

As he began to formulate his principles of cooking, the European experience was also making him more patriotic. "In the U.S., when someone asks you what you are, you usually say the country where your grandparents were born, but in Europe you say you're an American. In food, I realized my country was getting the short end of the stick, and for no reason."

He returned to New York in 1977, and took a job at Régine's, the first foreign outpost for the Paris restaurant. Michel Guérard was the executive chef, and Forgione began as a saucier, then three months later took over the kitchen as chef.

A year later, he met Buzzy O'Keefe, owner of the River Café, a floating restaurant in the shadow of the Brooklyn Bridge, offering an unobstructed view of the lower Manhattan skyline.

"O'Keefe said he had a good restaurant, but wanted a great restaurant. I realized, since it has 136 seats, I would have the buying power to develop the products I wanted to use."

He talked Paul Kaiser, an upstate New York poultry farmer, into raising the free-ranging chickens he still uses. And he began American Spoon Foods in Michigan to ship buffalo to New York.

"I wanted the great ingredients, and I began to believe that, to give American cooking a place in the future with what we've learned, we have to reach back to the integrity of yesterday."

His approach was validated by the late James Beard, who replaced the French masters as Forgione's guru and mentor. "Jim could remember all the foods that have disappeared that I'm now trying to have cultivated again. I look at the apples on the market, and there are so few, and he would tell me about the ones that used to grow in his yard in Portland."

While the size of his orders from the River Café encouraged his sources, the lack of control he could exert in the kitchen caused frustration. He wanted his own restaurant, and he wanted it less than half as large.

An American Place is not the first great restaurant to occupy the slightly underground Lexington Avenue site. When Forgione first knew it, the late famed Japanese chef Masa Kobayashi was creating paintings with his food for Le Plaisir. "I was so uncomfortable when I came to talk about getting the space, we went and sat under a tree." He made the room lighter in every way, starting by cutting in a large window in the front, filling it with natural arrangements of tulips and pussy willows, and mirroring the wall at the back to reflect light through.

The interior of An American Place is as much an expression of Forgione's personality as the food. The walls are covered in taupe silk, on which abstract squiggles in earth tones were painted by an artist. "Earth tones are a sense of reality to me, and I needed these colors in the restaurant. I wanted sandstone and clay, but with elegance."

The table appointments follow the same theme. Flower arrangements in terracotta vases look totally unarranged; they are as if someone had picked a handful of wild flowers. In contrast, the votive candles next to them are set on frilly paper doilies.

The setting is as serene and tranquil as Forgione's food is elegant. "Nouvelle cuisine is an influence in cooking, not a cuisine. The cuisine I do here is American, but why should I not be able to express myself in an artistic way? Cooking is an art form.

"I want to give American food of the future an integrity by looking to the past, but I'm cooking in the present. My food must reflect that present, and I don't do slavish recreations of historic dishes, even those dishes with distinct roots in the past."

Forgione's sauces are based on stock reductions and on a deft hand with spicing that allows the inherent flavors of his ingredients to meld together with subtlety. Even his bolder conceptions, such as a corn and chili sauce for charred buffalo, is softened with cream.

Forgione alternates a number of different breads each night, including cornsticks and a buttery brioche fired with a large quantity of cracked black pepper. "One of the aspects of American cuisine I love is the diversity of the baked goods. We probably have more than any other culture, and just baking white bread—be it in a loaf pan or for a baguette—is boring for us and for customers who come often."

One of his signature dishes is a pâté made from three smoked American fish—

whitefish, salmon, and sturgeon—magnificently arranged and garnished with their respective golden, red, and black caviars. "Some people have criticized me that my food is too pretty to be American, and it bothers me that they equate American food with slopping stuff on a plate."

And Forgione makes sure that does not happen. He works the sauce station in the kitchen, in a corner where he can pivot easily to see everything going on and inspect each plate. "My sous chef is Richard D'Orazi, who was executive sous chef at the River Café with me, and this kitchen works with a feeling of family. There is a much higher sense of accomplishment than I ever had before."

The restaurant's size also means that each plate can be garnished differently; there is no vegetable du jour. For grilled rib steaks, he creates timbales called Ladies Cabbage. "I read about it, and it is cabbage that is blanched twice to remove the 'skunk' from the cabbage."

While that dish is derived from the East, Forgione explores the nuances of each region of American cooking. In his version of Southwestern food, he layers thin corn crêpes and barbecued Texas wild duck into a torte, and then serves a wedge surrounded by a rich duck sauce laced with a hint of chili and made colorful with fresh corn and diced red and green peppers. His Cajun-inspired creation is soft-shelled crawfish, which are soaked in milk, salt, and Tabasco, and then deep fried. They are served with a spicy sauce and freshly baked cornsticks.

The visual presentation of his food is matched by the complexity of the textures and flavors. His warm lobster and frogs'-legs salad is served with warm tiny white beans in the center, surrounded by medallions of lobster arranged on miner's lettuce (similar to mâche), and with warm vinaigrette spooned over. The frogs' legs were crisply fried, and placed around the perimeter of the arrangement like guards. The fillet of Pacific king salmon was topped with fresh shiitake mushrooms and giant smoked Gulf shrimp to resemble a seascape.

Looking at the component parts of nineteenth-century dishes and then adding his special touch is part of his cuisine. One such dish is a veal steak topped with a julienne of Montana beef jerky and garnished with morsels of sautéed sweetbreads. "I added green and red peppers to enhance the Western nature of the dish, but it basically goes back to one served in St. Louis in 1860." Among other innovations, pears are poached in maple syrup and garnished with wild hickory nuts before being coated with a velvety custard sauce, and crêpes are wrapped around a pungent mélange of wild elderberries and pears with a textural accent of toasted almonds.

For other entrées, the inspiration is more from American life than from any region's food. Picnic quail combines the fried breasts of the tiny birds coated with potato-chip crumbs with the leg sections marinated and grilled. The garnish is a sharp mixture of pickled cucumbers, pickled tomatoes, and pickled peppers. While few people take quail on a picnic, the rest of the dish is reminiscent of everyone's traditional Fourth of July.

This same eclectic approach—updating and inventing, treating American foodstuffs with nouvelle skill—extends to the lengthy list of desserts. His Bread Pudding is an entire loaf of bread soaked in an egg mixture and baked, with the slices remaining intact when served in a warm Bourbon sauce. In his Apple Pandowdy the apples remain crisp and are highly seasoned with molasses and spices, placed between slices of sweetened bread, and baked in individual soufflé dishes.

Forgione ends each meal with a tray of sweets that are down-to-earth and old-fashioned. No American can look at chocolate-chip cookies, sugary pecan pralines, and squares of chocolate fudge without nostalgia, even if they are eaten in an elegant restaurant rather than around grandma's kitchen table. ∎

RECIPES FROM LAWRENCE FORGIONE

SUSUMU FUKUI

■ *La Petite Chaya* ■

I n the early 1970s, when the Japanese food rage was introducing sushi to Americans who would not even eat cooked fish a decade before, there was a small coterie of Japanese chefs forging a culinary alliance with the West. While the Japanese were apprenticing in French kitchens to master the teachings of Escoffier, their French maîtres were absorbing the artful presentation and insistence on freshness that spawned nouvelle cuisine.

But the Japanese discovered, back in their native country, that classic French food needed modification to appeal to their countrymen's palates. The hybrid has become known as Franco-Japanese, and chef Susumu Fukui at La Petite Chaya (*chaya* is the Japanese word for teahouse) in Los Angeles is this country's first and most able practitioner.

But the style Fukui brought from Japan in 1982 has been broadened by the ingredients and clientele found in California. Although the menu at the sleek restaurant reads "La Nouvelle Cuisine Franco-Japonaise," now terming it Franco-Japonaise à la California would be a more apt description.

"The abundance and freshness of California's ingredients and my own convictions and French training allow me to be flexible and constantly create a contemporary cuisine," says Fukui. (All of the chef's quotes were translated from Japanese by Petite Chaya manager Patrick Harrington and owner Yuji Tsunoda, and to them go my thanks.)

Fukui's art form is dual. He is a master at blending Eastern and Western ingredients so that they remain in harmony, but combine to form unfamiliar and exciting tastes, and his presentations of dishes range from those as precise as a medieval enamel to others as spontaneous as an Abstract Expressionist oil. Just when you think you've figured dinner and his dishes out, he will add a new element to the matrix.

Fukui, now thirty-four, was born in the apple country in Aomori, in the northern part of Japan. "My older brother was a master of Japanese sweet cakes for seven years before he took on the art of French pastry. He would often come home in his white jacket, bringing with him the necessary ingredients for making those wonderful pastries, and make cakes and pastry for his family. I shall always remember how different they were from what we were used to seeing in the cake shops, and how beautiful as well as tasty they were." The garb also impressed Fukui, since Japanese chefs were not uniformed in tall white toques.

"I would look in his many cookbooks, and soon French cuisine be-

La Petite CHAYA

LA NOUVELLE CUISINE FRANCO - JAPONAISE RESTAURANT & BAR

came as familiar to me as Japanese cuisine. Until then I had thought of studying art, being most interested in classical Japanese painting such as was seen in the Momoyama Era."

But, as French cooking emerged as his primary interest, he began an apprenticeship in the Fontainebleau Restaurant of Tokyo's Imperial Hotel. "It was different work, and I learned to know various meats, vegetables, and fish by their French names. The chef was French, Robert Caiyo, and as I listened to his French echoing throughout the kitchen, everything was new and fresh."

After a stint at Régence, moving up the classical French ladder chefs such as Paul Bocuse had established in Japan's French restaurants, Fukui moved to La Marée de Chaya. Also owned by Yuji Tsunoda, who comes from a restaurant dynasty dating back to the seventeenth century, La Marée de Chaya is the restaurant credited internationally with the development of Franco-Japanese food, and Chef Kihachi Kumagai was its leading proponent.

"He studied at Maxim's in Paris, working there at the same time as Wolfgang Puck, and he began creating dishes in the French manner but using Japanese ingredients."

When Tsunoda, who had started planning an American chaya in the late 1970s, approached Fukui about moving here, "I thought that where I was would not make much difference. I had developed identity and personality in my culinary presentation, which I thought would remain the same no matter where I worked."

But prior to crossing the Pacific Tsunoda broadened Fukui's style by providing him training at some of the finest classic Japanese restaurants in Tokyo—Kappo, Ichinao, and Tatsumura. The chef had been first intrigued with French food, and now was well schooled in the hybrid, but was still unfamiliar with the Japanese part of its roots.

When Fukui arrived in Los Angeles, he was "astonished by the wealth of fresh ingredients. I began to think of the different things that I could do with my culinary abilities and the fresh and different materials. In addition, Los Angeles was a city where the four seasons in the year that I was used to often blended to only two. I studied the seasonal availability of the different ingredients, and concentrated on how I could make the changing of the seasons more obvious on the plates."

To learn this, Fukui started haunting the central markets in downtown Los Angeles.

Not only did working with new produce present challenges to Fukui, he was also adding another country into the equation of the French and Japanese elements in his food. And the complex equation is resulting in a flexibility in his cooking not present when he arrived in this country.

"I must remember that this is not Japan, but America. I work as always on French principles, but my French training allows me to be flexible and constantly create a contemporary cuisine. I am putting aside the classical recipes, but not the training."

His Americanization has led to the creation of dishes in which the three countries are integrated by technique and ingredients.

It's easy to pass by La Petite Chaya, since the plain façade is as unadorned as a rice-paper wall. The gray stone floor and simple bentwood chairs are warmed by the bottle-green velvet banquettes in the main dining room and the panels of smoked mirrors. On some walls there are contemporary paintings reminiscent of California, as is the open and airy enclosed patio, the light from which brightens the otherwise dark room at lunch.

Throughout the restaurant, art objects, from Buddha heads to Tantric sculptures in contorted poses, are placed on pedestals and spotlit with precision. Flower arrangements get the same treatment, but they are spare and done with restraint, in contrast to the profusion of flowers filling most Los Angeles restaurants.

Fukui and his staff of sixteen use the same restraint, balancing colors, flavors, and textures and arranging the foods with simplicity to form cohesive dishes—for the eyes and the palate.

He is fond of lamb, and will combine it with bacon, fresh water chestnuts, Chinese kale, and asparagus in a vinaigrette made with rice vinegar and sesame oil. At the same time, he will take a rack of lamb and sauce it in a French manner with a chived cream sauce.

He does a red snapper en papillote, and includes bacon, potatoes, and fresh shiitake mushrooms as part of the surprise when diners open the crescents of parchment. Or as an appetizer he will use wonton skins in lieu of puff pastry for a mille-feuille of raw tuna with a mixture of colorful vegetables from tomato to daikon and carrot.

While the French elements in his cuisine can be detected, it is becoming more difficult to draw the line between the lightness derived from Japanese food and the same quality found in California.

Some of the newer dishes, such as an artichoke salad with crawfish, foie gras, and haricots verts, and the salad of raw mushrooms—both enoki and the more pedestrian varieties—in a red-wine vinaigrette seem at home in Los Angeles.

And the desserts derive from his French training, but now with a lighter base of ingredients. Although his terrine of chocolate, marbled with white chocolate and gaining textural diversity from chopped pistachio nuts, is sauced with both a sabayon and a raspberry purée, most of the desserts are light fruit fantasies elegantly arranged and made magical with some spun sugar.

La Petite Chaya, under Fukui's direction, is making a mark on American food in the eighties just as the style excited the palate of the Japanese a decade ago. ∎

RECIPES FROM SUSUMU FUKUI

ANNE GREER

■ *Nana Grill* ■

W hile other chefs are drawing from all re-
gional American foods as the basis for their updated innovations, Anne Greer
remains a specialist. She loves the directness and intensity of the ingredients and
flavors of Southwestern cooking. After writing a comprehensive book documenting
the traditional dishes, she has become the leading force in keeping the cuisine alive
by lightening and combining its larder with a deft and subtle hand.

"Fresh food is part of the modern world, and traditional Southwestern cuisine
has great integrity. What I do preserves the integrity of those ingredients and
traditions, but adds a dimension of newness by my personal interpretations."

And Greer's influence on Dallas, where she is concept consultant to the Anatole
Hotel and works in three kitchens with the staffs, has spread like a brush fire through
a forest of mesquite. Dishes such as her red-chili pasta salad and oysters topped with
a green-chili pesto sauce are showing up on as many menus as oysters Rockefeller
in New Orleans. Since she defines the Southwest as the area from California to
Louisiana, her cuisine is far more varied than the Tex-Mex of her adopted state,
where Greer, now thirty-eight, moved thirteen years ago after being born and raised
in Chicago.

"I think the ethnic communities in Chicago had an effect on the development
of my taste, and I learned to love strong flavors."

Greer, an art major in college, married and moved to Florida, and though she
had no formal training, cooking became her tension release from raising two sons.
She began "ghost catering" with an English friend, selling food to caterers who
would pass the dishes off as their own.

"My life was revolutionized in the mid-1970s when food processors first hit the
market and I began to realize their potential. I kept entering
cooking contests until I won $5,000 for a Tex-Mex
stuffing from Uncle Ben's rice, and that was
the money I needed to publish my own book.
It never occurred to me that a commercial publisher would be interested." *Culinary Renaissance* was self-published in 1975, and sold more
than seventy thousand copies.

By that time, Greer was beginning her exploration of Southwestern cuisine, having abandoned
a career as a painter. "I began doing television and

teaching cooking classes in San Antonio, where I had moved from Florida. Food in Texas was just beginning to become important, and there really wasn't a leader in the state since Helen Corbitt at the Greenhouse had died."

Greer used teaching classes around the region as a vehicle for learning about the food. "Each town is different, although many of the ingredients are the same. I would ask a Mexican American why they did a dish a certain way, and the answer would always be 'because my mother taught me.' Chilies and tomatillos are part of most of the region's food, then you start to find the variations. They put cabbage in tacos in San Antonio because there is a German influence, and the blue corn native to New Mexico and American Indian influence gives that region its distinctions."

Greer found even dishes as common as flan had variations. "In Texas it's made with reduced milk almost like condensed milk, and in New Mexico they mix eggs and milk together and it's much lighter."

"The cuisine of the Southwest changes with the proportion of Spanish and Indian settlers. The higher-class Spanish had all the spices the peasants didn't have, and things like cumin were considered prizes. The other variable in Southwestern cooking is the native chili pepper. You can only get poblano chilies in Texas and southern California, and the intensity of the chili determines a lot about the food."

Greer found there were marked differences in grilling over aged mesquite wood, the way they do in Texas, and over the mesquite charcoal used in California. "The charcoal is much hotter and dryer, so meats and fish have to be brushed with oil or butter to keep them moist, and the fat has a tendency to burn and give food a bitter taste."

What she also learned in her travels was that there was no adequate book chronicling the true Southwestern food, apart from a few with tortilla dishes, which she found were only a small portion of the cuisine.

Cuisine of the American Southwest was published in 1983, and won the R. T. French Company's Tastemaker Award in 1984 for the best book on American food. The book was co-published by Harper & Row and the Cuisinart Cooking Club, since Greer had been developing recipes for the food-processor company for five years.

But, by the time it was published, she had moved into her own style of cooking. "I felt the base had to be documented, but I'm not interested in re-creations. I'm a direct person and there's a directness to all my food. When I was a painter, my watercolors never had a studied look, and my food is like my art. It has a freedom, it's not controlled.

"At the same time, I'm contemporary and so is my cooking. In the same way that pizza is a traditional part of Italian cooking, the tortilla specialties are part of Southwestern tradition. But there is room to move that cuisine on and not make Southwestern cooking dated."

Her forum for the new dishes, a few of which were in her book, became the Anatole Hotel, owned by Dallas real-estate developer Trammell Crow. On the twenty-ninth floor of the new hotel tower is a restaurant with a panoramic view of the city. It is named the Nana Grill after a large painting of a reclining woman in the wood-paneled bar. The restaurant is a Southwestern grill, with an open kitchen in the center, where diners can see large veal chops and fillets of delicate salmon grilling over mesquite.

But it is in the presentation of the basic foodstuffs that Greer's imagination comes into play. The veal chops are sauced with papaya purée surrounded with a halo of dark cordon sauce made from a reduction of stock, and the salmon tops a green bed of lightly sautéed fresh tomatillos enriched with a little butter.

Some of her appetizers also rely on the grill. Her now famous oysters topped with a paste made from cilantro, green chilies and pine nuts are finished by grilling, and the smoky aromatic flavor of the mesquite imbues a creamy roasted corn soup, lightened with cream and thickened with cornmeal.

Even the Nana Grill's salads draw from the regional larder. A black-eyed-pea salad is served warm, garnished with artichoke hearts but flavored with cinnamon, a classic Southwestern spice. And her house salad is topped with chickpeas and dressed with a lime and coriander vinaigrette.

Even before Greer had the Nana operating to her standards, and the smell of mesquite out of her blond hair, the Anatole had her moving on to The Terrace restaurant on the ground floor of the new tower. In planning for this restaurant, she focused on the California style of Southwestern cooking in the same way that she had updated Texas cooking for the Nana Grill.

Some of her most popular dishes at The Terrace are an artichoke soup topped with toasted nuts, and two signature salads—one with red-chili pasta tossed with spinach and topped with goat cheese. The other is a warm chicken, avocado, and papaya salad with Oriental overtones from the addition of soy sauce and ginger to the dressing.

Greer's dishes have established a beachhead for nouvelle Southwestern cooking, and she believes Dallas could become as sophisticated a dining town as San Francisco. "Part of our problem here is self-image, and tourists thinking they should only eat tacos and chili con carne. With restaurants like Turtle Cove and the Routh Street Grill, we are all redefining Southwestern cuisine. Dallas is a sophisticated city, but until recently there were few good classically trained chefs. Now there are some, and they are starting to experiment with native ingredients because it's what we have that's the freshest." ∎

RECIPES FROM ANNE GREER

Shrimp in Tequila with Orange Beurre Blanc, page 138

Oysters with Green-Chili Pesto, page 144

Roasted Corn Soup, page 168

Artichoke Soup, page 173

Pumpkin Soup, page 174

Warm Black-Eyed-Pea Salad, page 179

Warm Chicken and Papaya Salad, page 190

Red-Chili Pasta Salad, page 198

Salmon with Tomatillo Butter Sauce, page 215

Veal Chops with Papaya Purée, page 225

Chicken Sauté, page 272

Cornbread with Chili, page 296

Minted Lime Sorbet, page 309

Pineapple-Orange Ice with Fresh Pineapple and Oranges, page 312

Grilled Apples with Minted Lime Sorbet, page 336

JIM HALLER

■ *The Blue Strawbery* ■

While many American chefs were drawing their nouvelle know-how from the kitchens of French masters, Jim Haller, owner-chef at The Blue Strawbery in Portsmouth, New Hampshire, trekked no farther than the Shaker village ten miles away.

"The Shakers were doing what we now term 'New American Cuisine' more than two hundred years ago. They used fresh herbs, and their whole philosophy was to take what's ordinary and make it extraordinary."

And "extraordinary" could describe The Blue Strawbery's success since Haller opened the doors fifteen years ago—having never cooked before except for a few private dinner parties. Six weeks later, *Boston* magazine raved about his innovative cooking. The restaurant, located on the waterfront in a narrow brick building constructed as a granary in 1797, has become the focal point for more redevelopment of the historic village, and the spelling of Strawbery comes from the Pilgrims.

Haller's motto is "the only ingredient you need to be a good cook is fearlessness." This has become the theme of his weekly menus as well as the two books he has written, which he declines to call cookbooks since "what I am giving is guidance and I refuse to call them recipes."

While the forty-eight-year-old Haller will acknowledge talent, he considers his culinary strength his ability to "taste something and duplicate it, or imagine how a dish will taste by looking at a pile of ingredients." He had no formal training as a chef, and limited education in any realm.

"I was born and raised in Chicago and quit school when I was fifteen, and was living in New York doing television writing for people like Merv Griffin and Mike Douglas. It sounds impressive, but when you consider it was eighteen years of my life and I can summarize it in one sentence it really wasn't."

Haller fell in love with Portsmouth because "after New York it was wonderful to walk into a town that was so vulnerable and trusting," and moved there awaiting more work as a writer. "Everyone wants some credentials, and mine was 'clever on the streets,' but when we decided to open the restaurant, there was a feeling of relief. I was thirty-three years old, and was really happy."

Haller's philosophy of cooking has two tenets: "Nothing should take longer to cook than it does to eat" and "Food should always be healthy, and taste luxurious."

He does not believe that certain foods cannot be paired with other foods, nor does he believe in chef's training. "Everybody has to have their own taste and develop that taste. Schools don't teach that fundamental. All they can do is show concepts from the teachers' tastes. That's why I don't believe in recipes. People get stopped and afraid if they don't have all the ingredients, instead of realizing the kitchen makes you a wonderful creator.

"I find it thrilling to see what my imagination brings me. When you bring your tactile, visual, and intuitive forces into play it gives you such an emotional payoff to know you've done everything yourself."

That is why Haller has not repeated one of his weekly menus since The Blue Strawbery opened its doors. Even the name is a reflection of his self-confidence. "I used to wear a piece of lapis around my neck in the shape of a strawberry, and someone told me lapis has the power to take away self-doubt. I was feeling very bummed out when I lost it, and that was about the time I was opening the restaurant. I decided the universe took it away because I didn't need it anymore."

Unlike chefs who tally a forty-hour week in two days, Haller insists his creativity can only be nurtured "if I'm not falling down dead from exhaustion." He only works four nights a week, and entrusts the menus to his sous chef on other nights, so he can spend time pursuing interests such as teaching cooking to the blind and working as a volunteer in a hospice.

"I even taught blind people how to flambé dishes by listening to the sounds of the sizzling in the pan, and I worked on a class for how to cook for the terminally ill so they and the people close to them could use the food as a way to share experiences."

When he turns his talents to the kitchen, he relies as much as possible on the bounty of seafood and other products grown in New England. "I first felt a kinship for the Shakers when I visited Eldress Bertha Lindsay. I had just 'created' parsnips with orange and brandy, and she showed me a Shaker cookbook containing almost the exact same recipe."

He says the Shakers made him aware of many foods, such as fiddlehead ferns and periwinkles, and imparted to him their dedication to freshness. "I grow more than forty different sorts of herbs in the summer, use local goats' milk, and scour the countryside for various squash. The local fishermen know if they've got something nutty in the nets to call me, and I have one person raising marvelous rabbits and another smoking Maine mussels."

Part of his experimentation is making his own butters from local cream. "I don't have the room in the kitchen to make my own bread, so I decided doing butters was the next best thing." He flavors them with spice combinations such as basil and nutmeg, or with nasturtium blossoms when in season.

"The seasonal aspects of New England cooking become boring during the winter, so I import more food from other areas than during the other seasons, but there's something so exciting when you spot the first signs of spring flowers and produce."

Although Haller considers his kitchen too small for breads, it is certainly large enough for his ice-cream machine. He has made ice cream from sweet potatoes, and sorbets from asparagus and cranberries.

Dinner at The Blue Strawbery is served to forty in a narrow brick-walled room lined with antique and primitive paintings consistent with the rough-hewn environment. It is served at two seatings and consists of six courses with a choice of three entrées. Although the table appointments are elegant and the linens are starched and pristine, each service plate is a different pattern of Wedgwood china.

"This began when we first opened, since we only had $2,700 to do the whole restaurant, including food and liquor for the first week. A friend worked for the company and gave us discontinued samples. I decided I liked the way it looked, so we continued to buy individual plates."

One Sunday, the first course was a sherried mussel cream soup, followed by a ramekin of snails with sun-dried tomatoes and garlic. The salad that day was a canary melon with cucumbers and apple soaked in homemade tangerine vinegar. "I don't believe in food that is forced, but this can be arranged so it looks like a rose, and I have nothing against food looking attractive."

He then gave diners a choice of tenderloin of beef with cèpes and a brandy sauce, or breast of duck with crushed almonds and raspberries in a crème de cassis sauce, or fresh artichoke hearts surrounding swordfish in a champagne cream sauce. Herbed new potatoes, carrots in honey, and fresh asparagus accompanied all.

"I bake all my vegetables in a 400-degree oven, tightly covered, and sprinkled with salt and pepper. It keeps more nutrients than even steaming them."

While his menus work in one-week cycles, Haller has been known to change the specific flavorings of the desserts after a few days.

Haller gives the same freedom of expression to the cooks who work with him. He is very proud that former assistants Mark Gardino, Burt Richardson, and Albert Boulanger are now commanding their own kitchens around the country, and he assumes sous chef Phillip McGuire will follow suit before long.

"If I can do anything for the people who work for me, it's to show them technique, and then send them off to pursue their own tastes, with my philosophy that nothing stumps me." ■

RECIPES FROM JIM HALLER

BRUCE LEFAVOUR

■ *Rose et LeFavour* ■

I f cookbook publisher Irena Chalmers is correct that "the Napa Valley is now revered the same as the South of France was in the past," then Bruce LeFavour's Rose et LeFavour, on the main street of St. Helena, California, is the region's three star dining spot.

One doesn't drop in for a snack at the thirty-seat restaurant marked by a bright green awning. Dinner is a three-hour six- to eight-course production. The menu changes daily. "I keep a page on each day we do, with comments from the diners on how successful the evening was to them. Certain dishes are placed on the menu again when the dominant or secondary flavor fits with my concept for the evening, but I don't think I've ever recycled an entire meal," says LeFavour, who mans the kitchen while partner Carolyn Rose moves deftly in the dining room.

LeFavour thinks of dinner at his restaurant as if he were creating a dinner party, and his kitchen reflects this hominess. In lieu of the usual gleam of steel, his space is bright yellow with matching enameled pots as well as industrial aluminum. He orchestrates each course so that the underlying flavors of one lead into the more dominant flavor in the next. His meals are unified, but with great subtlety. "Sure, I could do a small à la carte menu the way everyone else does, but I conceive of dinner as the total experience."

His wine list, perhaps the most comprehensive in the state, lists the best French châteaux next to local vineyards, and the cheese tray, which Rose explains to customers with great pride, will have a Santa Rosa goat cheese next to a rare Saison d'Or, a creamy French cheese made in the mountains near Geneva for a brief time each year after the frost coats the morning grass.

Rose et LeFavour is the third restaurant for this Amsterdam, New York, native, who never intended to become a chef and has no formal training as one. "As a kid I made things like floating islands for dessert, and always got a kick out of the kitchen. But after I got out of Dartmouth College I was stationed in France in the Army, and my interest in food was a result of the traveling I did in Europe. I pedaled my bicycle from three-star restaurant to three-star restaurant, and learned what really great food should taste like.

"I think you can learn a tremendous amount of cooking from books as long as you know the taste of quality. And from observing how the French arranged their food I developed my ideas for ornate plating. Part of the reason I want to keep the restaurant small is so that I can prepare the dishes to order, and spend the time needed for their presentation. Carolyn is my eyes in the dining room, and reports constantly the comments from diners and how each table is doing."

His first restaurant, The Paragon, began in Aspen, Colorado, in 1965, after LeFavour spent time in Austria writ-

Rose et LeFavour · Restaurant Français

ing a novel and trekking through the northwest territory of Canada. The principles he assimilated in France—using all fresh ingredients and a light touch—made the small restaurant a success. "I was cooking vegetables crisply even then. My wife, Pat, was a good baker, and we never took any shortcuts. The beef, pork, and lamb were wonderful in Colorado, and we were doing French-inspired food with Colorado ingredients the way people in California are using local products now. We did a lot of pâté and snails, but we also experimented with dishes like fresh duck with olives."

In 1973, LeFavour determined the mountain resort was losing its rural character, and was becoming overcrowded. His next restaurant site was Robinson Bar, Idaho, a village eighty miles north of Sun Valley, where he became an innkeeper in addition to a restaurateur.

"We had a self-sufficient farm adjoining the restaurant, and with the Jersey cows I raised I could make my own butter from cream, and use the freshest possible eggs because we kept about eighty chickens." In addition, he raised Rouen ducks, which he still finds preferable because of their low fat content; pigs; sheep; and vegetables. "It was a crazy area, and I was nuts for beginning a serious restaurant there. Custer County is about the size of Connecticut, and there were only two thousand people living in it. We really had to depend on people using the inn to support ourselves."

One of the dishes he developed there was Robinson Bar potatoes, his rendition of the classic potatoes poached in cream he had eaten and loved in France. "When you live in Idaho, you can only depend on the land for a few months out of the year, but there's no potato sweeter than one plucked right from the ground."

After five years in Idaho, LeFavour and his wife divorced and he decided the blossoming Napa Valley contained the serenity he still craves, plus the bounty of ingredients he was lacking. And the sort of restaurant he envisioned would have the intimacy of the inn he was abandoning.

The small storefront occupied by Rose et LeFavour was an old café, since a year's search had not uncovered the outdoor dining area he and Rose sought. There are but seven tables in the room, each with a different flower arrangement in an antique vase. Carolyn Rose works with a local florist to do the flowers each week, and the containers, like many of the plates on which the multi-course meals are served, were inherited from LeFavour's family.

"We wanted to create a room neutral enough so the focal point was the food and flowers, but elegant enough for the dining experience," said Rose. "It's a lengthy meal, intended for people to talk. But, for that odd couple who can't stand each other, they have things to look at and discuss." A house rule is that no smoking is allowed in the dining room until after dessert, at which time ashtrays are brought out if requested.

The first course one Sunday afternoon, when diners are seated between 1 and 3 P.M. rather than 6 to 8 P.M., as from Wednesday to Saturday, was a lightly smoked loin of rabbit with a warm kumquat vinaigrette. It was garnished with a julienne of lightly steamed green beans, and miner's lettuce, small leaves similar to mâche.

Following the rabbit was an arrangement of fresh seafood—mussels, scallops, petrale sole—with asparagus in a blood-orange sauce. And to continue his subtle thread of light fruit flavors, the sorbet that followed was a purée of fresh pears flavored with a rosemary and thyme brewed tea.

Next, medallions of pork were served with a complex blend of apple and lemon sauce and topped with slivers of ginger butter. The julienne of red and yellow peppers and gaufrette potatoes played off the flavors of the pork and provided a textural contrast.

While the dishes that day were primarily sautéed, LeFavour has begun to favor mesquite charcoal as a medium. "The flavor works so well with the game birds coming from the valley these days, and in using more grilled meats I am becoming more California in the sense it's now used."

But one of his favorite new products—the New York State foie gras—is used on many menus. He dresses it with vinaigrette to cut the richness and serves it with baby beets and sautéed beet greens or in a nest of local greens, such as mâche, and white chanterelles.

His cooking of fish follows the Japanese mode. Although he prefers most fish raw, he understands many diners do not, but very rare is the way all fish is served —from fresh salmon on a bright green asparagus cream sauce to yellowfin tuna done in a red wine sauce with beef marrow—unless otherwise specified.

The cheese tray follows the entrée, and while totally satisfying, the meal was not so overwhelmingly large that any diner would pass up the dessert cart, prepared daily by Ann Kathleen McKay to coordinate with LeFavour's plan for the courses preceding it.

"What I love about her work is the intensity of the flavors but the lightness balancing it." The pastries can range from luscious chocolate meringue tortes to blackberry tarts, and she tries always to have a poached fruit—such as pears in red wine with cloves, vanilla, and black pepper.

LeFavour is pleased with the limited but controlled operation of his restaurant. It allows him the time to make pear and raspberry vinegars and to visit the markets in San Francisco three times a week to secure products not grown in the Napa Valley. "Part of my joy in cooking is thinking of each meal as a totality, and planning a menu that works together and sauces that lead from one to the next with some logical order. I know a lot of chefs who can put together individual dishes, but I would get so bored doing the same thing even two nights in a row." ∎

RECIPES FROM
BRUCE LeFAVOUR

MARK MILLER

■ *Fourth Street Grill* **■**

As one would expect from a pioneer in California-style mesquite-charcoal grilling, you'll find swordfish and halibut on Mark Miller's menu at the Fourth Street Grill in Berkeley. But, if it's an African night, the sauce might be orange-lime with cloves, and on a Moroccan evening the same fish might be covered with tomato, coriander, sweet onion, and paprika.

Miller owns the one-story, sleek grill with Susan Nelson. Both once worked at Chez Panisse a few miles away, and now apply the French training learned from Alice Waters and Richard Olney to create non-Western ethnic cuisines with intense flavor and color combinations. While this is the aim for all his food, his monthly "regional dinners," a term purposefully vague to range from the glorification of the Pacific salmon to African dishes, are what he considers the test of his talents.

"The difference between a chef and someone who cooks is that there is a style and underlying philosophy of cuisine that pervades everything a chef cooks, and what first attracted me to primitive art—the intensity of the forms and colors—is what I look for in my own food."

For Miller, cooking is a practical application of his anthropological training. Now thirty-six, he was born and raised in Massachusetts, and was drawn to the Berkeley campus in 1967 to study Chinese art history and Japanese anthropology.

"I had wanted to be an anthropologist since I saw my first bark painting at the age of twelve. Chinese art was my training in formal aesthetics outside the world in which I was raised, but I knew I wanted to become involved with cross-cultural aesthetics."

He completed his bachelor's degree in less than three years, and used cooking as a release of tension, with his first experiments from the *New York Times Cookbook* and a paperback by James Beard. "I used to cook as therapy, and as a way of handling real materials to get an immediate result. When you're an academic always looking for approval from advisers, cooking could be a way of interacting socially and not caring about anyone's judgment."

After a year in graduate school at Berkeley and a year at Oxford, during which he worked on an archaeological dig in Scotland, Miller abandoned academia. He worked at the Williams-Sonoma store in San Francisco, and then began a newsletter, *Market Basket.*

"It didn't make it commercially, but it was years before its time in 1974. It was an in-depth examination of food, reviews of all the products on the market, and recipes. *Gourmet* was the standard then, and it didn't go into depth about anything and wasn't concerned with food."

He was studying food and wine with academic discipline in both California and Europe. "I now have a collection of more than a thousand books on the subject and believe you can learn a lot from books. Chefs should be able to conceptualize a taste by reading the way a musician can

Fourth Street Grill

hear a piece by looking at the score. I don't have to see it done; I have the ability to taste the finished product from the page, and have a good taste memory."

It was on this basis that Alice Waters, trail-blazing the use of California ingredients in what was basically French food, hired Miller as the third cook for Chez Panisse in 1975. "From Alice I learned a lot. She has perfect taste the same way some people have perfect pitch. She would make something better with a few adjustments. She also uses only great ingredients and I learned respect for seasonal things. Richard Olney is the only cook I know better than Alice, and he has an amazing ability to cook. It took him six years to train the butcher in his town in France to cut the meat the way he wanted it, and when I visited him in France we went to five cheesemakers before he liked the chèvre."

The system at Chez Panisse was that Miller, Waters, and Jean Pierre Moulez each did a dish a day for the set three-course meal, so during his three years there he created more than five hundred dishes.

"The real shock was my first experiences with restaurant cooking. It's different because of the stress, and the hours. Few jobs require ten to twelve hours a day with a schedule that must be maintained. At Chez Panisse we could never miss a day because there were no prep people to help us."

Miller's decision to leave Chez Panisse was owing to a difference in styles, and his developing confidence in his own tendencies. "It was a French restaurant, and 'Frenchifying' recipes took away from the intrinsic nature of the dishes I wanted to do. I didn't want food defined by creams and butters, and I have a natural penchant for using spices.

"It's like people who take a folk melody and orchestrate it. It loses brightness, intensity, and integrity when you try to translate it."

For Miller, cooking and anthropology had merged in his mind and talents, and the Fourth Street Grill opened in October, 1979, so "I could have a freer expression in cooking. It was an undefined restaurant, although it was one of the first mesquite grills. But it was in Berkeley, with a well-traveled clientele.

The restaurant was instantly successful, and it gave Miller the opportunity for the experimentation he craved. "Good chefs have an innate sense of balance, color, and form, in the same way artists do. And the whole is much greater than the sum of its parts. Nouvelle cuisine is based on the parts. But there can be an animalistic satisfaction from food, versus a cultivated satisfaction. That's why I collect nineteenth-century Navajo art. There's a strength in the design and a warmth and depth of expression I can relate to from my food."

While the Fourth Street Grill was popular, Miller was eager to expand, so he became a partner in the Santa Fe Bar and Grill in Berkeley, which opened in December 1980. "It was an attempt to disassociate myself even more from the French at Chez Panisse. I focused on South Atlantic cuisines, such as Caribbean, Latin, and Creole, with a little bit of the Southwest. These are homogeneous taste areas, which historically shared methods of cooking and ingredients. We had things on the menu from the Yucatán, and used to sell two hundred orders a day of Peruvian beef hearts en brochette. The cuisine was popular, we got good reviews, but I was too young and naïve to be running two restaurants."

After five months, Miller sold his interest in the Santa Fe to concentrate on the ethnic fare he wanted at Fourth Street. "In the last four years the restaurant has gotten stronger and better. There are certain dishes—like our Caesar salads, made with whole leaves of romaine and a thick shredding of Parmesan cheese, and our pastas—that people expect from us. It's almost impossible to change a restaurant around in terms of people's expectations."

But what he has done is attract clientele open to experimentation for his Friday dinners. "Ethnic food usually gets muddied because it's done ahead of time, and all our food—regardless of where it's from—is cooked to order. What I do is use my classical background to treat ingredients with that respect, using no dairy products or salt. We achieve the intensity of flavors with spices. Our only thread is my interest in the cooking of the tropical and subtropical areas, which means there's a lot of coriander and chilies on my plates. I love to have lots of flavors in one dish, such as a chicken salad made with mango and jalapeño chutney."

One way in which Miller expands culinary horizons is through traveling. He tries to visit two countries each year for the first time. "It's one thing to study food from books, but I really want to get the flavor of the people as well as their food." The sensual experiences are then reflected on his menus, but he finds certain restrictions as to ingredients frustrating. "In Bali and Burma I couldn't believe the foods in the markets; there must have been twenty kinds of pickles alone. And in Asia I never had a bad meal, even at what we would term a truck stop. Other parts of the world have a much higher level of food consciousness than we do."

His minimal, stark restaurant—almost the antithesis of European design—has only the mesquite charcoal grill as a constant. His dinners glorify ingredients discovered in foreign markets. Dishes from Morocco include such specialties as lamb simmered in saffron, garlic, onion, cinnamon, and other spices, with pistachio rice, and the traditional dish from Fez, bisteeya, which layers phyllo dough with pigeon, chicken, and almonds. Or he will plan an evening around a variety of California chili peppers and devise dishes such as duck smothered in jalapeño peppers and Yucatán white sausages, a variation on French boudin laced with coriander and chilies.

Miller's regional specialties are not all as exotic, however. He borrowed liberally from Paul Prudhomme, giving proper attribution, for a Creole evening featuring blackened redfish and chicken étouffée, and returned to French cooking for a Provençal evening, with bouillabaisse and grilled lamb with beans. ∎

RECIPES FROM MARK MILLER

Creole Marinated Fresh Crab or Shrimp, page 136

Scallop Seviche, page 141

Pepper Oysters, page 143

Yucatán Seafood Stew, page 162

San Remo Pasta with Roasted Tomatoes and Black Olives, page 196

Roast-Duck Pasta with Summer Vegetables, page 204

Lamb Pasta with Wild Chanterelles, page 205

PATRICK O'CONNELL

■ *The Inn at Little Washington* ■

Washington, Virginia, in the foothills of the Shenandoah Mountains, was first noted by those outside its region during the Civil War. Plaques indicating hostilities between North and South—Bull Run, Manassas, Second Manassas—mark the sides of the two-lane road providing access to the town of 150, a population figure that has remained constant for more than a century. The closest interstate highway is forty miles away.

But Washington is back on the map, and for the past seven years, diners have been reserving tables up to three months in advance at Patrick O'Connell's Inn at Little Washington. O'Connell is "trying to develop a regional cuisine based on elevating what is here in Virginia, or can be grown here," and with those products he "brings in the best, regardless of what country it comes from."

Perhaps owing to its location as much as to O'Connell's temperament, The Inn at Little Washington strives for the total dining experience of a three-star French auberge. "I know the time commitment people make to come here to dinner, and I want them to feel that they are eating in an elegant private home. I remember once reading that Ferdinand Point said he was not a chef at all, and that the true restaurateur is aware of every nuance, detail, and subtlety going on in the dining room."

"Reinhardt [O'Connell's partner, Reinhardt Lynch] has seated every guest since the day we opened seven years ago, and not one plate has left the kitchen without my inspection. The staff is told that every time they enter the room I want them to add grace to it, and I check every detail thirty minutes before we open at night down to the angle of the silverware and the freshness of each flower on the tables."

The "sacrifice" of the seventy-five-mile drive from "Big Washington" is because the bucolic location of the inn, built initially eighty years ago as a garage, which housed an antique shop prior to its renovation, was a decision O'Connell and Lynch took as a given in their lives. They had moved to a farm ten miles beyond the town fifteen years ago, to achieve the personal tranquillity antithetical to the frenetic restaurant business. "I began in theater, and this business is the same in many ways. It's living an odd existence different from the rest of the world. It's now been thirteen years without a Saturday or Sunday off, dining at midnight, and I feel both positive and negative things about that life. But, once the decision was made that I had to be in a kitchen, the rural farmhouse became the foundation of my life. It's the most serene and comfortable place on earth for me."

O'Connell first saw the village at the age of eight, almost thirty years ago. "I was born in Washington, the city that is, and my grandfather was a great Civil War history buff."

O'Connell grew up wanting to be an actor, and studied acting at Catholic University, but "something about it didn't satisfy me the way I thought it would. So many people were leading unhappy personal lives, and I did not get immersed into theater on schedule."

At the same time, he was supporting his theater studies by working in restaurants, starting with Mr. H's carry-out at the age of fifteen. "Fast food was just catching on, and this was the sort of place that still cut its own fries, made its own relish, and had a sense of pride in the quality of the food, albeit simple food."

What followed was seven years of what O'Connell terms a "proper American apprenticeship." He kept trading up restaurant jobs, and worked both as a waiter and in the kitchens. "Not that food work had much status then at all, though moving out of the grease of the kitchen and putting on a tuxedo seemed to have a little more. I began to realize what I loved was working with food."

The turning point for his career was ten years after that first carry-out. "I was having trouble with my legs, and they ached so I didn't think I could stand it for the rest of the evening, and I went outside the kitchen, put my feet up against the garbage cans, and suddenly I had made the decision. My legs stopped hurting and I knew I wanted my own kitchen."

The first step was a catering business tailored to the wealthy horse-farm owners in the counties around Middleburg, Virginia. "Reinhardt and I met in a Chinese cooking class while in college, and he had worked at a catering company and knew the logistics of catering, while I had worked in kitchens and had the preparation experience. While many firms now deliver total service, we were the first in this region to handle the party from beginning to end and pay attention to each detail.

"I remember renting birds and cages for one party at Oak Hill Plantation, James Monroe's house, and the last party we did had Princess Anne as the honorary chairman and Elizabeth Taylor as the guest of honor."

Many party guests trekked from the city, and liked the food and service. The firm was soon commuting to the capital for parties, and they realized they had lost sight of their goal of staying in the country.

In historic tradition, the restaurant's walls are painstakingly painted in faux bois, to make the plaster walls resemble wood, a style favored by George Washington and used extensively in Italian palaces. And the gold-leaf detailing sparkles from the light reflected from ruffled salmon-colored shades hanging over bare dark wood tables.

In 1983, they added a pebble and brick patio, with fountains and classical urns.

"Each inch of the interior was decorated and no detail was omitted, but I think we've succeeded in not making the restaurant seem studied."

And the same is true of O'Connell's food. "My clientele is very value conscious, and not as trendy as the people on the West Coast. They know the value of a dollar, and when they come here for dinner they want to be the focus of the evening. They're not coming to bow down to my work.

"But they have trust in me, and will try dishes on my menu that they might never try in another restaurant or make in their own homes."

An example is thinly sliced sautéed sweetbreads fanned with snow peas and mushrooms, or shad roe topped with crunchy slices of fried banana.

This sense of trust has grown with O'Connell's confidence in his own talents, although he had only one summer of formal training, at the Culinary Institute of America. "Seven years ago when I first visited the three-star restaurants of France

I was awe-struck, and realized there were so many areas of my food that needed development. By the fourth year I went to France I thought the same places were a colossal bore, so in 1983 we went to the Orient for the month the inn is closed. I emerged with a thrilling sense of confidence and a clear feeling of our place."

He also has an appreciation for the American palate, and how it differs from the European. "Americans are way ahead of the French in our appreciation of textures. Colors and textures have become an important part of my cooking."

He wraps salmon in crispy phyllo dough to avoid "all that soggy pastry I tasted with French en croûte dishes," and garnishes plates with flowers from chives and thyme as well as the herbs themselves. "I love cooking with flowers as well as herbs and not just decorating with them."

O'Connell wants The Inn at Little Washington to have "a sense of place strongly reflected," and many of his ingredients are grown in gardens of the townspeople. "We have wonderful local hams, and trout and all the fish from the Chesapeake are so close, but it's how I use the ingredients that makes our cooking different from what Thomas Jefferson was doing in Charlottesville two hundred years ago."

His rhubarb is transformed to an ethereally light mousse, and the local apples, when served as a garnish for the Virginia wild ducks, are cooked to preserve the tart crispness inherent in the local species.

The inn bakes breads daily, and is known for its wide array of fresh sorbets—sometimes fifteen or twenty on a given day. O'Connell will offer such flavors as Earl Grey tea served in a teacup as an intermezzo. Dessert flavors—such as blood orange, cassis, and grapefruit-Campari—are formed into quenelle-like ovals, arranged with appropriate fruit, and then raspberry sauce is shot over the top with the energy of an Abstract Expressionist painting.

"I want the meal to end on a dramatic note. The longer I'm in the restaurant business, the more I realize there is a correlation between theater and cooking. Both are based on the emotions of the audience and on using as many of their senses as possible. In both realms, the audience has no idea—or should have no idea—of the behind-the-scenes chaos.

"Someday I'd love to do a video or film about this subject, and the contrast between the front and back of the house. But I've never regretted giving up theater. My life now is far more satisfying, and it's a sense of loving to know I've enriched people's lives with my work." ■

RECIPES FROM PATRICK O'CONNELL

BRADLEY OGDEN

■ *The Campton Place Hotel* ■

S an Franciscans hailed Bradley Ogden's arrival as chef of The Campton Place Hotel in October 1983 with the enthusiasm usually reserved for superstar athletes. Everything from his hesitance about taking the job —"at first I thought, 'No way.' Twenty-one meals a week plus room service!"—to his ingrown toenails was reported in the papers.

And, within a few weeks after the lavishly renovated hotel opened, Bradley was a name to be bandied about in the Bay Area's active food community along with such nouvelle luminaries as Alice (Waters of Chez Panisse) and Jeremiah (Tower of the Santa Fe Bar and Grill and Stars).

What Ogden imported from An American Restaurant in Kansas City was a style of cooking apart from the grand French and mesquite grilling for which San Francisco is known. Ogden brought his own rendition of American cookery, far more inclusive than "California cuisine." He had Brie from Illinois, hams from Kentucky, and oysters from Massachusetts. His style of presentation was sophisticated, yet the substance of his food was both nutritious and wholesome.

"What I'm doing is taking old ideas and making them something new. American cuisine has been around for a long time, but it's now coming of age. There's a difference. I approach dishes acknowledging how much we need good French technique to elevate the concepts to a new height. Stocks, sauces, and reductions would not be the same if we had not been influenced by French food and techniques for all those generations."

For example, Ogden's pâté is made from smoked ham, pork, and currants soaked in port, but the loaf is still weighted for the classic French texture. And his wild mushrooms laced with sherry under an herbed breadcrumb crust are close to a stew, but the ingredients set it apart.

Ogden is personally set apart from his Bay Area contemporaries since his culinary instincts were developed entirely domestically. The thirty-two-year-old Traverse City, Michigan, native was one of seven children, and he and his twin brother had part-time jobs even in the first grade.

"I was raised in a little town of twenty thousand people and my father owned a dance hall, although he would rather have been a chef. When I graduated from high school I went to college for drafting, and while I enjoyed the drawing and designing, I didn't like the math. So I dropped out and took my first restaurant job—at a local Holiday Inn, where I also had to be the bellhop."

In 1972, he entered the Culinary Institute of America in Hyde Park, New York, and worked part time at a health-food store. "In some ways, that was more valuable than a lot of the restaurant work I had done. I learned a lot about nutrition, and balancing the nutritional benefits of my dinners, along with

concerns a lot of chefs have about color, texture, and taste, is very important to me.

"Even desserts can be healthy if you use good, fresh ingredients. And it was at that time that I started caring so much about freshness, and finding the best possible sources for food."

After the first year of the two-year program, Ogden dropped out of CIA and spent four years working at a series of management jobs. He completed the program in 1977, winning the school's prestigious Richard T. Keating Award.

"It was harder the second year. I had gotten married and we had one son and another child on the way, but I had grown up a lot. I knew I wanted to be in a first-class operation that produced fine food and was out for quality, but I hadn't defined my style at all."

His initiation into Kansas City, where he took a job at the Plaza Three Restaurant, was hardly as auspicious as his move to The Campton Place. A flood struck during his first week, wiping out the restaurant. He then went to a family-style restaurant serving 450 to 500 dinners on an average Saturday.

"It didn't give me the chance to cook the way I wanted to, but it certainly taught me organization."

A stint at a Sheraton Hotel in Springfield, Missouri, followed, but in 1979 he returned to Kansas City, this time to become sous chef at An American Restaurant at Hallmark's Crown Center. The menu was conceived by noted food consultants Joe Baum and Barbara Kafka, and after six months he was made executive chef with a free hand.

"In many ways, my style followed what the restaurant was all about. We emphasized the change of seasons, and presented good, fresh American food. That's what I started there, and that's what I'm continuing here."

One change in the move to California is the increase in his repertoire of ingredients. "It's hard to get good trout here; in Kansas it would still be kicking when they brought it in. But the fresh herbs and greens that come from the Napa Valley are superior to anything I've ever worked with."

With the peach-toned dining room of sixty-eight seats as only one of his responsibilities, Ogden operates from a kitchen as confined as the galley on a ship. A different assortment of breads—cornsticks, dill muffins, strawberry muffins, yeast rolls made with sweet potatoes—are baked three times a day, and the kitchen must fill room-service orders and feed employees in a basement dining room as well.

"I'm here by ten A.M., because it's important that I cook. It's the only way people in the kitchen will understand what my food is about." Before he arrives, the crew is already making all the fresh fruit jams and relishes used for breakfasts and garnishes, and vinegars such as raspberry, basil, and blueberry used in dressings.

During quiet times in other parts of the kitchen, ice creams and sorbets are churned, and meats and fish are both hot-smoked and cold-smoked.

A dish that symbolizes Ogden's approach to food is pheasant sausages made with veal and peppers, presented in medallions on a bed of lentils with a garniture of sliced tart apples and roasted chestnuts. "Keeping food simple and attractive, with the interest coming from the contrast of flavors, colors, and textures, is what I'm working toward. A change in my style over the past few years is that I think in terms of the complete dish and its presentation. The starch and vegetable I serve with the protein has to make sense for that dish."

So on any given evening, while the Campton Place menu might list only a dozen entrées, the kitchen is prepared to produce more than twice that number of side dishes. Baby grilled quails arrive under a thick blanket of crisp bacon on a bed of fried shoestring sweet potatoes. The sweetness of the potatoes is the perfect contrast for the hearty smokiness of the bacon and delicacy of the tiny game bird.

Medallions of rare lamb cut from the eye of the rack are placed over a verdant nest of collard and mustard greens wilted with malt vinegar, which cut through the richness of the meat.

Using greens, a staple of Southern kitchens, is characteristic of Ogden's democratic view. "As long as something is fresh, there are no second-class foods in this country, only second-class ways of preparing them."

Some of the other accompaniments include timbales of corn and grits, made as light as a soufflé, and corn spoon bread made with sour cream and buttermilk for additional richness and flavor. The grits are first cooked with garlic and cream to rid them of any similarity to library paste.

Catfish, hardly an option at most restaurants where the service plates are floral Wedgwood, can be fried crisp in a batter or hot-smoked as an appetizer over apple chips and hickory wood.

Desserts are displayed on a buffet table at the restaurant's entrance as if to say, "This is what you have in store, so make sure you leave room." The spice cake with orange curd is far spicier and lighter than any gingerbread, and the sauce contains no flour. It derives its thickness from the large number of egg yolks, its richness from butter, and its flavor from grated zest.

Flour is almost banned from Ogden's kitchen except for breads and pie crusts. One of his favorite desserts is a flourless chocolate pecan cake. "There will always be a place in any meal for a good dessert, but I want people to leave here satisfied but not feeling overly full, and by eliminating flour and making most sauces from reductions of stock, I think I can achieve that balance." ■

RECIPES FROM BRADLEY OGDEN

JEAN-LOUIS PALLADIN

■ *Jean-Louis at Watergate* ■

When Jean-Louis Palladin was cooking in his tiny native Gascony region of southwest France, the dishes were usually made from foods farmers and hunters would bring to his kitchen door. But now that his door is at the Watergate Hotel in downtown Washington, Palladin maintains he is an American chef—working with a French mind.

But Jean-Louis at Watergate, his forty-two-seat restaurant two levels below the elegant hotel lobby, does not just draw on crabs from the Chesapeake Bay and morels from Virginia. Palladin, who shakes his halo of brown hair to emphasize his point, says an artist cannot function with restrictions, including the price of the ingredients. So he imports fresh hearts of palm from Brazil and pounds of truffles from France, and finds Louisiana bayou fishermen who pick his crawfish one by one so they arrive unharmed by commercial harvesting techniques.

"I develop my food with my body. The food and the personality who makes the food is the same, and the personality comes through. That's why my food is changing as I become more American and I change."

Palladin was born in the small town of Condom in Gascony, a region best known for Armagnac brandy. His career was first influenced by his mother.

"My mother is a wonderful cook, and was a nurse during the week and worked in a restaurant on Sundays. One Sunday when I was twelve, I skipped mass to stay with her. The owner offered me work on the spot, and that was the beginning of my career."

The owner of that restaurant was René Sandrini, who became Palladin's mentor as well as closest friend. Palladin went to hotel school in nearby Toulouse at the age of fourteen, returning to Condom on weekends to work, and then apprenticed for short times at the Hôtel de Paris in Monte Carlo and the Plaza Athénée in Paris.

"In 1968, he showed me a fourteenth-century monastery he wanted to renovate, and we started work in May, right in the middle of the student uprisings in France. The restaurant was called La Table des Cordeliers, after an order of monks,

and although the town was small and we would only serve a few dinners during the week, as word about the food got out, we'd serve 350 dinners on a weekend."

For weekday dinners Palladin was likely to use the ducks, geese, cèpes, and game native to the region. "We did dishes like poulet farcie, and created really fantastic cooking for the working people of the area."

Even when the restaurant opened, however, Sandrini was suffering from kidney failure, and he died eight years later. During his illness, while still deferring to his wishes, Palladin really commanded the kitchen and started realizing his own ideas. In 1971 he was awarded his first Michelin star and a high rating in the Gault-Millau guide, adding the coveted second star in 1975.

"I started cooking two menus, so people could taste the regional cooking or the free cooking—since I don't like the term *nouvelle cuisine*—I was doing for myself."

Palladin was the wonder boy in a country that produces fine chefs in the numbers Canada spawns hockey players. "I didn't realize the difference between the press in France and this country until recently. Over there, when journalists recognize you as a good cook, you are allowed to occasionally make a mistake in one of your experiments. In the U.S., the pressure is on you every day, and your reputation over the years means nothing if a writer does not like an individual dish or meal."

It was reports in the French press that led Nicholas Salgo, owner of the Watergate, to Condom. And, after almost a year of negotiations, Palladin moved to Washington with no money and a pregnant wife.

Jean-Louis at Watergate operates as a semiprivate club for lunch, and at dinner offers almost as many fixed-price options as a Chinese restaurant—ranging from two-course dinners to five-course degustation dinners, in which each course is paired with the appropriate wine.

Diners are instantly greeted by lagniappes even before seeing menus. One night it can be crispy rings of squid tempura followed by toast topped with tiny fried quail eggs surrounded by a ring of caviar. The next night it could be toast with thin slices of Norwegian smoked salmon on a layer of anchovy or caviar butter, also served with the huge wedges of buttery brioche that precede the first appetizer of the evening.

Palladin changes his menu nightly, and the menus are written in his French schoolboy script with English translations typed beneath. "Recipes are only guidelines, and each time I do a dish I play with it and try something different. The first year I was in America I was learning what the American people liked, and I was also learning what was available to work with. No matter where the ingredient comes from, I demand the best quality, and I'm willing to pay for it.

"Although the products I had to work with in France were always the freshest, Condom was a small town, and I did not have the variety I would have had at a restaurant in Paris. Cooking in Washington has opened my eyes to new ideas. My imagination soars every day at the market. In France I had been using the same foods all my life, and now I have crabs from Maryland and hams from Virginia as well as foie gras from France and passion fruit from New Zealand. The world is my market."

One of his passions remains truffles, and during the height of the truffle season he will do $120-a-person ten-course dinners, with the delicacy from Périgord in nearly every dish, including a truffle ice cream adapted from a 1765 cookbook.

In a city where the restaurants are judged by who dines there and the size of the drinks more than the quality of the fare, the popularity of Jean-Louis is an exception.

And, even with the prices charged, Palladin's spendthrift attitude about ingredients places the restaurant in the red, a financial burden assumed by the Watergate complex. "Call it a loss leader," says Wolf Lehmkuhl, the hotel's managing director. In an article in the *Wall Street Journal* in 1984 costing out a Jean-Louis at Watergate meal, Lehmkuhl says the aim is similar to that of a supermarket luring customers by promoting items at a loss. In this case, they hope to attract top-dollar tenants for the apartment complex given such notoriety during the past decade.

The quality leads to a larger variety of tastes than is found in most restaurants in any city. On a given night the appetizers included in the various packages might range from a terrine of fresh morels filled with a healthy chunk of fresh foie gras, to slices of moullard liver sautéed and garnished with fresh peaches. Morels garnish lobster sautéed then sauced with cream and sun dried tomatoes. Palladin will use caviar butter both for fresh Belon oysters from Maine and a wedge of shad roe, a delicacy he only discovered after his move across the Atlantic.

On the menu along with the consommé is a soup of fresh pumpkin with turkey, Virginia ham, and duck breast. And with the poached salmon in a saffron cream sauce is something titled Maryland crabcakes, although they are bound with a mousseline of lobster rather than breadcrumbs. A delicate chicken breast in a sweet garlic sauce and accompanied by a garlic flan is listed, along with a heartier bird, a squab breast roasted rare and placed on a bed of sautéed cabbage with bits of Smithfield ham.

"I'm finding old American recipes and learning the concepts of American food, and then basing dishes in my style on them. I am learning how much I like to work with corn, bell peppers, and broccoli. And ingredients like ham hocks can be wonderful. But I must make these foods something lighter than they were before and something for now."

And that's what makes Palladin's food so exciting and credible. ∎

RECIPES FROM
JEAN-LOUIS PALLADIN

RICHARD PERRY

▪ *Richard Perry Restaurant* ▪

While he lived in Chicago and New York and worked as a publishing executive for McGraw-Hill during the 1960s, Richard Perry's chief recreation was going to restaurants. But none of the food was reminiscent of his Midwestern rural boyhood. So, to recapture those hearty tastes, in 1971 he started his own restaurant in St. Louis, where he had gone to high school.

His restaurant was originally called the Jefferson Avenue Boarding House, although the tall red brick 1897 building on a corner of Jefferson Avenue and a small alleyway housed a tavern and the only "boarders" lived in the apartment topping it. The name changed in 1981 to that of the proprietor and chef, then forty-one.

Richard Perry Restaurant is anchored in the American heartland, and is reflective of its development. As skyscrapers rise in the Missouri countryside almost within sight of grain silos, so Perry's menu has taken down-home fare and sophisticated it, lightened it, and made it his personal cuisine. It, like him, continues to draw flavors from the countryside. It is down to earth, not ethereal, but with a complexity and sophistication that balance its basic substance.

Although Perry has lived in many cities, some of his "fondest memories are those from the war, when my mother and I lived with her relatives on a farm in central Illinois. I remember a purity to that food that was missing from dishes at even the finest restaurants.

"On the farm, I used to help with the butchering, and I can remember my grandfather seasoning sausage in the smokehouse, and frying off bits to taste until it was just right. The icehouse was where all the seasonal canned goods—tomatoes, corn, relishes, jams, mincemeat—were kept, and I think that's when I first became attuned to taking a menu from the seasons."

Perry decided "it was restaurants that failed to provide good American food. The food never actually disappeared. It always flourished in the homes, particularly rural homes in the South and West. So it was my idea to combine the two: the food as I remember it tasted as a child and the atmosphere of an elegant restaurant. I thought it would be easy to run a restaurant, and when I realized it wasn't I was stuck."

His restaurant has dining rooms on the first and second floors, and during the summer there is a wooden-walled garden in the back planted with a border of fresh herbs. These are clipped for the kitchen and also give a fragrant perfume for diners selecting from an all-cold menu of such dishes as crudités with three fresh mayonnaises, fresh fruit with strawberry bread and cream cheese, and smoked-trout salad with dill sauce.

"I love the garden menu, and think it is moving in the direction all menus will go. The demarcations of appetizers and entrées are beginning to disappear. And if people want to order a few small dishes instead of the usual courses I encourage them to do so."

The interior space is intimate, with

RICHARD PERRY
Restaurant

dark brown walls, antique prints, and contemporary paintings. Most of the newer works are by Perry's friends.

The original restaurant concept was one prix-fixe dinner per evening, with many of the recipes carefully researched. "I used to pore over menus at the Chicago Historical Society, and St. Louis was the site of Tony Faust. Along with Delmonico's in New York, it was one of the great turn-of-the-century restaurants. It had the first electric lights west of the Mississippi, and a menu that went on for yards.

"I talked to people who had worked there, and also at the Planter's Hotel here. But a lot of food in this part of the country was in boardinghouses. People who would stay on the boats docked in St. Louis took their meals at boardinghouses." His early menus featured dishes like short ribs of beef and smothered chicken. "I used to joke about the names and pictured a chicken in a pillow case."

About six years ago, Perry decided his concept was not working. "I was reinventing the restaurant each night, and it was difficult and not successful in the long run. People were cautious about coming, since there were no choices." After five years in business, Perry was beginning to have confidence in his own taste, although he never sought formal training. Also, he realized he could retain the honesty of Midwestern food while still appealing to the increasingly light palate of his diners.

His approach to the kitchen is as unorthodox as serving up historical dishes. Rather than the structured hierarchy of a staff acceding to the chef's every wish, his young staff, all of whom he trained, are encouraged to push their own creativity. One evening, a dish of seafood sausage, with a blend of textures since the shrimp and scallops are both puréed and minced, was garnished with a few watercress leaves and some enoki mushrooms.

"I know who is cooking by just looking at the plate. This cook is Vietnamese, and his style of garnish is very Oriental. If another cook on the line completed the dish it would be entirely different."

Perry rotates three dishes off the menu each week, so within a few months the options will have changed completely. "I can't do the same dishes week after week, but a new menu each week would have us back to where we were before." Certain favorites, such as crisp fried shrimp on a sauce made with strawberry jam, have become such favorites they never rotate off.

The favorites are also on the lunch menu, along with such options as chicken hash with a poached egg, salmon dumplings served on noodles with fresh basil pesto, and a selection of the pâtés he makes daily. "The idea of a dumpling goes back centuries, but using puréed salmon as the base and saucing it with pesto is a fresher use of the form than chicken and dumplings. In the same way, chicken hash is lighter than corned-beef hash."

In addition to the charcuterie, his kitchen produces a daily variety of breads, ranging from a densely textured white bread to quick breads such as strawberry-applesauce, and a cracked-wheat loaf that may include different types of nuts.

The breads are dictated by the menu, which, in turn, follows the seasons. "I love to go to produce row about midnight. You get a feel for nature you can't get calling up a supplier and hearing what he has to offer."

Famed Belleville white asparagus grows right across the river from St. Louis, and Perry looks forward to the rhubarb and gooseberries of spring. But he tries to select the best for each season. "Although the spring and golden fall in the Midwest are wonderful, what I missed most living in California for a year was the blazing hot summer, when no amount of refrigeration can make you cool, and the winter, when the skies are gray, and the air cold and heavy with impending snow. These are times when nature in this part of the country challenges you to live well, and doing the most with the produce available is also a challenge."

One such dish he favors in winter is a mélange of root vegetables—parsnips, turnips, carrots—which he cuts into a fine julienne and then sautés in an onion butter.

For entrées, the basic heartiness of his fare is balanced by sophistication in the treatments. Grilled lamb chops are marinated in a combination of mustard and red currant sauce, which intensify the sweetness of the meat and produce a charred outer crust as a textural contrast with the rare lamb. In the same way, he marinates a duck breast in molasses and sauces it with port wine, shallots, and puréed dates.

"Part of the reason for changing my menu is that people are eating lighter today than they did a century ago, and all the heavy meat dishes I spent hours researching just don't appeal to the modern palate the way poultry and seafood do."

But desserts are one place where he still believes more is better. "Pastries, like stocks and reduction sauces, are the hallmark of a good restaurant, and what I try to do is capture elemental American tastes and concoct desserts with their spirit."

His bread pudding is paired with a raspberry sauce, and he also offers a bourbon chiffon pie that is light but heady from the liquor. He makes at least one fruit tart per evening, and is fond of white chocolate in all forms, especially a mousse.

His American spirit extends to the California wine list, which includes many small Napa and Sonoma vineyards that rarely ship beyond the Bay Area. "I think it's up to restaurants to encourage fine wine production, and I started the St. Louis Wine Forum so local restaurateurs could meet with vintners when they came through town and learn more about the wines. I also offer premium wines by the glass and encourage people to try a few during dinner. We've got to realize the prejudice against American wines in favor of French is the same thing people here had about American food. Both can be extremely complex and sophisticated." ∎

RECIPES FROM RICHARD PERRY

PAUL PRUDHOMME

■ *K-Paul's Louisiana Kitchen* ■

I n a city known for the old-world opulence of its restaurants, the line in front of K-Paul's Louisiana Kitchen in the New Orleans French Quarter seems all the more astounding. The ninety-two-seat dining rooms on two levels have Formica tables (which diners must share if not the number to fill one as a group), linoleum floors, ceiling fans, and a neon green-and-orange Dixie Beer sign in the window. The only decorations are murals on the ceiling by waitress Sally Lincks, illustrating and listing ingredients for some favorite dishes, such as a velvety oyster soup enriched with Brie and champagne and enlivened with scallions and red cayenne pepper.

The patrons of K-Paul's are firm believers that you can't eat ambiance, and the place has none in conventional terms. But what it does have, with a menu changing daily Monday to Friday evenings—at which time Paul Prudhomme and his wife, Kay, pack up their trailer and go camping for the weekend—is some of the most legendary food in this Mississippi Delta city known for eating.

Prudhomme, who seats his mammoth forty-four-year-old frame at a corner table with a telephone at his side, tastes every menu listing, even if the actual cooking is done by his assistants. And through his taste he has done more than anyone to tell Americans about the differences between city-bred Creole cooking and Cajun, its country cousin. Although he is beginning to believe that "we're now blending together into one New Orleans cuisine rather than keeping Creole separate from Cajun," Prudhomme's background is pure Cajun.

In addition to transmitting and popularizing the food cooked in his native Opelousas, Louisiana, Prudhomme has taken the cuisine one step further. He has defined its elements and continued to push the potential of those flavors to create a cuisine of supreme complexity based on traditional Cajun techniques and ingredients. One such

K-PAUL'S LOUISIANA KITCHEN

dish, blackened redfish, made by throwing a spice-coated redfish fillet into a very hot black iron skillet, was served to seven world leaders at the Williamsburg Economic Summit meetings in May of 1983.

The first bite of the dish is an assault on the palate, tangy and smoky, but overlaid on the tenderest of fillets, which remain succulent and moist on the inside. From beneath the brim of his blue denim hat, with a pin saying "Totally Hot," Prudhomme urges a second taste. This time, the aftertaste is one of sweetness, to which he says: "My goal is to make dishes taste round, so people get the sense of sweet and spicy in alternate bites. With the local taste for rich food I can't get too far from butter and cream, but every bite of a Cajun dish should taste different, should turn on a different part of your mouth."

Another example is his batter for frying catfish, enriched and thickened with spicy Creole mustard. It is far from traditional, although the fish it coats is entrenched in the Cajun repertoire.

"It's part of Louisiana tradition to set a good table, and about 250 years went by in the bayous with mothers teaching sons and daughters to become good cooks. The tastes of dishes changed to match the family's taste, and you would find a different gumbo on every stove. It's called 'pot cooking,' and the way you put things in and cook them is what makes it good." He explains that there are two basic types of Cajuns—land and sea Cajuns, depending on their proximity to the Gulf—within the twenty to twenty-three parishes of Louisiana comprising the Cajun country. The land Cajuns eat much more pork, and the sea segment are the ones who popularized such dishes as crawfish étouffées.

All the Cajun people, Prudhomme says in an accent native only to the bayou country, were originally from the South of France, and immigrated to Nova Scotia and then down the Mississippi River. "It's what 'Evangeline' is all about."

While Creole cooking contains influences from Spanish, Caribbean, French, and Black cultures, Cajun cooking remained an isolated pocket based on French peasant style but utilizing the ingredients available in Louisiana—especially the peppers.

In the heart of Cajun country is the McIlhenny family's Avery Island, where the familiar red-hot sauce with the diamond-shaped label—Tabasco—has been made for more than a century. Legend is that when the family returned to their salt-dome island after fleeing to Texas during the Civil War, the crops had been destroyed. Edmund McIlhenny found a pot of peppers brought from Mexico during the Mexican War and discovered that fermenting the ground peppers with salt for a few years, then mixing them with vinegar, produced a flavor that was not only hot, but most salable.

"The world of peppers is native to our world. They grow wild here and the Indians introduced them to the Cajun people. All hot peppers come from the same species and the different shapes and how hot they are is the result of how much sunlight and moisture they get."

Prudhomme began spicing the family pot with peppers when he was still a child. "I was the youngest of thirteen children, so I was the one left home to help my mother cook." And, since cooking was his only skill, he began it professionally at the age of seventeen by opening a hometown hamburger stand, Big Daddy-O's Patio. After a few years he started traveling the country working as a chef, and in the mid-1970s signed on as a cook for the Brennan family's Commander's Palace restaurant in New Orleans. He was soon executive chef for the restaurants in Houston and Atlanta as well.

Starting K-Paul's in 1979 was Kay's idea, and she ran it for the first year while he supervised the kitchen in addition to his duties at Commander's. There the fare was more Creole than Cajun. "Cajun uses more spices. Creole food has a lot of oregano, thyme, and basil, and both cuisines have the 'holy trinity' of celery, bell pepper, and onion. But the basis of Cajun cooking is the black roux formed by browning flour in oil. It gives a nutty taste."

Prudhomme maintains he cannot give times for the roux, since what he is after is the color. For some gumbos, it should be a walnut brown, while the color can be as deep as mahogany for other dishes. Prudhomme has simplified the technique, and now heats the oil until very hot to brown the flour to the desired color within six to eight minutes, less than a third of the time it previously required.

He may sound at times like a back-bayou chemist, but what Prudhomme is after is an intensity of flavor for his foods—and he gets it. Diners at K-Paul's begin with the house drink, if brave enough. The Cajun martini is either vodka or gin, in which hot peppers have marinated from twenty-four to forty-eight hours. The sharpness of the alcohol gives way, in the back of the mouth, to the lingering hotness.

It is a drink consistent with Prudhomme's philosophy about his developing cuisine: "The short taste of food should be clear, but then it should round out and, all of sudden, should go back to another taste and another part of the mouth. Most alcohol doesn't mix well with Cajun food, and we started this drink to prime the mouth for the flavors in the food."

In addition to the hot peppers, one product essential to many Cajun dishes is sausage—the highly spiced and smoked andouille sausage, the mild boudin, and the smoked tasso ham, which flavors red beans and rice, the traditional Monday lunch.

Prudhomme was so dissatisfied with the quality of commercially produced sausages that he began doing his own in 1982. "I couldn't find sausage with the sort of intense smoke I wanted, and I remembered when I was a kid a lot of grocery stores had smokers out back and made sausage. Boudin could be called the Cajun national snack food. The meal we used to eat on Saturday mornings was pork cracklings, baked sweet potatoes, and boudin."

Prudhomme says, "Cajun sausages are different from those in the rest of the world because we don't put herbs in them. We rely on peppers, garlic and onion." Andouille is made from pork, but back in the bayous it could be venison or beef as well. "There was no electricity or refrigeration when I was a kid, and we used to have parties, called boucheries, to make sausage. Three families would get together and make it, since there was no way to keep the meat fresh."

Prudhomme's method for making andouille involves cold-smoking it at 38 degrees for five to six hours, and then turning the heat on. The result is a sausage with the fire of pepper and garlic balanced by a great smokiness.

His Boudin, usually white and made from rice and pork to which the pork blood is sometimes added for a red sausage, is for more delicate, and includes liver for richness.

He uses the sausages in dishes of his own invention. Andouille is sauced with tomato purée to allow its natural peppery pungency to emerge, or it can be baked with apples and cream.

But the main purpose of the sausage is to give the desired flavor to his gumbo and jambalaya. Gumbo's only constants are the dark roux and filé powder, made from sassafras, or fresh okra, when available, as a thickening agent. The protein can vary from shrimp and crab to chicken and sausage.

"Dishes like gumbos and jambalayas were a way of stretching a meal to feed a crowd. One chicken and a piece of ham goes a lot further when it's mixed with all that rice."

In addition to making his own sausage, Prudhomme carefully controls the sources of ingredients. He buys his veal calves from a local dairy so he can ensure the animals were fed no chemicals and the meat could not have been inadvertently frozen in transit.

His rabbits are raised in a similar manner, and he works with Dan Crutchfield's Hollow Creek Organic Farm in Mississippi for the majority of his vegetables.

"This guy loves to cross vegetables, and he watches over the fields of wild garlic to keep the grass clean."

Prudhomme does not make his own pastas, since "to me that's like growing rice. It's silly to do it when there are such fine ones on the market."

The food at K-Paul's is less traditional Louisiana and more Paul Prudhomme than when the doors opened. "I find us now refining and creating a tremendous depth in our cooking. Stocks are reduced to almost a glaze now.

"I can't travel anywhere without picking something up. Ideas come in and then I use New Orleans thinking and ingredients to make it a Louisiana dish. I don't think you can be creative and not travel. And my traveling is the reason for the change in our food. Before, my imagination worked totally off this area."

He gave as example a shrimp bread he judged in a local cooking contest. While the dish was poorly executed, the idea was something he began to work with. And the curries that routinely pop up on the nightly menus were a souvenir from his two-week residency at Annabel's in London, a swank private club.

Some of his adaptations result from limiting his operation to dinner. "Red beans are not a night-time dish, but people love them. So I cook them in a seafood stock, purée them, and call it 'Monday lunch gravy.' I use it to top fried fish and poached oysters." He uses the basically bland taste of pasta as a base for a rabbit sauce, made with a light tomato flavoring, or a sauce with six varieties of fish and shellfish. "I prefer to use a lot of small chunks of things with pasta, and then let the sauces make them work together."

Introducing people around the country to his food is part of his zealous dedication to American cuisine. "I'm trying to enforce the validity of American food, and instill as much pride in our food as other countries have in theirs."

In the summer of 1983, Prudhomme packed up his staff and kitchen for a

San Francisco field operation, and the lines matched or even exceeded those in New Orleans. However, the enterprise was a financial disaster, with losses nearing $40,000 for lodging and shipping.

"My fantasy is to spend six months on the road each year, and my real fantasy is to make part of that time in Europe so we can turn the tables and tell them what our food is about."

But he has no plans to rent linens and install crystal chandeliers in New Orleans. "What I stand for here is good, honest food." ∎

WOLFGANG PUCK

■ *Spago* and *Chinois on Main* ■

Hollywood is where everyone wants to be the star attraction—including Wolfgang Puck, who planned his restaurants with the kitchens in the middle of the dining rooms. In addition to owning two of the most popular yet dissimilar restaurants in Los Angeles, he consults with a hotel chain, designed the food for a luxury airline, and placed a copy of his restaurant in the busiest section of Tokyo.

It's a Wednesday night, but Spago is jammed, with a row of Rolls-Royces and Mercedeses in the parking lot. Zsa Zsa Gabor leans across the row of Villeroy & Boch plates on the counter artfully arranged by Puck, wearing his trademark baseball cap, to give the thirty-five-year-old Austrian-born restaurateur a peck on the cheek. Mark Peel, whom Puck entrusts with Spago's kitchen while he is manning the woks at Chinois on Main in Santa Monica, calls for the pickup of plates for Don Knotts and the cast from *Three's Company,* who are sitting at a corner table overlooking the smoggy skyline and Sunset Boulevard.

Puck grills fresh tuna steaks to be covered with a basil and tomato vinaigrette and spoons garlic sauce around Columbia River salmon, while to his left cooks pull pizzas from his hardwood-burning ovens. But these are no ordinary pizzas. They are made with combinations like duck sausage, fresh tomatoes, mozzarella, basil, and garlic; or smoked salmon and golden caviar; or double-blanched garlic, prosciutto, tomatoes, red peppers, red onions, and California goat cheese.

Spago—Italian slang for pasta—opened in 1981, after Puck's reputation was established. His training began in Austria at his mother's knee as she kneaded dough as pastry chef for a hotel in the resort town of Maria Wörth, near Klagenfurt. "I would follow the chefs around, and decided I wanted to become a pastry chef, but couldn't find an apprenticeship, so at fourteen I went to hotel school and then moved to France."

For the next decade, Puck got some of the best hands-on training possible—at L'Oustau de Baumanière in Les Baux de Provence, at Hôtel La Réserve in Beaulieu sur Mer on the French Riviera, at the Hôtel de Paris in Monte Carlo, and at Maxim's in Paris.

"It was at Baumanière that I really started to realize the potential food had, and it was the first time I started to really like cooking. We used only fresh vegetables and everything was cooked to order, and fifteen years later that's still how I believe a restaurant must work."

He credits chef Raymond Thuilier with his dedication to freshness. "We worked lunch and dinner six days a week, and Thuilier had only started to cook professionally when he was fifty, so he didn't have the rigidity of many men his age in the kitchen."

By contrast to the training at Baumanière, Puck says La Réserve was "very elegant, but run like an army." He "didn't like Paris because all I could afford was a little room, but Maxim's was so well known I could hardly turn it down. And what I had hoped would happen did," he said with his impish grin. "I got a job offer to come to the U.S."

That entry job was as chef at La Tour in Indianapolis, Indiana, and Puck was nineteen at the time. "I was so hyper then, I used to scream and yell constantly in the kitchen."

Puck was hired as chef at Ma Maison in Los Angeles in 1975. "It was losing $18,000 a month when I got there, and three months later it grossed $150,000."

What he brought to Ma Maison was the nouvelle cuisine he had observed at the time he was leaving France. His duck salad became so popular that other restaurateurs were dropping in just to eat it. "It was a new style of French cooking for this area, and the lightness of it appealed to the health-fad people out here," says Puck, although his own apron reads "Never Trust a Skinny Cook."

"After four years at Ma Maison I began to think 'If I'm doing the same thing for the rest of my life I'll go crazy,' so I decided I'd write a cookbook." Puck's *Modern French Cooking,* published by Houghton Mifflin, kept him occupied for two years, but his basic boredom remained, as did his need to constantly seek new challenges.

One challenge was Spago. The building had been a Russian-Armenian restaurant. It now boasts a modern trompe l'oeil painting of pipes on its façade and is filled with vibrant, colorful works by young California artists.

The concept for his Spago menu is an extension of the name: Food can be fun, and should not be pretentious. But presentation is as important as the combinations of flavors on a plate. He garnishes dishes with sprigs of the fresh herbs used in the sauces, and sautées delicate enoki mushrooms as the textural contrast to paper-thin slices of raw beef for carpaccio.

While his allegiance may have shifted from France to Italy, his loyalty to the ingredients produced in his adopted state transcends all cuisines. "It's not entirely stocked by California, but almost everything comes from the West Coast for both restaurants."

Along with his continued explorations of styles indebted to nouvelle cuisine, Puck created pastas and pizzas. Ravioli is stuffed with lobster mousse, noodles are sauced with smoked salmon and golden caviar, and calzone is stuffed with a mixture of three cheeses, eggplant, artichokes, and thyme.

But even when Spago was only a few months old, Puck was moving on to his next project. "I decided if I could be Austrian and cook French food, then I could do Italian, too." And with that successfully proven, why not Chinese?

Chinois on Main, near the water in Santa Monica, opened in October of 1983. Puck now stir-fries as well as sautés, but though the menu is Chinese-inspired, as Spago nodded to Italy, both restaurants could describe their cuisine as "Puckian."

The interior of Chinois on Main combines a pair of $25,000 Chinese cloisonné cranes and an antique Buddha head over the bar with rotating displays of contemporary art. Cool jade green and fuchsia are the primary colors, the latter reflected from state-of-the-art neon lighting tubes placed in corners. Behind the open kitchen with a copper hood over the stove, and seats around the counter almost like a sushi bar, is a stylized tile mural portraying bamboo in tones of green, plum, and black.

Although Chinois on Main has seventy-five seats, in contrast to the 140 at Spago, the atmosphere is as electric and the room is just as noisy. And Puck and Richard Krause, in command if Puck is at Spago, tend the woks and grills.

Many of the dishes on Chinois on Main's menu could come from the menu of the corner Chinese restaurant, but what makes them special is Puck's treatment. His spareribs are charcoal grilled and then coated with a honey glaze. They veritably fall off the bone. His Cantonese roast duck has a sweet-and-sour sauce, but it is made with fresh plums enlivened by the bite of dried mustard greens.

The majority of menu items are his own creations, using the vocabulary of Chinese ingredients—sesame oil, rice vinegar, fermented black beans, bok choy, and ginger.

"When we first thought about a Chinese restaurant, I wanted to spend a lot of time in Hong Kong. But what I then did was start experimenting with all Oriental ingredients to get what I was after."

One of his favorite appetizers is a blending of East and West. Oysters are dusted with flour flavored with curry, and then sautéed in butter, placed in their shells on a purée of cucumbers and cream, and finished with a dollop of red caviar. Swordfish is grilled with ginger and the zest of orange, but has a hint also of fresh mint, and tender calf liver is stir-fried with cashews, pine nuts, and bok choy.

The blending of East and West extends to the dessert options. He offers a sampler of three styles of crème brulée—flavored with ginger, mint, and mandarin orange; and fruit desserts such as fresh melon in plum wine with a mint-tea sorbet.

In addition to the restaurants, Puck developed the food for Regent Air, a luxury airline that began operating between New York and Los Angeles in 1983. And he is the restaurant consultant to Texas millionaire Caroline Hunt Schoellkopf, who owns the Bel-Air Hotel in Los Angeles, the Remington in Houston and the Mansion on Turtle Creek in Dallas.

All of his activities are united by a constant philosophy: "What I am doing is my personal statement, and the most important thing is to cook what people like to eat. I'm very much an idealist, and think everyone should have their own style." ■

RECIPES FROM WOLFGANG PUCK

MICHAEL ROBERTS

■ *Trumps* ■

L os Angeles is becoming known as the city where the food served is so minimal and light that, to quote one diner, "You never get satisfied or full; you crave Chinese food two hours later." But that cannot be said for Trumps, where Michael Roberts's culinary philosophy could be dubbed "nouvelle down-home."

And not down-home to a particular region. His food has elements of ethnic heritages from Cuban to Eastern European. On them the thirty-five-year-old native New Yorker overlays sophistication from his classic French training and his own inventive combinations of ingredients.

Now a general partner as well as chef at Trumps, Roberts's style was influenced by some of the wishes of the four original partners. For example, Waldo Fernandez, a well-known Los Angeles interior designer responsible for Trumps's stark and sleek interior, longed for the plantains of his Cuban childhood. Roberts arranges the crisp double-fried slices with stripes of fresh golden and black American caviar. For additional flavor and textural contrast, he added a scoop of refried beans and a dollop of sour cream. While the intent is Cuban, the dish, which has become one of the signature dishes at Trumps, is a variation on the popular caviar, sour cream, and crispy potato skins that have become almost a cliché in California.

Improvisation in the kitchen is not Roberts's first artistic endeavor. He graduated from New York University in 1971 with a degree in music, after studying the piano from age six and the bass from age ten. "I was playing the piano and composing a bit, but there was little work and cooking seemed like an easy form of expression. I had no formal training, but picked up Julia Child, volume 1, when it came out, and by the time I had worked my way through it, she was there with volume 2."

He landed a job at Lady Astor's in New York in 1975. "It was a huge splash with all the downtown trendies. My experience was at a Greenwich Village restaurant which had closed quickly, but was something I could call experience. There was another guy in the kitchen who had worked in a mediocre French restaurant, and we were the cooks."

After six months, Roberts decided a career in the kitchen was what he wanted, and found a school in France run by the French government, which offered a nine-month program. "It was a totally classical French school. Even though it was the mid-seventies, they talked about nouvelle cuisine but took the attitude that they were creating a foundation. And certain techniques had to be mastered or you were doing a bad nouvelle and bad classic."

Filled with desire to have his own restaurant, Roberts left France since he "couldn't see starving in France to be third cook on the line in a famous restaurant. I wanted to be a chef." And, after two years at One Fifth Avenue in New York, he moved to Los Angeles in 1979.

The job he had gone there for never materialized. After a few months of filling his time with riding lessons, he became involved with a short-lived but critically successful restaurant called Le Soir. Then, through Michael McCarty, owner of Michael's in Santa Monica, Roberts met the consortium of investors who were starting Trumps: Jerry Singer, who had a catering company called Moveable Feast; Doug Delfeld, who owned a popular casual restaurant; Fernandez; and Sheldon Andelson, an attorney and University of California regent.

"This was my first opportunity to really design a menu according to my concepts, and I got to run with a lot of the ideas I was starting to make popular at Le Soir. Even though it had a French name, my pet peeve is that if something is to be taken seriously in this country, it had to be French. It's time to knock down the temple of food the French have created beyond their shores.

"At Le Soir, the first thing I did was translate the menu. And I started certain dishes there which are still on my menu with updating and variations. I did a salad with smoked chicken, shrimp, endive, and a walnut-oil dressing. Moving to California, I began to see the sky was the limit because the ingredients here were more varied than in any other city in the country."

Trumps opened in October of 1980. It is not only packed for lunch and dinner, but is also credited with popularizing the civilized pastimes of afternoon tea and eclectic aftertheater dinners.

The atmosphere of the restaurant changes radically from day to evening.

During the day, light floods in from skylights, and pots of dwarf magnolia trees or baskets of pink and white hydrangea warm the bar area, where the same beige textured burlap used for the comfortable banquettes upholsters armless sofas. A forest of ficus trees breaks the achromatic environment, which extends to the natural straw placemats and small thorny cacti on the tables.

At night, the environment changes from bright and bustling to romantic and intimate. The only lights in the room are flickering candles on the tables and pin spots on the paintings. The room seems to disappear, and the 130-seat restaurant gains its energy from the people dining.

Regardless of the time of day, Roberts's food remains avant garde. His cooking is rustic with the rough edges taken off, and his use of meats and starches could make Trumps the first nouvelle steakhouse in the country. At lunch, the composed salads range from his original smoked chicken to preserved duck with mixed beans and roasted peppers, warm scallops dressed with a bacon vinaigrette, and a hearty warm chicken-and-potato.

Roberts is a master at mixing textures as well as flavors. While his smoked salmon and scrambled eggs are not unlike those found in many New York delis, his potato pancakes are joined with goat cheese and slices of sautéed apple. A dish popular at both lunch and dinner is a salmon tartare, a blend of the freshest possible salmon with flavor elements such as capers and onion. And his fried cornmeal cakes with chicken and clams are another example of a successful mixture. The infusion of saffron with the chicken and clams is reminiscent of the flavor of a paella, but the corncake base is a cross between New England johnnycakes and Southern corn-bread.

There's a Hispanic influence in his omelet made with tomato, cilantro, shredded beef, avocado, and potato. And Creole cooking forms the basis for his rendition of bread pudding, and for the sauce scented with vanilla and sassafras into which fingers of duck, cooked Chinese-style with moist meat and crispy skin, are dipped.

Roberts also borrows from himself. An early dish was a veal roast served with roasted garlic in a lemon sauce, garnished with a julienne of candied lemon peel. The same flavoring was then administered to a chicken breast.

While many entrée preparations at Trumps are grilled, one cannot term it a "grill restaurant." "I have a kitchen large enough to do a variety of preparations, and choose a cooking method according to the flavors I want the dish to have. I think scallops are best sautéed, and swordfish is one of the best fish to grill because it absorbs the delicacy of the smoked flavor so well."

French training aside, Roberts's concept for desserts is that richer and simpler are better. Some of the most popular desserts are his old-fashioned pecan pie, as dense as any found on the Mississippi Delta, and ice-cream "trumpets," homemade sugar cones inverted on scoops of ice cream made richer with a coating of fudge sauce.

"People were told for years by restaurants what they wanted to eat. What I'm doing is actually giving them what they want to eat, but doing it with my style." ■

RECIPES FROM MICHAEL ROBERTS

ROBERT ROSELLINI

■ *Rosellini's Other Place* ■

Part of art is its poetic and metaphysical content, and while many chefs pay lip service to the creativity that makes cooking an art form, Robert Rosellini's basis for his cuisine is the overlay of poetry on technology. Rosellini's relationship with food begins with controlling how it is grown and extends to creating most dishes without recipes. Instead, he sets a goal for the flavor he wants achieved and adds complementary essences until it meets his satisfaction. His eighty-five-seat restaurant in the commercial district of Seattle has no chef or sous chef to oversee operations when he is not present in the kitchen; he has a staff who understand his philosophy and go their separate ways to create the components of the menu, which changes twenty times a year, twice for each of the ten climatic seasons he has identified in the area.

Although his methodology and kitchen practices might be unorthodox, the diner's experience at Rosellini's Other Place proves that, as with all successful works of art, it can have meaning to the spectator as well as the creator. When eating roast elk with a sauce made from the reduction of grape skins that had been pressed for a Washington Cabernet Sauvignon, the diner experiences a contrast of flavors, with the underlying sweetness from the sauce contrasting with the inherent gaminess of the animal. The dish is a success, even if the diner does not know the chef believes that "for a truly wild animal the sauce should evoke that animal charging through the forest."

The restaurant is called Rosellini's Other Place so as not to confuse it with Rosellini's Four-10, the restaurant started by his father, Victor, more than twenty years before Robert served his first meal in 1974. "I was almost born into the restaurant business. I'm the fourth generation," says Robert, now thirty-eight years old.

But he did not enter the business directly. Rosellini graduated from the U.S. Merchant Marine Academy in Kings Point, New York, and after two years as an ensign in the Navy was considering careers in navigation and oceanography when he took a trip to France in 1968.

After reading the late Roy Andries de Groot's article "Have I Discovered the World's Greatest Restaurant?" Rosellini wanted to eat at famed Jean and Pierre Troisgros's Les Frères Troisgros in Roanne.

"There was a magical quality in that restaurant. The food, service, and wine were excellent but there was more. They had integrated themselves into a unique whole.

"I had been looking for something to really give my life to, and I noticed there was a quality in their excellence that made me feel alive in a very special way. So I made a commitment to myself and stayed in Europe.

"I could have stayed twenty years. I immersed myself, and said I would not come up for air until

I had the answers. I saw clearly that for someone who wanted to learn the essence of a subject, school wasn't the place to get it. I just dove in."

Rosellini worked with Chef Émile Shild in Geneva, and for six years remained in Europe, working with every aspect of the restaurant business, from 4 A.M. stints with butchers to afternoon visits with cellarmasters to probe their styles.

When he returned to Seattle to open his restaurant in 1974, his central theme was set. "Technology allows poetry to express itself, and only after a long time does this relationship begin to reach reality. Quality is the window I look through to examine everything, for only with quality in the raw ingredients can my dishes begin to express my spirit."

To control the quality, he owns a fishing company and engages farmers within a few hours' drive to Seattle to produce everything from herbs and berries to game birds and veal to his exact specifications. And their proximity to the city is important for more than ensuring the freshness of the ingredients. "I want harmony with my surroundings, and I want to reflect the local area. If all Seattle restaurants served stone crab, there would be nothing exciting about going to Florida."

He began a game farm, since there were no fresh birds or fur game available, and he believed "there is nothing interesting about an animal raised in a domestic environment." He now features pheasant, quail, squab, and ducks in addition to elk and venison. "I have direct access to the people doing things for me, and we work together. My fishermen treat their fish like infants, and it makes such a difference if the fish arrive without a scale missing."

He claims his veal, raised in Marysville, Washington, is the lightest possible color because he insists the animals be fed 100 percent goats' milk as a diet.

But these farms and fishing companies have turned the poet of the kitchen into a businessman as well. His primary aim is to supply the Other Place with its needs, but then the remaining products are marketed to other area restaurants. This is important to Rosellini both to ensure that all products will be used by someone at their moment of perfection, and to keep the businesses viable for his own use.

But it's doubtful any chef could copy one of Rosellini's dishes from tasting, or from a casual observation in the kitchen. "I establish parameters and a context of thinking, and we usually have nine people working the kitchen. All of them want to be chefs, and the greatness of a dish is the expression of the wholeness of the person creating it. If they are just following an order, they cannot put their whole self into a dish."

Rosellini admits that a failing of his system is that it renders repeating a successful dish difficult, since there are no written recipes, except for baked goods that require exact measures. "The concept for my sauces is simplicity and articulate brevity; it's the Japanese principle of Shaboni. This is something I've learned over the years. Eight years ago my food was much fancier and more cluttered."

He has determined a style of sauces based on nuts and fruits as the best complements to meats, and uses herbs to bring out the flavor of fish. On a particular evening, calf liver was sauced with prunes, cognac, and almonds; medallions of veal with parsnips, filberts, and local marion berries; and king salmon fillet was simply broiled with thyme butter.

His adherence to intensity of flavor continues to the desserts, which he admits are growing in popularity. "What makes my business is that people come here and can get what they want, but they get it my way. I think desserts, especially chocolate, can be rich and deeply flavored but maintain a sense of lightness within the density."

What he prefers are fruit desserts, since they harmonize with the fruits used in his sauces, and can be as fresh and local as the other components of the meal.

Lunch is tailored to the businessmen working in surrounding office buildings, with options ranging from an omelet to fish of the day, either poached or broiled. "I think about lunch in terms of what people like to eat at that hour, but dinner is strictly what I want to do."

In the hours between the two meals, Rosellini's kitchen staff is frequently busy putting up vinegars. He began dabbling with flavored vinegars made from wine, cider, and berries when he realized vinegar was one component of his sauces that he was not controlling, and he was continually disappointed with those found on the commercial market.

"Last year I had two hundred gallons of Chardonnay grapes at the AV Winery, and we turned it into white-wine vinegar with very good results. What I am looking for is a product which is high-toned but totally reflects the aroma and flavor of the product being used, and commercial vinegars upset the balance of my ingredients."

A concession to efficiency is freezing certain berries for use in sauces and sorbets. "When berries are included in a sauce, they are cooked for the flavor, not the texture, and some berries, such as marion berries, have a season that can be as short as one week, while the foods they complement can be seasonal for a few months. So I do freeze the berries, and find it consistent with my principles."

Freezing fruits is not the only change he has adopted in the past few years. He says his entire temperament has mellowed, partly in response to what he perceives as the success of his production system, and partly from structuring his kitchen staff along unorthodox lines.

"Somebody's enthusiasm for food should hit each plate that comes out of my kitchen. It should be as sharp and professional as the edge of a samurai's sword. And when it's that way it's magical.

"But I've gotten gentler over a period of time. I've learned to swing my sword without the blade always exposed." ∎

RECIPES FROM ROBERT ROSELLINI

JIMMY SCHMIDT

■ *London Chop House* ■

Hearing the corn grow at night and swiping a neighbor's raspberries when the supply on his own Illinois farm was depleted gave Jimmy Schmidt, chef at Detroit's London Chop House, a reverence for nature beyond the utility of freshness for a finished dish. He considers the role of the chef is to create dishes "in which all the ingredients collide at the precise time to enhance all parties concerned. I use techniques and talents to really deliver food at its peak, and part of that is experimentation to realize what the peak of each food is."

He has philosophical qualms about preparing fish, after becoming a licensed scuba diver and seeing them swimming in their natural habitat. "The most I can do is to present the fish in its natural clarity, and in a style that enhances the texture and flavor of the fish. My presentation is the fish's final bow, and I want it to be in a way harmonious with nature and the environment in which the animal lived."

And he discovered, while searching for the peak time to serve lamb, that it is better if the racks (eventually to be served with a reduction sauce of lamb stock, veal stock, and fresh herbs) were aged for an extra thirty days after being delivered. "It's more tender, not gamey, and there's a little sweetness to the lamb after five or six weeks."

Schmidt uses a scientific approach in tandem with the quest for natural harmony. But the London Chop House, founded in 1938 by Lester Gruber and now owned by Lainie and Max Pincus, is far from the serene setting one would equate with this poet of foods. It has all the physical hallmarks of a steakhouse that has fueled the stomachs of America's heartland for more than a century.

Located in downtown Detroit, near the imposing Renaissance Center and blocklike Ford Auditorium, the 170-seat restaurant is a dark basement cavern, with tables jammed close together and a noisy bar along the length of one wall. Soft paisley tablecloths add another jumbled element to the eclectic interior. Gruber and his wife, Cleo,

amassed a collection of paintings ranging from portraits of red onions and heads of garlic to reclining nudes. Added to the oils are rows of caricatures by Hy Vogel, who has been around since the restaurant began, of everyone from visiting stars such as Raymond Burr and Joe E. Lewis to those regular customers whose faces are known only to others in the coterie.

If diners could ever become bored by the visual details, there is an aural component as well. There is live music every night, with the soft tinkling of Cole Porter and George Gershwin by a lone pianist. A disco band arrives at 11 P.M. as one section of tables is removed to reveal a parquet dance floor, which is quickly jammed with dancers as tuxedo-clad waiters deftly weave their way through with trays.

Schmidt landed in the kitchen at the London Chop House in 1977, still viewing it as a way station back to his home in Illinois to finish a degree in electrical engineering he began working toward five years before. Now thirty, he has abandoned thoughts of engineering.

His cooking began, however, as a lark. "I was raised on a farm near Champaign, Illinois, where my father was a part-time farmer and a part-time printer with the University of Illinois Press. As a child we'd be directed to go pick the wild asparagus in the spring, and we'd drive the car over walnuts to break the husks in the fall. The seasons were marked by what crops we had to harvest, and Thanksgiving was always special because my uncle had a cabin in the woods and we would eat the pheasants and ducks he had hunted and hung during the fall."

After a year in engineering, Schmidt decided a summer in France was the sort of break from science he needed. "I wanted to go to Europe just to goof off, and I thought cooking would be a way to learn the history and culture." He was accepted at Luberon College in Avignon, and attended cooking seminars while also studying wine at the Maison du Vin in the same city.

It was at Avignon he met Madeleine Kamman, the legendary trainer of chefs who became his mentor. "I was scared at first. The first thing I ever made was a vinaigrette, and I had no idea what one was. I kept looking around, did what the other students did, and then studied like crazy at night. But what I liked was the immediate results of cooking. You could plan something out and make it work. But it was still a lark; I always thought I would be an engineer."

He returned from France with food and wine diplomas in either hand in the summer of 1974, and by winter was moving to Boston with his bike and back pack to study further with Kamman at her newly founded school, Modern Gourmet, Inc., and supporting himself by working at her instantly popular restaurant, Chez la Mère Madeleine.

"I did anything and everything I could to keep mind and body together. I washed dishes two nights a week and assisted in the nonprofessional classes when I wasn't working as one of the restaurant's senior staff members."

Kamman met Lester Gruber on a trip to Detroit, and it was with her blessing that Schmidt accepted a job at the London Chop House in June, 1977.

"Lester was another important influence on my life. We used to get together on Sundays to taste old ports and talk about his ideas for the restaurant. I would try to recreate what his imagination had dreamed up. It was detective work at first, since I was not old enough to have seen food as he had seen it and the quality that once was. I was out to please him, since he was my boss, but I was also after the wisdom that came from all those years he had on me."

The challenge Gruber promised certainly materialized. Although the restaurant had a national reputation for quality, the chef who had been commanding the kitchen for more than thirty years emphasized steaks and fried seafood. No sauces were done at all. "I went through everything on the menu and rebuilt each recipe. We started making our own mayonnaise, then baking breads fresh for lunch and dinner, then making our own fettuccine."

At this point, there is practically nothing Schmidt does not control in the kitchen. In the downstairs storeroom, with shelves of the finest ingredients, such as Corcellet raspberry vinegars and bins of coffee he selects green and has roasted for him twice a week, are urns of Zinfandel red-wine vinegar and a chef's blend made with red and white wine to which long orange chili peppers and cloves of garlic add pungency. On a nearby shelf are wax-coated rounds of cheese, so they can be aged to what he deems the perfect point. And an outside smoker allows him to both cold- and hot-smoke ingredients like lake trout from northern Michigan or duck breasts over his own combinations of hickory and apple woods.

He cannot do any canning, owing to health-department regulations, but he does pickle cucumbers and zucchini, and keeps an ice-cream maker churning fresh ice creams, including a caramel with which he stuffs poached pears and which he coats with a champagne sabayon sauce.

Schmidt's style of cooking would be different if his restaurant were located in Florida or New York. He tries to use almost all ingredients from the Midwest. "I don't serve what I call 'airline food.' If you have everything flown in it loses its identity. We try to get the best sources we can, and certain things do come by plane. The oysters are sent by a friend of mine in Maine who knows my standards, but the lamb and buffalo come from Michigan. We have good supplies of pickerel, perch, and whitefish locally, and all the golden caviar comes from the Great Lakes."

Schmidt works with Marilyn Hampstead, the owner of Foxhill Farms in nearby Jackson, Michigan, to parcel her acreage each spring according to his needs. "We buy the seed for greens like arugula and radicchio, and tell her what herbs we'll need. Summer is when nature really gets rolling around here. It's a muddy state so there are tons of wild mushrooms, even beyond the famous Michigan morels, and I love cooking with wild mustard greens about two inches high, and dandelion crowns."

In 1983, many of these ingredients traveled with him to San Francisco, where he took part with other chefs in a dinner benefiting the American Institute of Wine and Food. Schmidt's garniture for the lamb he was preparing with Bradley Ogden was originally morels, but even in mid-May none were available, owing to the late spring that year. He left for San Francisco while Michigan farmers were gathering fiddlehead ferns, his second choice, by the bushel basket. They arrived just in time to be cleaned and sautéed for the dinner.

He approaches each dish the way an artist conceives a painting. There is the subject, but the background creates a contrast with the dominant flavor and contributes to the unity.

For the lamb, he makes a sauce with a reduction of part lamb and part veal stock, so the flavor of the lamb is complemented by the sauce but it remains subtle. Into the sauce he whisks a compound butter with fresh rosemary and oregano. The herbs impart their fresh pungency, and are then strained out so as not to detract from the velvety texture of the slow reduction.

In the same way, he uses ginger and nutmeg, which he thinks "were meant to be together," as a foil for the full flavor of a soufflé made with dried apricots. "Apricots are not as flashy as the rest of the fruits, and the glory they achieve in a soufflé is accentuated by the ginger and nutmeg.

"Building up the background flavor structurally reinforces the dish. It's not at the immediate forefront of the taste, but hits the palate a few seconds behind. The focus of the dish always wins, because I've stacked the decks in its favor, and also because the created dishes build from the backgrounds and do not attract attention to them."

The background can be a textural as well as a flavor foil. He garnishes a slice of sautéed fresh foie gras, buttery and still rare in the center, with a stir-fried mélange of red cabbage, Belgian endive, red onion, and chervil moistened with hazelnut oil and balsamic vinegar.

Schmidt believes there is an element of theater in the restaurant kitchen. Just as an actor's performance in a role changes from night to night, so he sees each piece of food he handles as an individual unit, and treats it as such. "Cooking is thinking, and you're dead the moment you begin to think every rack of lamb takes fifteen minutes. They're all different, and it's a constant approach of your energies to meet the needs of the food."

Although he still looks far more youthful than his thirty years, Schmidt now feels as if he has hit the stride of his cooking, as he continues to make it more polished and consistent with his principles. "Madeleine Kamman used to say our personalities should come out on each plate. While I agree with her, I also want the environment and personalities of the food to emerge."

Schmidt believes that food should never be forced, and a dish is best presented with ingredients raised with it, or, if meat, on which the animal was fed. He is very fond of a saddle of rabbit dish sauced with morels. "This is really Michigan-style food. The morels are from the same environment as the rabbits, and there's a contrast between the lightness and silkiness of the meat and the resiliency of the mushroom. In the same way, I combine duck and pheasant rather than doing either alone. The duck is firmer and heftier in flavor, but the birds are related. And making quenelles of the two is a hybrid of the tastes and enhance both textures and flavors."

One of his favorite spring dishes is a sauté of morels with fiddleneck ferns, sauced with a hint of sherry and crowned with delicate puff pastry as a neutral textural contrast. "This dish epitomizes what I am trying to do. The sherry gives the dish a rounder flavor, the pastry becomes a liaison between the two, and the two main ingredients maintain their own identity. Who knows? They may have shared the same plot of moss at one time."

While he enjoys spending time on dishes such as fricassee of lobster and scallops or goujonettes of Dover sole with mushrooms, potatoes, and artichokes, he is also a realist. The waiters' trays carry more filet mignons and broiled lobsters than the dishes Schmidt creates with such sensitivity. And such "Continental" vestiges as veal

Oscar and onion soup get more takers than breast of pheasant and duck or salmon poached with sherry, dill, and cucumbers.

"There's a mess of fried zucchini sticks and shrimp cocktails going out of here each night. But I'd like to think my quest for the finest ingredients will make the difference in simple preparations the way it does in food that really shows my style."

James Beard wrote six years ago that "in my opinion the finest restaurant in the country is not in New York or San Francisco as you might expect, but in Detroit." At that time, Schmidt had just taken command of the kitchen. And with that dean of American cookery's feelings about freshness and innovation, his raves would surely be as high as a soufflé if that article were written today. ∎

RECIPES FROM JIMMY SCHMIDT

LYDIA SHIRE

■ Seasons ■

It's a wintry Boston Saturday, with gray skies making the red brick buildings of Quincy Market and Faneuil Hall seem all the duller. North End housewives vie for position in front of the fruit stalls with the city's young trendies, who hold shopping bags from the hall's boutiques.

Watching the scene from Seasons, the two-tiered dining room on the top of the New Bostonian Hotel, was Lydia Shire, the restaurant's executive chef. If "restaurant food" in the U.S. is losing its pejorative connotation, it's owing to restaurants like Seasons and chefs like Shire, who have chosen careers in hotel dining rooms for the freedom they can provide.

"I love hotels, and have picked hotels because of the equipment and ingredients I can specify, without fearing that things will go to waste, and the space I can have in a kitchen is so much larger than any restaurant this size could give me if not part of a hotel."

So while diners at Seasons might be looking across at Faneuil Hall's sign for Durgin-Park, a Boston landmark serving Indian pudding and slabs of roast beef at communal tables, the fare they are sampling from Shire's kitchen are dishes like pâté of rabbit with leeks, foie gras and fresh rhubarb, or veal chop with Gorgonzola cheese and deep-fried artichokes.

Seasons is named for the seasonally changing menus, each placed within a menu cover with a watercolor depicting Quincy Market during that time of the year. But it might also be named for the increasingly complex use of seasonings Shire is giving to her food. While drawing from the New England larder for produce and seafood, Shire has become intrigued with explorations of the world's range of spices and how she can combine them to achieve dishes with complexity, intensity, and balance. "Food must be fun to eat, but I always want to maintain the sense of balance I learned from classic French cooking. So, if lobster is seasoned with aromatic and strong Thai spices, I discovered a sauce like a hollandaise works well with it to achieve that balance. I was not after a Thai dish but my version of a lobster dish."

The style of cooking Shire has reached at thirty-six, and the success she now enjoys, follow almost two decades of difficult personal and professional decisions. Born and raised in Brookline, a Boston suburb, she married right out of high school at seventeen, and promptly had three children. "When I was divorced five years later, I knew I wanted to work. It never occurred to me anyone would ever support me."

Spring at Seasons

She had no formal training in any skill, but had always enjoyed cooking. "Both my parents are commercial artists, and my father is actually the cook in the family. We always ate good food, and fresh food. We only had asparagus in the spring, and I still remember the smell of spaghetti with garlic sauce filling the house.

"When I was married, my fun was having people over to dinner, and I read cookbooks instead of novels. I also started to become interested in wines, and was happiest when I was in the kitchen."

After her divorce, she and her children moved back to Boston from New York, and she realized selling towels during the day and working as a cocktail waitress at night were not fulfilling. "I heard Maison Robert was opening in September of 1971, and I talked them into hiring me as the salad girl, and promptly realized I hated salads. I quit, and realized I should go to cooking school. I set my sights on Cordon Bleu in London, and kept calling and badgering them until they accepted me. I then hocked my diamond ring and moved to London for a year."

While disappointed that the school was "for rich girls who want to cook well and not professionals," she acquired enough formal training to land a job back at Maison Robert, located in the old Boston City Hall, first manning the broiler and then the sauté station in Bonhomme Richard, the less fancy of the restaurant's two dining rooms. She became chef for that room at age twenty-six.

"For an American girl to get that job in a French restaurant was the first proof I had that people really thought I could cook, and I worked with the head chef, Jacky Robert, the nephew of owner Lucien Robert. He is an absolute master, and the finest cook I've ever worked with." Jacky is now chef at Ernie's in San Francisco.

"He taught me that once you become a chef you learn to taste with your eyes. If a sauce is too reduced or a dish needs pepper you can tell it from looking at the plate, so the plate never leaves the kitchen in that condition. Working with Jacky and getting classical French training from him is the best education I could have had. I learned why things were done, and I began to think in terms of maximizing taste."

Shire says Maison Robert was her true school, but it was a very strictly structured kitchen, with little room for experimentation. Julia Child was one of her frequent patrons, and recommended her to the owners of the Harvest Restaurant in Harvard Square. The restaurant manager was Henry Ball, who has played a role many times in her professional life.

"It gave me a chance to explore my own interests, but I failed miserably as a kitchen manager and quit because I was so unhappy. I could do things like pompano espagnol rather than the Dover sole I was so bored by at Maison Robert, and if I wanted to do Vietnamese spring rolls one night there was no one there to tell me not to. It was at the Harvest that I became convinced the problem was that food today is to look at rather than eat, and my food is to be eaten."

But her management problems overshadowed the thrill of cooking, and in 1977 she quit to become chef at the Café Plaza, the small but fancy dining room in the Copley Plaza Hotel, and has not strayed from hotel dining rooms since that move.

"It was a tiny kitchen set up for one cook, so the control I had was wonderful. That was when I started to experiment with different sauces and develop my own style with them. Mixing pan juices into hollandaise was a novelty then."

Within three years, the restaurant went from no stars to four stars, and Gus Saunders, noted Boston food authority, said it was the best hotel dining room in Boston.

Her next career move was dictated by personal choices. After her return from England, her children had gone to live with their father, and for the past ten years, Shire has lived with Fred King, who is now the maître d' at Restaurant Jasper. King became temporarily ill, and Shire quit her job so they could move to Florida. But after one winter, a brief time cooking at Elaine's in New York, since old friend Henry Ball had married the celebrity restaurateur, and then in Rhode Island, they moved back to Boston.

Shire then again became allied with Jasper White (with whom she had worked for six weeks at the Biltmore in Providence, Rhode Island) at the Parker House, a hotel determined to raise its culinary image. "It was the best job I ever had, and Jasper and I worked together designing the menus. I was the best sauté cook in the city and felt at my prime. I remember one Saturday night when we did 250 dinners, and the kitchen was so hot, but I had the best feeling."

Then in 1981 White left and Shire became head of the kitchen. The culinary community knew when White became executive chef at Seasons Shire's time at the Parker House would end. "Seasons is the direct influence of Jasper's ideas and my experience cooking, and what has changed since he started his own restaurant is that I've become more ambitious and my food has grown so much in complexity."

Shire is increasingly interested in drawing flavors from all cuisines, and then combining them for a personal result. Her clam and oyster bisque is flavored with curry powder, even though the soup cycles back to tradition with the garnish of crisp biscuits like those served in Boston oyster bars with chowders. While her lobster dish is flavored with Thai spices, her duck is cooked with ginger and scallions from the Chinese repertoire, and rabbit is enlivened with Indian spices.

But not all Shire's dishes are drawn from non-Western cuisines. Thinly sliced salmon is baked with a lemon-herb mousseline sauce, and dishes such as a seafood ragout combine lobster sausage with clams and spinach tortelloni.

"I want people's taste buds to be excited, and part of that excitement is from unexpected combinations of flavors and textures." ■

RECIPES FROM LYDIA SHIRE

JEREMIAH TOWER

■ *Santa Fe Bar & Grill* and *Stars* ■

Jeremiah Tower finds it amusing when people describe the food at the Balboa Café in San Francisco or Santa Fe Bar & Grill in Berkeley as the "new light cooking."

"The classical principles of how food is prepared never change and have never changed. The basic tenet of Escoffier was keep it simple, and if you really follow the rules, classical food is really light."

And Tower's appreciation of classical cuisine, a style now served at the third kitchen under his command, Stars, near the Civic Center and Opera House, came not from formal training or reading books, but from the sort of palate one develops from eating the best food in Europe as a child.

"My father was in international business, and by the time I was sixteen I'd been on board the *Queen Elizabeth,* the *Liberté,* and the first-class sections of every other first-class ocean liner. I remember once on the *Queen Elizabeth* I made friends with the steward, so I'd go to both seatings for dinner, and we lived at the Hyde Park Hotel in London for six months when I was eight, and I used to help the floor waiters serve. My parents really appreciated good food, so I grew up knowing all the tastes of the best dishes executed in the best possible way."

After attending Kings College at Cambridge, Tower came back to the U.S. and finished his B.A. at Harvard. During college, cooking was a hobby, and his first fascination with the performing arts came when he was cooking for friends who were dancers. One evening Dame Margot Fonteyn was a surprise guest.

"I stayed at Harvard for graduate school and tried to major in underwater architecture, and figured California would be about the only place to practice it. I moved here in 1972, right at the start of the recession, and was absolutely broke; down to my last $5."

He heard the newly opened Chez Panisse was looking for a chef, and he interviewed with Alice Waters. "The kitchen was two of us—Willy Bishop, an out-of-work beatnik artist, and me. I learned to cook by doing it all, and when necessary the dishwashers became cooks."

Tower, now forty-two, says that the bounty of ingredients for which the Bay Area is now famous was then in its early stages. "An Oriental couple would swap us wild mushrooms for dinners, and people would show up with baskets at the kitchen door. But there was nothing new to the food. We were doing French regional cooking using California ingredients, and that goes back to the emphasis placed on freshness in classical French food."

In Tower's lasting memory of his stint at Chez Panisse "it was so chaotic

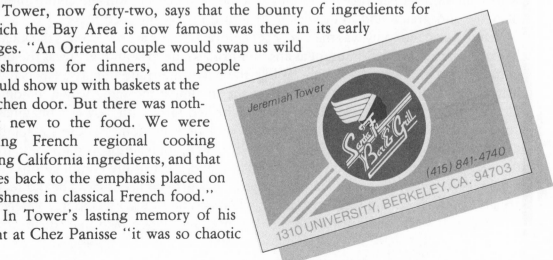

that I didn't have a chance to think for two years."

He left in 1977 and moved to London to work on the Good Cooks series for Time-Life Books.

When he returned to San Francisco in 1978, it was to start his own restaurant, and he was drawn to the downtown area near Davies Hall, then under construction. He met Doyle Moon, an interior designer.

"Doyle was one of the partners in the Balboa Café, and he wanted to turn it into a grill with a small dining room. It was not the restaurant I wanted—it was too much of a singles bar—but transforming it was proof to the partners that I could do a restaurant on my own."

The Balboa Café, on the section of Fillmore Street now considered trendy, off the Union Street shopping district, was built in 1914, and folklore has it that during Prohibition, the café's customers had keys to "safety deposit boxes" behind the bar. It had been in the Carmiganis family from its opening to its sale to Moon and his partners in 1975. While quiet during the day, with white paper placed bistro-style over the tables and a rack of newspapers near urns of flowers so solitary diners have reading material, the Balboa is body to body at night.

The menu Tower created, with pastries added from his kitchen at the Santa Fe Bar & Grill once he took command across the bay, made Balboa a stylish café. It's known for the best hamburgers in the Bay Area; dishes such as lime-marinated chicken, grilled, topped with an oozing pat of coriander butter, and served with crisp french fries; and fish, bought from the highly praised Monterey Fish Company, such as salmon with a mustard and chive butter sauce.

After being noted, if not making headlines, with the success of Balboa Café, Tower was again sidetracked to rework the kitchen and menu at the Santa Fe Bar & Grill, opened by Mark Miller with Doyle Moon. Miller had sold his interest to concentrate his energies on his Fourth Street Grill, and after his departure what had been a fine grill restaurant slipped in quality.

The mesquite grill was in place, and for lunch Tower repeated much of the Balboa concept, with simple grilled fare and such special dishes as black bean cakes topped with sour cream, tomato salsa, and sprigs of fresh cilantro, now considered one of his signature dishes.

The Santa Fe, on one of Berkeley's main drags, looks like a stucco Taj Mahal, with a tile-floored bar at one end and a domed circular area in the center in tones of beige and green, and light wicker furniture in the entrance foyer.

Once again, not only was the decor set before Tower's arrival, so was the kitchen. Miller had wanted the restaurant as another grill, so the mesquite grill was the prime cooking area in the small kitchen. "I like the flavor mesquite imparts, especially on fish. It tastes almost lemony, and is aromatic in almost the same way a lemon is."

The fixed menus at Santa Fe are simple grilled fare, with Tower's imagination appearing in the flavored butter toppings and presentation. "There's something about mushrooms, parsley, garlic, and butter that cannot be improved upon, so that's the seasoning I use for my mushroom ragout, and most of my combinations come from old French books, some dating back to the fourteenth century. The old recipes are always the best, and I get so amused when people think of raspberry vinegar as a new fad. It was made during the Renaissance, and with a bird like squab, that is very rich, you need an acid balance so raspberry vinegar is a wonderful marinade."

But the daily specials were where Tower pushed his own creativity, using the ingredients he sees coming into the California market in such variety and freshness. He serves poached fish with purple basil sauce, and blanches a variety of vegetables to serve as a warm salad, or enlivens simple grilled sturgeon with a butter made from roasted red chilies and chives.

Both restaurants with which he was associated were grills, and what Tower longed for was a "high brasserie, with the wonderful feeling of the bistros and brasseries in Paris, but modernized. I think the restaurants of tomorrow are the ones featuring old food reworked so we can eat it today, like the specials at Santa Fe and what I did ten years ago at Chez Panisse. Food has gotten away from things that make you feel comfortable, like big carts of foods wheeled up to ladle out as much as you want, or sausages brought to the table on a board. I kept thinking about wanting to recapture the generosity of the brasserie, but lightening the food so it appeals to us today."

Even dishes like cassoulet can be lightened by skimming off the fat rather than breaking it back into the dish, says Tower. Stars, which opened in July of 1984, includes what Tower considers American bistro food, such as gumbo and ravioli stuffed with puréed sweetbreads or brains. "Dishes can have rich flavor from stocks instead of fat.

"What made Chez Panisse famous was reworking French regional meals with a lighter touch and California ingredients, and there was no reason that same freshness couldn't be done again."

The look of Stars, with gold stars in a dark green carpeting, even looks like an updated bistro. There are a forty-foot bar and white paper on the tablecloths, but there are also skylights and a profusion of fresh flowers to brighten the space for the California eye.

With all the dishes Tower has created, the return to a more closely aligned French style is a return to his childhood, as tempered by an adulthood of being a chef. "It's a shame, but certain dishes just cannot be reworked. American chickens don't work for coq au vin; and the meat is not the same, so that's why navarin of lamb is lost forever. But we can still do blanquette de veau, and there's no reason that can't be on the same menu as a hamburger." ∎

RECIPES FROM JEREMIAH TOWER

Black-Bean Cakes, page 155

Grilled Sonoma Goat Cheese in Vine Leaves, page 157

Warm Vegetable Salad, page 180

Raclette Gratin with Radicchio Salad, page 181

Poached Fish with Tomatoes and Purple Basil, page 263

Raspberry and Fig Gratin, page 333

Warm Mixed Berry Compote, page 344

BARBARA TROPP

■ China Moon ■

Barbara Tropp walks through an empty room, formerly a French restaurant, with blueprints under her arm, fabric samples stuffed into her briefcase, and holding teacups and plates in her hands. She envisions her restaurant, China Moon, scheduled to open in the spring of 1985. She sees it as filled at midnight with the chicly dressed coming from the nearby San Francisco Opera and the designer-jeans set, all sipping wine with bowls of wild rice stir-fried with wild mushrooms and Chinese greens. The now imaginary customers and the food represent the dual sides of the owner and chef Barbara Tropp's personality. As she puts it: "It's kind of like me. The substance will be California, but the spirit is definitely China."

She describes the restaurant as a Chinese bistro. It will incorporate the French connotations of the atmosphere with the Eastern influences in the food. But Tropp does not think of *bistro* in Western terms. "There's a pulsating side of Asia you don't get in America's Chinese restaurants. I remember in Taipei the food stalls around a temple being jammed at 1 A.M., and people eating in front of a statue of Buddha. There's a potency to that experience that prettily garnished plates of vapid food don't have."

Tropp defines China Moon as "food as entertainment, with the cooks and staff the actors and the exposed kitchen the center stage. Our plot and centerpiece is the food."

A restaurant is hardly what the thirty-six-year-old Tropp could have envisioned a decade ago, when her first foray to the Orient was as a graduate student in Chinese studies working for a doctorate at Princeton after graduating from Barnard College.

"My interest in cooking was preceded by an interest in China. I was born and raised in Springfield, New Jersey. I wanted to play with Chinese dolls as a child, and was mesmerized by slides of Buddhist sculpture in high school.

"My mother was a doctor and my grandmother did the cooking. I was raised on wheat-germ milkshakes, and the only spice used was paprika because the color was pretty."

During the 1960s she was a vegetarian, and only became fascinated with food when she lived with a Chinese

family while studying at Taiwan National University. "Po-Fu was an old man with two wives, and he had retired from the Shanghai bank and spent his days in the pursuit of pleasure. He was responsible for awakening me to food, and when I returned to Princeton I was a confirmed eater, but had no interest in cooking."

Teaching herself to cook became an emotional link to Taiwan, and she realized that "not a cookbook on the market described the foods I ate every day, nor did any of the books place any emphasis on technique.

"What I wanted to do for Chinese cooking was what Julia Child did for French. And like what Julia had done, I felt the book had to be written by an American. There had to be the kind of distance and broad-based interest that took the quirkiness of the Americans into account."

She gives as example that "no Chinese sweets appeal to the American palate; it's sort of a black hole in their cuisine." That's why her book, *The Modern Art of Chinese Cooking* (William Morrow), includes a chapter on "East-West Desserts" that are Western in mode and Eastern in mood. And that aim has carried through to her plans for China Moon, which will offer fresh desserts based on fruit. "Chinese home cooking features fresh fruit, and the tartness and sweetness are right after the oil-based cooking, while butter and cream desserts don't work." Her ice creams, such as fresh pear topped with a pinot noir sauce, are made on the concept of an intermezzo sorbet, with half and half and no egg yolks, but much more lemon juice than normally called for "to bring the taste of the fruit to the fore." In the same way, her pastry tarts are not made with pastry creams. But she loves small cookies, and adds rice flour to them for extra crunch.

Another concept for her wine bar stems from the essay Gerald Asher, wine editor for *Gourmet* magazine, wrote for her book. She will pair Western wines with Eastern food, as he suggested.

But creating restaurant concepts was not the intent of her volume. She was solely interested in the documentation of authentic Chinese food and technique.

"Chinese cooking is based on an infinite number of hands, and small dishes like dim sum take all those hands. But home-style cooking is simple, since one or two people are preparing a meal in a relatively small amount of time. But simple does not imply mundane. It's not pretentious and doesn't seek to put on a show, but presentation and the emphasis on fresh ingredients are always there."

Tropp felt very comfortable, therefore, in California during the late 1970s, with the general insistence on freshness.

"I've often said I had to open a restaurant so I could eat food out that had fresh water chestnuts. You read in old journals about the quality of *gwo chi* in food, and it's the quality of freshness and life in the food the Chinese prized above anything else.

"But no one in my kitchen is going to carve a radish into a rabbit and I am not interested in ketchup, sugar, and cornstarch sauces. Banquet foods are painful to prepare, and I would rather have a stew of spareribs than a bird's nest. I cooked one Peking duck in my life and that was enough." And anyone who opens the clay casserole to the aroma of her spareribs with fermented black beans and garlic would agree.

While she was documenting authenticity, her emphasis on artfulness and natural-ness in Chinese food found a following in San Francisco, and Tropp began catering and teaching. "Rather than eating spinach raw in salads, I was teaching students how to briefly stir-fry it with red onions, and rather than eating just Italian-inspired cold pasta salads, my students were making Szechuan noodles with scallions. It's a recipe I developed to feed my fellow graduate students at Princeton when the only thing I had large enough to make the noodles in was the kitchen sink." Her personal inventiveness was grafted onto classical culinary philosophy.

"After working on the book for almost five years, I felt a void after it was published, and started looking for the next step in my life. The book is the founda-tion of the restaurant, and the food I'll be creating for China Moon represents what I have become since the book. I'm gutsier and more spontaneous, more willing to experiment, and so the dishes I make are gutsier."

But always keeping a toehold in classicism, Tropp maintains the validity of her improvisations by likening them to jazz and contemporary art. "The food is built on the premise that you have to understand the way you cook. You can't have a synthesis until you have mastered the basics.

"But what I am seeing now is a ying-yang between our predilections for food and classical Chinese technique. Grilling is an old Chinese thing, but it is also 1980's California."

Her first step in realizing the restaurant was meeting Paul Bernstein, a psycholo-gist working in real estate, who became her partner and handles the business opera-tions for the corporation. Combining culinary talent with business acumen was a start in the process, but just the beginning. "The days when you could start a restaurant by hanging out a sign are long gone, and it took us two years to amass the number of backers needed in addition to government loans."

Then came finding a space. The first China Moon site was near the Civic Center and Opera House, in close proximity to the Hayes Street Grill and Stars. After a year of construction delays, work began and then the space had to be abandoned because of problems with the landlord. A few months of searching uncovered nothing in the area, so the pair began a city-wide search from the docks near the financial district to the trendy Union Street area, finding a new space in between the two.

It was difficult for Tropp to remain enthusiastic with all the changes in plans. "If I wanted to go into the real estate business I would have. But I'm in this business to have a kitchen under my command and be a chef."

She knew what she wanted, but she had never worked in a professional kitchen. That was why her second step became her maiden voyage into a restaurant kitchen, an experience that shaped the unorthodox structuring of her own kitchen.

"I had to find a place to apprentice, and I trained at Greens, the Zen Center–run restaurant at Fort Mason. The restaurant ran as part of Zen practice, and it was a kitchen without ego. It was a group of untrained cooks. Everyone who worked in the kitchen would taste, and the dishes had the wisdom of the combined tastes of the whole kitchen."

After that experience Tropp found the traditional hierarchy of the Western chef and the underlings taking orders from the authority figure totally against her spirit. "I see my role as an orchestra leader. I'm there to get everyone working in harmony, but they all have their solos. I do not consider myself a feminist, and would still resist the label. I'm not an angry woman; I'm simply a strong woman. I've never been discriminated against or found a roadblock put in my way on account of my being a female.

"My observations of professional kitchens have politicized me to a certain degree. It is a strikingly male world, and I like the way women work together in a kitchen. It is hard work, and the issue really boils down to the fact that like many women executives I am a communicator. Woman do that with fluid ease, and talk about things by their nature. My staff are also communicators and that's a lot of the oil on which my own kitchen runs."

Plans for the space call for the diners to cross the bar and enter the dining room, with aubergine and celadon tiles on the floor. They will see Tropp and her line of cooks—dressed in colorful and individual outfits rather than white jackets and toques—stirring woks and taking skewers off grills. "It's an alternative to the Western kitchen and the traditional Chinese restaurant. It will offer the unexpected, and the whole aim is to delight. I plan to run it as much for my staff as the clients. They, too, must be satisfied."

China Moon will be a different restaurant each night, with the dishes falling into categories that remain constant. There are the *hsiao-chir,* the "little eats, which literally means food to make the wine go down." And the appetizers served with the wines will be such nibbles as fire-dried walnuts or spicy hazelnuts, baby spring rolls stuffed with red bell pepper and coriander. But the sauce is made with French Dijon mustard. "I find Chinese mustard bitter, as I do dried Chinese orange peel, so I use fresh orange peel in all my dishes."

After two summers in Kyoto, Japanese country cooking is important to her, so long amethyst Chinese eggplants will grill alongside more traditional skewers of Japanese yakitori.

"I'm not a bland person or a bland cook. So my tastes run to northern Chinese rather than southern." But then there's her personal spirit. She dislikes steamed rice, so the starch at her tables will be either wild rice or a risotto with Chinese flavorings, but she loves the concept of shao mai dumplings, and now fills her steamed circles with a delicate fish paste flavored with ginger rather than the traditional bland pork.

The entrées will include a cold poultry salad such as smoked squab with pickled sugar snap peas or a Chinese bonbon chicken garnished with glass noodles in a French-style chive vinaigrette sauce.

She incorporates many Western foods into Eastern dishes, such as baby new potatoes in curried pork stew, or white Oregon chanterelles in a stir-fry with Santa Barbara shrimp, red bell peppers, and fresh Chinese mustard greens. Bulgur wheat and kasha are used as much as rice, and a favorite starch is savory pan-fried scallion breads.

The dishes on which her food is served emphasize the individuality. She haunted Chinatown shop basements for unusual patterns of Chinese blue-and-white plates, but desserts are on pink glass flanked by celadon teacups. "Teas are very important to me, and they should be orchestrated with dishes as carefully as wines."

Tropp's orchestration and attention to nuance will underpin China Moon as much as her personality. "No point of the menu is automatic or thoughtless. I want to give great and unexpected tastes, and that takes painstaking attention." ■

RECIPES FROM BARBARA TROPP

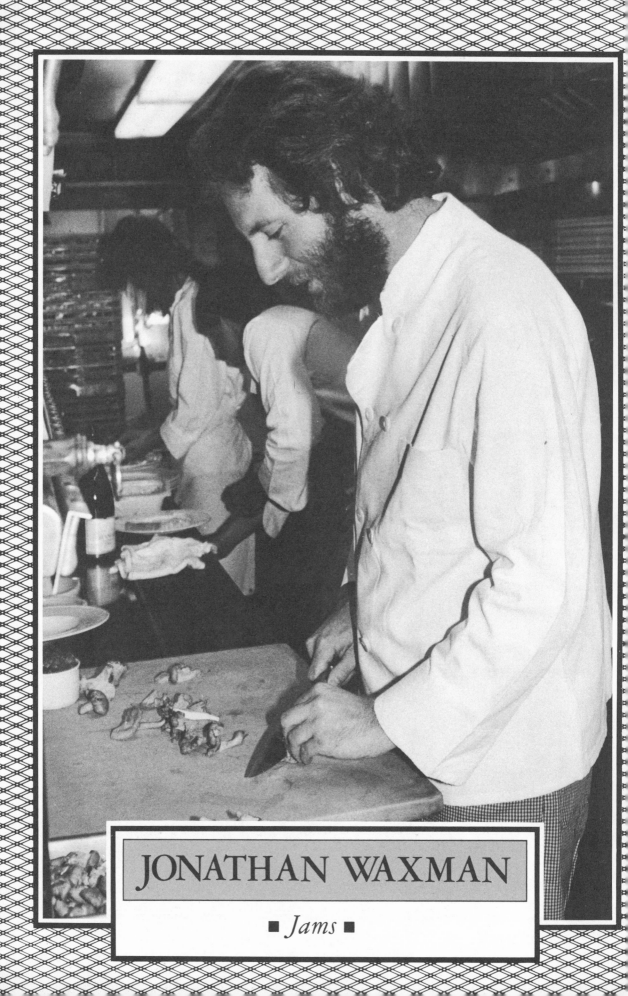

JONATHAN WAXMAN

■ *Jams* ■

When Jams hung its orange awning over Seventy-ninth Street on New York's chic Upper East Side in January 1984, New Yorkers finally had a chance to eat the casual California food they had read about. And it was not being prepared by just any casual observer of the food phenomenon, but by one of its leading practitioners, Jonathan Waxman.

Waxman had been the chef at Michael McCarty's much-heralded Michael's in Santa Monica. And the thirty-three-year-old Waxman had even been born in Berkeley, where much of the state's culinary ferment took place. But, in order to feel the independence other chefs had moved to California to discover, Waxman decided to launch an outpost on America's opposite shore. "If I had stayed in Los Angeles I would always have been Michael's clone, and in New York I can bring my style of cooking and not have the entire food community compare it to dishes I did years ago when I was at Michael's."

The style of the food, and the ambiance of the restaurant, still have the freshness and lightness of California, but no New York location could offer the airiness of the temperate climate. Jams (an acronym for Jonathan and Melvyn, Waxman's partner and former wine merchant, Melvyn Master) is starker. Waxman's work space is open at the far end of the first floor, with strong lights creating an eerie glow reflecting off the pink and gray tiles when diners enter.

From the first day Jams opened its doors, Waxman discovered there were differences between New York and Los Angeles greater than the climate. "New York is such a cosmopolitan place, but it doesn't have a sense of humor. All of the restaurateurs here, as good as they are, take themselves so seriously, and I think food can be fun and is fun."

It was the fun of food that attracted Waxman from the beginning, since he had no intentions of becoming a cook and rather stumbled into it. He first wanted to become a jazz trombonist. "Although I had always cooked as an amateur, my first professional experience was in Hawaii in 1974, where I started to work in restaurants so I could lie on the beach all day."

After music, he worked on a degree in political science, but found himself in the Berkeley library reading cookbooks instead of political theory. "I got an old Gault-Millau guide, and fell in love with the idea of guys steeped in tradition, and fell in love with the idea that a chef could do anything."

Waxman also admits he wanted to go to Paris for a while. So the answer to both desires was enrolling at La Varenne cooking school. But his real training was in the kitchen of Ferdinand Chambrette in his small restaurant about thirty miles from the Swiss border. "It was just the chef and me working from 7 A.M. to midnight, and I must have seen every technique there was to learn. He taught me how to make sauces, and I'm amazed I'm still in the restaurant business after learning how much work it is. It's a real slavery operation."

Homesick, he returned to California in 1977, and landed a job as day head of the kitchen at the Domaine Chandon restaurant, which had just opened in the Napa Valley. "It was like the French restaurants I had known, and the experience taught me how to run a kitchen." From there he moved back home to Berkeley to do a stint, as did so many others, with Alice Waters at Chez Panisse.

After another sojourn in France, this time in Grasse for two months, Waxman returned to Los Angeles. "I found the produce and other ingredients that had so impressed me before were not there. The French oceans were more polluted, and I missed cooking with the vegetables from California."

He used many of them for the salads that made Michael's famous, such as grilled chicken with fruits and vegetables, pigeon in a creamy dressing, and chicory topped with hot goat cheese in a walnut vinaigrette.

Waxman originally planned to open a casual bistro in Greenwich Village, and spent months seeking a site. The Seventy-ninth Street location had been an Italian restaurant, and "while I didn't want to be chic again, we'd been through months of looking for a location, so we modified our concepts for the interior more than the food."

The menu is limited to a half-dozen starters and entrées changing frequently, if not nightly, after Waxman's trips to the markets. One evening, fresh New York foie gras was topped with a sauté of shiitake mushrooms, and pasta was tossed with bay scallops, golden caviar, and fresh chopped basil. The same scallops were paired with oysters from the same Long Island waters to be tossed warm with greens. Salads can be as simple as baby beets and oranges arranged on red leaf lettuce with a vinaigrette.

The entrées are primarily grilled over mesquite charcoal or are quickly sautéed, and Waxman has adjusted his portion size to fit the larger New York appetites. The interest in his dishes comes from the combinations of flavors in the simple butter and cream sauces, such as the blood-orange juice and shallots on swordfish or the ginger and lime in a cream sauce prepared for striped bass. For meats, however, he's just as likely to contrast textures and add roasted red peppers in an olive-oil sauce to a plate with a paillard of veal or crunchy endive to an Oriental-inspired sauce for duck breast.

"You don't realize how much you know unless you start to practice it for yourself. There's an energy that comes from running your own kitchen and you keep pushing to develop yourself. I want food that is light and light-hearted but excites people without being pretentious.

"There's a whole world of food that's honest and relies on simple combinations of good ingredients, and that's what I'm all about." ■

RECIPES FROM JONATHAN WAXMAN

JASPER WHITE

■ *Restaurant Jasper* ■

W hen asked why he left a series of prestigious hotel restaurant jobs to open Restaurant Jasper in the fall of 1983, chef-owner Jasper White has a simple answer: "I had to go to the bank and borrow all this money so I could make a roast chicken. Food is love and giving, and I remembered the chicken dinners my Italian grandmother would make in New Jersey, and no head of food and beverage would ever let me make one."

White's grandmother, born in Rome, instilled in him the feeling that cooking was almost his "destiny in life." Few young chefs of thirty-one had had White's experience in a variety of posh eateries when he opened the restaurant. While he terms his food "just my personal style," many people have analyzed his menu as "nouvelle New England." He is drawing from the endless variety of seafood, as tempered by Boston's ethnic mix, and coming up with dishes updated from bland traditional fare.

His lobster sausage is as fat as any of its Italian pork cousins, and is served with the traditional cabbage garnish used with pork sausage in North End of Boston homes. Squab with oysters dates back to colonial times, but he updates it with a Zinfandel sauce. "One of the first recorded dishes from this region was the Carpetbagger, which combined beef and oysters, and the rare squab breast resembles beef in flavor and texture."

It's not surprising that White would hold an affinity for the dish, since his professional life was one of a wanderer, if not a carpetbagger, for more than a decade. His first restaurant job was at age twelve, butchering and washing dishes in an inn in Pennsylvania owned by his father. "I had the image of myself as Beetle Bailey then, as if the kitchen was the army. But I knew I wanted to work with food, and just kept moving around the country. I had country-club jobs from Florida to Seattle, and by the time I went to the Culinary Institute of America in 1974 I was already a pro in the kitchen."

From his early training, White adheres to the traditional discipline and respect of the restaurant kitchen. "I'm slow about moving chefs up fast, and believe in the traditional respect given the chef," but "I worked for some I thought were jerks along the way."

One clear exception was Yves Lansac, for whom White worked at the Bank of America's restaurant in San Francisco. "He was the other influence on my life besides my grandmother. She had her own vegetable garden, and was fanatical about cooking and growing things on her land. She taught me respect for ingredients, and

Lansac reinforced that by teaching me that a cuisine was a personal thing between the chef and the food."

When the two influences are combined in White's cooking, the result is "a continual move to simpler and more traditional flavors without being boring. I love garlic and the aromatics such as rosemary and thyme, and much of the fish and game birds in New England lend themselves to the sort of treatment I like to do."

He first started cooking with these ingredients when he moved to Boston in 1978 to work in the restaurant at the Copley Plaza Hotel. When the Copley Plaza sent him to open the Biltmore Hotel in Providence, R.I., he began a lasting friendship and collaboration with Lydia Shire. "Certainly there are differences between our styles, and I tend to like foods more highly spiced than she does, but our minds are so in tune that we talk to each other when we're developing new seasonal menus to make sure we don't have the same dishes."

Both White and Shire left the Biltmore after only six weeks, and moved to the main dining room at the Parker House Hotel in Boston. "Dunfey had just taken it over, and they were out to prove a dining room could produce more than rolls." After developing a menu, he became a consultant to Dunfey and revamped menus from San Mateo, California, to the posh Berkshire Place Hotel in New York.

"I had to take over at the Berkshire Place when the chef quit, and after less than two months I was really turning the place around. Then the public-relations agency told them they had to have a French chef running the kitchen to have any status in the New York market. I quit that week."

White had tired of the traveling life of a consultant as much as fighting the snobbery of French food, and he missed Boston. He accepted the job of launching the Bostonian Hotel's Seasons restaurant, and the culinary community bet it wouldn't be a week before Shire would leave the Parker House to join him. She did, and became executive chef at Seasons when White opened Restaurant Jasper.

"My return to Boston was as much for the ingredients as anything else. The products were a lot of the same things I grew up with, and I can't wait for summer each year. The flavors of the Rhode Island corn and the blueberries from Maine are as good as anything grown in California. And there's something about fish from these cold waters that makes the flesh so succulent."

White also likes the Boston climate, since it gives him the freedom to totally change his style to match the seasons. "In the winter I can cook far more gutsy and hearty foods, and it's far more Italian in style. When we get to spring everyone waits for the first shad roe, and I love its nutty flavor. But I think it needs the kick I give it with chopped capers and anchovies whipped into the butter sauce."

But White's innate love of strong flavors ("garlic goes without saying; I love it and use it in just about everything") is balanced by his formal training and love for delicate terrines and mousses. "These take more skill than heart, but I try to balance the two tendencies in my food."

One list of appetizers reflected both tendencies. There were a hearty fried polenta topped with chicken livers; fresh tortellini stuffed with ricotta and sauced with rabbit—one of his signature dishes; and a salmon pâté wrapped in pale green leeks.

His sense of New England is reflected in many dishes. His creamed lobster soup is a velvety broth totally devoid of flour thickening and containing an entire sliced lobster tail with the light, crisp vegetables. Topping it are biscuits made with cornmeal, molasses, and salt pork. All the ingredients for a traditional Cape Codder's meal are there, but his delicate hand elevated the dish. The same is true for the lobster salad matched with fresh papaya, which enhances the sweetness of the crustacean.

"There's a traditional balance of flavors and densities you must have with food on an à la carte menu. What I want to do is please people, and the variety of personal tastes coming into the dining room is far greater than my personal taste."

On the list of entrées is the roast chicken "so revered in France but considered so plebeian." His "five spices" are not the blend found in Chinese restaurants; he does use star anise, but also Western herbs. Many entrées are accompanied by Freddie's Potatoes, named after headwaiter Fred King, who invented the dish of large-cubed potatoes and roasted garlic, which adds nutty pungency to the tubers.

White is spending most of his energies now rethinking desserts. "I always hated pastries, and maybe the reason was so many hotel pastry chefs produce the same dishes, no matter what the chef tells them and no matter where the hotel is located. What I want to do is think of desserts as I do the rest of the meal, create a balanced list for people who want light or heartier things."

He started making his own ice cream. "I'm calling it a tortoni although it does not contain the crushed macaroons, and I think of desserts now in terms of a balance of flavors, textures, and even temperatures." In New England fashion, he is wrapping apples in pastry, and also creating a lighter dessert akin to an apple charlotte. His repertoire of poached fruits goes beyond the noble Seckel pear, to fresh figs that could be found on many a Roman menu.

"When you own your own restaurant, you can control so much more. I don't have to get approval on any item I want to have on the menu. A lot of people were turned off in this conservative city because I don't have a dress code, and on a Saturday night people will be dining in silk shirts and no ties.

"Sophistication has to do with dining and not dressing up, and I think my food is something a little more modern for Boston—in every way." ■

RECIPES FROM JASPER WHITE

Lobster Sausage with Cabbage, page 130

Oysters with Caviar, page 142

Rabes in Garlic and Olive Oil, page 182

Grilled Lobster, page 212

Squab with Oysters and Zinfandel, page 280

Spinach and Cheese Breadsticks, page 292

Freddie's Roast Potatoes, page 302

Grilled Leeks, page 303

Seckel Pears in Late-Harvest Riesling, page 332

BARRY WINE

■ *The Quilted Giraffe* ■

arry Wine's first experience with snails was hardly with the mollusks he now combines with fennel or leeks and perfumes with garlic as a first course at The Quilted Giraffe. In 1968, the then twenty-five-year-old Milwaukee native rejected his training from University of Chicago law school and architecture school at Columbia to turn entrepreneur. His project was to market a snail encrusted with rhinestones, dubbed the "Living Jewel."

"After you gave it water it became a pet, and if it rained while we were shipping it, it would come alive," he recalled, while gently immersing quarters of duck into barely simmering duck fat. He was preparing a confit, which he would serve with polenta in lieu of the creamed garlic potatoes of the past. The dish appears in many of the eight- to ten-week menu cycles in this sixty-seat New York restaurant.

Wine is part of the coterie of American chefs who are self-trained and entered the profession quite by accident. A lone framed trapunto giraffe in the sleek second-floor dining room is the only vestige of a series of unrelated events. But the "doing your own thing" spirit of the sixties is the restaurant's foundation.

Susan Wine, a Barnard College graduate whose art gallery spawned the first restaurant on the bottom floor of their New Paltz, New York, house, takes all reservations and serves as hostess in the evening. And diners frequently glimpse daughter Winifred, now fourteen, and son Thatcher, twelve, taking their shaggy gray-and-white dog Eloise out the front door for an evening walk. The restaurant occupies the first two floors of what was a greasy coffeeshop named the Bonanza, and the family live on the two floors above. "We moved to New Paltz so we could be a family, and the system we have now is the only way we can maintain a family in the city," says Susan, a perky brunette in her mid-thirties.

The Wines' emphasis on family is why The Quilted Giraffe breaks two rules of successful restaurants—neither lunches nor weekend dinners are served. After the last diners depart, usually about 1 A.M., on Friday nights, the family pile into a station wagon and head for New Paltz, about ninety miles north of Manhattan.

They moved there in 1970 and began the restoration of the first of what was to be a succession of four Victorian houses. Thus began their living pattern: Barry practiced law on the first floor of the house, and the family lived above.

"It was a town of five thousand, and most of my practice was wills and criminal work for the students arrested for marijuana," Barry said.

As they renovated houses they became their own best tenants, and Susan ran an art gallery and toy store specializing in children's quilts. The idea

the Quilted Giraffe

New York

for the restaurant sprang from the proximity of the Culinary Institute of America, just twenty minutes away in Hyde Park.

"We had hired a teacher from CIA to run a restaurant, which we thought would bring people into Susan's shops, and a month before it opened he backed out of the deal. I knew absolutely not the slightest thing about food; I didn't know we had to wash spinach. But we hired two graduates of the school and opened on a Friday night. On Saturday morning I knew I was hooked, and I'd also caught a glimpse of how much work it would be."

But the Wines did have experience as lovers of food, and were frequent patrons of New York restaurants while leading what Susan describes as "the Upper West Side young professional life of shopping at Zabar's and eating out a lot" before their New Paltz years.

What created the dishes at the original Quilted Giraffe was Barry's ability to "eat something and then come back to the restaurant and duplicate it. We were the typical French restaurant of the time, with roast duck, maybe with a banana sauce; chicken Kiev; and veal Cordon Bleu."

He shudders when he looks at the scrapbook of old menus, but the restaurant quickly gained fame in New York. Brian Vanderhorst's review in the *Village Voice* put New Paltz on Manhattanites' culinary circuit.

After a 1977 trip to the three-star restaurants of France, the Wines set the food and ambiance of restaurants run by the Troisgros brothers and Roger Verge as their goal. The move to Manhattan, in order to have the freshest ingredients daily and the clientele for the increasingly complex dishes, was the next logical step.

As in the best French restaurants, Wine decides which pattern of Fitz and Floyd china a particular dish is served on. His Beggar's Purses, scoops of Beluga caviar placed on feather-light crêpes and tied into purses with slivers of scallion, are fit for the Ming Dynasty plates, for example.

The title of that dish is part of the underlying humor that extends from Wine to his food. He has fashioned chocolate to resemble sausages, and served them with rounds of poached sweetened egg white to complete the breakfast analogy. And his Crêpes Sole are garnished with vegetables cut to look like shoe laces.

But name and dish titles aside, The Quilted Giraffe is one of New York's most serious restaurants, awarded four stars by *New York Times* critic Marian Burros in 1984.

Wine's philosophy, as he continually innovates dishes, is "using the best ingredients we can find and handling them with respect, love, and care. We are probably one of the country's biggest users of fresh truffles, caviar, and all sorts of fresh wild mushrooms."

In addition, the Wines have turned their weekend home into a working farm, starting with flowers in 1983, and putting in six thousand plants for a vegetable garden the next summer. "This is not California, and if we can supply ourselves from July to November I'll be happy."

While some of his purveyors are the same ones he has used since 1974, he is constantly looking for sources. "The market determines what we can do; that's the reality of any restaurant."

While Wine's standards were set by the French elite, he does not emulate their menus. "We're an American restaurant because we're American, the rest of the staff is American, and the menus are printed in English. And like this country we draw influences into our food from the melting pot of ethnic groups. We see ourselves as a modern restaurant and create dishes regularly, and I see our sauces are even lighter now than they were two years ago. In the past I emphasized the meat taste, but our sauces are not as reduced and they rely more on a greater quantity of fresh herbs as a method of making food more interesting."

But The Quilted Giraffe's menu balances consistency with innovation. While Wine immediately embraced the recently produced fresh foie gras from New York, frequently sautéing it with wilted lettuce and cassis, certain dishes such as a breast of duck, a rack of lamb, and a New York strip steak have been on the menu for years. What changes is their preparation. "In the past I might have done duck with Armagnac or a cherry sauce, and now I'm serving it with fried plantains and hot peppers."

Wine's flirtation with Oriental ingredients has moved into a full romance. Dishes such as lobster and lotte with ginger and scallion or paper-thin slices of rib eye wrapped around a scallion were early successes. He now is fond of fresh yellowtail, served with a simple sauté of spaghetti squash, and fresh tuna. "We even bought Japanese lacquer plates for some of the dishes, so we're presenting them in an Oriental fashion."

While lightness is part of the appeal of Oriental food, most of the desserts are rich. From the beginning, Wine has made all his own ice creams and sorbets, ranging from blueberry maple and kiwi sorbet to cinnamon and coffee ice cream. He also has modernized such classics as strudel, filling it with a purée of prunes cooked in red wine with candied lemon peel, apples, pears, and ginger.

A large kitchen staff enables him to enhance the presentation of his dishes. Centered on a plate is likely to be a basket of thin waffled potatoes, hot and crisp, filled with barely steamed flowerets of broccoli and cherry tomatoes.

The story of Barry and Susan Wine and of their restaurant, with some of its recipes, will be published by Random House in 1986.

"There's a fine line between personal and homey, and even though this is our home, we never want people to feel we're too folksy," says Susan. But the clientele is happy with the personal service; even a woman who asked for snails for dessert got them, without a raised eyebrow. ∎

RECIPES FROM BARRY WINE

PART II

THE
RECIPES

*T*he dishes created by the twenty-four chefs profiled in the first section of this book are as diverse —both in their conceptions and the degree of skill required to duplicate them—as the chefs' personalities and philosophies of cooking.

In general, the recipes are surprisingly simple relative to the superb tastes of the finished products. There is very little specialized equipment called for, since restaurant kitchens work with the pots, skillets, blenders, and food processors most of us have in our batterie de cuisine. Theirs are just larger.

What make the dishes special is the exciting and frequently unexpected combinations of ingredients. In the same way that tubes of paint produce masterpieces when the brushes are held by a genius, so onions, garlic, racks of lamb, and fillets of salmon are elevated to elegance by skilled cooking and inspired combinations.

If there is one constant to the recipes it is the chefs' insistence on high quality raw ingredients. In this respect, many American chefs learned a great deal from European masters, whose restaurants built reputations on the fertile regions from which they were drawing their foodstuffs. Supermarkets in this country are keeping pace with restaurant suppliers. While a decade ago the home cook would have to trek to a nearby Chinatown for fresh snow peas or to an Italian market for a bunch of fresh basil, these ingredients are now among those routinely carried in the produce section.

Credit for this must go to a great extent to produce wholesaler Frieda Caplan, who along with her daughter, Karen, runs Frieda's Finest, a specialty produce supply house in Los Angeles, known by its lavender-and-black labels. In 1962, Caplan renamed the Chinese gooseberry the kiwi fruit, and then began merchandising Jerusalem artichokes as "sunchokes," thus increasing the popularity of that vegetable.

During the past twenty years, Caplan has been responsible for many firsts in the area of produce, including marketing ideas such as moving tofu from the dairy case to an area next to the bean sprouts and ginger root with which it would most frequently be used.

While Caplan can be singled out for praise for her role in expanding our produce options, there has been a general growth in the variety of fresh meats and fish during the past years. In Dallas in 1984, at a meeting of the Food Marketing Institute, the trade organization representing the country's 29,000 supermarkets with gross annual sales of $2 million a store or more, the trend discussed by retailers most often was the supremacy of the superstore. Stores now offering flowers, fresh pastas, homemade baked goods, and a complete selection of imported wines and cheeses are becoming as common as drug departments were in the 1960s.

Most recipes in this book would not have been possible to duplicate, or certainly to duplicate without trips to specialty food stores, even five years ago. In the future, such ingredients as a wider variety of game birds and meats, fresh foie gras, and scallops with roe will be as easy to obtain as racks of lamb and fresh ducks are today.

ORGANIZATION OF THE RECIPES While you can cook along with any individual chef by consulting the list of his or her recipes at the conclusion of each profile, the recipes in the book are organized according to category rather than personality. More often than not, we are looking for an appetizer to start a meal or a dessert to end it rather than a total menu plan. The recipes have been divided to facilitate that quest.

But there are certain idiosyncrasies to the organization. The little dishes are clearly hors d'oeuvre or small appetizers. But it is possible, as I have done many times, to select a few, for either their compatibility or contrast, and turn them into a dinner. Richard Perry believes "we are moving away from the concept of set courses, and more towards wanting to sample a number of different tastes." That is perhaps the reason for the popularity of the sampling dinners at such restaurants as Barry Wine's Quilted Giraffe and Jean-Louis Palladin's Jean-Louis at Watergate, as well as for diners ordering nothing but "little dishes" at Barbara Tropp's China Moon.

At the same time, some of the heartier fare listed as appetizers on the chefs' menus have been integrated into entrée chapters, with the number of servings modified for appetizers and entrées. These recipes, with a simple salad, I felt, could become lunches or light suppers.

SHOWCASING A COURSE Many of the dishes in this book are new ways of preparing foods served often. If you take a few extra moments to whisk together a sauce for sautéed salmon or blend the ingredients for an ice cream or sorbet, the end result is one of excitement and fresh flavors.

But, in many other instances, the dishes form the showcase course of a meal. Most of us today follow the advice food writers have been giving for years: to put the energy for a meal into one course or dish. These recipes fit that formula. The dish can be the appetizer, followed by a simple salad, grilled entrée, and store-bought dessert, or with a slice of warm goat cheese your bravado can be the salad course.

When planning a meal, select the dishes to be showcased first, and build the dinner or lunch around them. If the meal centers on a simply prepared roast or poached fish, the interest can come from the soup and the side dishes that accompany the protein. If, on the other hand, you care to place your energies in an elaborate entrée, the accompaniments should remain plain and simple so as not to compete with the centerpiece or take time away from its execution.

ADVANCE PREPARATION Few generalizations can be made about the chefs in this book, or about their recipes. But one is that chefs do not think about advance preparation, since they pride themselves on the fact that everything is cooked to order and no dishes on their menus are held in steam tables. While this is fine if you have a kitchen staff, or care to serve as one while guests enjoy food at the table, neither of these options is likely at home.

Taking that into account, I have adapted the recipes so as much of the work as possible can be done in advance—as much as a few days in advance. But most dishes do require a certain amount of last-minute cooking and assembly, which can be little more than mixing the contents of two bowls together or quickly sautéing ingredients that were "prepped" and kept in plastic bags in the refrigerator overnight.

Another generalization, which ties in to the overall lightness of the chefs' creations, is that stock-reduction sauces are important. One of the shackles of classic French food was the flour-laden sauces that are an integral part of it. In their stead are sauces made from intensely flavored stocks cooked for many hours, frequently enriched with cream or thickened with butter. In most kitchens I observed while interviewing the chefs, stockpots and free-standing cauldrons are kept bubbling around the clock to provide the bases for soups and sauces.

Stocks take less skill than filling water glasses on the dining-room table, and I cannot stress enough their importance to the taste of the finished dishes. Certain stocks, such as chicken and veal or beef, should always be kept on hand frozen. Since many recipes call for a few tablespoons, part of a batch can be frozen in ice-cube trays and then unmolded into plastic bags. Then you learn to know the measure for your individual cubes. Stocks that form a particular sauce for a dish must be done in advance, to make the last-minute procedure only a few moments between courses. Recipes for the more commonly used stocks are given at the beginning of the soup chapter, while stocks for individual sauces accompany the recipes.

But never throw out leftover sauce if it is a stock reduction. For a dish such as Bradley Ogden's Crisp Peppered Duck or Robert Rosellini's Veal Medallions with Apple-Vinegar Sauce, once a batch of sauce has been made, the dish can be made a second time in a matter of minutes.

PRESENTATION The third generalization about these chefs is that they give care and attention to the presentation of food. They believe you start to eat with your eyes the moment a plate arrives on the table, and the garnishes and arrangement of the dish instantly create the first sensual response, before a fork is lifted or an aroma is savored.

But, once again, they are basing serving on the availability of a large number of hands to sprinkle nuts on top of a salad or arrange a flower from slices of sautéed sweetbread and crisp snow peas.

Arranging one platter, rather than six individual plates, is not one-sixth the time, but it is certainly less. In addition, there is a visual impact when a platter is ceremonially brought into the dining room that is every bit as exciting as placing an individual dish before a diner.

In cases where appropriate, I have suggested how dishes can be arranged on platters as well as individual plates. Some of the more elaborate salads should be done for each person, but they can be kept chilled in the refrigerator for a few hours before serving.

PAIRING FOOD AND WINE Restaurateur Richard Perry commented that we who serve at home have a great advantage over the restaurant when it comes to what wines best suit a meal. "You are serving a variety of courses, but everyone is eating the same thing at the same time, while our wine steward is asked by a party of four to recommend one wine, and people at the table are eating everything from steak to salmon," Perry lamented.

His point is very well taken, and I'm a firm advocate of the idea that food and wine are natural partners. But a hearty red wine to accompany a slab of prime ribs of beef is not as difficult to choose as a wine to best enhance some of the complex dishes in this book.

Part of the fun of the dinners frequently fed to friends while testing recipes for this book was the pairing and discussions about wine with David Vaughan. He is a very knowledgeable wine writer and wine teacher in the Washington area, who provided all the wine suggestions listed with the recipes.

We would start by reading the recipe, and select what wine to serve. But we frequently found the combination of flavors led to a second, and better, choice. With the exception of a few suggestions from the chefs themselves, David Vaughan gets all the credit for wine selection. He was also kind enough to write some general guidelines for the section that follows. ■

by David Vaughan

Balance is the key to pairing food and wine. Neither the food nor the wine should overwhelm the other with intensity of flavor. Thus you would avoid serving a Zinfandel port with fillet of sole. Similarly, a light, mildly flavored Italian white wine, such as Soave, might not be much of a complement to your venison in a green peppercorn, garlic, and tomato sauce. Choose a savory, intensely flavored wine to accompany a dish of the same description, and serve a light, mildly flavored wine with a light, mildly flavored dish. In deciding whether your dish is strongly flavored, consider the sauce. A chicken breast prepared in a delicate Champagne sauce would require a much milder-flavored wine than it would if prepared with the green peppercorn, garlic, and tomato sauce mentioned above.

CLASSIFICATION OF WINES BY INTENSITY OF FLAVOR

White Wines

Light Intensity Sylvaner and Pinot Blanc from Alsace; Muscadet and Gros Plant from the Loire; Entre-deux-Mers, Bordeaux, and Bordeaux Supérieur from Bordeaux; Vernaccia, Verdicchio, Orvieto, Frascati, Pinot Grigio, Trebbiano, and Soave from Italy; most white jug wines.

Medium Intensity Riesling from Alsace; Vouvray; Côtes du Rhône and Côtes du Rhône Villages, Bourgogne Blanc, St. Veran, Mâcon Blanc, Pouilly-Fuissé, Mâcon Villages, Mercurey, Rully, and ordinary Chablis from Burgundy; mild-flavored Graves from Bordeaux; German Kabinett; certain Chenin Blancs, and mildly flavored Sauvignon Blancs and Fumé Blancs from California.

Intensely Flavored or Assertive Sancerre and Pouilly Fumé from the Loire; strongly flavored Graves from Bordeaux; first- and great-growth white Burgundy (including Grand Cru Chablis) in superb years; white Châteauneuf-du-Pape, Hermitage, Crozes-Hermitage, and Condrieu from the Rhône; Gewürztraminer, Riesling, Muscat, and Pinot Gris from Alsace; Chardonnay and certain strongly flavored Sauvignon Blancs or Fumé Blancs from California.

Red Wines

Light Intensity Pinot Noir from Alsace; Samur, Chinon, Bourgueil, and St. Nicholas-de-Bourgueil from the Loire; Valpolicella and Bardolino from Italy; certain light Beaujolais, Beaujolais Supérieur, and Beaujolais Villages; many light jug reds.

Medium Intensity Good Beaujolais, Beaujolais Villages, and Grand Cru Beaujolais; Burgundy of ordinary quality (often labeled Côtes de Nuits, Côtes de Beaune, Fixin, Gevrey-Chambertin, Morey-St. Denis, Chambolle-Musigny, Vosne-Romanée, Nuits-St.-Georges, Pernand-Vergelesses, Aloxe Corton, Beaune, Pommard, Volnay, Santenay, Givry, Mercurey or Rully); Bordeaux of ordinary quality (often labeled Médoc, Haut Médoc, Graves, St. Julien, Moulis, Listrac, Bourg, Blaye,

Margaux, St. Émilion, or Pomerol); milder-flavored Côtes du Rhône and Côtes du Rhône Villages; average Chianti, Barbera, Dolcetto, and Nebbiolo from Italy; Pinot Noir and Petite Syrah from California; Rioja from Spain; Cabernet Sauvignon from South America and Eastern Europe.

Intensely Flavored/Assertive Châteauneuf-du-Pape, Côte Rôtie, Hermitage, Crozes-Hermitage, and Cornas from the Rhône; wines from the great Bordeaux châteaux in good years; wines from the great Burgundy vineyards in good years; Barolo, Amarone, Brunello di Montalcino, and great Chianti from Italy; certain estate wines from Rioja in Spain; Cabernet Sauvignon, Petite Syrah, and Zinfandel from California.

As with much of the standard learning on wine, the maxim "white wine with fish, red wine with meat" is only half true. Red wine should generally be avoided with fish as it contains tannin, which reacts with substances in the flesh of the fish to cause a bitter or metallic flavor in the mouth. However, the fact that fish almost always calls for white wine doesn't mean that meat automatically calls for red wine. A chicken breast or veal in a delicate white wine sauce might find a better companion in a white Burgundy.

Another principle is that extremely tart and dry wines tend to go well with salty foods—hence Champagne with caviar and Muscadet or Chablis with oysters. A good German wine at the drier end of the spectrum, such as a Kabinett, will have enough flavor to match that of ham and sufficient acidity to counterbalance the saltiness.

Another principle is never to serve a dry wine with a sweet food. The sugar in the food will accentuate the acidity in the wine, making the wine taste sour. For the same reason, desserts should always be less sweet than the accompanying wine. A delightful combination experienced recently was a lush, sweet late-harvest Riesling from Château St. Jean in California with a lemon mousse.

The order of service of wines is also important. In general you want to have lighter, more subtle, and delicate wines and dishes earlier in the meal while the palate can still appreciate them, and richer, heavier, more strongly flavored wines and foods later.

An important aspect of choosing wine to accompany a meal is deciding whether you are going to emphasize the wine or the food. If the main point of the evening is the food, you might wish to err slightly on the side of having your wine less strongly flavored and less distinctive than the food. If, on the other hand, you wish to show off your wines, you might select foods that do not compete with the wines for your guests' attention.

If you are serving a truly great wine, you might wish to serve it with only cheese —the classic companion to wine. Here are some traditional wine and cheese affinities which you might bear in mind. A full-flavored Chèvre is well matched by a pungent Sancerre or Pouilly Fumé from the Loire River in France. The traditional companion to English Stilton cheese is vintage Port. Roquefort is often served with sweet Sauternes, and Creamy Muenster cheese can be served with a spicy Gewürztraminer from Alsace. We recommend a Cheddar, Parmesan, or flavorful Camembert with a California Cabernet or Zinfandel, an Italian Barolo or a big French Rhône. As you can see, in matching wine with cheese you follow the same principle—match the intensity of flavor of the wine to the intensity of flavor of the food. ∎

HORS D'OEUVRE AND APPETIZERS

Most cooks today have moved away from heavy hors d'oeuvre to mop up many martinis before dinner to baskets of raw or blanched crudités and a wedge of cheese with a glass of Champagne or wine. Not only does a lighter approach to before-dinner snacking not fill the guests, it also eliminates the time previously spent on elaborate canapés.

If you are taking the vegetable route, some of the salad dressings in the book, such as Amy Ferguson's Hazelnut Vinaigrette, make excellent dips for the vegetables.

But another approach is to serve your first course in the living room on small plates while guests are gathering and enjoying a drink. This can be a cold dish, such as Mark Miller's Creole Marinated Shrimp or Lawrence Forgione's Terrine of America's Three Smoked Fish, or a hot dish such as Anne Greer's Oysters with Green-Chili Pesto or Barbara Tropp's spicy Grilled Chicken Wings with Orange Peel and Garlic.

I am a fan of this approach, and have served mugs of soup as well, since it cuts down on time spent at the dinner table with a few dinner partners and increases time for guests to interact in a larger group.

If serving small dishes at the table, keep in mind that the appetizer is the overture to the courses following. Since the goal for any menu should be balance, it begins with the first bite. If your entrée is very light and simple, the first course could be something as elaborate and rich as Jimmy Schmidt's sautéed foie gras with a garnish of vegetables, Barry Wine's Caviar Beggar's Purses, or Richard Perry's Cheesecake with Smoked Salmon.

More often than not, however, you want to keep the first course on the light side. This can be done either with light dishes or with small amounts of a rich and/or richly flavored dish. Jasper White's Oysters with Caviar falls into the former category, while Jeremiah Tower's Black-Bean Cakes are clearly the latter. ■

Seafood
Shao Mai
Dumplings

Makes 30, to serve 6 to 10
as an appetizer

BARBARA TROPP, China Moon   Appetizers are my favorite part of a Chinese meal, which is why I'm addicted to dim sum parlors. These steamed dumplings are better than any others I've tasted. Rather than being filled with bland pork, they are stuffed with a delicate fish purée, given a healthy dose of spicing with ginger and pepper, and some crunch from fresh water chestnuts. They look beautiful topped with some red pepper, and are given additional flavor if you choose to sprinkle them with minced coriander. They are like a Chinese version of quenelles or gefilte fish, and make a wonderful hors d'oeuvre for a party.

Wine choice: Champagne or Muscadet.

1 pound unseasoned fresh fish paste (see Note)

2 teaspoons finely minced fresh ginger

1 hefty whole scallion, finely minced

8 fresh water chestnuts, cut into peppercorn-sized dice (about ½ cup), or ½ cup diced jícama

1 teaspoon kosher salt

⅛ teaspoon freshly ground pepper

1 tablespoon Chinese rice wine or dry sherry

30 to 35 paper-thin, round dumpling wrappers, or wonton wrappers cut with a cookie cutter

Garnish: finely diced red bell peppers and chopped fresh coriander

Combine the fish paste, ginger, scallion, water chestnuts, salt, pepper, and wine, stirring in one direction until well-blended. To test for the desired flavor, poach a dab of the mixture in simmering unsalted water, then adjust the seasoning if you wish.

To form each dumpling, put a scant tablespoon of the filling in the center of a round wrapper. Bring the wrapper up on four sides to form a loose 4-lobed cloverleaf, then press each rounded lobe toward the filling to form a cupcake-like dumpling with eight scalloped edges. To decorate, turn the dumpling upside down and press the exposed fish gently into either the diced bell pepper or the chopped coriander.

Arrange the dumplings ½ inch apart in concentric circles on an oiled steamer tray, alternating the green- and red-crowned dumplings for a pretty effect. Steam the dumplings over medium-high heat for 15 minutes, then turn off the heat and let them rest in the covered steamer for 5 minutes.

For a richer flavor, spoon a few drops of a mixture of 1½ tablespoons soy sauce, 1 tablespoon unseasoned Japanese rice vinegar, and ¼ teaspoon Chinese or Japanese sesame oil on top of each dumpling just before serving.

Note: Tropp can buy fish paste in San Francisco's Chinatown markets, but not all of us are that lucky. I grind salmon, sea bass, or any mild, good-tasting fish fillet in the food processor until smooth. The freshness of the fish is more important than what species it is.

Caviar
Beggar's Purses

*Makes 12, serves 3 or 4
as an appetizer*

BARRY WINE, The Quilted Giraffe   The feather-light crêpes are filled with
Beluga caviar, which implies most of us would have to become beggars after paying
for the dish. While Beluga is wonderful, red salmon caviar gives you the same sense
of having the caviar melt away in your mouth, at about a fraction of the price.

The little pouches look adorable on the plate, and when popped into the mouth
—the way Wine says they should be eaten—you get the caviar taste along with some
cream and a little sparkle from the chive.

Wine choice: Sparkling California wine, such as Piper Sonoma or Domaine Chandon.

CRÊPES

½ cup pastry flour

Pinch of salt

2 eggs

¾ cup milk

1½ teaspoons clarified butter,
melted

I n a mixing bowl combine the flour, salt, and eggs, stirring
with a wooden spoon until you obtain a very smooth paste.
Gradually add the milk, whisking constantly, until the batter
is smooth. Allow it to sit at room temperature for 1 hour, then
stir in the butter.

Heat a seasoned crêpe pan over medium heat. Using a
paper towel lightly dipped in melted butter, grease the pan.
Using a ¼-cup measure, pour just enough batter into the pan
to lightly coat the bottom. Immediately pour the excess back
into the uncooked batter, since the proper amount of batter
will cling to the pan. Cook the crêpe until it is lightly browned
on the first side. Lift with a small spatula or the point of a knife
and flip the crêpe over for 15 seconds. If you find your first
crêpe is too thick, use a little additional milk to thin the batter
to the proper consistency.

Stack the finished crêpes between sheets of wax paper. If
you are not using them immediately, wrap the stack in plastic
to keep them from drying out.

BEGGAR'S PURSES

12 crêpes, trimmed to a
diameter of 4½ inches

12 long chives

4 tablespoons good-quality
caviar, such as Beluga

1½ tablespoons crème fraîche,
or sour cream

¼ cup clarified butter

2 lemons

Blanch the chives in hot tap water for 10 seconds, or until
they are limp.

Lay a trimmed crêpe on a plate, and spoon 1 teaspoon of
caviar into the center. Then spoon a small dollop of crème
fraîche onto the caviar.

If you are right-handed, grasp the edge of the crêpe between the thumb and forefinger of your left hand, using your
right hand to pleat the edge. Tie closed with the chive, about
½ inch from the top. Trim away excess chive. Repeat with the
remaining crêpes. Refrigerate the purses for up to 8 hours if
you wish. Allow them to sit at room temperature for 1 hour
before they are to be served.

Heat the clarified butter gently until warm, and dip the
purses into it to warm them slightly. Serve with a slice of lemon
on top of each.

Fried Plantains and Caviar

Serves 6

MICHAEL ROBERTS, Trumps While purists maintain fine-quality caviar should just be eaten with a spoon, lesser varieties at lesser costs may be ingredients for cooking. In this dish, the combination of flavors is as wonderful as the look of the plate, with all the colors in rows. It's like the appetizer of sour cream and caviar on fried potato skins, only better. When serving this dish, it's best to give some instruction, and suggest to people that they mix it up to get all the flavors at once on their fork, rather than being dainty.

Wine choice: California Fumé Blanc.

½ cup dried black beans

1 small onion

1 clove garlic, peeled

1 teaspoon salt

3 ripe plantains

2 cups vegetable or peanut oil

1 cup sour cream

6 ounces golden whitefish caviar

6 ounces black American sturgeon caviar

1 red onion, peeled and sliced into thin rings

Wash the beans well in a strainer, and place them in a covered saucepan with the onion, garlic, salt, and 3 cups of cold water. Bring the beans to a boil and simmer them, covered, for about 2½ hours, or until they are tender but not mushy. Remove the onion and garlic, drain well, and mash the beans with a fork.

Peel the plantains and cut on the diagonal into ½-inch-thick slices. Soak them in salted water for 30 minutes. Pat them dry with paper towels.

Heat the oil in a deep skillet, and when hot add the slices of plantain. Fry them until golden, drain on paper towels, and smash with the back of a spoon until they are ¼ inch thick. Refry for 30 seconds and drain well.

To arrange: Place a row of plantains down the center of each plate or the platter, with strips of the beans, sour cream, and the two caviars alongside them, alternating colors. Garnish with slices of red onion across the center of the plate.

Terrine of America's Three Smoked Fish

Serves 12 to 15

LAWRENCE FORGIONE, An American Place This is hardly inexpensive, but it does feed quite a crowd, and is so easy to make. Most of the work is done by the man behind the deli case when he slices off the smoked fish.

While the overall taste is from the smoked fish, it's much more delicate and subtle mixed with the fresh fish and cream. And the terrine looks elegant with stripes of orange smoked salmon and white smoked sturgeon, and little mounds of caviar around the slices.

I've served this as part of a buffet dinner, and found that, while the caviar adds to the flavor, it's not really necessary. The terrine and dressing passed separately are still flavorful.

Wine choice: French white Burgundy or California Sauvignon Blanc.

Terrine:

1½ pounds firm, white fresh fish (monkfish, sole, halibut)

½ pound smoked whitefish

2 egg yolks

3 egg whites

1¼ cups heavy cream

½ cup chopped parsley

1½ teaspoons salt

6 drops Tabasco

Pinch of ground white pepper

1½ pounds smoked salmon, cut into ½-inch-thick slices

1½ pounds smoked sturgeon, cut into ½-inch-thick slices

Dressing:

2 egg yolks

1 tablespoon cold water

1 cup vegetable oil

6 tablespoons white-wine vinegar

2 cups sour cream

2 teaspoons salt

½ teaspoon ground white pepper

Garnishes:

¼ cup chopped parsley

2 hard-boiled eggs, yolks and whites chopped separately

1 medium onion, finely chopped

½ cup fresh whitefish caviar (golden)

½ cup fresh sturgeon caviar

½ cup fresh salmon caviar

Chill all the terrine ingredients thoroughly. Purée the fresh fish, whitefish, and egg yolks in a food processor fitted with a steel blade until it becomes a smooth paste. With the food processor running, add the egg whites, one at a time, and the cream, stopping the machine to scrape the sides of the bowl from time to time. Add parsley, salt, Tabasco, and pepper.

Lightly butter the sides and bottom of a 12-by-3-by-4-inch terrine mold or loaf pan. Spread a layer of mousse ½ inch thick on the bottom. Top with a layer of smoked salmon. Cover the salmon with half the remaining mousse mixture, then add a layer of sturgeon, and finish the top with the remaining mousse. Rap the pan a few times on the counter to compress the mixture, and cover the mold with a double layer of buttered heavy-duty foil.

Put the mold in a baking pan, and pour in hot water halfway up the sides of the mold. Bake at 350 degrees for 45 to 60 minutes, or until a cake tester comes out clean. Cool the terrine to room temperature and then chill, pouring out the liquid that has accumulated in the pan.

For dressing: Mix the yolks and water in a blender or food processor. With the motor running, add the oil in a very slow stream as if making a mayonnaise. Then add the vinegar. Scrape the mixture into a mixing bowl and stir in the sour cream and seasonings. If the dressing is too thick, thin with a little milk.

To serve: Thinly cover the bottom of the chilled serving plates with a little dressing. Cut ½-inch-thick slices of the terrine and center the slices on the plates. Surround them with chopped parsley, egg yolks, egg whites, and onion. Alternate caviars in small mounds around each terrine slice.

Cheesecake with Smoked Salmon

Serves 6 as an appetizer, 4 as an entrée

RICHARD PERRY, Richard Perry Restaurant   There are certain foods just made to go together, and cream cheese and smoked salmon—called *lox* where I come from—fall into that category. But rather than being heavy heaped on a bagel, this cheesecake is so light, and the leeks and cheese add to the combination. Instead of thinking of it as a cheesecake with all the dessert connotations, think of it as a mousse. That's what the texture is like, and the flavor from the salmon permeates every bite.

Wine choice: California Chardonnay.

For the loaf pan:

1 tablespoon butter

3 tablespoons breadcrumbs

2 tablespoons freshly grated Parmesan cheese

The cheesecake:

14 ounces cream cheese

2 eggs

3 tablespoons heavy cream

½ cup chopped leeks, white part only

3 tablespoons unsalted butter

¼ pound smoked salmon, cut into small dice

2 tablespoons Parmesan cheese

¼ cup grated Gruyère cheese (imported, not processed)

1 tablespoon finely minced black truffle (optional)

½ teaspoon white pepper

½ to 1½ teaspoons salt

Butter a loaf pan (12 by 3 by 4 inches) well. Mix the crumbs and cheese and sprinkle on the pan until the sides and bottom are well covered. Turn the pan upside down over the sink and rap to shake out excess crumbs.

Let the cream cheese sit at room temperature for 3 hours to soften. Place the cream cheese, eggs, and cream in a mixer bowl or in a food processor fitted with a steel blade. Beat them until smooth and fluffy.

Sauté the leeks in butter in an 8-inch skillet until they are soft and translucent, about 5 minutes. Fold the leeks into the cheese mixture with the diced smoked salmon. Add the Parmesan, Gruyère, truffle if used, and pepper. Add salt a little at a time, and taste, since smoked salmon varies in its saltiness.

Preheat the oven to 300 degrees. Pour the cheese mixture into the loaf pan and place the pan in a baking pan in the oven. Pour hot water into the baking pan until it comes halfway up the sides of the loaf pan. Bake the loaf for 1 hour and 40 minutes, turn off the oven, and let it sit in the oven for an additional 1 hour. Remove it from the oven and let it sit at room temperature for at least 2 hours before unmolding. Or prepare it a day in advance and reheat it in a 300-degree oven for 20 minutes or until warm but not hot, then unmold.

Mille Feuille of Fish with Mustard Vinaigrette

For 4 people

SUSUMU FUKUI, La Petite Chaya   This dish looks so pretty when you put it on the plate you barely have the heart to dig into it. Like puff pastry, the crispy fried wonton skins will crunch in your mouth. They are much lighter than the buttery layers of pastry, and that's why they go so well with the delicate fresh fish. The mustard dressing gives a lift to the dish.

Wine choice: French Sancerre or Pouilly Fumé, or a California Sauvignon Blanc.

Peanut oil for deep frying

8 wonton wrappers

¼ daikon (Japanese radish)

¼ carrot

2 cucumbers

5 ounces fresh tuna

3 tablespoons rice vinegar

½ cup safflower oil

3 tablespoons coarse-grained prepared mustard

Salt and pepper to taste

4 spears asparagus

½ tomato

Heat the peanut oil in a skillet, and when hot fry the wonton skins one at a time, holding them between two metal spatulas to make sure they do not lose their shape. Fry them until golden and drain on paper toweling.

Peel the daikon, carrot, and cucumbers, seed the cucumbers and cut them into fine julienne. Sprinkle the tuna with salt. Set it aside for 15 minutes, then wipe off any salt and moisture and slice it thin.

In a bowl, mix together the vinegar, oil, mustard, salt and pepper, and whisk until thick and well combined.

Blanch the asparagus for 3 minutes, and peel, seed, and chop the tomato.

To assemble: Mix the julienned vegetables together and arrange them on individual plates in an even layer. Place slices of tuna around the edges of the plate on top of the vegetables, and place a fried wonton skin over each. Top with a layer of fish on top of the wonton, then add another wonton skin, and a spear of asparagus and sprinkling of tomatoes on top. Place some of the vinaigrette on each slice of fish and serve.

Note: The wonton skins can be fried and the vegetables and dressing prepared in advance.

Salmon Tartare

Serves 4 to 6

MICHAEL ROBERTS, Trumps   The steak is always a minor part of my fondness for steak tartare; I love the flavors of the anchovies, capers, horseradish and spices. The same is true here, only the fresh salmon with a lot of parsley adds to the whole rather than serving as the binder. Even in this world of sushi mania, there are still people around with an aversion to raw fish. One of these appeared at my table the night I first made this recipe. A portion was whisked to the kitchen to become a "salmon burger" by being sautéed in a little olive oil. It pleased the guest, and I also cooked the leftovers that way the next day for lunch, since the salmon had lost some of its freshness.

   This makes a wonderful hors d'oeuvre with cocktails.

Wine choice: California Sauvignon Blanc or Alsatian Gewürtztraminer.

1 pound salmon fillet

1 bunch fresh parsley

4 anchovy fillets

4 tablespoons minced shallots

3 tablespoons capers

2 tablespoons horseradish

2 tablespoons grainy prepared mustard

6 drops Tabasco

Freshly squeezed lemon juice to taste (at least 2 tablespoons)

Salt and pepper to taste

Chop the salmon fine by hand. Chop the parsley, anchovies, and shallots fine. Add the whole capers, horseradish, and mustard, and stir well. Mix with the salmon, and add Tabasco, lemon juice, and salt and pepper. Serve with toast points, or with crackers as an hors d'oeuvre.

Lobster Sausage with Cabbage

Serves 12 as an appetizer, 8 as an entrée

JASPER WHITE, Restaurant Jasper   These sausages are listed as appetizers, the way White serves them, but I could certainly eat them as an entire meal. The flavor and color of the red pepper makes the lobster taste even sweeter and look pinker, so the plate is very attractive with the green cabbage.

The celery and carrots add some crunch to the dish, and the cabbage brings it further down to earth. It's fun to watch people's faces with the first bite. They see something on the plate that looks like a bratwurst, but the aroma is unmistakably lobster.

Wine choice: California Chardonnay or Sauvignon Blanc.

3 two-pound lobsters, killed according to procedure on p. 135

1 red pepper

1½ sticks unsalted butter

½ teaspoon finely chopped garlic

1 stalk celery, finely chopped

½ medium carrot, finely chopped

3 teaspoons chopped fresh parsley and chervil (if you have no fresh chervil, use parsley alone)

Salt and freshly ground pepper to taste

6 cups finely sliced green cabbage

Break off the tails of 2 lobsters. Remove the meat from the shells and set it aside. Cook the whole lobster and the remaining claws and bodies about 7 to 8 minutes in boiling salted water. Remove every speck of meat from the shells, and cut it into pieces the size of a dime.

Roast the red pepper under a broiler, until the skin is charred all over, and then wrap it in a dish towel and cool for 5 minutes, or until cool enough to handle. Peel, skin, and remove the seeds and ribs.

Purée the red pepper with the raw lobster meat in a food processor fitted with a steel blade, or in a blender. Set it aside.

Heat 8 tablespoons of the butter in a sauté pan or 12-inch skillet and add the garlic, celery, and carrot. Sauté them over medium heat for 3 to 4 minutes, keeping them crunchy. Remove them to a large bowl and cool to room temperature.

Mix the vegetables with the raw lobster purée, the cooked lobster meat, the parsley, and chervil. Season the mixture with salt and pepper.

Pack loosely into sausage casings (see Note), since the mixture expands as it cooks, or butter 8-by-12-inch rectangles of heavy-duty aluminum foil and place some of the filling at one long side of each. Roll the foil to encase the filling, twisting the ends tightly.

Poach the sausages in simmering water for 10 minutes, and drain. Heat a few tablespoons of butter in a sauté pan and cook the sausages an additional five minutes over low heat. Unwrap them before sautéing if cooked in foil.

Bring a large quantity of salted water to a boil, and blanch the cabbage for 30 seconds. Drain it well, pressing to extract as much water as possible. Heat the remaining butter in a sauté pan or 14-inch skillet and sauté the cabbage in the butter until tender, about 10 minutes. Season with salt and pepper to taste.

Serve the sausages with the sautéed cabbage.

Note on sausage casings: Before using pork or lamb casings, rinse in cold water to remove the salt they are packed in. Then soak the casings in puréed papaya for 24 hours. Papaya contains an enzyme that tenderizes the casings. Then rinse again in cold water. White says for this small amount of sausage a machine is not necessary, and a pastry bag fitted with a sausage nozzle works well. The sausages and cabbage can be prepared separately a day in advance and reheated slowly.

Poached Spiny Lobster in White Wine with Blue Corncakes

Serves 4 as an appetizer or 2 as an entrée

BRADLEY OGDEN, The Campton Place Hotel   Blue corncakes are not actually blue, they are blue-gray, and not finding blue cornmeal—a staple around Santa Fe, New Mexico, and elsewhere available in specialty food stores—should not deter you from making this dish. Stoneground yellow cornmeal works just as well. The resilient lobster and crunchy, barely cooked vegetables with some fresh dill and the cream sauce make this an interesting variation on creamed seafood. It looks so pretty to have the chunks of lobster and vegetables on top of the corncakes.

Wine choice: California Chardonnay.

BLUE CORNCAKES

1⅓ cups blue cornmeal

1 cup all-purpose flour

1½ teaspoons kosher salt

1 teaspoon granulated sugar

¾ teaspoon ground white pepper

3 eggs, separated

1 cup milk

4 tablespoons melted butter

½ cup bacon fat or clarified butter

SAUCE AND LOBSTER

Sauce:

1 cup heavy cream

¼ cup dry white wine

2 tablespoons dry white vermouth

1 tablespoon minced shallots

½ teaspoon minced garlic

Poaching the lobster:

1½ cups dry white wine

1½ cups water

1 lemon, thinly sliced

Mix the dry ingredients, and stir in the egg yolks, milk, and butter. Beat the egg whites with an electric mixer at medium speed until they are frothy, and then increase the speed until they form stiff peaks. Fold them into the beaten mixture.

In a 10- or 12-inch skillet, heat bacon fat or clarified butter over medium heat. Drop the batter into the hot fat, shaping into circles 2 inches in diameter. Cook on one side until the edges become golden brown, then turn and cook for an additional 30 seconds.

Repeat the procedure until all the batter is used up. You should have 12 corncakes. Remove them to a warm oven, or they can be made a day in advance and reheated for 10 minutes at 275 degrees before serving.

Mix all the sauce ingredients in a small heavy saucepan. Place it on medium heat and bring the mixture to a boil. Reduce the heat to low, and simmer the sauce until the volume is reduced by half, and the sauce is thick enough to coat the back of a spoon.

Combine all the poaching ingredients except the lobster tails in a saucepan and simmer for 15 minutes. Strain the broth, and return it to the pan, discarding the solids, and poach the lobster tails for 3 to 5 minutes just to cook them partially. Cool them and remove the shells. Cut the lobster meat in half lengthwise or into chunks.

To finish the dish: Place the butter in an 8-inch skillet over medium heat, letting the butter heat until it is sizzling. Add the celery, shallots, and scallions, and stir-fry a few seconds. Add the lobster, wine, and seasonings, and heat through. Add 1½

1 carrot, peeled and coarsely chopped

1 onion, coarsely chopped

2 stalks celery, coarsely chopped

6 sprigs parsley

3 bay leaves

1 teaspoon whole black peppercorns

2 lobster tails, 6 ounces each (see Note)

Finishing:

1 tablespoon unsalted butter

2 tablespoons celery, cut into ⅛-inch diagonal slices

1 teaspoon minced shallots

1 tablespoon sliced scallions

1 tablespoon dry white wine

Kosher salt and freshly ground black pepper to taste

For garnish: Sprigs of fresh dill

cups of the broth and bring the mixture to a boil.

To serve, arrange 3 corncakes on a plate. Top with the sauce and place the cooked lobster in the center. Garnish with a sprig of fresh dill.

Note: Spiny lobsters are not easy to find, but lobster tails can be substituted, or a whole Maine lobster can be dismembered before poaching. The claw meat should be removed, and the body can be kept for a fish stock or lobster bisque. Substitute one 1¼-pound Maine lobster for the two lobster tails.

The corncakes, sauce, and poaching of the lobster can be done in advance. The only last-minute preparation in this dish is the finishing of the lobster and assembly.

Lobster Mousse
with
Parsley Sauce

Serves 8 to 10

JEAN-LOUIS PALLADIN, Jean-Louis at Watergate   There's no fish as sweet as lobster, and cream brings out all of the sweetness. What's so wonderful about this dish is how light the mousses are, and how refreshing the parsley sauce is with them. One time, when wanting an elegant course for a basically Mexican meal, I did the sauce with some cilantro as well as parsley, and it was spicier and gave an entirely new taste to the dish.

Wine choice: French white Burgundy.

1 pound fresh lobster meat (about 2 large tails)

2½ to 3 cups heavy cream

Salt and freshly ground black pepper to taste

2 bunches parsley

3 ounces chicken or fish stock, or consommé (pages 160, 161)

Run the lobster meat through a meat grinder or food processor fitted with a steel blade, and then pass through a sieve to remove any fiber. Put the purée back into the food processor after chilling it well, and with the motor running, slowly add 1 to 1½ cups of the cream and salt and pepper to taste, keeping the mixture light and not thinning it too much. Do not process after the cream has been added or the mixture will turn to butter. Place it in buttered individual molds and set aside.

For the sauce, trim the tough stems off the bunches of parsley and blanch it in boiling water for 30 seconds. Drain it, and purée in a blender or food processor fitted with a steel blade. Add the remaining cream and the stock, and season to taste with salt and pepper. Heat slowly but do not boil.

Place the mousses in a baking pan, and pour in hot water until 1 inch up the sides of the molds. Bake at 275 degrees for 15 minutes, or until the centers are warm and the mousses are set. Remove them from the oven and allow them to sit for 10 minutes. Carefully unmold them onto plates, and spoon the sauce around them.

VARIATION: Freeze the sauce in ice-cube trays and insert a cube into the center of each mousse before baking. The sauce will ooze out almost like butter from chicken Kiev. If this is done, add 10 minutes to the baking time.

Crabcakes with Tomato Butter

Serves 8

JEAN-LOUIS PALLADIN, Jean-Louis at Watergate Washington, D.C., my home, is near the eastern shore of Maryland on Chesapeake Bay, and pounding away at hard-shelled crabs and savoring the local delight of crabmeat bound with bread-crumbs and deep fried are signs of summer. Palladin's crabcakes draw their inspiration from this tradition, but they are far lighter and more delicate. The little ovals are bound with tomato-flavored lobster purée, and topping them with tomato butter is a rich reinforcement of the flavor.

The cakes should be baked at the last minute, but the mixture and butter can be done in advance.

Wine choice: California Chardonnay or Sauvignon Blanc.

1 live lobster (1¼ pounds), or a 12-ounce lobster tail

Salt and freshly ground black pepper to taste

½ cup heavy cream

2 fresh ripe tomatoes

1 bunch chives

2 pounds fresh lump crabmeat

¼ cup extra-virgin olive oil

1 pound unsalted butter

1 six-ounce can tomato paste

Kill the lobster by placing a sharp knife where the tail meets the body and cutting off the tail to sever the spinal cord. Remove the raw flesh from the tail and claws, and save the shell and body for making stock. Cut the meat into small pieces, and purée it in a food processor fitted with a steel blade. Season it with a little salt and pepper. Pass the lobster through a sieve and return it to the food processor. Add the cream and blend in short spurts for about 4 seconds, scraping down the sides of the bowl as needed.

Peel the tomatoes and cut the outer meat into a fine julienne, or chop it fine. Discard the seeds, but save the remaining flesh for the butter. Chop the chives fine, and pick over the crabmeat to remove any shell and cartilage.

Mix the lobster and cream with the crab, julienned tomato, and chives. Form the mixture into 24 round cakes, about ¾ inch thick, and place them on a baking sheet brushed with olive oil. Set them aside.

Place the butter, the remaining tomato flesh, and the tomato paste in a food processor fitted with a steel blade, and blend until smooth. Heat the mixture in a saucepan, over medium heat, until the butter is melted; stir to keep blended. Adjust the seasoning with salt and pepper. The tomato butter can be made to this point and refrigerated, tightly covered with plastic wrap. Reheat before serving.

Place the crabcakes in a 400-degree oven until slightly browned, about 5 to 7 minutes. Let them sit on the sheet for 3 to 5 minutes, and then remove them with a spatula. Top the cakes with tomato butter.

Creole Marinated Fresh Crab or Shrimp

Serves 6 to 8

MARK MILLER, Fourth Street Grill   This is one of the easiest and prettiest dishes I've ever placed on a buffet, not to mention delicious. The pickled vegetables perk up the seafood, and the pimentos and carrots make the dish look like a bowl of confetti. I've served this as a light supper by mounding it on a bed of greens and placing some sliced tomatoes and hard-boiled eggs around the plate.

Wine choice: California Sauvignon Blanc.

3 to 4 large fresh crabs, or 2 pounds fresh shrimp

¾ cup finely diced celery

¾ cup finely chopped pickled Italian gardiniera vegetables

12 finely chopped peperoncini (pickled Tuscan pepers)

4 chopped whole canned pimentos or roasted and skinned red peppers

4 large cloves of garlic, minced

½ bunch finely chopped parsley

Juice of ½ lemon

2 tablespoons fresh oregano

½ cup extra-virgin olive oil

4 to 6 tablespoons white-wine vinegar, to taste

Salt and pepper to taste

Cook the crab or shrimp in boiling salted water and let cool to room temperature. Clean. Purists can chop the vegetables individually, or the celery, gardiniera vegetables, peperoncini, pimentos, garlic and parsley can be chopped with a few pulse actions in a food processor fitted with a steel blade. Be careful not to chop the ingredients too fine.

Mix lemon juice, oregano, olive oil, vinegar, salt and pepper in a jar. Shake vigorously to combine. Mix seafood and vegetables with the dressing for a few hours.

Note: Both the seafood and vegetable marinade can be prepared up to a day in advance and kept tightly covered in the refrigerator. But do not combine them until a few hours before serving time or the seafood will absorb too much of the flavor.

Strawberry Shrimp

Serves 6 to 8 as an appetizer

RICHARD PERRY, Richard Perry Restaurant   Perry adds and deletes dishes from his menu, except for this one, because it's such a favorite with his clientele. And it drew raves when I made it. There's a slightly spicy undertaste to the batter, and this contrasts with the richness of the sauce. The sauce is a variation on sweet-and-sour, but strawberry preserves have a deeper flavor than most sugar-based sauces.

Wine choice: California Chardonnay.

Batter:
2¼ cups flat beer
1 tablespoon salt
1½ tablespoons baking powder
1 tablespoon sugar
1¾ cups high-gluten bread flour
¼ teaspoon cayenne pepper

Combine all the batter ingredients, beating with a whisk until smooth, and refrigerate overnight, tightly covered with plastic wrap.

Sauce:
1½ cups strawberry preserves (preferably homemade)
½ cup red-wine vinegar
1½ teaspoons soy sauce
¼ cup ketchup
1 clove garlic, minced
1½ teaspoons horseradish

Combine all the sauce ingredients in a pan, and heat slowly until the mixture comes to a simmer. Reserve off heat, or refrigerate.

The Shrimp:
2 pounds large shrimp
Flour
Oil for deep frying

Garnish:
Sliced strawberries and watercress

Peel the shrimp, leaving the tails intact. Devein, split, and flatten. Dip the shrimp in flour, then in the batter, and fry them at 350 degrees until golden brown. Put ¼ cup sauce on each plate and top with shrimp. Garnish with sliced strawberries and watercress.

Note: The sauce can be prepared up to four days in advance and refrigerated, and the batter must be done the night before.

Shrimp in Tequila with Orange Beurre Blanc

Serves 6

ANNE GREER, Nana Grill at the Anatole Hotel   The presentation is dramatic, with shrimp hanging over the sides of small cornbreads, surrounded by an orange beurre blanc that is ever so slightly sweet to balance the hint of chili in the cornbread. This is really a very subtle dish, and changed my guests' expectations of what Southwestern food is all about.

Wine choice: California Sauvignon Blanc or French Pouilly Fumé.

1 recipe cornbread, baked in individual bundt molds (page 296)

1½ pounds red Spanish shrimp

2 cups white vermouth

¼ cup tequila

3 tablespoons butter

2 scallions, white part only, sliced thin

Sauce:

3 tablespoons reserved liquid from the shrimp

3 tablespoons white-wine vinegar

¼ cup white wine

1 cup plus 1 tablespoon fresh orange juice (approximately 2 oranges)

1 tablespoon diced orange zest

2 sticks unsalted butter, at room temperature

Salt to taste

Pinch cayenne pepper

2 to 3 tablespoons heavy cream

Make the cornbreads.
Shell and devein the shrimp, keeping the tails on. Set them aside, and reserve 6 to 8 of the shells.

Bring the vermouth, tequila, and butter to a simmer in a 12-inch skillet. Add the scallions and shrimp, and boil for 1½ minutes, moving the shrimp around constantly. Remove the shrimp with a slotted spoon and keep them warm.

Boil the liquid, adding the reserved shrimp shells, until it is reduced by half. Reserve 3 tablespoons for the sauce, saving the rest for another use.

Combine the shrimp liquid, vinegar, white wine, orange juice, and orange zest in a small heavy saucepan, and bring it to a boil. Simmer for about 5 minutes, until the liquid is reduced by half, and lower the heat to medium low. Gradually whisk in the butter, about 2 tablespoons at a time. Keep the heat low enough so the sauce never starts to simmer, or it will become thin and separate. Add salt to taste, a pinch of cayenne pepper, and a few tablespoons of cream. Set the sauce aside to keep warm.

To assemble the dish: Place a ring of cornbread in the center of each plate and spoon sauce around the bread. Hang shrimp over the edge of the cornbread with their tails on the plate. If desired, sprinkle with more orange zest simmered with a little sugar and tequila until tender.

Note: The cornbreads can be prepared a day in advance and reheated for a few minutes before assembling, or they can be frozen and reheated.

Seafood Sausages

Serves 6

RICHARD PERRY, Richard Perry Restaurant The texture of these sausages is similar to that of a French boudin blanc, but they are more interesting since the seafood is both puréed and chopped. There's very little in them except seafood, so that's the flavor you get, with the addition of mushroom.

Wine choice: California Chardonnay or French white Burgundy.

1¼ pounds fresh shrimp

1 pound bay scallops

2 tablespoons vegetable oil

2 tablespoons butter

¼ pound mushrooms, washed and minced

1 shallot, minced

¼ cup fresh breadcrumbs

1 to 1½ teaspoons salt

½ teaspoon Tabasco, or other hot pepper sauce

¼ teaspoon nutmeg

2 egg whites

1½ to 2 cups heavy cream

Shell the shrimp and devein them. Wash the scallops and pat them dry with paper towels.

Heat the oil in a 12-inch skillet and sauté ¾ pound of the shrimp for 1 minute, stirring, until they have turned pink. Chop them coarse and set aside.

Melt the butter in a 10- or 12-inch skillet. When the butter foam starts to subside, add the mushrooms and shallot and sauté until tender, about 3 minutes. Put the mixture in the bowl of a food processor fitted with a steel blade. Add the breadcrumbs, remaining raw shrimp, scallops, salt, Tabasco, and nutmeg. Purée; add the egg whites and mix well. Add the cream through the feed tube gradually, using only as much as the mixture will hold and still remain a thick purée. If it begins to look thin, stop adding the cream.

Put the mixture into a bowl and stir in the sautéed shrimp.

Cut heavy-duty aluminum foil into 6 pieces, 6 by 8 inches. Butter the inside of the foil heavily and divide the sausage mixture, placing it lengthwise down the middle of the pieces of foil. Seal the foil tightly by crimping the edges.

Bring 2 quarts of water to a boil in a saucepan with a cover. Add the sausages and regulate the heat so the water is barely simmering. Cover the pan and simmer the sausages for 15 minutes. Turn off the heat and let them stand for 10 minutes in the water. Unwrap and put them in a buttered pan with buttered parchment or wax paper over them to keep them warm.

To serve: Slice the sausage into rounds and arrange the slices across each plate, garnishing with a few extra shrimp if desired.

Bourbon Shrimp

Serves 4 to 6

AMY FERGUSON, Charley's 517   You don't think of cooking with bourbon except to lace a fruitcake, but there's a sweetness in the corn mash that brings out all the flavor in the shrimp and makes them even sweeter. This is an extremely easy and fast dish, and the addition of dill and cream to the sauce gives it a fresh, light taste. The only trick is removing the prawns or shrimp before they become over-cooked and tough.

Wine choice: California Chardonnay or Sauvignon Blanc.

1 pound prawns or jumbo shrimp

2 tablespoons unsalted butter

½ cup bourbon

2 teaspoons tomato paste

1 cup heavy cream

1 tablespoon chopped fresh dill

Salt and white pepper to taste

Additional sprigs of dill for garnish

Peel the shrimp and devein them. Wash under cold running water and pat them dry with paper toweling.

In a sauté pan or skillet, heat the butter over medium-high heat until sizzling and add the prawns. Sauté for 1 minute, until they just begin to turn pink, and add the bourbon. Raise the heat to high and sauté until the liquid is reduced to a few tablespoons, about 1 minute.

Add the tomato paste and cream, and continue to cook for 1 minute. Remove the shrimp or prawns from the pan with a slotted spoon and set them aside to keep warm. Reduce the sauce by half, then add the chopped dill and season with salt and pepper to taste.

Spoon the sauce over the shrimp and garnish with additional sprigs of fresh dill.

Moules Rodrique

Serves 6

AMY FERGUSON, Charley's 517   It's amazing what a few tomatoes and mushrooms do to a classic French mussel dish. I love mussels, and drinking the broth after the seafood is eaten, and this sauce is one of the best fish soups I've ever tasted. It has a lot of character from the vegetables and herbs. With a tossed salad and some French bread, this could be a light supper.

Wine choice: French white Burgundy.

4 dozen mussels

1 cup veal stock (page 160)

1 cup white wine

3 garlic cloves, minced

3 medium shallots, minced

To clean the mussels, start by discarding any that are not firmly closed. Scrub each mussel well with a stiff brush under running cold water. Then, with a small knife, scrape off the beard that extends from between the sides of the shell. Set the mussels in a bowl of cold water for 1 to 2 hours, so they will rid themselves of sand or mud.

1 cup fresh diced tomatoes,
skinned and seeded

1 cup sliced mushrooms

½ cup minced scallions

3 sprigs fresh thyme, or 1½
teaspoons dried thyme

2 bay leaves

Juice of 1 lemon

6 tablespoons unsalted butter

Place all the ingredients except the butter in a skillet or Dutch oven, and cover. Steam, shaking the pan from time to time, until the mussels open, about 6 minutes. Uncover the pan after 3 minutes to stir the mussels.

Remove the mussels to a serving bowl, discarding any that did not open, and whisk the butter, cut into 12 pieces, into the sauce. Pour the sauce over the mussels and serve in bowls.

Scallop Seviche

Serves 6

MARK MILLER, Fourth Street Grill The reason I like this version of seviche, the classic South American marinated seafood dish, is that the sweet peppers give it so much color at the same time that the coriander adds an additional flavor to the marinade. Unlike most recipes I've tried, this one calls for marinating the scallops for only one hour. They come out very tender, but do not have the "cooked" taste of a longer marination. If you want them more opaque, marinate longer, but do not add the remaining ingredients until just before serving.

Wine choice: French Sancerre or Pouilly Fumé.

1½ pounds fresh scallops

1½ cups fresh lime juice, or to
cover

3 cloves finely chopped garlic

1½ red bell peppers, cut into
julienne strips

2 mild green chilies,
deveined, seeded, and cut into
julienne strips (Anaheim is
the most widely available
mild chili)

¾ bunch fresh coriander,
stemmed and coarsely
chopped

2 fresh tomatoes, cored and
chopped

2 or 3 jalapeño chilies, finely
chopped

¾ cup olive oil

Place the scallops in a glass or stainless-steel bowl, add the lime juice and marinate for 1 hour. Add the remaining ingredients, mixing thoroughly, and serve immediately.

Should be eaten within 2 to 3 hours.

Oysters with Caviar

Serves 6

JASPER WHITE, Restaurant Jasper This is one of my favorite first courses when I have more money than time, since the elegance comes from the fresh chilled oysters and caviar rather than from any elaborate kitchen work. The slightly salty taste of the caviar brings out the delicacy of the oyster, and the carrots and parsley add some color to the topping, making it look even more festive.

Wine choice: California sparkling wine or French Champagne.

18 to 24 oysters, shucked

1 cup Champagne vinegar

2 tablespoons finely chopped shallots

2 tablespoons finely chopped carrots

2 teaspoons freshly cracked black pepper

¼ cup chopped parsley

6 tablespoons caviar

Shuck the oysters and place each on one shell on a bed of crushed ice. Mix the vinegar, shallots, carrots, and pepper. The caviar will be salty, so no salt is needed in the dressing.

Spoon the vinegar mixture over the oysters and sprinkle them with parsley. Put a dollop of caviar on each oyster and serve immediately.

Roast Willipa Bay Knife-and-Fork Oysters

Serves 4

LAWRENCE FORGIONE, An American Place My eyes popped out when this dish arrived at the table one evening at An American Place. The oysters, from a bay in the Pacific Southwest, were about 8 inches long, and rather than one bite, each one was about a half dozen, eaten with a knife and fork. They are warm and flavorful, with the slightest hint of pepper and lemon in the buttery sauce.

The treatment works just as well for the Blue Point oysters I could find in the market. A bonus is that your hands are not in jeopardy since no shucking is required.

Wine choice: California sparkling wine or French Champagne.

12 giant Willipa Bay oysters
or 24 Blue Point Oysters

2 tablespoons dry white wine

8 tablespoons (1 stick)
unsalted butter, at room
temperature

4 drops Tabasco

4 tablespoons chopped fresh
parsley

2 tablespoons freshly squeezed
lemon juice

4 turns from a peppermill
(about ⅛ teaspoon)

Wash each oyster well and scrub the shell under cold running water. Arrange the oysters, flat side up, on a bed of rock salt on a cookie sheet, and roast them in a 375-degree oven for 7 to 10 minutes, 4 to 5 minutes for smaller oysters, or until they open. Remove the tray from the oven and let it sit for 5 minutes, or until the oysters are cool enough to handle. Remove the top shells, holding the oysters over a bowl to collect any liquor that seeps out.

Strain the oyster liquor through a fine strainer or cheesecloth into a small saucepan. Add the white wine and bring the mixture to a boil, then lower the heat and add the butter, whisking until smooth. Remove from the heat and add the remaining ingredients. Spoon the butter sauce over the oysters and serve.

Pepper Oysters

Serves 4 to 6

MARK MILLER, Fourth Street Grill   Pepper oysters are great for a party, since the flavor is even better and deeper if it is made a day in advance. And the flavor is such a surprise. The first bite is peppery, then you begin to taste the garlic. But you never lose the taste of the oyster.

Wine choice: California Sauvignon Blanc.

20 to 24 fresh oysters

2 tablespoons black
peppercorns

3 large cloves garlic, peeled

½ teaspoon salt

3 tablespoons olive oil

3 bay leaves

2 tablespoons freshly squeezed
lime juice

Shuck the oysters and reserve the shells and juice. Strain the oyster liquor through a strainer lined with cheesecloth. Place the juice in a sauté pan or 12-inch skillet and bring it to a boil. Add the oysters and poach them gently, about 2 to 3 minutes, until their edges begin to curl slightly. Remove them with a slotted spoon, set aside, and reserve the liquor.

In a mortar, grind the peppercorns, garlic, and salt to a rough paste. Add ½ cup oyster liquor and continue to grind for 1 minute.

Add olive oil and bay leaves to the remaining liquid in the pan and bring it to a boil. Add the spice mixture and return the oysters to the pan. Remove from the heat and immediately add the lime juice. Cool the oysters to room temperature or refrigerate before serving.

Serve either on the half shell, or on a lettuce leaf.

Oysters with Green-Chili Pesto

Serves 6

ANNE GREER, Nana Grill at the Anatole Hotel Many restaurants in the Southwest are adding Greer's creation to their menus, and they are adding it for a reason: the flavor of the topping, only slightly hot since these green chilies are not high on the heat scale.

The sauce is also versatile, and nachos with it are one of my favorite hors d'oeuvre to make in a hurry.

Wine choice: Alsatian Gewürztraminer, French Pouilly Fumé, or California Chardonnay.

Green-chili pesto:

2 cloves garlic, peeled

4 ounces Parmesan cheese, about 1¼ cups grated

6 mild green chilies, or 2 (4-ounce) cans mild green chilies, drained

½ to ¾ cup pine nuts

½ cup parsley, or ¼ cup fresh cilantro leaves

2 to 3 tablespoons safflower oil

The oysters:

2 dozen fresh oysters, shucked and on the half shell

Using a food processor fitted with a steel blade, start the motor and drop the garlic and cheese through the feed tube. Process until the cheese is finely grated. Remove the stems and seeds from the chilies and discard them. Add the chilies to the work bowl, along with the nuts, parsley (or cilantro), and oil. Process until the mixture is a smooth paste. It may be refrigerated for 1 week.

Spread 2 to 3 teaspoons of the pesto on top of each oyster. Either place the oysters on a grill until they are barely cooked and the topping is hot (about 5 to 7 minutes, depending on the heat of the grill and the size of the oysters), or place the oysters in a 500-degree oven for 3 to 5 minutes.

VARIATIONS:

Nachos with the pesto: Spread nacho chips (large round corn chips) with the pesto. Top them with coarsely chopped cooked shrimp and shredded Monterey jack cheese. Place 6 to 8 inches from the broiling element and heat until the cheese is melted, about 3 minutes.

Green-Chili Chicken: This can be done either for oven-baked chicken, or for chicken on a grill. Spread the pesto on the chicken breasts for the final 5 to 8 minutes of cooking time. In the oven, the topping should be nicely browned.

Fresh Duck Foie Gras with Beets and Beet Greens

Serves 6

BRUCE LEFAVOUR, Rose et LeFavour   Until testing recipes for this book, I had never cooked with the American foie gras produced on a farm in upstate New York and available from butchers. Each liver is more than a pound, and when raw it has the same buttery consistency as French foie gras, though derived from ducks rather than geese as in France. It cooks quickly, and the trick is to get the pan very hot and just sear it for a few seconds on a side. Any longer and it will virtually melt away before your eyes.

I like this recipe since the sweetness of the beets balances the richness of the foie gras, and the vinaigrette dressing adds additional excitement.

Wine choice: Alsatian Gewürztraminer.

15 baby red or golden beets with greens

2 tablespoons unsalted butter

Salt and pepper

2 teaspoons Dijon mustard

2 shallots, finely chopped

2 tablespoons aged sherry wine vinegar

2 tablespoons walnut oil

¼ cup peanut oil

6 slices fresh foie gras, about ⅜ inch thick

Flour (about ½ cup)

1 tablespoon minced chives for garnish

Wash the beets well under running water and cut the leaves from the beets, leaving 1 inch of the stems attached. Ideally, the beets should be about ½ inch wide and 1 inch long. Once they are cooked, split them in half or cut them into pieces of those dimensions if they are larger. Reserve the greens, and cook the beets in vegetable stock or salted water until barely tender, about 10 minutes for baby beets, longer for larger beets. Cool, peel, and reserve the beets.

Discard the damaged or very tough outer beet greens. Heat the butter in a sauté pan or 12-inch skillet and add the greens. Cook them over medium heat, lifting and turning, until they are wilted and tender. Toss them with salt and pepper and set them aside.

For the vinaigrette: Whisk together the mustard, shallots, vinegar, and oils until the dressing is combined and thick. Set aside. The recipe can be made ahead to this point, but the beets and greens should not be mixed with the dressing. Set aside, covered, in the refrigerator.

Place a nonstick sauté pan or 12-inch skillet over medium-high heat and allow it to become very hot. Sprinkle the foie gras with salt and pepper and dust with flour, shaking off the excess. Place the foie gras in the pan and cook for 10 to 15 seconds on a side to form a crust. The foie gras should still be rare. Remove it from the pan and set it aside.

To serve: Toss the beets and beet greens with about 3 tablespoons of the dressing and divide them among 6 plates. Place a scant tablespoon of dressing on the plate next to the beets, and place a slice of foie gras on the dressing. Garnish with chopped chives, and serve immediately.

Foie de Canard with Endive and Chervil

Serves 6

JIMMY SCHMIDT, London Chop House Fresh foie gras is so buttery that a little acidity—like balsamic vinegar—actually brings out the richness. The vegetable mixture, with the nutty flavor from hazelnut oil and the crunchy vegetables, gives each bite a little contrast. It also looks pretty on the plate, with the vegetable mixture next to the slices of foie gras.

The only caution is to get the pan very hot and cook the foie gras for only a few seconds on a side. You really sear it rather than cook it, or it will just melt away into the pan.

Wine choice: Alsatian Gewürztraminer.

½ cup hazelnut oil

2 cups julienned red cabbage

½ cup julienned red onion

Salt and freshly ground pepper

¼ cup balsamic vinegar

4 tablespoons clarified butter

8 ounces fresh foie gras, cut into 6 slices

2 cups julienned Belgian endive

1 bunch chervil, broken into sprigs

In a sauté pan or 12-inch skillet, heat the hazelnut oil over medium heat. Add the cabbage and onion and sauté them for 5 minutes, until the onion is translucent and the cabbage is cooked but still slightly crisp. Season them with salt and pepper and toss with vinegar. Place them in a mixing bowl and set aside.

In a sauté pan or large skillet, heat the clarified butter over high heat. When it is very hot, add the slices of foie gras and cook very quickly, turning almost immediately. The foie gras should not cook for more than 15 seconds on a side.

Remove the slices, add the endive and chervil to the cabbage mixture, and distribute the vegetables on serving plates. Place slices of foie gras on top of the vegetables and serve immediately.

Apple-Ham Pâté

Serves 12

BRADLEY OGDEN, The Campton Place Hotel   The attraction of this pâté is how light it is, in addition to being enlivened by the slightly smoky flavor from the ham and the sweet flavor from the port and currants. The texture is like classic French pâtés, but it comes from the apple rather than from large quantities of fat.

Wine choice: California Zinfandel or California Chardonnay.

¼ pound smoked ham, sliced ⅜ inch thick and cut into ⅜-inch-wide strips

4 cups water

¼ cup dried currants

¾ cup ruby port

1¾ pounds ground lean pork shoulder

¼ pound chopped beef suet

¼ pound chopped fatback

½ cup heavy cream

¼ cup brandy

2 eggs, lightly beaten

2 Pippin apples, cored, peeled, and diced (Delicious can be substituted)

½ cup dry white wine

1½ teaspoons minced garlic

1½ teaspoons salt

1 teaspoon freshly ground black pepper

¼ teaspoon ground nutmeg

½ teaspoon ground allspice

¾ pound sliced bacon

For garnish:

Huckleberry relish or chutney

Sprigs of fresh chervil or parsley

Soak the ham strips in cold water for 1 hour. Soak the currants in port for 1 hour; drain both, reserving the port.

In a food processor fitted with a steel blade, purée the pork, suet, and chopped fatback in two batches. Into each batch of puréed meat pour half the reserved port and half the cream. Process each mixture for 30 seconds, until smooth and paste-like. Combine the two batches.

In a small saucepan, warm the brandy and ignite it. Allow the flames to die down, and add the brandy to the meat mixture. In a large bowl combine the meat mixture, the eggs, apples, white wine, garlic, salt, pepper, nutmeg, and allspice. Stir the mixture with a wooden spoon or mix with your hands until well blended.

Line a loaf pan (12 by 3 by 4 inches) or 8-cup pâté mold with bacon strips, reserving some strips for the top. Put about 2 cups of the pâté mixture on the bacon strips in the bottom of the pan to form an even layer. Lay 3 strips of ham in the mold. Repeat with another layer of pâté, and another layer of ham strips. Finish with another layer of bacon. Cover the pâté with a lid or with a double layer of heavy-duty foil.

Preheat the oven to 300 degrees. Place the mold in a baking pan, and pour in hot water to go halfway up the side of the pan. Bake for 2 hours, remove the foil, and bake an additional 30 minutes, to an internal temperature of 160 degrees. Cool the pâté on a rack for 1 hour. Replace the foil, weight the pâté with another pan filled with weights or cans, and refrigerate it overnight.

Unmold the pâté. Slice and garnish with relish and chervil.

Note: This can be made up to 3 days in advance, and kept tightly covered in the refrigerator.

Duck-Liver Mousse

Serves 10 to 12

JONATHAN WAXMAN, Jams   This mousse, which can be served in wedges with toast points at the table, makes a wonderful hors d'oeuvre for a cocktail party. I've started molding mousses in buttered springform pans rather than molds, since you can eliminate the step of dipping into hot water, and the top can be decorated well in advance.

   While the mousse is rich, the apples make it lighter than most I have tried, and the slight undertastes from the walnut oil and Calvados are delicious.

Wine choice: French red Burgundy.

2 pounds duck livers

2 tablespoons walnut oil

4 apples, such as McIntosh or Delicious

8 tablespoons (1 stick) unsalted butter

1 teaspoon sugar

¼ pound walnuts, toasted for 10 minutes in a 350-degree oven

2 tablespoons Calvados or apple brandy

Salt and pepper to taste

Wash the duck livers, pulling off any fat or removing any dark spots with a knife. Pat them dry on paper towels.

   Heat the walnut oil in a sauté pan or large skillet over high heat. Add the livers and sauté until they are springy to the touch but still rare in the center, about 4 minutes, stirring constantly. Set aside.

   Peel and core the apples and slice them thin. Melt the butter in another sauté pan or skillet over medium heat and add the apple slices. Sauté them until tender, about 5 to 7 minutes, add the sugar, raise the heat to high, and cook until the sugar caramelizes and browns.

   Purée the duck livers, apples, walnuts, and Calvados in a food processor fitted with a steel blade, or pass them through a food mill. Season the mixture with salt and pepper to taste and pour it into a mold. Chill overnight.

   Note: The mousse can be made up to 2 days in advance and kept covered with plastic wrap in the refrigerator. For the best flavor, take it out at least 30 minutes before serving.

Goose-Liver Pâté

Makes 1 pâté, serving 6 to 8 as an appetizer

JIM HALLER, The Blue Strawbery What is unusual, and addictive, about Haller's pâté is the combination of flavors. The herbs and bacon give the livers a fresh taste, and the veal is not as strongly flavored as the liver so the dish has a balance.

Wine choice: French Sauternes.

1 pound goose livers

10 tablespoons (1¼ sticks) unsalted butter

½ teaspoon salt

½ teaspoon black pepper

2 cloves garlic, finely minced

1 sprig fresh thyme, or ¼ teaspoon dried

Pinch of paprika

½ pound bacon

¾ pound mushrooms, chopped

½ pound chopped veal

1 egg

¼ cup chopped scallions

¼ cup chopped parsley

2 tablespoons heavy cream

Juice of 1 lemon

4 tablespoons cognac or other brandy

1 tablespoon chopped basil, or ½ teaspoon dried

1 tablespoon chopped tarragon, or ½ teaspoon dried

1 tablespoon chopped thyme, or ½ teaspoon dried

Sour cream for garnish (optional)

Wash the livers well and pick them over to remove any fat or dark tissue. In a sauté pan or 12-inch skillet, melt 6 tablespoons of the butter over medium-high heat. When it is sizzling, add the livers, seasoning them with salt, pepper, 1 clove of the garlic, thyme, and paprika. Cook until the livers are brown and springy to the touch, but still slightly rare in the center, about 5 minutes, stirring often. Set aside.

Cut the bacon into ½-inch slices and fry it until crisp. Remove it with a slotted spoon and drain it on paper toweling. Pour off the grease, and add the remaining butter to the skillet. Heat it until sizzling and add the chopped mushrooms. Stir until brown, and add the chopped veal to the skillet, breaking up the lumps and cooking until the meat is cooked through and no red remains. (You can use leftover veal and chop it, Haller says.) Pour off any liquid, and immediately add the egg to the skillet to cook it slightly. Crumble the bacon and add it to the skillet.

In a food processor fitted with a steel blade, purée the livers and bacon mixtures with the remainder of the ingredients. It should be a smooth pâté, but do not overprocess.

Press the mixture into a buttered springform pan and chill it. Remove the sides of the pan when you are ready to serve, and spread the pâté with sour cream, if desired.

If the pâté is served as an appetizer, Haller suggests orange slices for a color contrast on the plate.

Note: The pâté can be made up to 2 days in advance and kept, covered with plastic wrap, in the refrigerator. Do not unmold it until you are ready to serve. The flavor improves if it is allowed to stand out for 30 minutes before serving.

Sweetbreads in Puff Pastry

Serves 6

JACKIE ETCHEBER, Jackie's   There's no question puff pastry is elegant, no matter what is filling it, and I think one of the great advances for cooking was when bakeries and commercial firms starting selling it a few years ago. It's easy to work with, and the crunchy cases are such attractive holders for an appetizer like this one.

The flavor from the sweet port cream sauce with the pungency of the morels—much heartier than their fresh counterparts—makes people who say they'll never eat sweetbreads come back for more.

Wine choice: California Chardonnay or French white Burgundy.

2 pounds sweetbreads

3 ounces French dried morels

½ pound puff pastry (defrost for 30 minutes at room temperature if frozen)

1 egg

Salt

3 cups port wine

2 cups heavy cream

Pepper

4 tablespoons unsalted butter

The night before cooking, wash the sweetbreads and place them in a bowl of cold water. Refrigerate overnight. The next day, remove the white membrane covering the sweetbreads and the tubes connecting the two lobes. Bring 4 cups of water or chicken stock to a boil and add the sweetbreads. Simmer them for 10 minutes, and then remove them with a slotted spoon and plunge them into a bowl of ice water. When they are cool enough to handle, remove the remaining membrane, and the sweetbreads should separate into about 1-inch pieces. Set them aside.

Cover the morels with hot water and soak them for 3 hours, then wash to make sure all grit is removed, cut off the stems, and roughly chop them.

Cut the puff pastry into rectangles ¼ inch thick by 4 inches by 3 inches and score the tops lightly in a diamond pattern. Beat the egg with a little salt and brush it on top of the rectangles. Place them in a 350-degree oven for 20 minutes, or until golden brown.

Bring the port to a boil, and reduce it over medium heat until only ¼ cup of liquid remains. Add the cream, and reduce it over medium heat for 15 minutes, or until reduced by half and thick enough to coat the back of a spoon. Season with salt and pepper, and add the chopped morels.

Heat the butter in a sauté pan or skillet over medium heat. When the foam starts to subside, add the sweetbreads and sauté them for 3 minutes.

Split the pastry shells and spoon the sweetbreads onto the bottom halves. Spoon the sauce over them and replace the tops of the shells.

Grilled Chinese Chicken Wings with Orange Peel and Garlic

Serves 6 as an hors d'oeuvre, 3 to 4 as a light main course

BARBARA TROPP, China Moon   Chicken wings, regardless of the problems of what to do with the bones, are one of my favorite hors d'oeuvre for a party, since they can be made in huge batches with little more work than a few. This is the best way of cooking—and eating—them I've tried, and I've been taking them on picnics as well as serving them at home. They are spicy, and the slight taste of orange makes them all the more interesting. Tropp uses fresh orange peel rather than the dried found in Chinese markets, and I agree with her that the clean taste is better. If you can't grill the wings, there's enough flavor from the marinade so that using the oven broiler will not detract.

If you want to serve them for a meal, rather than as a snack, a bowl of Stir-Fried Wild Rice with Chinese Greens (page 299) goes well.

Wine choice: California Chardonnay, California sparkling wine, or French Champagne.

2½ tablespoons finely minced fresh orange peel

1½ tablespoons finely minced fresh garlic

¼ cup Chinese or Japanese sesame oil

2 teaspoons finely minced fresh ginger

2 hefty scallions, cut into 1-inch lengths and crushed with the side of a cleaver

2 teaspoons Szechwan brown peppercorns, roasted in a dry skillet over moderate heat until fragrant, then pulverized in a mortar and sieved to yield about ¼ teaspoon ground Szechwan pepper

2 tablespoons soy sauce

¼ cup corn or peanut oil

3 pounds (about 15) fresh meaty chicken wings

Roasted Szechwan Pepper-Salt (see following recipe)

Grind the orange peel, garlic, and sesame oil in a mortar for several minutes to release the oils. Scrape the mixture into a large bowl and add the ginger, scallions, peppercorn powder, soy sauce, and corn or peanut oil. Stir to combine the mixture, then set it aside for 30 minutes to blend the flavors.

Cut off the wing tips and reserve them for stock, then cut the wings into two pieces at the joint. Add the chicken wings to the marinade and toss to coat them. Cover them with plastic wrap and leave at room temperature for 4 to 8 hours, or in the refrigerator overnight. Turn them occasionally, and bring them to room temperature before grilling.

Grill the wings over medium-hot coals until brown, about 6 minutes. Then turn them over and grill the second side until the juices run clear when the wings are pierced with a fork. Baste them with the marinade occasionally throughout cooking.

Serve the wings with a dish of Roasted Szechwan Pepper-Salt for dipping.

Roasted Szechwan Pepper-Salt

Makes ¼ cup

BARBARA TROPP, China Moon   While most peppers add pungency to a dish, Szechwan peppercorns are also aromatic, and there is no substitute for them. This recipe is used as the seasoning for many of Tropp's dishes at China Moon, and as a dipping medium for Grilled Chinese Chicken Wings with Orange Peel and Garlic (see preceding recipe). The recipe calls for crushing the mixture in a mortar, and she considers this far preferable, for taste, to grinding it in a food processor fitted with a steel blade. In both cases, the mixture must be sieved to remove the pepper-corn husks.

Please note the recipe calls for kosher salt. "We use it exclusively at China Moon on account of its mild, good taste. If substituting sea salt or table salt, use only half as much as they are twice as salty."

2 tablespoons Szechwan
brown peppercorns
¼ cup kosher salt

Roast the peppercorns and salt in a dry heavy skillet over moderate heat, stirring frequently, until the salt turns off-white, about 5 minutes. The peppercorns will smoke; do not allow them to burn.

Pulverize the hot mixture in a mortar until fine, then sieve. Leftover pepper-salt may be stored in an airtight jar and used as seasoning.

Potato Pancakes, Goat Cheese, and Apples

*Serves 4 as an appetizer, 2 as a
light supper*

MICHAEL ROBERTS, Trumps   I've served this as a light supper, and love the richness of goat cheese with the hearty potato pancakes, and the crunch of the apples with the softness of the other ingredients. It seems everyone loves potato pancakes, and many recall them from childhood topped with applesauce or sour cream. This dish is definitely a "comfort food."

Wine choice: French Pouilly Fumé or Sancerre, or California Sauvignon Blanc.

1 large baking potato

2 eggs

¼ cup flour

¼ cup cream

2 tablespoons finely chopped onion

Salt and pepper to taste

4 tablespoons clarified butter

2 apples, such as green or red Delicious

½ pound goat cheese, cut into 12 slices and brought to room temperature

Peel and finely shred the potato with a grater or with the shredding blade of a food processor. Beat the eggs together with the flour, cream, and onion. Add the potato and salt and pepper.

Melt 2 tablespoons of the butter in a 10- or 12-inch skillet over medium heat, and when hot, add the batter 2 tablespoons at a time, forming ovals. Sauté the pancakes on medium heat on both sides until they are cooked through, about 8 minutes. Repeat with the remaining batter, and keep the pancakes warm.

Peel the apples, core, and slice each into 8 slices. Sauté them in the remaining butter until golden brown.

To serve: Divide the pancakes and apples into 4 portions, and top the pancakes with slices of goat cheese.

The dish can be prepared up to 3 hours in advance, and the pancakes and apples can be reheated in a 300-degree oven for a few minutes, although it is best served immediately.

Onion Tart

Serves 6 to 8

JONATHAN WAXMAN, Jams The flaky texture of the puff-pastry shell makes this a better version of the classic onion quiche. I've served it both hot and cold, used it as part of buffet dinners, and taken it on picnics.

Wine choice: A dry white from Alsace.

2 Maui or Bermuda onions (about 1½ to 2 pounds)

8 tablespoons unsalted butter

Salt and pepper to taste

¼ pound puff pastry (frozen can be used)

2 egg yolks

¼ cup heavy cream

Peel and thinly slice the onions. Melt the butter in a large covered skillet or Dutch oven over low heat. When the butter is melted, add the onions, tossing them to coat well. Cover the pot and cook over low heat for 10 minutes. Remove the cover, raise the heat to medium, and sauté the onions until tender, stirring occasionally. This will take 20 to 30 minutes. Season with salt and pepper.

While the onions are sautéing, roll the puff pastry (you will have to let it defrost if frozen) ⅛ inch thick. Arrange in a pan, crimping the edges, and bake it at 350 degrees in a tart shell blind or false-bottom tart pan for 25 minutes, or until the pastry is golden.

Combine the egg yolks and cream with the onions and pour the mixture into the pastry shell. Bake the tart at 350 degrees for 25 minutes, or until a knife or cake tester comes out clean.

Note: The pie shell and filling can be made a day in advance. Keep the pie shell in a dry place, and refrigerate the filling, covered with plastic wrap, in the refrigerator.

Feuilleté of Morels and Fiddlehead Ferns

Serves 6 to 8

JIMMY SCHMIDT, London Chop House   This dish epitomizes spring to me, with delicate little green fern shoots mixing with the hearty morels that seem to sprout up out of nowhere. This appetizer is so elegant when it arrives at the table, with the puff pastry boxes enclosing the velvety filling livened with a bit of sherry.

Frozen puff pastry, very easy to use and found in every supermarket, makes this a most easy dish to prepare.

Wine choice: California Chardonnay.

1 pound fresh morels

1 pound fiddlehead ferns

½ pound puff pastry (frozen can be used)

1 egg yolk, beaten slightly

½ teaspoon salt

6 tablespoons unsalted butter

½ to ¾ cup Amontillado sherry

2 cups heavy cream

White pepper to taste

De-stem the morels, reserving the stems for another use, and if they are very large cut them in half lengthwise. Wash them well under cold running water, and allow them to drain on paper toweling. Cut the stems of the fiddleheads 1 inch from the heads. Soak them in cold water to loosen the outer membranes, and clean off all the brown skin. Set aside.

Cut the puff pastry dough into 6 to 8 rectangles, and place them on an ungreased cookie sheet. Allow them to defrost if frozen, then score the tops lightly in a diamond pattern, and brush with an egg wash made from the egg yolk and salt. Place the cookie sheet in the center of a preheated 350-degree oven for 20 to 30 minutes, or until the pastry is brown. Cut off the tops and remove any excess pastry from the insides of the shells. Set them aside at room temperature. This can be done up to four hours in advance, and the shells can be stored in the oven once it has cooled.

Melt 2 tablespoons of the butter in a sauté pan or 12-inch skillet, and when the foam starts to subside, add the fiddleheads. Sauté, stirring constantly, until they are just tender, about 2 minutes, then add 2 tablespoons of the sherry. Remove from pan and set aside, reserving any juices that accumulate.

Melt the remaining butter and sauté the morels over high heat until tender. Add them to the fiddleheads.

Place the remaining sherry in the pan and reduce it over high heat until only a few tablespoons remain. Add the cream, and reduce it over low heat until the volume is reduced by half and the sauce coats the back of a spoon. Add the morels and fiddleheads to the sauce and season them with salt and white pepper to taste.

Place the puff pastry shells on serving plates. Spoon the vegetable mixture onto the bottom halves of the shells, and replace the tops, slightly askew. Serve immediately.

Black-Bean Cakes

Serves 6

JEREMIAH TOWER, Santa Fe Bar and Grill When I first ate this dish at the Santa Fe Bar and Grill, lover of refried beans that I am, I was amazed that anything made with beans could have this much intensity. I like to fry the cakes in rendered duck fat rather than olive oil, since that adds an even earthier taste to the spices and smokiness in the beans. They look dramatic on the plate, with sour cream, red salsa, and sprigs of fresh cilantro, and all the accompaniments work with the taste of the cakes.

Wine choice: French red Rhône, or a glass of chilled beer.

1½ pounds black turtle beans

6 tablespoons olive oil

1 medium onion, coarsely chopped

3 slices bacon or pancetta

6 cups chicken or duck stock

Salt to taste

2 serrano chilies, seeded under cold running water and finely chopped

3 tablespoons ancho chili powder

1½ tablespoons cumin powder

Pepper to taste

1 cup sour cream

1 cup tomato salsa (found on the Mexican shelves of supermarkets)

1 bunch fresh cilantro

Wash the beans well in a strainer, picking them over carefully.

In a heavy 3-quart saucepan, heat 3 tablespoons of the olive oil, add the onion and bacon, and cook for 3 minutes over medium heat. Add the beans and enough stock to cover them, and salt to taste, if unsalted stock is used. If you are using canned stock, no salt should be added. Cook the beans, covered, over low heat until tender, about 1½ hours, stirring occasionally. Drain off any excess liquid, and put the bean mixture through a meat grinder or food mill to make a smooth paste. Season the paste with serrano chilies, ancho chili powder, cumin, salt, and pepper.

Take enough paste to roll into the size of a golf ball, and pat the rolled balls between two sheets of waxed paper until they form cakes ⅛ inch thick.

Heat a seasoned crêpe pan or Teflon-coated skillet over high heat. Add the remaining olive oil and cook the bean cakes on each side for about 1 minute, or until crisp. Drain them on paper toweling.

Serve with a dollop of sour cream in the center of each cake, a bit of salsa on top of the sour cream, and sprigs of cilantro around the cake.

Note: The paste can be prepared up to two days in advance and refrigerated, tightly covered, but the cakes should be fried at the last minute. If you cannot find pure ancho chili powder, commercial chili powder, preferably Gebhardt's, can be substituted, but then reduce the cumin by half.

Grilled Chinese Eggplant with Spicy Szechwan Peanut Sauce

*Serves 8 to 12 as an hors d'oeuvre,
4 to 6 as a light main course*

BARBARA TROPP, China Moon Part of my fun in researching this book was wandering through Chinese markets in San Francisco with Barbara Tropp, learning how to select the best ingredients and watching her deal with the merchants. Chinese eggplants, almost amethyst in color, long and slender, are sweeter and contain smaller seeds than other varieties, but I have made this dish with small Japanese and Italian eggplants and it was equally delicious. While the flavor from the mesquite grilling adds immeasurably to the dish, the oils and sauce are interesting enough so that the oven broiler can be substituted.

Wine choice: California Zinfandel or California Chardonnay.

6 long Chinese eggplants or
12 small Japanese or Italian

Five Flavor Oil

Coriander sprigs

Spicy Szechwan Peanut Sauce

Without removing the caps, which will serve as a decorative note, slice the eggplant lengthwise evenly in half. Brush the cut sides liberally with the flavored oil, then place the cut side down on a baking sheet. This may be done an hour ahead and the eggplants left at room temperature.

Just before grilling, brush the cut surfaces again with oil. Grill, cut side down, over medium coals until the cut surface is golden brown and marked by the grill and the top is tender to the touch, about 5 minutes.

To serve, cut the eggplant into diagonal wedges and reassemble, marked side up, on the plate. Garnish with coriander and serve the peanut sauce in a dip dish alongside.

FIVE-FLAVOR OIL

6 tablespoons corn or peanut oil

2 tablespoons Chinese or Japanese sesame oil

1 hefty scallion, cut into 1-inch lengths and crushed with the side of a blade

4 quarter-size slices fresh ginger, smashed with the end of a knife handle to release juices

½ teaspoon dried red chili flakes

1 teaspoon Szechwan brown peppercorns

Heat the oils in a small, heavy saucepan over medium heat. When they are hot enough to foam a single chili flake, remove the pan from the heat. Add the scallion, ginger, chili flakes, and peppercorns, and stir to combine. When the foaming subsides, cover the oil a full day or two before straining. Strain, pressing down to extract the oil, then discard the solids.

The oil keeps indefinitely refrigerated, and should be used at room temperature for fullest flavor.

Note: The oil can be used for dressing cold poultry salads and marinating cold vegetables.

SPICY SZECHWAN PEANUT SAUCE
Makes ¾ cup

1 tablespoon finely minced garlic

2 tablespoons finely minced fresh coriander

¼ cup unseasoned peanut butter

¼ cup plus 1½ teaspoons soy sauce

2¼ tablespoons sugar

¼ teaspoon Chinese rice wine or dry sherry

2 to 3 teaspoons hot chili oil

Blend the ingredients until thoroughly emulsified and smooth, either by hand or in a food processor fitted with a steel blade. Taste, and adjust the taste if necessary with an extra dash of soy sauce or sugar to obtain a full, rich, spicy flavor.

If you are making the peanut sauce in advance, use the lesser amount of chili oil as the sauce will grow spicier as it sits.

Refrigerate the sauce to store it, but allow it to reach room temperature before serving.

Grilled Sonoma Goat Cheese in Vine Leaves

Serves 6

JEREMIAH TOWER, Santa Fe Bar and Grill While sun-dried tomatoes are hardly new in Italy, they are a recent addition to the list of American trendy ingredients, and I use them in everything from pastas to salads to this appetizer, where they spark up the pungency of goat cheese. The key to the success of this dish is making sure the cheese is well wrapped, so it doesn't ooze out onto the grill. It is truly sensuous to scrape out the cheese with bread rounds, a sophisticated version of grilled-cheese sandwiches.

Wine choice: French Sancerre or Pouilly Fumé, or a California Sauvignon Blanc.

6 fresh white goat cheeses, in round shapes (4 to 5 ounces each)

12 pieces sun-dried tomatoes in olive oil

1½ cups olive oil

12 grape leaves, stems removed

24 slices of French bread, rubbed with oil and baked in a 350° oven until golden brown, about 7 minutes

Gently pound the tomatoes with the side of a cleaver or the flat side of a meat pounder until they are very thin and long.

Dip the goat-cheese rounds in olive oil, placing a flattened tomato on the top and bottom of each round. Wrap the cheese with grape leaves, using 1 or 2 to cover. Drip olive oil on the leaves, and grill the packages for 5 minutes on each side.

Serve the cheeses on additional grape leaves, using the croutons to scoop out the melted cheese.

STOCKS AND SOUPS

S oups—from a light consommé clearly intended as a prelude to the entrée to a hearty gumbo that could suffice as a supper in a larger quantity—are my favorite first courses for dinners. It's a shame that, as many cooks have cut back on the number of courses served, they have eliminated the soup course. The vast majority of soups can be prepared up to a few days in advance and are a light way to begin a meal.

Creamed soups, branching off the French repertoire, provide a rich but bland background for more spirited ingredients. This is the case in Anne Greer's Roasted-Corn Soup, in which the cream allows the roasted flavor of the kernels to emerge, or Patrick O'Connell's Red-Pepper Soup, in which the cream serves as a balance to the chili pepper.

Every culture uses soups and stews as a way of stretching protein to feed a crowd. And dishes such as Paul Prudhomme's Seafood Filé Gumbo and Mark Miller's Yucatán Seafood Stew are modern renditions of this concept.

The key to a successful soup is the complexity given it by a good stock, and recipes for basic stocks follow. If it is not possible to make stock, it still helps soups' flavor if the canned stock is simmered with chopped vegetables and herbs for even 15 minutes. To date, no canned stocks are adequate, and flavored bouillon powders are even lower on the scale.

Many cooks do a disservice to soups because they believe that the longer the soup simmers the better. This is true of the stocks forming their base, but simmering soups for hours renders the ingredients flavorless and is the procedure that makes cream soups feel heavy. Once the soups are made, they should not be allowed to boil for more than the time specified. Or they can be cooked slightly less and then simmered for a few additional minutes in the reheating process.

Stocks

That special flavor we associate with food eaten in good restaurants is more often than not obtained from homemade stocks. They are the foundation for soups, the braising liquid for stews, and, in the new style of cooking, the basis for sauces.

In addition to adding flavor, making them can save money. I keep plastic bags in the freezer at all times, with scraps of meat and meat bones in one, chicken and poultry scraps in a second, fish in a third, and slightly-past-their-prime vegetables—such as the last carrot in a bag, which is slightly soft, or the dried-out sprigs of parsley—in a fourth. When the bags reach capacity it's time to do a stock.

But doing a stock does not require more than physical presence in the house, since once it comes to a boil, it may need skimming for the first few minutes, but then does its own thing while the cook watches television or reads. And cooking may be stopped at any time and continued later.

As mentioned elsewhere in this book, some stock should be frozen in ice-cube trays, and when the cubes are solid they can be moved to plastic bags to save space. This is for the recipes calling for less than 1 cup. By melting a cube you can learn the capacity of your trays. I suggest for the remainder of a batch that you freeze it in washed-out milk cartons, so you know the capacity is 1 quart. Stocks may be kept frozen for months.

The only general rules are: Don't let the stock boil rapidly or fat will become incorporated, and don't cover the stockpot until the liquid has cooled or it can become sour.

I have not included salt in any stock recipe for a reason: since so many stocks are reduced for sauces, the resulting sauce may become too salty. ■

Basic Meat Stock

Makes 3 quarts

5 to 6 quarts water

4 to 6 pounds of one of the following:

> Chicken bones and skin (If you don't have enough, buy the packages of backs and necks in the supermarket. They're the cheapest.)
> Beef and veal bones and scraps
> Veal bones and shanks for veal stock

2 carrots, scrubbed and cut into 2-inch sections

2 medium onions, peeled and halved

2 stalks celery, with leaves

3 sprigs thyme

1 bay leaf

8 sprigs parsley

3 unpeeled garlic cloves

12 whole peppercorns

Bring the water, meat, and bones to a boil in a tall-sided stockpot, and reduce the heat to medium. As the liquid starts to simmer, scum will rise to the surface. Skim it off with a slotted spoon or ladle, and after a few minutes it will stop. Then add the rest of the ingredients, return to a simmer, and simmer partially covered.

With chicken stock, you will get a good flavor after 2½ or 3 hours, but meat stocks can go for up to 6 or 8 hours. Boiling water should be added if the liquid goes below the level of the ingredients. Strain out the solids, and refrigerate until the stock chills; remove the fat before freezing.

GLACE DE VIANDE AND FOND DE VEAU

Meat glazes are nothing more than stock that has been reduced to the point of being a syrup after being strained and degreased. A batch of 2 quarts of stock will become less than a cup of glacé de viande, and a teaspoon or so of the glacé adds much flavor to sauces or stews. Make glacé from beef or veal stock, but not fish or poultry.

Basic Fish Stock

For fish stock, some wine is added and some of the vegetables are deleted. The method is the same, and the stock should simmer for 2 to 3 hours.

4 pounds fish trimmings

2 onions, peeled and halved

1 cup dry white wine

Juice of ½ lemon

1 sprig thyme

6 peppercorns

2 stalks celery

4 sprigs parsley

4 quarts water

LOBSTER STOCK

For the fish bones in the preceding recipe substitute lobster bodies and shells, breaking them up into small pieces.

Consommé

Makes 2 quarts

JEAN-LOUIS PALLADIN, Jean-Louis at Watergate Making consommé is no more difficult than boiling water, and it is an elegant first course, especially if followed by a rich entrée. This one has intense flavor from all the vegetables and meat. I've taken Palladin's tip to use consommé in many sauces rather than plain stock.

½ pound carrots, scrubbed and cut into 2-inch pieces

½ pound celery, scrubbed and cut into 2-inch pieces

½ pound leeks, washed well under cold running water, trimmed 1 inch above the white end, and cut into 2-inch pieces

1 pound onions, cut in half and roasted in a 450-degree oven for 20 minutes

6 cloves garlic, peeled

5 pounds bones (beef and veal for meat, and fish and lobster shells for fish)

1 quart V-8 juice

3 quarts water

Salt and pepper to taste

For clarification:

¾ pound chopped vegetables (same proportions as above)

¾ pound ground beef (or chopped raw fish for fish consommé)

¾ cup V-8 juice

1½ cups egg whites (save yolks for another use)

Put all the consommé ingredients together in a large pot, and simmer for 6 hours for meat consommé and about 1 hour for fish. Strain.

To clarify the consommé, place all the clarification ingredients in a pot and mix well. Add the hot consommé base and bring it to a simmer over low heat. Do not let it actively boil, but let it simmer for 45 minutes. Strain the liquid carefully through cheesecloth, ladling it from the pot rather than pouring it.

Note: Consommé can be frozen for up to six months, and as with stocks, freeze some of it in ice-cube trays for adding small amounts to recipes.

Clam and Oyster Bisque

Serves 6 to 8

LYDIA SHIRE, Seasons The addition of just a little curry powder makes this a far more interesting soup than most seafood bisques. The curry is a hint in the steam, and livens the broth, but it does not overwhelm the seafood's delicacy.

Wine choice: French white Burgundy or a California Chardonnay.

16 oysters

16 cherrystone clams

1 cup white wine

¼ pound (1 stick) unsalted butter

½ cup chopped onions

3 shallots, chopped

½ cup chopped leeks, white part only

1 tablespoon curry powder

3 egg yolks

¾ cup heavy cream

Salt and pepper to taste

Scrub the oysters and clams well with a hard brush under cold running water. Open the oysters over a bowl to reserve the liquor. Strain the liquor through a cheesecloth-lined sieve and set it aside. Steam the clams open with the wine. It should take about 4 minutes. Discard any that do not open.

In a 2-quart saucepan, melt the butter and sauté the onions, shallots, and leeks with the curry powder over low heat for 5 minutes, or until the onions are translucent. Add the stock from the clams, strained through cheesecloth, and bring the mixture to a boil. Simmer for 5 minutes, and then add the oysters with their liquor and bring back to a simmer. Cook for 1 to 2 minutes, until the edges of the oysters begin to curl.

Cool slightly, and then put the mixture, along with the clams, through a meat grinder, or grind in a food processor fitted with a steel blade. If using a food processor, you want to chop the soup but not purée it, so just a few pulses will do.

Beat the egg yolks with the cream and stir into the hot soup. Heat over a low flame until the mixture thickens slightly, but do not let it come to a boil or the egg yolks will curdle. Adjust the seasoning with salt and pepper, and serve with little round cream biscuits and garnish with a little chopped parsley.

Note: The soup can be made a day in advance and reheated very slowly over a low flame, making sure it never comes to a boil or the egg yolks will curdle.

Yucatán Seafood Stew

Serves 6

MARK MILLER, Fourth Street Grill The great thing about fish stews and soups is that almost any combination of fish works equally well as long as the procedure is followed. This version is more highly seasoned than those from Europe. I've sometimes changed the proportion of one fish to another, substituted Atlantic species for the Pacific varieties he calls for, added more or less seafood, and it comes out just as well. What makes the stew so appealing is the spicing of the broth and the aroma from the coriander mixing with that from the fish.

Wine choice: French red Beaujolais or white Rhône.

1 head garlic

½ pound fresh monkfish

½ pound tuna fillet

½ pound rock cod fillet

½ pound lingcod fillet

¾ cup olive oil

1 medium onion, chopped

3 bay leaves

2 allspice, crushed, or ½ teaspoon ground allspice

1½ to 2 quarts fish stock or chicken stock

2 bunches fresh coriander

8 to 12 clams, Manila or Littleneck, well scrubbed under cold running water

8 large tomatoes, grilled or placed in a 500-degree oven until almost black, then roughly chopped

½ cup freshly squeezed lime juice

2 pasilla chilies, roasted under a broiler until the skin is black, peeled and cut into small julienne strips (jalapeño chilies can be substituted)

1 dozen mussels, soaked for 2 hours in cold water with 2 tablespoons cornmeal, then scrubbed and debearded

1 lobster (1½ to 2 pounds), boiled for 5 minutes in salted water, cut into pieces in the shell

8 large shrimp or prawns, boiled for 2 minutes, peeled and deveined

6 large oysters, removed from the shell

6 small fresh squid, cleaned (see procedure, page 268)

Toast the garlic head, placing it on a baking sheet in a 350-degree oven for 10 to 15 minutes, depending on the size of the head. Allow it to cool for 10 minutes, or until cool enough to handle, then pop the cloves from the skins. They should pop out easily. Then chop the pulp fine. Set it aside.

Remove the skin and bones from all the fish, and cut it into 1-inch cubes.

In a large sauté pan or deep Dutch oven with a cover, heat the oil over medium heat. Add the onion, toasted garlic, bay leaves, and allspice, and sauté them for about 10 minutes over medium heat, until the onion is translucent. Do not brown. While the onion is sautéing, heat the fish stock in a 2-quart saucepan.

To the sauté pan add 1 bunch of the coriander, stems tied with kitchen string, along with the clams and grilled tomatoes. Add 2 cups of the heated fish stock, cover, and simmer to open the clams, about 5 minutes. Discard any clams that did not open, and replenish the fish stock as needed to keep the ingredients covered. You will need most of it. From this point on, the cooking procedure is a matter of minutes.

Add the monkfish, lime juice, and chilies. Cook for 2 minutes, then add the mussels. Cover and steam for 2 minutes until they open, and discard any that did not open. Add the remaining fish, lobster, shrimp, oysters, and squid. Remove the tied bunch of coriander, then cook the stew, covered, for 3 minutes, until the fish is done, and serve. Garnish with sprigs of the remaining fresh coriander.

Spicy Smoked-Marlin Soup

Serves 4

BARRY WINE, The Quilted Giraffe   I adore the taste of smoked fish, and this is one of the few recipes that use it in soup. The broth is elegantly clear, but packed with the flavor of the fish and the spiciness of ginger, jalapeño pepper, and cilantro. It is elegant to serve, with all the little bits of seafood and vegetables floating in it.

Wine choice: Alsatian Gewürztraminer or spicy white from the Rhône.

For the broth:

1½ ounces smoked marlin

2 cloves garlic

1 tablespoon fresh ginger, peeled

½ green pepper

½ to 1 teaspoon chopped jalapeño pepper

1 sprig cilantro

1 quart water

Salt and pepper to taste

For garnish:

1½ ounces smoked marlin

1 lobster tail, cooked and shelled

4 to 8 mussels

4 to 8 slices daikon (Japanese radish), peeled

¼ red pepper

¼ green pepper

Tsu-mamina (Japanese radish sprouts), washed

½ cup cooked black beans

Chop all the broth ingredients roughly and simmer them gently in the water for 10 minutes over low heat. Strain the liquid through a coffee-filter-lined sieve, so it will be as clear as possible. Correct the seasoning with salt and pepper, the amount of salt depending on the saltiness of the smoked fish.

For the garnish: Cut the smoked marlin and lobster tail into small pieces the size of a dime.

Scrub the mussels well, and put them in a bowl of cold water for a few hours. Trim off the beards, and steam them with ½ cup water in a covered saucepan for 3 minutes, or until they open. Discard any that do not open.

Cut the raw daikon and red and green peppers into attractive shapes. Arrange all the objects artfully in the bottom of a warm soup bowl, and scatter the tsu-mamina and black beans across them.

Heat the broth to the boiling point and pour it gently into the bowls so it will not disturb the arrangement. Let the soup sit a moment before serving so the solids will heat through.

To cook black beans: Wash 4 tablespoons of dried black beans and let them sit covered with water overnight. Or wash the beans and bring them to a boil. Let them sit covered off the heat for 1 hour, and then simmer for 1½ hours or until tender. For this small quantity of black beans, canned could be substituted.

Note: The broth can be prepared a day in advance and refrigerated, and the garnishes can be made at the same time and kept in separate bowls (or in a large bowl separated by layers of wax paper).

The daikon and tsu-mamina are available at Japanese markets.

One-Pot
Fish Soup

Serves 6 to 8 as a soup, 3 or 4 as
a main course

JIM HALLER, The Blue Strawbery   With the fragrance of saffron perfuming the steam from the pot, this soup always reminds me of the Portuguese fish restaurants in New England. I love the heartiness of the broth, flavored with lots of garlic (open to personal interpretation, of course) and vegetables. And the nice part about the soup is that it calls for bottled clam juice rather than a long-simmering stock, so it can be put together in a matter of minutes. A loaf of crusty garlic bread and a salad are all you need to turn this into a supper.

Wine choice: French white Rhône or a red Beaujolais Villages.

4 tablespoons olive oil

4 ripe tomatoes

1 green pepper

1 carrot

6 cloves garlic, peeled and minced

1 medium onion, chopped

1 teaspoon saffron

1 teaspoon freshly ground black pepper

½ cup dry sherry

1 cup dry white wine

2 cups clam juice

1 pound bay scallops

½ pound crabmeat, picked over

6 to 8 clams, scrubbed well under cold running water

6 to 8 mussels, scrubbed well under cold running water and debearded

1 two-pound lobster, cut into sections

½ cup freshly grated Parmesan cheese

Salt to taste

2 to 3 cups cooked rice or cooked curried rice (optional)

In a large soup pot, heat the oil over medium heat. Slice and add the tomatoes and green pepper, and after peeling the carrot, shave it into the pot with a vegetable peeler. Add the garlic, onion, saffron, and pepper, and sauté the mixture over medium heat until it thickens (about 10 minutes), stirring occasionally.

Add the sherry, white wine, and clam juice. Bring the mixture to a boil, and add the shellfish. Return to a boil, cover the pot, and simmer for 5 minutes, until the clams and mussels have opened. Discard any that have not opened.

Add the Parmesan cheese and salt, and simmer uncovered for 3 minutes. Serve as is, or ladle over rice or curried rice.

Corn and Oyster Soup with Dill

(Serves 6)

BRADLEY OGDEN, The Campton Place Hotel For two such dissimilar ingredients—corn from the fields of Kansas and oysters from the seacoasts—they have a lot in common: delicate, sweet flavor. This comes through in the soup. One sip tastes like a corn chowder, the next tastes like a richer oyster bisque, and the freshness of dill is perfect with the flavors of both. It's a very elegant soup to serve, with the oysters floating in the dish, and quite easy to prepare.

Wine choice: French white Burgundy or California Sauvignon Blanc.

8 tablespoons (1 stick) unsalted butter

4 cups corn, freshly cut (approximately 12 ears) or frozen corn. Do not substitute canned corn.

1 tablespoon kosher salt

½ teaspoon ground pepper

1 teaspoon Tabasco

4 cups heavy cream

1½ cups milk

18 Blue Point or Cotuit oysters, shucked, with the liquor reserved

¼ cup fresh chopped dill

Melt the butter in a 2-quart saucepan. Add the corn, salt, pepper, and Tabasco, and cook for 10 minutes, sautéing lightly and stirring often. If using frozen corn, cook 5 minutes longer. Add the cream and milk and bring the mixture to a slow simmer for 30 minutes. Remove it from the heat and cool it slightly. Blend the mixture in a blender or food processor fitted with a steel blade, and strain it through a fine sieve.

Before serving, heat the soup and add the oysters and their liquor, strained through a cheesecloth-lined sieve. Cook until the edges of the oysters start to curl, about 2 minutes, correct the seasoning, and garnish with fresh dill. Place 3 oysters in each bowl and pour the soup over.

Note: The corn soup base can be made in advance and refrigerated, but the oysters and their liquor should be added at the last minute.

Seafood Filé Gumbo

Serves 8 as an appetizer, 4 as an entrée

PAUL PRUDHOMME, K-Paul's Louisiana Kitchen Gumbo (the word coming from the African word for okra) is thickened either with the vegetable for which it is named or with filé powder. The latter is made from ground sassafras leaves, and was first used by the Choctaw Indians. I personally prefer filé, since the texture of okra may be a taste Southerners are born with but Northerners sometimes find it difficult. There are as many variations on gumbo as there are families in the Cajun country, so use this recipe more for guidance than exact ingredients. As with most fish soups, I've substituted various fish for those called for.

Although I always use unsalted butter, margarine is what is used traditionally for making the base, since it is oilier and gives the base a distinctive taste and texture. There's a smoky undertaste to gumbo that makes it different from all other fish soups, as well as the spicing.

Wine choice: California Sauvignon Blanc or French red Beaujolais.

1 pound medium shrimp with heads and shells, or ½ pound without heads

5 cups fish stock (page 160)

1½ teaspoons ground cayenne pepper

1½ teaspoons paprika

1 teaspoon salt

½ teaspoon white pepper

½ teaspoon black pepper

½ teaspoon dried thyme

½ teaspoon dried oregano

1 bay leaf, crumbled

¾ cup margarine

2 cups chopped onions

2 cups chopped celery

2 cups chopped green peppers

3 tablespoons filé powder

1 tablespoon Tabasco

1 teaspoon minced garlic

1¼ cups tomato sauce

1½ cups crabmeat, picked over (about ½ pound)

1 dozen oysters, shucked (optional)

1⅓ cups cooked rice

Peel and devein the shrimp and rinse well. Use the shells and heads for the seafood stock, and refrigerate the shrimp, covered with plastic wrap, until you are ready to use them.

In a small bowl combine the cayenne, paprika, salt, peppers, thyme, oregano, and bay leaf, and set the mixture aside.

In a 4-quart heavy soup pot, melt the margarine over medium heat. Add the onions, celery, and green peppers. Turn the heat to high and stir in the gumbo filé, Tabasco, garlic, and seasoning mixture. Cook for 6 minutes, stirring constantly. Reduce the heat to medium, stir in the tomato sauce, and continue cooking an additional 5 minutes, stirring. (During this time, the mixture will stick to the bottom of the pan. Scrape well, since the scrapings add to the gumbo's taste.)

Add the stock and bring the mixture to a boil, then reduce the heat to low and simmer 45 to 60 minutes. Add the seafood, turn off the heat, and let it sit undisturbed for 6 to 10 minutes. Serve ladled over rice in soup bowls.

Note: The gumbo can be made in advance up to the addition of the seafood, and refrigerated. When you are ready to serve, bring the soup to a boil, lower the heat to a simmer, and add the seafood. Turn off the heat, cover the pot, and let it stand for 10 minutes to cook the fresh ingredients.

Roasted-Corn Soup

Serves 8

ANNE GREER, Nana Grill at the Anatole Hotel The first time I made this soup it was winter, and while I managed to find fresh corn, I roasted it in the oven. The soup was excellent, with the added cornmeal and green chili giving it thickening and sparkle. But grilling the corn a few months later over a mesquite fire turned an excellent dish into an exquisite one. The smoky, aromatic flavor of mesquite is an undertaste with every sip, and it always surprises guests when they take the first.

Wine choice: California Chardonnay, at the oaky end of the scale.

Red-pepper garnish:

3 red bell peppers, roasted and peeled

1 tablespoon tomato paste

1 to 2 teaspoons paprika

Dash of cayenne pepper

1 egg yolk

1 to 2 tablespoons safflower oil

The soup:

2 poblano chilies, roasted and peeled by method above, or canned green chilies

10 to 12 medium ears of fresh corn, unshucked

2 sticks unsalted butter

4 large cloves garlic, roasted in a 350-degree oven for 15 minutes, peeled

1½ tablespoons stoneground yellow cornmeal

2 cups chicken stock, preferably homemade

2 cups heavy cream

Salt and pepper to taste

Roast the peppers by placing them under a broiler or in a 500-degree oven, turning occasionally, until the skins are charred and black. Place them in a tea towel for 15 minutes or until they are cool enough to handle, and then remove the skin, seeds, and ribs. Purée the peppers with the tomato paste, paprika, cayenne, and egg yolk. Add enough oil to achieve a consistency that can be forced through a squeeze bottle to form a ribbon atop the soup. Taste and adjust the seasonings. Set aside.

Roast the poblano chilies. Set aside 2 strips of poblano or canned chilies per serving for the garnish.

Soak the unshucked corn about 10 minutes, then drain it thoroughly. Pull away some of the husk, without removing all. Insert 1 tablespoon of butter in each ear of corn. Roast the corn on an outdoor grill or on a baking pan in a 450-degree oven for 12 to 20 minutes, or until it is tender. The time will vary with the cooking medium. Scrape all the kernels from the cobs. Set aside 1 cup to finish the soup.

Purée the remaining corn, chilies, peeled cloves of roasted garlic, cornmeal, and chicken stock in a blender or food processor fitted with a steel blade. This will probably have to be done in a few batches. Combine the purée with the cream and heat to a boil. Add the reserved whole corn kernels and salt and pepper to taste. Simmer for 2 minutes.

The thickness of the soup depends on the starch content of the corn. If it is not thick, add a bit more cornmeal. And if it is too thick, thin with a little stock or milk.

To serve, garnish each serving by piping a ribbon of red-pepper purée across the top, and float 2 strips of roasted poblano chili.

Note: The soup can be made up to 2 days in advance and reheated slowly, but do not let it cook or reduce. Reheat it just to the boiling point. After it has sat in the refrigerator, it may have to be thinned with a little additional milk or stock.

Curried Apple and Onion Soup

Serves 8

MARCEL DESAULNIERS, The Trellis I usually add apples to my curried dishes, since the sweetness of the fruit goes so well and seems to cool down the heat of the curry. What I like so much about this soup is that you can adjust the heat according to what you're serving after it. If the main dish is delicate, you don't want to kill the palate by making the soup too hot. The commercial curry powders available in supermarkets are on the mild side, while those found in Indian markets will be much hotter. I've started making my own, since curry powder is a blend of spices, and most Indian cookbooks have the proportions to use.

Wine choice: Alsatian Gewürztraminer.

5 stalks celery, chopped

½ onion, chopped

1 leek, white part only, rinsed well under running water and chopped

1 tablespoon vegetable oil

5 tablespoons unsalted butter

½ cup flour

1 tablespoon curry powder, or to taste

3 quarts chicken stock, heated

3 medium onions, sliced

2 Granny Smith apples, peeled, cored, and sliced ¼ inch thick

½ cup heavy cream

Salt and pepper to taste

Heat a sauté pan over medium heat, and add the celery, chopped onion, leek, and oil. Sauté the vegetables over low heat for 6 to 8 minutes, or until the onion is translucent.

In a soup pot, melt 4 tablespoons of the butter on low heat. Add the flour and curry powder, and cook over low heat for 10 minutes, stirring often. Slowly add 1 quart of the chicken stock and whisk until smooth. Add the sautéed vegetables and simmer the mixture over low heat for 45 minutes, stirring occasionally.

Purée the mixture in a blender or food processor fitted with a steel blade, or pass it through a food mill. Set it aside.

In a heavy stockpot, melt the remaining 1 tablespoon of butter and sauté the sliced onions over low heat until they are transparent, about 10 minutes. Add the remaining 2 quarts of stock and boil gently over medium heat until the liquid is reduced by half, about 20 minutes. Add the celery purée, sliced apples, and heavy cream. Simmer for 10 minutes, and adjust the seasoning with salt and pepper.

Note: The soup can be made a few days in advance and quickly reheated, but do not let it simmer for too long. Also, if reheating, you will find the flavors become a bit stronger, so decrease the amount of curry powder when initially making it.

Wild-Mushroom Soup

Serves 6

WOLFGANG PUCK, Spago   Cream-of-mushroom soup is a French classic, but our perceptions of it have been colored by years of its ghastly canned versions. This soup is a more flavorful variation on the French theme. After trying both chanterelles and shiitake—the two wild mushrooms Puck recommends—I prefer the shiitake. They have a more pronounced flavor when diluted with liquid, and their pungency blends well with the cream.

Wine choice: California Chardonnay.

1 pound chanterelle or shiitake mushrooms

Juice of 1 lemon

2½ tablespoons unsalted butter

3 medium shallots, minced

2 sprigs fresh thyme, leaves only

½ bay leaf

Salt and freshly ground pepper

3 cups heavy cream

2½ cups chicken stock

1 teaspoon cornstarch, dissolved in 1 tablespoon cold water

Clean the mushrooms and sprinkle them with the lemon juice. Slice ½ cup of the mushrooms and reserve. Coarsely chop the remaining ones in a food processor fitted with a steel blade, or by hand.

Melt 2 tablespoons of butter in a heavy 2-quart saucepan, and lightly sauté the shallots. Add the chopped mushrooms, thyme leaves, and bay leaf. Sauté them over medium heat for 10 minutes, or until the liquid has evaporated. Add salt, pepper, cream, and chicken stock. Bring the mixture to a boil over medium heat, stirring frequently. Reduce the heat to a simmer and cook for 20 minutes. Whisk in the cornstarch and continue to simmer for 10 minutes longer.

Sauté the reserved mushroom slices in the remaining butter, and season them with salt and pepper to taste.

Correct the seasoning of the soup and serve it garnished with sautéed mushroom slices.

Note: If you are making the soup in advance, do not add the cornstarch until reheating it, or the soup will thin out in the refrigerator.

Chinese Noodle Soup with Toasted Almonds and Deep-Fried Ginger

Serves 4 to 6

BARBARA TROPP, China Moon Like most of Tropp's dishes, this one is not authentically Chinese. "It's what I think a Sung poet might have sipped on a spring day." Regardless of that, it's the most interesting chicken soup I've ever made. It could serve as a meal in itself, eaten with chopsticks with the broth sipped from the bowl. The coriander and ginger enliven it, and there is a blend of textures in the soup with the vegetables and noodles.

Wine choice: California Zinfandel or French red Rhône.

1½ to 2 pounds fresh whole chicken breasts, with skin and bones

1 scallion, cut into 2-inch lengths and crushed with the side of a cleaver

1 quarter-size slice fresh ginger, pounded lightly

⅛ teaspoon brown Szechwan peppercorns

½ pound very thin cooked egg noodles, or 6 ounces dry People's Republic of China-manufactured mung-bean noodles ("bean threads" or "glass noodles")

¼ pound fresh baby bok choy leaves, fresh spinach leaves, or leafy ribbons of Napa cabbage

6 cups simmering rich chicken stock, seasoned to taste with Roasted Szechwan Pepper-Salt (page 152)

¼ cup finely julienned fresh ginger, deep-fried in 375-degree corn or peanut oil until crisp, drained on paper

¾ cup loosely packed fresh coriander leaves

⅓ cup sliced almonds, toasted in a 350-degree oven for 7 to 10 minutes, or until golden

To cook the chicken: Combine the scallion, ginger, peppercorns, and enough cold water to cover the chicken in a heavy 2- to 2½-quart saucepan. Bring the water to a boil, simmer 5 minutes, then add the chicken. Cover the pot tightly and turn off the heat. Let the chicken steep undisturbed for 2 hours.

Remove the chicken to a plate to cool, and discard the water or save for stock making. Carefully remove the skin and bone, then separate the fillets. Discard the membrane and tendon from the fillets and trim the breast pieces of fat and cartilage. Slice the chicken across the grain into slices ¼ inch thick.

If you are using mung-bean noodles, soak them in boiling water to cover for 5 minutes; cut the noodles in half, rinse, then drain well.

Blanch the greens in boiling unsalted water until supple, about 5 seconds, then drain them and refresh in cold water to stop the cooking action. Press them gently to remove excess liquid.

Just before serving, swish the egg or mung-bean noodles in the simmering stock to heat through, then place portions in the center of deep soup bowls. Ring the noodles with the blanched greens and top with the slivered chicken. Apportion the stock among the bowls, sprinkle the fried ginger threads and coriander around the chicken, and scatter the nuts on top.

Serve immediately.

Red-Pepper Soup

Serves 8

PATRICK O'CONNELL, The Inn at Little Washington   Part of the appeal of this soup is its vivid red color, deeper than any cream-of-tomato soup. And when you taste it the overall sensation comes from the pungency of the herbs and peppers, made slightly hotter with jalapeño chilies.

Wine choice: California Sauvignon Blanc or Alsatian Gewürztraminer.

¼ cup olive oil

1 cup chopped onions

1 tablespoon fennel seed

¼ teaspoon thyme

½ bay leaf

½ teaspoon minced garlic

1 tablespoon chopped fresh basil

6 red bell peppers, seeds and ribs removed, diced

2 tablespoons minced jalapeño pepper, seeds removed under cold running water

¼ cup flour

5 cups chicken stock

¼ cup chopped fresh tomato, peeled and seeded

2 teaspoons tomato paste

½ to 1 cup heavy cream

Salt, pepper, and a pinch of sugar to taste

Splash of Sambuca liqueur

In a heavy saucepan, heat the olive oil over medium heat and add the onions, fennel seed, thyme, bay leaf, garlic, basil, red pepper, and jalapeño pepper. Sauté the vegetables over low heat until they are wilted, about 10 to 15 minutes. Add the flour and stir the mixture over low heat for 10 minutes to cook the flour.

Add the chicken stock, whisking until smooth, along with the tomatoes and tomato paste. Cook the soup over medium heat, partially covered, for 45 minutes. Purée it in a blender or food processor fitted with a steel blade, or pass it through a food mill. Return the purée to the pan, add the cream, and simmer for 10 minutes.

Adjust the seasoning, and add a splash of Sambuca just before serving.

Note: The soup can be made up to 2 days in advance and reheated slowly. Do not add the Sambuca until you are ready to serve.

Artichoke Soup

Serves 6

ANNE GREER, The Terrace at the Anatole Hotel   While the ritual of eating artichokes is enjoyable, putting them in a creamed soup is an alternative for the flavor with far less bother. The soup is light, and the flavor of vegetables from a good homemade stock enhances the taste of the artichoke.

Wine choice: California Sauvignon Blanc or Chenin Blanc.

4 large fresh artichokes, or 2 packages of frozen artichoke hearts (do not substitute canned artichokes)

4 tablespoons butter

1 tablespoon flour

2 cups chicken stock

1 cup heavy cream

1 tablespoon minced parsley

1 teaspoon lemon juice

½ teaspoon salt

¼ teaspoon white pepper

½ cup pine nuts (for garnish)

In a large enameled or stainless-steel pan, bring 2 quarts of water to a boil. Trim the stem ends of the artichokes and wash them well. Salt the water and add the artichokes. Cover the pan and simmer for 35 to 45 minutes, until the artichokes are cooked and a knife point can pierce the stem with no resistance, or boil according to package directions if using frozen artichokes. Drain the artichokes upside down in a colander, and let them cool until they are easy to handle. Pull the leaves off the heart, and scrape the hairy choke away and discard. With a spoon scrape the bottom of the artichoke leaves to get the edible meat off. Place the hearts and scrapings in a blender or food processor fitted with a steel blade and purée them until smooth, adding a little of the stock if necessary.

In a saucepan, melt the butter and add the flour, stirring over low heat for 2 minutes to cook the flour. Whisk in the stock and cream, and bring the mixture to a simmer over low heat. Add the parsley, lemon juice, salt, pepper, and artichoke purée.

While the soup is heating, sauté the pine nuts in a little butter to toast them, or place them on a baking sheet in a 350-degree oven for 7 minutes.

After the soup comes to a simmer, simmer for 5 minutes and serve, garnished with the toasted pine nuts.

Pumpkin Soup

Serves 8

ANNE GREER, Nana Grill at the Anatole Hotel   Until I ate this soup, I always thought of pumpkin, with cinnamon and nutmeg, as a heavy pie filling. Pumpkin is actually very delicate, and the soup has a lovely pastel orange tone.

Wine choice: California Sauvignon Blanc or French Pouilly Fumé.

1½ to 2 pounds fresh pumpkin (see Note)

2 sprigs each fresh rosemary and oregano, or ½ teaspoon of each dried

4 cups chicken stock

1 tablespoon flour

2 tablespoons unsalted butter

½ cup milk

1½ teaspoons salt

Pinch of cayenne pepper

White pepper to taste

1 cup half-and-half or light cream

Garnish:

4 fresh tomatillos

1 tablespoon unsalted butter

Roasted spiced pecans

Peel the pumpkin and cut into 2-inch cubes. Place them in a saucepan with ½ cup water. Cook, covered, over low heat until the pumpkin is tender, about 25 minutes. During the last 10 minutes, add the herbs and chicken stock to the pan. Discard the herbs if fresh, and purée the pumpkin with the flour in a blender or food processor fitted with a steel blade. Then combine the purée with the butter, milk, and seasonings. Simmer the soup over low heat, uncovered, for 20 minutes, stirring occasionally. Stir in the half-and-half, bring the soup back to a simmer, and adjust the seasonings.

For the garnish, slice the tomatillos very thin, and sauté them in hot butter for a few seconds. They should be heated through, but not mushy.

To serve, fan 4 slices of tomatillo across the top of the soup in each bowl, and place a small number of the pecans below the slices in the bowl.

Note: While fresh pumpkin is called for, a combination of canned pumpkin and fresh acorn squash works well. If you are using canned pumpkin, cook the squash as above, and add the pumpkin with the chicken stock; do not cook it with the squash.

The soup can be made up to 2 days in advance and slowly reheated. Do not allow it to simmer.

Pumpkin Soup with Turkey, Virginia Ham, and Duck Breast

Serves 6

JEAN-LOUIS PALLADIN, Jean-Louis at Watergate The most interesting thing about this soup is that it tastes different with every sip, depending on which of the slivers of ingredients you have in your spoon. With one taste, you get the smokiness of the ham, with another, the richness of the duck. This soup looks very attractive to serve, with all the bits floating on top of the thick, creamy base.

Wine choice: French red Burgundy or Grand Cru Beaujolais.

1 duck breast
1 medium onion, sliced
1 shallot, sliced
6 ounces raw turkey breast
6 ounces Virginia ham
1 pound fresh pumpkin
2 cups chicken stock or consommé (pages 160, 161)
Salt and freshly ground black pepper to taste
1½ cups heavy cream
Nutmeg to taste

Remove the duck meat from the bones, and cut it into small strips. Set them aside, and cut the skin into small pieces.

Place the duck skin in a 2-quart pan and cook it over medium heat to render the fat. When it has been rendered and the cracklings are crisp, pour it into a bowl. Then put 2 tablespoons of the fat in the pan and sauté the onion and shallot for 2 minutes. Divide both the turkey and ham into two parts, and cut one half of each into a fine julienne and set aside for the garnish. Roughly chop the remaining portions. Divide the pumpkin also, peeling and cubing ¾ pound, while finely dicing the remaining ¼ pound for the garnish.

Add the chopped ham and turkey and cubed pumpkin to the pan with the onion, and sauté the mixture for 10 minutes over low heat, until the onions are translucent.

Add half the stock and some salt and pepper, and simmer for 20 minutes, adding a little water if necessary. Add the cream and the remaining stock, and simmer for 5 minutes. Purée the mixture in a blender or food processor fitted with a steel blade. Season with salt and pepper to taste.

In a small saucepan, cook the finely diced pumpkin in salted water until tender, about 10 minutes. Drain it and plunge it into cold water to stop the cooking action; drain again. In a sauté pan, heat 3 tablespoons of the remaining duck fat and sauté the julienne strips of duck, turkey, and ham together over medium heat, stirring constantly, about 2 minutes, or until cooked. Do not overcook.

Place some of the soup in each soup bowl, and top with an arrangement of the meats and pumpkin. Sprinkle with nutmeg.

Note: The soup can be made a few days in advance, and slowly reheated over a low flame; stir occasionally. Keep the meats in separate dishes, and decorate each bowl with them. You do not have to reheat them, since they are small enough to be warmed by the hot soup.

SALADS

Salads in American restaurants were traditionally nothing more than mixed greens, or wedges of iceberg lettuce topped with—rather than tossed with—dressings. If you were lucky, the dressings were homemade, and if your tab was high enough, chances are the salad might be tossed at tableside with much fanfare and a few grinds from an absurdly large peppermill.

Most of the neglect in what was a meat-and-potatoes diet was due to the lack of popularity of greens, and concomitantly the lack of variety available. The influence of California in American cuisine is far older than the California cuisine now being popularized. The nation's Garden of Eden is also the birthing ground of such popular dressings as Green Goddess, and Caesar Salad. And when chef's salad started in that state following World War II, one could hardly anticipate that the ham and hard-boiled eggs would be supplanted by smoked lake trout or warm lamb.

In California today, as elsewhere in the nation, salads made from interesting combinations of greens and proteins are being eaten as light meals and as appetizers, in addition to providing more interesting options for the separate salad course. While few restaurants have adopted the French custom of a separate cheese course, many have begun serving salad after the entrée in the French fashion, and adding cheese—either warm or cold—to the salad itself. Wolfgang Puck's salad with warm goat cheese is almost synonymous with the new California cuisine, while in the Bay Area the European influences on Jeremiah Tower's cooking are evident in the use of warm Swiss raclette with colorful radicchio.

Serving artfully arranged individual salads is an easy medium as an art form. Your palette is whatever greens are the freshest, and the presentation is up to the cook's imagination. In all the salad recipes given here, the types of greens are merely the chef's suggestions for the general theme, and no salad recipe should be ignored because the vegetables are out of season. ∎

Green Salad with Hazelnut Vinaigrette Dressing

Serves 6

AMY FERGUSON, Charley's 517 The nutty oil, nuts, and mild vinegar make this an excellent dressing when a salad is being served after the entrée. It becomes a bridge between the entrée and the sweet dessert to follow. The dressing is also delicious as a dipping sauce for crudités, or for topping cold asparagus as an appetizer or salad course.

Wine choice: California Chenin Blanc or Chardonnay.

Greens:

2 heads radicchio

1 bunch mâche

1 bunch watercress

Dressing:

1 cup hazelnuts

3 tablespoons sherry-wine vinegar

3 tablespoons Madeira

1 tablespoon Dijon mustard

½ teaspoon sugar

Salt and white pepper to taste

1 cup hazelnut oil

Wash and dry the greens. Arrange them on a plate with the radicchio fanning out from the center with the leaves extending outward, and pile the mâche and watercress in the middle.

Place the hazelnuts on a cookie sheet and toast them in a 350-degree oven for 10 to 12 minutes, or until they are brown. Let them cool, and then chop them fine in a food processor fitted with a steel blade or by hand. Set them aside.

In a bowl, mix the vinegar, Madeira, mustard, sugar, salt, and pepper. Slowly whisk in the oil, beating until thickened. Then whisk in the hazelnuts.

Spoon on top of the salad.

Fall Salad

Serves 6 to 8

JACKIE ETCHEBER, Jackie's   What makes this salad so attractive is the combination of colors and shapes in the bowl. Bacon and ginger in the dressing add even more flavor and texture.

Wine choice: Alsatian Riesling or Gewürztraminer.

½ pound bacon

½ cup sherry-wine vinegar

2 ounces fresh ginger, peeled and cut into a fine julienne or grated

1 clove garlic, minced

Salt and pepper to taste

1 cup vegetable oil

1 bunch curly endive, washed and torn into small pieces

10 ounces fresh spinach, washed and destemmed

12 baby carrots

1 red pepper, cut into rings

1 green pepper, cut into rings

8 cherry tomatoes

¼ pound snow peas, stringed and blanched in boiling water for 30 seconds, then refreshed in ice water to stop the cooking action

Cook the bacon until crisp. Drain it on paper towels; crumble it and set it aside. In a bowl, mix the vinegar, ginger, garlic, salt, and pepper. Whisk in the oil and set the dressing aside. Toss the bacon with the endive and spinach and mix with some of the dressing. Arrange the greens in a bowl, with the baby carrots, rings of peppers, cherry tomatoes, and snow peas around the edges. Serve, and pass additional dressing separately.

Warm Black-Eyed-Pea Salad

Serves 6

ANNE GREER, Nana Grill at the Anatole Hotel   Black-eyed peas are often thought of as just soul food, but I found this to be one of the most sophisticated of salads. The flavoring of the beans, with equally lowly pork hocks and cinnamon, permeates them and contrasts with the dressing. In some ways, this is similar to many warm spinach salads dressed with bacon, and adding the sliced artichoke heart creates a prettier dish.

Wine choice: California Sauvignon Blanc.

1 pound dried black-eyed peas (do not use canned)

2 smoked pork hocks, or 1 ham hock

1 medium onion, peeled

2 cloves garlic, peeled

1 teaspoon salt

1 stick cinnamon

3 large fresh artichokes

½ pound bacon

1 tablespoon Dijon mustard

1 tablespoon Worcestershire sauce

3 tablespoons red-wine vinegar

1 pound baby spinach, washed, with tough stems removed

Wash the dried beans well in a sieve, and place them in a saucepan with the pork or ham hock, onion, garlic, salt, and cinnamon stick. Add 6 cups of water and bring to a boil. Cover, and simmer the beans for 1 hour, or until they are tender but not mushy. Remove and discard the onion, garlic, and cinnamon. Drain the beans, and keep them warm. Let the hock cool. Cut the meat from it into a fine dice, and set it aside.

In another saucepan, boil the artichokes in a large amount of water for 35 to 40 minutes, or until a knife easily pierces the base of the stem. Drain the artichokes upside down, and discard the leaves and prickly choke. Cut the hearts into vertical slices and set them aside.

Cut the bacon slices into 2-inch lengths, and fry them in a skillet until crisp. Remove the bacon bits with a slotted spoon, and drain them on paper towels. Reserve the fat. In the hot fat, brown the pieces of meat removed from the ham or pork hocks, and add to the bacon bits.

Mix the mustard, Worcestershire sauce, and vinegar in a bowl. Slowly whisk in the bacon fat, stirring until the mixture is smooth and thick.

To assemble individual salads: Divide the spinach leaves on the plates, and mound 1 cup of the black-eyed peas on each. Place slices of artichoke heart around the peas, and spoon the warm dressing over the salads.

Note: The salads can be arranged on plates and kept at room temperature for two hours. The beans can be done a day in advance and tossed with the dressing. They should be reheated in a 250-degree oven before mounding on the plates.

Warm Vegetable Salad

Serves 6

JEREMIAH TOWER, Santa Fe Bar and Grill   This is one of my favorite salads for a buffet, since the vegetables are cut into small pieces so the salad does not overwhelm the plate. It is visually pleasing as well, with a great variety of colors, shapes, and textures mixed together.

Wine choice: California Chardonnay or French white Burgundy.

¼ to ½ cup each of green beans, julienne of carrots, 1-inch sections of asparagus, fava beans (shelled), cauliflower, and broccoli (broken into small flowerets)

Dressing:

2 tomatoes, peeled, seeded, and finely chopped

2 shallots, finely chopped

1 tablespoon mixed fresh herbs, such as tarragon, thyme, basil, and parsley

¼ cup lemon juice

Salt and pepper to taste

½ cup olive oil

Mix all the vegetables together until well combined, and set them aside.

Combine all the dressing ingredients, and stir well.

Bring 2 quarts of salted water to a boil, and add the vegetables. Blanch them for 3 to 5 minutes, drain, and plunge them into ice water to stop the cooking action. Then drain again, mix with the dressing, and serve immediately.

Note: The vegetables can be cut up a day before and kept in plastic bags in the refrigerator, and the dressing can be made in advance as well. But, for the freshest taste, they should be cooked at the last minute.

Baby Beets, Red Leaf Lettuce, and Orange Salad

Serves 6

JONATHAN WAXMAN, Jams   This salad looks so attractive on the plate, with deep red beets and red-tinged lettuce contrasted with slices of bright orange. The sherry-wine vinegar in the dressing is not as harsh as other vinegars, and blends well with the sweetness of the beets and fruit.

Wine choice: A white wine from Alsace.

1 pound small baby beets,
about 1 inch in diameter, or
larger beets

2 heads small red-leaf lettuce

6 to 8 sweet oranges

¼ cup extra-virgin olive oil

2 tablespoons sherry-wine
vinegar

Salt and pepper to taste

Chopped fresh chervil or
parsley

Scrub the beets well and cut off the greens 1 inch above the top. Place the beets in a saucepan with salted water and bring it to a boil. Lower the heat to a simmer and poach the beets until barely tender, about 10 minutes for baby beets, and longer for larger ones. Cool them and peel. Cut up the beets if large into 1-inch chunks.

Wash and dry the lettuce leaves.

Juice half of one orange and reserve the juice. Peel and section the remaining oranges, removing the white membranes. Set the sections aside.

To assemble: Combine the beets, orange juice, olive oil, vinegar, and orange sections. Toss the mixture until well blended and season with salt and pepper to taste. Arrange the lettuce on salad plates and pile the beets and oranges in the center, sprinkling with chervil or parsley.

Note: The beets can be cooked and the other ingredients can be prepared up to a day in advance, keeping them separated in plastic bags in the refrigerator. But do not mix the beets and dressing until serving time, or they will become too strong.

Raclette Gratin with Radicchio Salad

Serves 6

JEREMIAH TOWER, Santa Fe Bar and Grill, Stars   This variation on the warm cheese–cold greens salad is richer than most, since Swiss raclette is a heavy and creamy cheese. Using radicchio and Belgian endive, two rather bitter greens, makes the cheese taste all the more creamy and sweet.

Wine choice: French Sancerre or Pouilly Fumé or California Sauvignon Blanc.

2 heads radicchio

4 Belgian endives

¾ cup good-quality olive oil

2 tablespoons freshly squeezed
lemon juice

½ teaspoon salt

¼ teaspoon pepper

6 ounces imported Swiss
raclette cheese, cut into even
slices

Separate the leaves of radicchio, wash them, and drain well on paper toweling or spin them in a salad spinner. Repeat with the spears of endive, keeping them separate from the radicchio. Arrange the greens on salad plates with the endive forming a circle from the center of the plate, points toward the edges, and a smaller circle of radicchio in the middle.

Whisk the olive oil into the lemon juice until the mixture is thick, then season with salt and pepper. Pour over the salads lightly.

On a cookie sheet place the cheese slices in the top of a preheated 500-degree oven for 1 minute, or until the cheese has melted. Place a slice in the center of each circle of radicchio. Serve immediately.

Note: The salad plates can be arranged in advance and stored, covered with plastic wrap, in the refrigerator. The salads can be dressed while the cheese is melting in the oven.

Rabes in Garlic and Olive Oil

Serves 6

JASPER WHITE, Restaurant Jasper What I like about rabes, also called rapini and broccoli rabe, is the spicy quality. Cooked this way, they can be served as a salad, used as part of an Italian antipasto, or eaten—the way White likes them—on a sandwich with hot ham. When I serve them as a salad, the plates look prettier if garnished with a few leaves of bright red radicchio.

2 pounds rabes

2 teaspoons finely chopped garlic

½ cup extra-virgin olive oil

Juice of 1 lemon

Salt and freshly ground pepper to taste

Trim the bottoms off the rabes so they are about 3 to 4 inches long. Blanch them in a large quantity of boiling salted water for 3 minutes, then drain, and plunge them into ice water to stop the cooking action. Drain well.

In a sauté pan, sauté the garlic in the olive oil for 5 to 7 minutes over low heat, until it is cooked and slightly brown. Pour the oil and garlic over the rabes and sprinkle with lemon juice, salt, and pepper.

Chill well.

Zucchini and Grapefruit in Raspberry-Honey Dressing

Serves 4

JIM HALLER, The Blue Strawbery This dressing is one of the best I've ever found for a fruit salad, and since it is slightly pink, it looks pretty on the grapefruit and pale slices of zucchini. I've served the salad with fish dishes, since there's a slight acidity that complements them, and it's wonderful as part of a brunch—served either as a separate course or as part of a buffet.

Wine choice: German Mosel or Rheingau.

1 head romaine or 4 heads Bibb lettuce

4 to 6 medium zucchini

1 large sweet grapefruit

3 tablespoons raspberry vinegar

Wash the lettuce and pat it dry or spin it in a salad spinner. Cut the zucchini into a fine julienne or use the julienne blade of a food processor. Do not shred in the food processor or it will be too fine. Peel the grapefruit, and remove all membranes.

Arrange the lettuce on a platter or individual plates, and

3 tablespoons Champagne
vinegar

½ cup raspberry preserves

1 tablespoon honey

2 tablespoons prepared
mustard

1 cup vegetable oil

place the zucchini around the edge. Make a flower from the grapefruit in the center of the platter, and set it aside in the refrigerator.

Whisk the vinegars with the preserves, honey, and mustard until smooth. Slowly add the oil in a thin stream, whisking until the dressing is thick. This can be done in a blender or food processor fitted with a steel blade.

To serve: Drizzle dressing over the salad and pass additional dressing separately.

Goat-Cheese Salad with Arugula and Radicchio

Serves 6

WOLFGANG PUCK, Spago I serve this salad following the entrée, and it becomes a combined salad and cheese course. The color combination with the white cheese, red radicchio, and greens is dramatic, and the cheese has a robust flavor after being marinated in the oil and thyme. If you can't find fresh tarragon, other herbs such as basil, chives, or even parsley work well in the dressing.

6 ounces fresh goat cheese,
cut into equal slices

⅓ cup extra-virgin olive oil

1½ teaspoons fresh thyme
leaves

Freshly ground pepper

3 small heads radicchio

⅓ pound arugula or mâche

Vinaigrette

1 tablespoon Dijon mustard

1 teaspoon fresh tarragon,
chopped fine

1 tablespoon sherry-wine
vinegar

1 egg

Salt and freshly ground white
pepper

½ cup almond oil or
extra-virgin olive oil (or a mix
of the two)

Marinate the slices of goat cheese overnight in the ⅓ cup olive oil, thyme, and pepper.

Wash the radicchio and arugula or mâche and pat them dry on paper towels or spin in a salad spinner.

For the dressing: In a medium bowl, whisk together all the remaining ingredients except the ½ cup oil. Add the oil in a slow stream, whisking constantly, until the dressing is thick and blended. Adjust the seasoning and set the dressing aside.

Toss the greens with enough dressing to coat them lightly and divide them among the salad plates.

Heat a nonstick sauté pan, and add 2 tablespoons of the olive oil from the marinated goat cheese. Sauté the slices over medium heat for 30 seconds on each side, or place the slices in a 450-degree oven for 1 minute.

Top each salad with a slice of hot goat cheese and serve them immediately.

Asparagus and Sautéed Cheese with Grapes and Green Peppercorns

Serves 6

MICHAEL ROBERTS, Trumps   I've served this salad as an appetizer, and it's a surprising turnaround of expectations. The asparagus is bright green, but thoroughly chilled, and the cheese is warm. The dressing comes out a pale green, and is both pungent and sweet.

Wine choice: French Sancerre or Pouilly Fumé.

¾ pound asparagus, preferably pencil-thin stalks

1 jar green peppercorns in brine, drained (1½ ounces)

2 cups seedless white grapes

½ cup vegetable oil

Salt and pepper to taste

6 ounces raclette or aged goat cheese

2 eggs, lightly beaten

¾ cup fresh breadcrumbs

½ cup clarified butter

Trim the asparagus, breaking off any tough ends, and steam or blanch it in boiling water until it is cooked but still crisp. Immediately plunge it into a bowl of ice water to stop the cooking action. Drain and chill it.

In a blender, or food processor fitted with a steel blade, purée the green peppercorns and grapes. Slowly add the oil until the dressing is thick, and season to taste with salt and pepper. Set the dressing aside.

Cut the cheese into equal portions, dip in the egg and then in breadcrumbs. Heat the butter in a sauté pan or skillet, and sauté the cheese for about 30 seconds on each side, until the crumbs are brown.

To serve: Arrange the asparagus on plates, top them with cheese, and pour on the dressing.

Marinated Bay Scallops in a Nest of Greens

Serves 6

BRUCE LeFAVOUR, Rose et LeFavour   This salad, which I've also served as an appetizer, is one of the most subtle and dramatic presentations I've ever constructed. The rings of greens around the mound of scallops, dotted with balls of cucumber about equal in size, vary in shade of green and shape of the leaves. The scallops are equally subtle, since they are marinated in just lime juice rather than with hot peppers as for seviche. I love the way they taste after being marinated just the hour LeFavour calls for, but if you want them more opaque—and looking "cooked" —leave them in the lime juice longer.

Wine choice: California Sauvignon Blanc or Alsatian Gewürztraminer.

1½ pounds fresh New England bay scallops

4 limes

Salt and pepper to taste

3 shallots, finely chopped

1 or 2 cucumbers

40 sugar snap or snow peas

2 Belgian endives

1 head escarole

Dressings:

4 teaspoons Dijon mustard

2 tablespoons sherry-wine vinegar

6 tablespoons peanut oil

2 tablespoons lemon juice

6 tablespoons heavy cream

Scallop or lobster roe, poached and sliced, or chopped tomato for garnish

Wash the scallops in a strainer and pat them dry. Squeeze the limes, and in a glass or stainless-steel bowl combine the scallops, lime juice, salt and pepper. Chop the shallots fine and add one-third of them to the scallops.

Cover the bowl with plastic wrap and refrigerate.

Cut the cucumbers in half vertically and scrape out the seeds. With a melon baller, cut out balls and place them in a bowl with a light dusting of salt. Set the cucumbers aside at room temperature.

String the peas and cut them into fine shreds, longer but the same width as matchsticks. Bring 2 quarts of salted water to a boil, and with the shreds in a strainer, hold them in the water for 30 seconds. Immediately dump them into a bowl of ice water to stop the cooking action.

Peel off and discard the outer leaves of the endives, slice the heads in half lengthwise, cut out the cores, and slice the leaves into a julienne ¼ inch wide. Set them aside.

Cut the escarole in half lengthwise and remove the yellow and white center leaves. Reserve the rest for another salad, and cut the centers into 2-inch sections.

Make two dressings: In one bowl mix together 2 teaspoons of the mustard, salt, pepper, vinegar, and half of the remaining shallots. Whisk in the oil vigorously until the ingredients are well combined. In another bowl, mix the remaining mustard and shallots, the lemon juice, cream, salt, and pepper. Set both dressings aside.

Assembly: Toss the pea pods with the vinegar-oil dressing, using enough to just coat them, and toss the endive and escarole with the lemon-cream dressing in the same manner. Place the scallops in the center of each plate or one platter. Tuck the cucumber balls in with the scallops, and build a "nest" with the snow peas around the scallops. Scatter the escarole and endive around the snow peas, and garnish with the roe or chopped tomatoes on top of the scallops.

Warm Bay Scallop and Oyster Salad

Serves 4 as an appetizer, 2 as a supper

JONATHAN WAXMAN, Jams   The most enticing thing about this salad is how the flavor of the seafood becomes part of the dressing, so every bite of the greens reminds you of the delicate scallops and oysters poached in it. I've served this as an appetizer-cum-salad course, and also as a light supper. The most attractive way to present it is on a mixture of green and red lettuces, such as radicchio and red leaf with watercress, spinach, and Belgian endive.

Wine choice: California Chardonnay or Sauvignon Blanc.

16 oysters

½ pound bay scallops, or sea scallops cut into thirds vertically retaining their circular shape

4 cups assorted red and green lettuce leaves

Vinaigrette:

3 tablespoons white-wine or champagne vinegar

2 tablespoons hazelnut oil

4 tablespoons olive oil

2 tablespoons peanut oil

Juice of 2 lemons

1 teaspoon chopped tarragon

1 teaspoon chopped marjoram

1 teaspoon chopped thyme

1 teaspoon chopped basil

Salt and pepper to taste

Clean and shuck the oysters and rinse the scallops. Wash the lettuce and arrange it on individual plates or a platter.

Combine all the ingredients for the dressing in a large sauté pan or skillet. Bring the mixture to a simmer over low heat, and add the oysters and scallops, simmering until the edges of the oysters start to curl and the scallops are opaque. This will only take 2 minutes or less. Be careful not to overcook.

Spoon the seafood decoratively onto the plate, and pour the dressing over it. Serve immediately.

Salad of Smoked Lake Trout

Serves 6 as an appetizer, 3 or 4 as an entrée

JIMMY SCHMIDT, London Chop House   The smoked fish is savory and rich, and the colors, flavors, and textures of the vegetables it is arranged with make this a wonderful salad. I've served it as the first course for an elaborate brunch or dinner, and as lunch itself. The addition of cream to the dressing softens it, so it is not a harsh contrast to the delicate fish.

Wine choice: California sparkling wine or French Champagne.

6 bunches watercress, hard stems trimmed, washed

⅓ pound red onions, peeled and cut in a fine juliene

3 ounces baby spinach, stemmed and washed

¾ pound smoked lake-trout fillet, skinned and defatted

6 chanterelles, stems trimmed washed, and cut into quarters (or sixths if large)

1 cup extra-virgin olive oil

3 tablespoons fresh lemon juice (1 lemon)

2 cloves garlic, pressed through a garlic press

Salt and pepper to taste

3 tablespoons heavy cream

The greens and onion can be tossed together, then divided among the plates, with the slices of smoked trout and chanterelle sections placed on top. Or, for a more artistic presentation, Schmidt places the watercress across the top of each plate with a pile of red onion centered on the plate. The spinach leaves fan out from the onion, with the base of the leaves toward the center. The slices of smoked fish are arranged across the spinach, parallel to the watercress, with the chanterelle sections on top of the fish.

To make the dressing: Whisk the olive oil slowly into the lemon juice. Add the garlic and salt and pepper. Whisk in the cream. Spoon a few tablespoons over each salad.

Note: The salads can be arranged on plates up to 5 hours in advance, and stored in the refrigerator covered with plastic wrap. To serve, remix the dressing and spoon over the salads immediately before serving.

Corn and Lobster Salad

Serves 4

MICHAEL ROBERTS, Trumps   There's nothing as delicious as fresh corn right off the stalk, and you can still find it in many parts of the country. Raw corn makes this salad crunchy, and it goes beautifully with the morsels of lobster. What I love about the salad most is the dressing, with its hint of vanilla and brandy added to the creamy vinaigrette.

Wine choice: California Fumé Blanc or California Gewürztraminer.

2 live lobsters (1¼ to 1½ pounds)

1 head chicory

2 ears corn

1 pint lobster stock (page 160)

½ vanilla bean, slit in half

⅛ cup brandy

1 tablespoon lemon juice

2 tablespoons crème fraîche or sour cream

¼ cup vegetable oil

Salt and pepper to taste

Bring a large pot of salted water to a boil and plunge in the lobsters. Bring the water back to a boil and boil for 12 to 15 minutes, depending on the size of the lobsters. Remove them from the water and let them sit until they are cool enough to handle. Remove the tail and claw meat, and set it aside. Reserve the shells and bodies for making lobster stock for the dressing.

Wash the chicory and break it into bite-size pieces, and cut the corn from the cobs with a small, sharp knife. Set both aside.

In a heavy 1-quart saucepan, combine the stock, vanilla bean, and brandy. Cook the stock over medium heat until the liquid is reduced to ¼ cup. Remove the vanilla bean, and when the liquid has cooled, add the lemon juice and crème fraîche or sour cream. Whisking constantly, add the oil and beat until thickened. Add salt and pepper.

To serve: Arrange chunks of lobster on a bed of lettuce either on individual plates or on one large serving dish. Sprinkle with the corn kernels and spoon the dressing over. Serve immediately.

Note: Cooking the lobsters and making the lobster stock can be done up to 2 days in advance.

Crawfish, Squab, and Sweetbread Salad

Serves 6 as an appetizer, 4 as a light meal

SUSUMU FUKUI, La Petite Chaya   Most salads that involve protein keep it to one genre, but this one has many interesting components. It looks so pretty with the tiny crawfish, slices of squab, and morsels of sweetbread mixed with the various vegetables, and the simple vinaigrette dressing blends it all together.

Wine choice: Alsatian Gewürztraminer or Riesling or a California Sauvignon Blanc.

2 pairs sweetbreads
40 crawfish
1 head red leaf lettuce
½ bunch curly endive
1 head radicchio
2 cucumbers
1 carrot
2 turnips
2 squab breasts
½ pound mushrooms
¼ pound haricots verts
2 tablespoons sherry-wine vinegar
½ cup olive oil
2 tablespoons peanut oil
2 teaspoons Dijon mustard
Salt and pepper to taste
2 tablespoons vegetable oil

The night before, wash the sweetbreads and cover them with cold water. Refrigerate them overnight, and then peel off the white membrane as much as possible; remove the tube connecting the two lobes. Bring 1 quart salted water or chicken stock to a boil, and add the sweetbreads. Bring the water back to a simmer and poach the sweetbreads for 10 minutes. Remove them with a slotted spoon and plunge them into ice water to stop the cooking action. Peel away any remaining membrane, and the sweetbreads should separate into 1-inch pieces. Set them aside.

Cook the crawfish in boiling salted water or court bouillon for 3 minutes. Drain, and when they are cool enough to handle, break off the heads and pop out the tails, leaving 4 to 6 whole for a garnish.

Wash and dry the salad greens, breaking them into small pieces. Peel and seed the cucumbers and cut them into a thick julienne. Peel the carrots and turnips, cut them into a thick julienne, and blanch them in boiling salted water for 3 minutes, so they are slightly cooked, and drain.

Remove the breasts from the squabs, if whole, reserving the leg sections for another use. Roast the squab breasts in a preheated 350-degree oven for 10 to 15 minutes, or until they are medium rare. Set them aside.

Slice the mushrooms into quarters and trim the ends off the haricots verts. In a bowl, whisk together the vinegar, olive oil, peanut oil, mustard, salt and pepper.

To assemble: Heat 2 tablespoons of vegetable oil in a large sauté pan over medium-high heat. Add the vegetables and sauté them until the mushrooms are cooked. Add the crawfish and sweetbreads, and sauté the mixture for 2 minutes. Add the dressing, and season with salt and pepper if needed. Arrange the greens on a platter or plates and top with the vegetable mixture. Slice the squab breasts and arrange the slices on top. Garnish with 1 whole crawfish per plate, or arrange the crawfish around the platter.

Note: Except for the final sauté, all the parts can be prepared in advance a day before and kept refrigerated separately, tightly covered.

Warm Chicken and Papaya Salad

Serves 8 as an appetizer, 6 as a lunch or supper

ANNE GREER, The Terrace at the Anatole Hotel   The ginger and orange in the dressing give a sparkling flavor to the chicken and fruits alike. I've served this salad with shrimp in place of the chicken, and toasted almonds instead of the sesame seeds, and all variations have been successful. This is a wonderful lunch salad or could be part of a brunch buffet, since the fruits make it light.

Wine choice: California Sauvignon Blanc or Chardonnay.

The dressing:

1 shallot

1 tablespoon Dijon mustard

¾ teaspoon salt

¼ teaspoon freshly ground white pepper

6 to 8 fresh orange sections, all membrane removed

⅜ cup white vinegar

½ cup freshly squeezed orange juice

1¼ cups vegetable oil, preferably safflower oil

2 teaspoons freshly grated ginger root

The salad:

3 tablespoons sesame seeds

8 chicken breast halves

2 tablespoons peanut oil

2 red bell peppers, cut into fine julienne strips

2 tablespoons imported soy sauce

2 avocados, ripe but firm

3 papayas, ripe but firm

2 heads Bibb or 1 head Boston lettuce, washed and separated into leaves

In a blender or food processor fitted with the steel blade, purée the shallot, mustard, salt, pepper, and orange sections. Add the vinegar and orange juice, and slowly add the oil, beating until the dressing is combined and thick. Stir in the ginger root and set the dressing aside at room temperature. Or make it a day in advance and refrigerate.

In a wok or 12-inch skillet, toast the sesame seeds for 3 minutes, or until they are lightly brown. Remove them and set aside.

Bone and skin the chicken breasts, removing all fat and tendons. Pound them lightly to an even thickness, and cut them into strips about 3 inches long and ½ to ¾ inch wide. Heat the peanut oil, and sauté the chicken and red-pepper strips until barely done, about 2 minutes. Turn off the heat, and add the soy sauce.

Peel and slice the avocados and papayas. Arrange the lettuce leaves on individual plates, and arrange slices of the fruit around the edges of the plates. Pour the dressing into the pan with the chicken and peppers and heat the mixture, but do not let it boil or the dressing will separate.

Mound the chicken and peppers in the center of the greens, drizzling some of the dressing on the avocado and papaya slices. Sprinkle on the sesame seeds and serve immediately.

Grilled Chicken Salad

Serves 4

JONATHAN WAXMAN, Jams   What makes this salad unusual is the taste of the grilled chicken with the pretty assortment of vegetables and fruits. Although it has the same ingredients, the salad comes across to those eating it as far heartier than a chicken and fruit salad, and there's some added zest from the cilantro. If you can't cook the chicken on a grill, second choice is to broil it in the oven broiler rather than bake it.

Wine choice: Alsatian white or German Mosel or Rheingau.

1 head red leaf lettuce

2 bunches mâche or watercress

1 bunch cilantro

1 ripe avocado

1 ripe papaya

1 ripe mango

2 oranges

2 nectarines

1 lime

1 cup extra-virgin olive oil

2 chicken breasts, boned but not skinned

Salt and pepper to taste

Wash the lettuces and dry on paper toweling or in a salad spinner. Clean the cilantro, and break it into small sprigs, discarding the stems. Peel the avocado, papaya, and mango, and slice them. Peel and section the oranges, removing the white membranes. Slice the nectarines.

Juice the lime and mix the juice with olive oil. Marinate all the fruit together in the lime and oil for at least 30 minutes.

Sprinkle the chicken with salt and pepper and grill it over hot charcoal until it is golden brown, about 6 minutes on the skin side and about 3 minutes on the underside. Slice the chicken across the grain and keep it warm.

To assemble: Place the lettuce and mâche on a platter. Arrange the fruit on the lettuce and top with the sliced chicken. Pour over any remaining marinade and garnish with the cilantro sprigs.

Warm Lamb
Salad

Serves 6

WOLFGANG PUCK, Spago   The combination of warm lamb, imbued with the flavor of mustard and herbs, with piquant sun-dried tomatoes and Parmesan cheese makes this salad hearty enough to please true meat-and-potatoes eaters, but it's still light and a salad for the increasing number of people who live on salads. There's no question that the dish is best with freshly roasted lamb, but I've also served it as a way to use up and stretch leftover leg of lamb; warm it in a 200-degree oven for a few minutes.

Wine choice: French red Bordeaux or California Cabernet Sauvignon.

1 pound boned lamb shoulder, boned leg of lamb, or any lean lamb

2 tablespoons Dijon mustard

4 sprigs fresh thyme

Freshly ground pepper

Salt

3 bunches arugula

3 bunches mâche

1 large head curly endive, tender inside leaves only

½ cup vinaigrette (page 183)

6 tablespoons sun-dried tomatoes, cut into fine julienne

½ cup freshly grated Parmesan cheese

Brush both sides of the lamb with the Dijon mustard. Sprinkle it with thyme leaves and pepper. Cover the lamb tightly with plastic wrap and refrigerate it overnight. Sprinkle it with salt and place it on a rack in a small roasting pan in a 450-degree oven for 20 minutes, or until it is medium rare. Remove it from the oven and let it rest for 15 minutes before carving.

Wash the salad greens and dry them on paper toweling or in a salad spinner. Tear them into bite-sized pieces. Toss the greens with enough vinaigrette to coat them lightly.

To serve: Arrange the salad greens on a large platter or 6 individual plates. Slice the lamb thin and arrange it in the center of the greens with the julienne of tomatoes over the top. Sprinkle with grated cheese.

PASTA
AND
PIZZA

The controversy may never be resolved as to whether the Italians were brought pasta from one of Marco Polo's travels, or if the Europeans and Chinese developed it independently of one another. But neither Marco Polo nor the Chinese courts he visited could have imagined that the basic egg-and-flour dough—made in some recipes with semolina for some added resiliency to the cooked noodles—would be flavored with red chilies or sweet potatoes or topped with sauces from lamb and wild mushrooms to sweetbreads and artichoke hearts.

Interesting pastas are not new to this country, they are just becoming increasingly popular. One of the trendy dishes of the 1970s, appearing on menus from Maine to the Mexican border, was pasta primavera. It was not an import, but was created by Sirio Maccioni, owner of New York's Le Cirque restaurant, in 1975. The mélange of spring vegetables in a Parmesan cream sauce was one of the first times pasta was seen on other than Italian menus.

Vegetable pastas, such as those prepared by Jackie Etcheber and Robert Rosellini, are their personal versions of Maccioni's basic idea. And, for any recipe calling for egg or spinach pasta, I'm a fan of the many fresh pastas available from pasta stores or in the refrigerator case of the supermarket from such national firms as Pasta & Cheese.

And then there are the recipes calling for pastas of other flavors, and these do need a turn or two of a pasta machine, although the food processor has simplified the dough-making for pasta as it has for pie crusts. Making pastas is a great release of aggression on a rainy Sunday afternoon.

While the ancestry of pasta may be as culturally interwoven as a plate of linguine, we do know pizzas were developed in the south of Italy around Naples in the seventeenth century, with buffalo-milk mozzarella cheese added as a topping about two hundred years later. But they began, and were popularized in this country, as peasant snack food. Pizza was hardly topped with such luxuries as the smoked salmon and golden caviar Wolfgang Puck uses at Spago.

Pizzas with unusual toppings were another California innovation, with Alice Waters's café Chez Panisse in Berkeley starting the trend. By 1983, restaurants in Minnesota, Washington, D.C., and Boston were making up combinations. ∎

Pasta with Winter-Vegetable Sauce

Serves 6 as an appetizer, 4 as an entrée

BARRY WINE, The Quilted Giraffe   There are delicacy and natural crispness to winter vegetables like celery root and fennel that add much to pasta, and the color from red pepper brings the plate visually to life. While Parmesan cheese is a natural with most pasta and vegetable combinations, I feel it detracts from the delicate flavors of this one, and if you're spending the money for truffles, you certainly want to be able to taste them.

Wine choice: Alsatian Riesling, French Sancerre or Pouilly Fumé.

1 medium celery root

2 bulbs fennel

4 medium leeks

6 black truffles

3 cups heavy cream

1 red bell pepper

Salt and freshly ground white pepper

1 pound fettuccine or linguine

Fresh chervil

Peel the celery root and cut it into ⅛-inch-thick slices. Cut the slices into attractive random shapes.

Cut the fennel bulbs in half, and discard their hearts. Separate the layers and cut them into a coarse julienne. Slice the leeks in half lengthwise, discarding the green part. Wash them well under cold running water, separating the root-end layers to rid the leeks of all hidden grit. Slice the leeks on a diagonal.

Slice the truffles about 1/16 inch thick.

Bring the cream to a boil over low heat in a heavy 3-quart saucepan. Turn off the heat and add celery root, fennel, leeks, and truffles. Cover the pot and allow the mixture to sit for 30 minutes without disturbing.

Remove the seeds and ribs from the red pepper and cut it into fine julienne strips. After the vegetables have steeped in the cream, add the red pepper and reheat the mixture, seasoning with salt and pepper to taste.

Bring a large pot of salted water to a boil. Add the pasta, and return to a boil. Cook until al dente, about 30 seconds if pasta is fresh.

Serve the sauce over the pasta, and garnish with fresh chervil if available.

Note: Although best if served immediately, the sauce can be prepared through the steeping procedure a day in advance and reheated gently. Add the red pepper at that time.

Vegetable Pasta

Serves 8 as an appetizer, 6 as an entrée

JACKIE ETCHEBER, Jackie's This dish looks like a party when placed on the table, with the red and green pasta, colorful vegetables, and bits of bacon. The taste is reminiscent of a lighter version of pasta carbonara, from the smoky bacon base, but it's lighter and fresher, with all the vegetables giving it an exciting texture. I've served this for buffet dinners, and it makes the simplest roast meats seem more elegant.

Wine choice: California Chardonnay or French white Burgundy.

½ pound broccoli, stems peeled, cut into slices and flowerets

½ pound cauliflower, cut into flowerets

½ pound zucchini, sliced ⅓ inch thick

2 tablespoons unsalted butter

½ pound mushrooms

¼ pound bacon, cut into 2-inch pieces

1 green pepper, cut into ½-inch pieces

1 red pepper, cut into ½-inch pieces

4 sprigs fresh basil, chopped

½ pound tomato rotini

½ pound spinach rotini

Salt and freshly ground pepper to taste

Bring a large quantity of salted water to a boil and blanch the broccoli, cauliflower, and zucchini for about 4 minutes, or until the vegetables are cooked but still crisp. Drain and quickly plunge them into a bowl of ice water to stop the cooking action. Drain them again and set aside.

In a skillet or sauté pan, melt the butter and heat it until the foam starts to subside. Add the mushrooms and sauté them until tender. Add the mushrooms and their cooking juices to the blanched vegetables.

In another skillet, cook the bacon until crisp. Remove the bacon pieces with a slotted spoon and add the green and red pepper to the pan. Sauté them until tender, and set them aside. Add the chopped basil to the pan.

Bring a large quantity of salted water to a boil and add the pasta, cooking it until al dente. Drain the pasta and toss it with the other cooked ingredients. Season with salt and freshly ground black pepper.

Note: The vegetables can be blanched in advance and reheated with the bacon fat and peppers. If reheating, cut back slightly on their blanching time. The pasta should be cooked at the last minute.

Pasta with Wild Mushrooms

Serves 6

JONATHAN WAXMAN, Jams   The savory earthiness of wild mushrooms, and the various colors and shapes of such species as fresh morels and chanterelles or cultivated shiitake, make this a wonderful dish. There's even a surprise flavor when you begin to sense the walnut oil, and the fresh herbs then give you another surprise and make the taste fresher. I like using a combination of mushrooms, but if you're using just one variety, I'd suggest shiitake, which are now available all year.

Wine choice: California Sauvignon Blanc.

1 pound wild mushrooms

½ cup walnut oil

1 shallot, minced

1 clove garlic, minced

Salt and pepper to taste

1 cup heavy cream

1 tablespoon sherry

1 sprig fresh thyme

1 sprig fresh tarragon

1 teaspoon chopped fresh basil

1 pound linguine or fettuccine

Clean the mushrooms and slice them into sections if they are large, but do not slice fine. Heat a sauté pan or skillet over high heat and add the walnut oil. When the oil is hot, add the mushrooms and sauté them until barely tender, stirring constantly. Add the shallots, garlic, salt, and pepper and sauté another minute. Then add the cream, sherry, and herbs, and let the sauce simmer for 2 minutes to blend the flavors.

Cook the pasta al dente and toss it with the sauce. You can make the sauce up to 2 hours in advance since the heat of the pasta will reheat it.

San Remo Pasta with Roasted Tomatoes and Black Olives

Serves 6 as an appetizer, 4 as an entrée

MARK MILLER, Fourth Street Grill   This is one of the most exciting and unusual pasta dishes I've ever made. The slight spiciness from the red-pepper flakes in the pasta itself forms a basis for the topping, light but intensely flavored from the combination of sun-dried and roasted tomatoes and olives. Eating it reminds me of sitting on a terrace overlooking the Mediterranean, and it's very easy to make.

Wine choice: French red Rhône or California Zinfandel.

RED-PEPPER PASTA

1½ cups flour

1½ cups semolina

2 teaspoons salt

4 eggs

2 tablespoons oil

1 to 2 tablespoons red-pepper flakes, ground in a mortar until powdery

TOMATO AND OLIVE SAUCE

½ cup fruity virgin olive oil

2 cups roasted fresh tomatoes (cooked in a 400-degree oven on a cookie sheet for 30 minutes, then peeled)

Chicken stock (if needed)

1 to 2 tablespoons chopped garlic

1 to 2 tablespoons red-pepper flakes, or to taste

6 ounces sun-dried tomatoes packed in oil, cut into a fine julienne

½ cup fresh basil leaves

50 Gaeta olives or Nyons olives, pitted and chopped

Freshly grated Parmesan cheese

If you are making the pasta by hand, mix the flour, semolina, and salt well. Break the eggs into the center and incorporate all the flour, adding oil and pepper to the liquid. Knead the dough.

Or place all the ingredients in a food processor fitted with a steel blade and process until the dough begins to form a ball, then process 60 seconds. Remove the dough from the work bowl, press it into a ball, wrap it in plastic wrap, and refrigerate for at least 3 hours. Then roll.

Bring a large quantity of salted water to a boil. If the pasta is freshly made, it will be cooked al dente almost as the water comes back to a boil. If it has been dried or frozen, it will take a few minutes to cook. Drain the pasta and keep it warm.

In a large sauté pan or skillet, heat the olive oil and add the roasted tomatoes. Add a little chicken stock if the tomatoes seem too dry. Add the garlic, red-pepper flakes, and sun-dried tomatoes, and cook for a few minutes, until the garlic has lost its raw taste. Add the basil leaves and turn off the heat. Toss with the pasta and olives, and serve with freshly grated Parmesan.

Fettuccine with Tomatoes, Basil, and Garlic

Serves 6 to 8 as an appetizer, 4 as an entrée

ROBERT ROSELLINI, Rosellini's Other Place   This is one of my favorite fast dishes: the sauce cooks in the same time it takes for the water for the pasta to come to a boil. The sauce is velvety, and enlivened by the tomatoes, which are barely cooked.

Wine choice: French Bordeaux or red Burgundy.

4 cloves garlic, peeled and minced fine

3 tablespoons chopped fresh basil leaves

1½ cups mushrooms, sliced

1½ cups heavy cream

3 medium tomatoes, peeled, seeded, and diced

1½ pounds fresh fettuccine

Salt and pepper to taste

Freshly grated Parmesan cheese

Bring a large quantity of salted water to a boil. While water is heating combine the garlic, basil, mushrooms, and cream in a heavy saucepan. Bring the mixture to a boil and simmer, stirring frequently, until the sauce has reduced by one-third and coats the back of a spoon.

Turn off the heat, and add the tomatoes to the sauce.

Add the fettuccine to the boiling water, cooking until it is just al dente. If the pasta is very fresh, this is no more than 30 seconds. Drain it well, and toss it with the sauce. Add salt and pepper to taste. Sprinkle with Parmesan cheese.

Red-Chili Pasta Salad

Serves 6 to 8

ANNE GREER, The Terrace at the Anatole Hotel   I've never been enamored of cold pasta salads because the basic pasta has no taste, but this one is not only given some zip from the chili powder, it also has a deep, rich color. It looks beautiful when mixed with spinach leaves, and the cilantro in the dressing adds a wonderful flavor accent and balances the chili taste. Greer uses Gebhardt's chili powder, and the flavor is far better than any others I've tried.

Wine choice: California Zinfandel or Italian Barolo.

THE RED-CHILI PASTA

2 cups unbleached flour

1 cup semolina flour

5 tablespoons pure ground red chilies or Gebhardt's chili powder

1 teaspoon cumin (omit if using Gebhardt's)

1½ teaspoons salt

4 large eggs

1½ tablespoons vegetable oil

Additional flour as needed

Cornmeal

THE DRESSING

1 clove garlic, peeled

2 sprigs fresh cilantro or parsley

¼ cup white-wine vinegar

1 tablespoon orange juice

¼ to ½ teaspoon salt

⅛ teaspoon cayenne pepper

1½ teaspoons dry mustard

⅔ cup vegetable oil

THE SALAD

Dressing (above)

½ recipe red-chili pasta, cooked, drained, and cooled

⅓ cup pine nuts

1 tablespoon vegetable oil

1 medium zucchini, cut into julienne strips

10 spinach leaves, cut into strips

60 to 80 spinach leaves (about 1½ pounds), washed and stemmed

8 ounces goat cheese, preferably California

4 tomatoes, seeded and chopped

Using a food processor fitted with the metal blade, combine the flours and seasonings. Then add the eggs and oil and process to make a smooth ball, adding more flour as needed. Knead in the processor for 60 seconds. Wrap the dough, divided into 2 or 3 portions, in plastic wrap, and let it rest for 20 minutes in the refrigerator. Process the dough through a pasta machine, choosing a fettuccine or spaghetti width, and sprinkle with cornmeal to prevent sticking.

Either cook the pasta or freeze it on flat trays. When it is frozen, divide it among plastic bags. The dough can be cooked directly from the frozen state.

Grush the garlic and finely chop the cilantro or parsley. Mix them with the vinegar, orange juice, salt, cayenne pepper, and mustard. Whisk in the oil, beating until the dressing is thick and smooth. Set it aside. This can also be done in a processor fitted with a metal blade.

Mix ½ cup of the dressing with the pasta and chill. Sauté the pine nuts in the oil and 1 tablespoon of the dressing until golden. Toss the nuts with the pasta, zucchini, and cut spinach leaves. For each plate: Line the plate with 10 spinach leaves and top them with pasta salad. Crumble the goat cheese on top and place some chopped tomatoes in the center. Pass extra dressing separately.

Note: If you are using red chili peppers instead of powder, toast them on a cookie sheet in a 250-degree oven for 8 to 10 minutes. Then remove the seeds and stems and grind them in a food processor.

Crabmeat with Tomatoes and Cheese on Corn Capellini

Serves 12 as an appetizer, 8 as an entrée

MARCEL DESAULNIERS, The Trellis   This dish is the most interesting permutation on an enchilada I've ever made, and looks wonderful when placed on the table. There's a crunch to the corn pasta, and the flavors of the crabmeat and fresh herbed tomato sauce make it very sophisticated. While the basil is excellent, I've sometimes made it more Southwestern by substituting cilantro.

Wine choice: California Chardonnay or Sauvignon Blanc.

3 tablespoons clarified butter

1½ pounds lump backfin crabmeat, well picked over

¾ cup sliced scallions, white part only

3 cups fresh tomatoes, peeled, seeded, and diced

1½ cups Fresh Tomato Sauce (recipe follows)

Corn Capellini (recipe follows)

¾ cup grated Monterey jack cheese

In a sauté pan or 12-inch skillet, melt 1½ tablespoons of the butter and sauté the crabmeat until hot. Set it aside and keep warm.

In another pan, melt the remaining butter and sauté the scallions over low heat for 4 to 5 minutes, stirring occasionally. Add the tomatoes and sauté for 2 minutes, until they are hot but not mushy. Add the tomato sauce, bring to a simmer to combine, and set the mixture aside.

Cook the pasta in a large pot of boiling salted water for 1 minute, and drain.

Place the pasta on a serving plate. Top with the crab and the tomato mixture, and sprinkle with the grated cheese. Serve immediately.

The final preparation of this dish only takes a few minutes, and should be done at the last minute, but the tomato sauce and pasta can be made up to 2 days in advance. Once the pasta has dried, it will take longer to cook.

FRESH TOMATO SAUCE

1 tablespoon butter

1 tablespoon olive oil

½ cup finely diced onions

2 cloves garlic, minced

3 cups fresh tomatoes, peeled, seeded, and diced

1 tablespoon chopped fresh basil

Salt and freshly ground black pepper to taste

Heat the butter and oil in a saucepan, and when they are hot add the onions. Sauté over medium heat for 4 to 5 minutes, stirring often, until the onions are translucent. Add the garlic and cook an additional 3 minutes. Add the tomatoes and basil, and bring the mixture to a simmer. Cook, uncovered, for 20 minutes, stirring occasionally.

Purée the mixture in a blender or food processor fitted with a steel blade, or press it through a food mill. Season with salt and pepper. Any sauce left over from the recipe will keep in the refrigerator for 3 days.

CORN CAPELLINI

1 cup corn flour (masa harina)

In a large mixing bowl, combine the two flours and the salt. Make a well in the center, and break in the eggs. Mix with

2 cups all-purpose flour

1 teaspoon salt

5 eggs

a fork, and then by hand, until all the flour has been incorporated, and the dough forms a ball. Remove the dough from the bowl, and place it on a floured surface. Knead by hand until the dough is soft and smooth. This can be done in a food processor fitted with a steel blade. Cover it, and allow it to relax for 1 hour in the refrigerator.

Roll the dough through a pasta machine, and cut into capellini.

Angel-Hair Pasta with Goat Cheese and Broccoli

Serves 4 to 6 as an appetizer or vegetable side dish

WOLFGANG PUCK, Spago I've served this dish as a combination vegetable and starch with entrées, and as a separate pasta course. The flavor is very delicate, and the broccoli flowerets make it most attractive to serve. While it doesn't matter with most pasta dishes if another width is used, I've found you need angel hair for this one since anything thicker makes it taste doughy in the mouth.

Wine choice: California Sauvignon Blanc or French Pouilly Fumé.

½ cup extra-virgin olive oil

½ pound (about 3 cups) tiny broccoli flowerets (reserve the stalks for another use)

¾ cup strong chicken broth

1 teaspoon fresh thyme leaves, plus 4 to 6 sprigs to use as garnish

Freshly ground pepper

3 tablespoons unsalted butter

4 ounces goat cheese, crumbled

10 ounces angel-hair pasta

1 tablespoon pine nuts, toasted in 350-degree oven for 7 to 10 minutes, as garnish

Heat the oil in a sauté pan or 12-inch skillet and sauté the broccoli for 1 minute over high heat. Add the stock and bring it to a boil. Add thyme leaves, pepper, butter, and goat cheese. Stir the mixture until the cheese melts, and remove it from the heat. The broccoli should be cooked but still slightly crisp.

Cook the pasta until al dente in a large quantity of boiling salted water. It should be done as soon as it floats to the surface. Drain it and toss with the sauce. Divide the pasta among the plates and garnish it with pine nuts and a sprig of thyme.

Pasta with Sweetbreads and Artichokes

Serves 8 as an appetizer, 6 as an entrée

WOLFGANG PUCK, Spago After trying both cheeses Puck recommends, I prefer the blue cheese since it gives a more interesting bite to the sauce and enhances the flavors of the artichoke hearts and sweetbreads without overwhelming them. This is one of my favorite pasta dishes, and delights guests who are not accustomed to finding these ingredients as part of a pasta presentation. It's a rich dish, while not being heavy.

Wine choice: French Sancerre or Pouilly Fumé, California Sauvignon Blanc, or Alsatian Gewürztraminer if blue cheese is used.

12 ounces sweetbreads

6 cups water

½ teaspoon peppercorns

½ bay leaf

¼ medium yellow onion, chopped

½ medium carrot, chopped

½ stalk celery, chopped

1 sprig parsley

1 sprig thyme

Salt

8 medium or 4 large artichokes

½ lemon

Freshly ground white pepper

Flour

5 tablespoons unsalted butter

3 tablespoons olive oil

2 cups chicken stock

2 ounces blue cheese or well-aged goat cheese

1 pound angel-hair pasta

Soak the sweetbreads in cold water overnight in the refrigerator, covered with plastic wrap. Drain the sweetbreads and rinse them under cold water.

Bring 6 cups of water to a boil with the peppercorns, bay leaf, onion, carrot, celery, parsley, thyme, and a pinch of salt. Add the sweetbreads and cook them for 4 minutes, or until they are medium rare. Remove them with a slotted spoon and plunge them into a bowl of ice water to stop the cooking action. Carefully pull off the white membrane covering the sweetbreads and remove the tube connecting the two lobes. As you peel them, they will separate into pieces 1 to 2 inches in size. Set them aside.

Cut the stems off the artichokes, and trim the leaves down to the hearts. Rub the exposed surfaces with the cut side of a lemon to prevent discoloration. Cook the hearts in boiling salted water until they are barely tender, about 20 to 30 minutes, depending on the size of the artichokes. Remove them with a slotted spoon, and plunge them into ice water to stop the cooking action. When cool enough to handle, carefully remove the hairy choke and cut the hearts into ¼-inch slices.

Cut each piece of sweetbread into 3 or 4 slices. Season them with salt and pepper and dust them lightly with flour. Heat 3 tablespoons of butter in a sauté pan or large skillet over medium heat. Raise the heat to high and add the sweetbreads. Sauté them until golden brown, remove with a slotted spoon, drain on paper toweling, and keep them warm.

In another sauté pan, heat the olive oil and remaining butter. Sauté the artichoke slices until they are lightly browned. Season them with salt and pepper, and remove them from the pan. Pour off the excess fat and deglaze the pan with the chicken stock. Add the cheese and reduce by the stock by one-third.

Cook the pasta al dente in a large quantity of salted water. Since the angel hair are so thin, they are cooked almost immediately as the water returns to the boil. Drain well and toss the pasta with the sauce.

To serve: Fan a few artichoke slices around the edge of the plate and heap the pasta in the center. Top with slices of sweetbreads.

Note: The artichokes and sweetbreads can be prepared a day in advance and refrigerated, tightly covered. The sweetbreads should be reheated on a cookie sheet in a 350-degree oven for 5 minutes, and the artichokes will be reheated by the sauce; drain them with a slotted spoon.

Prawns in Garlic Sauce with Fettuccine

Serves 8 as an appetizer, 6 as an entrée

AMY FERGUSON, Charley's 517   The tomatoes and cream give the sauce the same pink blush as the shrimp, and you expect it to be very delicate. The basil and garlic give the flavor some excitement, but are not so overwhelming that you lose the blend of flavors as a result. This is a very quick sauce to make, and a tossed salad is all you need to make it dinner.

Wine choice: French white Burgundy or California Chardonnay.

18 to 24 prawns or jumbo shrimp (1½ to 2 pounds)

½ cup olive oil

4 cloves garlic, crushed and minced

1 cup white wine

2 ripe tomatoes, peeled, seeded, and diced

2 tablespoons chopped fresh basil, or 1½ teaspoons dried

Salt and pepper to taste

2 cups heavy cream

3 tablespoons unsalted butter

1½ pounds fresh fettuccine, cooked al dente

Garnish: Freshly grated Romano cheese and fresh basil sprigs

Shell and devein the prawns, washing them well. Heat the olive oil in a large skillet. Add the prawns and garlic and sauté them, stirring constantly, for 1 minute, until the prawns begin to turn pink. Add the wine, tomatoes, basil, salt, pepper, and cream, and cook over medium heat until the prawns are cooked through, about 3 minutes. Remove the shrimp from the pan, and reduce the sauce for about 2 minutes over medium heat, until it coats the back of a spoon. Whisk in the butter, stirring until the sauce is smooth. Toss the pasta and prawns with the sauce to heat through. Garnish each serving with about 1 tablespoon of freshly grated Romano cheese and a sprig of fresh basil.

Roast-Duck Pasta with Summer Vegetables

Serves 6

MARK MILLER, Fourth Street Grill The richness in this dish comes from duck, an animal I've rarely seen mixed with pasta, and it is as colorful as any cream-sauced pasta primavera when it comes to the table but is much lighter. The vegetables and fresh herbs with the duck are a fabulous combination of textures and flavors.

Wine choice: California Zinfandel or French red Rhône.

1 duck, quartered (5 to 6 pounds)

¼ cup olive oil

1 large red onion, thinly sliced

2 large red bell peppers, seeded and cut into thin strips

1 pound mushrooms, quartered

Salt

3 cups chicken stock

3 cloves garlic, finely minced

3 large tomatoes, seeded and cut into large dice

3 small to medium yellow squash, sliced into thin rounds

3 small to medium zucchini, sliced into thin rounds

4 carrots, cut into thin strips and blanched until soft

1 pound freshly shelled peas, blanched for 1 minute

1 cup fresh basil leaves, chopped, or a mixture of fresh oregano and thyme, with extra sprigs for garnish

3 tablespoons unsalted butter

1¼ pounds fresh egg pasta, cooked (fettuccine or linguine)

In a 450-degree oven, roast the duck for 45 minutes. Remove it and set aside until cool enough to handle. Remove all the meat from the bones, discarding the bones, fat, and skin. Or add the bones to your chicken stock to make it richer. Cut the meat into strips and set it aside.

Using a large sauté pan or two small ones, heat the olive oil. Add the red onion, red peppers, mushrooms, and a little salt, and sauté for 2 to 3 minutes, tossing constantly. Add the stock, garlic, and tomatoes, and boil for 3 minutes on very high heat to reduce the liquid. Add the yellow and green squash, duck meat, and carrots, and simmer for 2 minutes. Add the peas, basil, and butter, and cook, tossing, for 30 seconds. Serve the mixture over the cooked pasta and garnish with fresh sprigs of basil.

To cook pasta, bring a large quantity of salted water to a boil. Add the pasta, bring back to a boil, and cook until al dente, only 30 seconds to 1 minute if the pasta is fresh.

Note: The duck can be roasted and the sauce can be totally prepared a day in advance and kept, tightly covered, in the refrigerator. Reheat slowly.

Lamb Pasta with Wild Chanterelles

Serves 6 as an appetizer, 4 as an entrée

MARK MILLER, Fourth Street Grill   Lamb and wild mushrooms are a piquant and flavorful combination, and this dish has a double dose from the dried and fresh fungi. The dish is rich and hearty enough to be classified as a "comfort food," but it's lighter than most stews, since the sauce is merely a reduction of the stock with some red wine and herbs.

Wine choice: French red Bordeaux.

2 cups lamb stock (see note)

½ cup dried imported cèpes

¼ cup olive oil

1 pound fresh chanterelles (if out of season, morels or shiitake can be substituted), chopped

Salt and pepper

4 tablespoons unsalted butter

¼ cup light red wine, such as Pinot Noir

1 tablespoon finely chopped garlic

2 tablespoons mixed fresh herbs, such as thyme, oregano, parsley

1 pound lamb meat

1 pound fresh egg pasta

chopped parsley (optional)

Heat the lamb stock to a boil in a small saucepan, shut off the heat, and add the dried cèpes. Set aside for 30 minutes. Remove the cèpes from the stock with a slotted spoon, and strain the stock through a piece of cheesecloth to remove the grit. Rinse the cèpes, rubbing to dislodge any further grit, and chop them fine.

Heat a 12– or 14–inch skillet over high heat, then add the olive oil, chopped chanterelles, a little salt and pepper, and 1 tablespoon of the butter to help them brown. When the mushrooms are browned, add the red wine, and cook until it is almost evaporated. Then add the chopped garlic, herbs, lamb stock, and cèpes, and simmer over medium heat for 15 minutes.

Cut the lamb into thin strips, and add them to the pan, along with the remaining butter. Cook for only 1 minute, to keep the lamb rare.

While the sauce is reducing, add the pasta to a large quantity of boiling salted water. Cook until it is al dente and drain.

Toss the pasta with the sauce, and garnish with a little chopped parsley, if desired.

Note: The sauce can be prepared, but without adding the lamb, a day in advance.

While many cooks have veal and chicken stock in the freezer, few have lamb stock, since it is rarely called for. Since the lamb meat for this dish must be perfectly lean and free from fat, my suggestion is to buy a half leg of lamb and then use the bones and scraps for making the stock. Follow the recipe for Basic Meat Stock (page 160), and be aware that lamb stock will need frequent skimming at first.

Pork with Cranberries, Pine Nuts, and Sweet-Potato Fettuccine

Serves 8

MARCEL DESAULNIERS, The Trellis   This dish, while not complicated at all to prepare, has some of the most interesting combinations of textures and flavors. The crispy fried sweet-potato slivers tie to the sweet flavor of the sweet potatoes added to the pasta dough, and the cranberries are a zesty, as well as colorful, inclusion.

Wine choice: California Cabernet or Zinfandel.

4 pounds boneless loin of pork, cut into ¼-inch-thick slices

1 cup vegetable oil

Salt and freshly ground pepper

½ pound cranberries, fresh or frozen and defrosted, cut in halves

4 teaspoons sugar

4 tablespoons unsalted butter

1 pound peeled sweet potatoes, cut into julienne strips and blanched for 5 minutes in boiling salted water

1 recipe Sweet-Potato Fettuccine (recipe follows)

½ cup pine nuts, toasted in a 350-degree oven for 7 to 10 minutes

SWEET-POTATO FETTUCCINE

½ pound unpeeled raw sweet potatoes

4 cups all-purpose flour

1 teaspoon salt

3 large eggs

Cornmeal

Dip the pork slices into the oil, then season with salt and pepper. Set them aside.

Combine the cranberries and sugar, and bring them to a boil in a 2-quart heavy saucepan, cooking until they are mushy and thick. Set them aside.

Melt the butter in a large sauté pan or skillet, and when bubbly add the sweet potatoes. Sauté them until they are crispy and golden brown, about 4 minutes. While the potatoes are sautéing, grill the pork over a low fire until it is cooked through. Be careful the fire is not too hot or it will toughen the meat.

Bring a large quantity of salted water to a boil and add the fettuccine, cooking until it is al dente, which is no more than 30 seconds if the pasta is freshly made, and may take 45 seconds to 1 minute if the pasta has been allowed to dry.

Either on individual plates or a large platter, place the cooked pork slices on the pasta. Garnish with the sweet potatoes, cranberries, and pine nuts.

Cook the sweet potatoes in boiling salted water for approximately 45 minutes, or until they are very tender. Remove the potatoes from the water, and when they are cool enough to handle remove the skins and purée the potatoes in a food processor fitted with a steel blade or pass them through a food mill.

In a large bowl, combine the flour and salt. Make a well in the center and add the eggs. Add the purée and knead the mixture by hand until the dough forms a ball. This can be done in a food processor, in which case the dough can be kneaded for 60 seconds or until pliable. Or remove the dough from the mixing bowl and knead by hand on a floured board.

Cover the dough and allow it to relax for 1 hour in the refrigerator, covered with plastic wrap.

Roll the dough through a pasta machine, and cut it into fettuccine. Sprinkle it with cornmeal to prevent sticking.

Pizza Dough

Makes 4 eight-inch pizzas

WOLFGANG PUCK, Spago   This recipe produces the best pizza crust I've ever tasted, regardless of what is put on top of it. It is thin, chewy, and crisp, with a slightly nutlike flavor. If possible, bake the pizzas directly on pizza stones or tiles, available in kitchenware stores, or heat the cookie sheets before placing the pizzas on them.

3 cups all-purpose flour
1 package dry or fresh yeast
1 teaspoon salt
1 tablespoon clover honey
2 tablespoons olive oil
¾ cup water
additional olive oil

Place the flour and yeast in a mixing bowl, or the bowl of an electric mixer fitted with a dough hook. Add the salt, honey, olive oil, and water. Mix well until the dough forms a soft ball.

Transfer the dough to a lightly floured surface and knead until it is smooth. Place it in a buttered deep bowl and allow the dough to rest, covered with a clean dry towel, for 30 minutes.

Divide the dough into 4 equal parts. Roll each piece into a smooth, tight ball, and place them on a flat sheet or dish, covered with a damp towel, and refrigerate until baking time. This can be done up to 6 hours in advance, but the dough should be removed from the refrigerator 1 hour before baking so that it will reach room temperature.

Lightly flour a work surface, and using the fleshy part of your fingertips, flatten each dough ball into a circle, approximately 6 inches in diameter, leaving the outer edge thicker than the center. Lift the dough from the work surface and gently stretch the edges, working clockwise, to form 8-inch circles. Place on pizza paddles or baking sheets, and brush the surface with olive oil. Top as desired.

Bake the pizzas in a 500-degree oven for 10 to 12 minutes, or as directed, until the crust is golden brown and the topping is bubbly.

Prosciutto Pizza

Serves 4 as an appetizer

WOLFGANG PUCK, Spago In some ways, cheese and tomato make this a classic pizza, but the use of fresh ingredients elevates the dish to one of the most complex imaginable in flavor, although very easy to make. It also looks so pretty, with the various vegetables and prosciutto arranged on the crust.

Wine choice: Italian Barolo or Chianti or California Zinfandel.

1 recipe Pizza Dough (see preceding recipe)

2 red bell peppers, julienned

½ cup extra-virgin olive oil

1 tablespoon dried red pepper, crushed fine in a mortar

¾ pound fresh whole-milk mozzarella

¼ pound Fontina cheese

4 large cloves garlic, blanched for 3 minutes in boiling water

½ bunch fresh basil leaves, chopped (½ cup)

6 ripe Italian plum tomatoes, sliced very thin

6 ounces prosciutto, cut into fine julienne strips

1 medium red onion, cut into fine julienne strips or rings

4 ounces fresh goat cheese, crumbled

Make the pizza dough according to the recipe.
Sauté the red bell peppers in ¼ cup of the olive oil until they are limp, about 5 minutes. Set them aside. Mix the remaining oil with the crushed red pepper and set it aside.

Grate the mozzarella and Fontina cheeses. Mix them together and reserve. Slice the garlic paper-thin and set it aside.

After forming circles with the pizza dough, brush them with the olive-oil-and-pepper mixture. Spread the mixed cheeses on top, reserving 1 cup of cheese. Sprinkle with the basil, top with the tomatoes, prosciutto, red peppers, red onion, and garlic. Dot with the goat cheese, and finish by sprinkling with the reserved cheese.

Bake the pizzas in a preheated 500-degree oven for 15 to 17 minutes, or until the crust is golden brown and the tops are bubbly. Cut the pizzas into wedges and serve immediately.

Note: Pizzas make wonderful hors d'oeuvre, and if you are serving them as such, I suggest forming the dough into rectangles, and then cutting the pizzas into squares.

The pizzas can be prepared and kept in the refrigerator up to 3 hours before being baked. If they are chilled, add 3 minutes to the baking time.

Pizza with Smoked Salmon and Golden Caviar

Serves 4

WOLFGANG PUCK, Spago The pizza crust, with some chives added for a slightly oniony accent, is a crisper alternative to the usual toast points served with smoked salmon. It is amazing how the warmth of the pizza crust brings out the flavors of the fish in a way serving it cold does not. Once you've mastered Puck's delicious pizza dough, making this recipe is very easy, and the results draw raves.

Wine choice: California Sauvignon Blanc, Alsatian Pinot Blanc, or French Pouilly Fumé.

2 to 3 ounces smoked salmon

1 tablespoon minced chives

1 recipe pizza dough (page 207)

4 tablespoons extra-virgin olive oil

6 tablespoons sour cream or crème fraîche

4 heaping tablespoons Great Lakes golden caviar

1 heaping teaspoon black caviar

Have the salmon cut into paper-thin slices and reserve. Knead two-thirds of the minced chives into the pizza dough, and shape the dough into 8-inch circles as directed in the master recipe. Brush the center of each circle with olive oil, and bake the crusts, preferably on pizza stones, in a 500-degree oven for 8 to 10 minutes, or until golden. When they are baked, transfer the pizzas to heated serving plates.

Spread the surfaces with the sour cream or crème fraîche, and arrange slices of salmon decoratively over the top of the sour cream. Place a spoonful of golden caviar in the center of each pizza, then spoon a little of the black caviar into the center of the golden caviar. Sprinkle the top of the salmon with the remaining chives.

GRILLED, BROILED, AND SMOKED ENTREES

There's no question that holding a hunk of meat over an open fire is the way all cuisines started, and as Barbara Tropp notes, grilling is very California 1980s, but it's also ancient Chinese.

While most people mean grilled when they say "barbecued," in the Southwest it has an entirely different meaning. "Barbecue in Texas is actually smoking for a long time over low heat," says Anne Greer. The word *barbecue* comes from the Spanish and Haitian word *barbacoa,* which refers to the latticework grill on which the meats were placed over the open pit fire.

The increased popularity of grilling and broiling is part of a general concern for health. The fat drips from meat and fish rather than being reabsorbed into the tissue (although a study by the American Cancer Society in 1982 placed all high-heat cooking methods under suspicion, since the chemicals produced by broiling and grilling are the same as those in cigarette smoke and industrial pollution). The grilling craze also ties in with our interest in intensified flavors, since the mesquite or hickory on which meats are cooked adds complexity.

For the most part, broiling and grilling are interchangeable, but not always. Dishes such as Jean-Louis Palladin's Fresh Broiled Cod with Eggplant Caviar needs the delicacy of broiling, since the grilled taste would overpower the sauce, and Amy Ferguson's Smoked Wild Boar with Currant Sauce requires a long smoking, since the meat would not be as flavorful if cooked in an oven or broiler.

One of the great boons to the home cook during the past few years has been the number of exotic woods one can buy for the grill. While hickory has been around for years, finding chips of grapevines, mesquite, apple, and cherry is now common. All chips added on top of a charcoal fire should be soaked in water before being used, or else they will instantly flame and not give the smoked flavor wanted. ■

Grilled Bluefish Fillet with Fennel and Roasted Chestnuts

Serves 8

MARCEL DESAULNIERS, The Trellis   All the components of this dish are easy to prepare, and what makes it so wonderful is the combination of flavors and textures. Bluefish is very delicate and buttery, and this ties in with the chestnuts, while the fennel adds some crunch along with its own special character. I've done the bluefish in a preheated broiler as well as on the grill, and the dish does not suffer from it.

Wine choice: California Sauvignon Blanc or French Pouilly Fumé or Sancerre.

8 bluefish fillets (10 to 12 ounces each)

1 cup olive oil

1 cup vegetable oil

½ cup lemon juice

Salt and pepper

16 whole chestnuts, roasted, peeled, and sliced, or French cooked chestnuts, vacuum packed, if fresh chestnuts not in season

2 tablespoons clarified unsalted butter

2 tablespoons minced shallots

8 individual fresh fennel stalks, cut in 1½-inch diagonal slices

Marinate the fillets in olive oil, vegetable oil, lemon juice, salt, and pepper for 30 minutes. While the fish is marinating, roast the chestnuts after cutting X's on both sides with a sharp knife. Place them in a baking pan, sprinkle ¼ cup of water on top of them, and put them in a 450-degree oven for 15 minutes. Remove the pan from the oven and peel the chestnuts quickly, since they only peel easily when hot.

Place the fish, flesh side down, on a prepared grill or skin side up in a preheated broiler. Cook 4 to 8 minutes, depending on the thickness of the fillets. Then turn them, and grill them an additional 3 minutes. Hold them in a warm oven.

Melt the butter in a sauté pan, and sauté the shallots for 2 to 3 minutes. Add the chestnuts and fennel, and sauté them for 5 minutes. Adjust the seasoning with salt and pepper.

Place the fillets on individual plates, and garnish with fennel and chestnuts.

Grilled Lobster

Serves 4

JASPER WHITE, Restaurant Jasper   If you believe, as I do, that many things taste better if cooked on a grill, then you'll love this simple method. The shells come out slightly charred and grilling seems to intensify the sweetness of the crustacean. White's trick is to salt the butter rather than the lobster, so the salt is more evenly distributed. He lets the butter for this, or any drawn butter sauce, come to a simmer to mix the milk solids with the fat and salt.

Wine choice: California Chardonnay.

4 live lobsters (1¼ to 1½ pounds each)
Vegetable oil
Freshly ground black pepper
Drawn butter

To select a lobster: Pick up the lobster by its back, and if the claws are drooping and the movements are slow, choose another.

Take a sharp knife and put the tip where the body meets the tail, with the blade facing the head. Split the body, then turn the knife around and split the tail. Remove the head sack and intestine. If the lobster has roe, remove some of it and place it in the head so that it will cook faster. The meat of the lobster usually cooks faster than the roe.

Lightly brush the shell and tail meat with oil, and place the lobster, shell side down, over hot coals. Cook until the tail meat is translucent, about 5 to 6 minutes. Cover the lobster halves with pie tins, or a double layer of heavy aluminum foil. Cook an additional 3 minutes, until the lobster is done.

To serve: Break off the legs and claws and shell them. Arrange the meat over the body and grind some black pepper over the lobster. Serve with drawn butter that is salted to taste.

Fresh Broiled Cod with Eggplant Caviar

Serves 8

JEAN-LOUIS PALLADIN, Jean-Louis at Watergate   The eggplant-and-pepper sauce is a light and elegant topping for the cod, and the sauce itself is so flavorful I've served the chilled leftovers with wedges of toasted pita bread as an hors d'oeuvre. The recipe calls for baby eggplant since they are sweeter and the seeds are not as large. I've used both the Japanese and Italian varieties with equal success.

Wine choice: California Chardonnay or French white Burgundy.

8 cod fillets (6 to 8 ounces each)

¾ cup extra-virgin olive oil

Salt and pepper to taste

2 pounds baby eggplants

2 red bell peppers

2 green peppers

4 shallots

Wash the cod fillets and pat them dry. Brush them with olive oil, and season them with salt and pepper to taste. Set aside.

Peel the eggplants and cut off the caps. Remove the seeds with a spoon if large, and cut the eggplants into small cubes. Cut the peppers into thin strips, and chop the shallots. Heat ½ cup of the olive oil in a sauté pan over medium heat, and cook the peppers until limp, about 5 to 7 minutes. Add the eggplant cubes, sprinkle them with salt and pepper, and reduce the heat to low. Cook slowly until the eggplant is mushy, about 15 minutes. Purée the mixture in a blender or food processor fitted with a steel blade.

In a preheated broiler, broil the cod fillets for about 3 minutes on a side, depending on thickness.

Put a bed of the eggplant caviar on each plate and lay a piece of the cod on top of it.

Note: The sauce can be prepared a day in advance and then reheated over a low flame. Stir occasionally.

Rockfish with Escargots

Serves 6

ROBERT ROSELLINI, Rosellini's Other Place What appeals to me about escargots, more than the snails themselves, is mopping up the garlic-and-parsley sauce with crusty bread. In this dish, the sauce is more delicate (although it has all the right ingredients for the flavor), so it does not overwhelm the fish but adds some sparkle to it. This is a very easy and quick preparation that wows guests with its elegance.

Wine choice: California Chardonnay or French white Burgundy.

6 rockfish fillets (7 to 8 ounces each)

3 tablespoons vegetable oil

Salt and pepper

½ cup dry white wine

24 large French snails, quartered (canned may be used)

2 tablespoons chopped parsley

2 cloves garlic, chopped

Juice of 2 lemons

4 tablespoons unsalted butter, cut into pieces

Brush the fillets with oil, and sprinkle them with salt and pepper. Place them in a preheated broiler and broil until the fish flakes, about 3 minutes per side. Do not overcook; take them out when the centers are still slightly rare, since they will continue to cook.

In a saucepan, boil the wine until it is reduced to half its original volume, and add the snails, parsley, garlic, and lemon juice. Simmer the sauce for a few minutes to reduce further, and then beat in the butter, bit by bit, until it is fully incorporated. Do not let the sauce come to a boil or it will separate.

Top the fillets with the sauce and serve immediately.

Note: The sauce can be prepared 1 hour in advance, and held over hot water.

Rockfish with Prawns

Serves 6

ROBERT ROSELLINI, Rosellini's Other Place   The slightly pink cast to the sauce and the pink succulent prawns on top of the flaky fillets make this a truly dramatic dish to place in front of a diner, but it's deceptively easy to prepare and the combination of textures makes it as interesting to eat as it is flavorful.

Wine choice: California Chardonnay or French white Burgundy.

18 prawns, Monterey Bay or Hawaiian Blue, or large shrimp

1 tablespoon unsalted butter

4 tablespoons olive oil

1 small onion, minced fine

1 cup dry white wine

2 cups heavy cream

Salt and freshly ground white pepper

6 yellow-eye rockfish fillets (6 ounces each)

1 cup water, or water and white wine

Shell the prawns and devein, washing them well. In a sauté pan or skillet, heat the butter and 1 tablespoon of the oil. When they are hot, sauté the shells until golden brown, stirring often. Reduce the heat to low, add the onion, and sauté for another 10 minutes, until the onion is translucent. Add the wine, and simmer until the liquid is reduced to 3 tablespoons. Then add the cream and simmer over medium heat until the volume is reduced by half, stirring frequently. Strain the mixture through a fine sieve, pressing firmly to remove all the juices. Season with salt and pepper, and set the sauce aside.

Place 1 cup of water, or water and white wine, in a 12-inch skillet, and heat until boiling. Add the prawns or shrimp and poach them for 2 or 3 minutes, until they just turn pink. Remove them with a slotted spoon and keep them warm.

Brush the rockfish with the remaining olive oil and season them with salt and pepper. Broil them in a preheated broiler until they flake, 3 to 4 minutes on each side.

To serve, place a rockfish fillet on each plate, top with 3 prawns, and spoon the sauce over the top.

Note: The sauce can be made in advance and either kept warm or chilled and reheated slowly over a low flame.

Salmon with Tomatillo Butter Sauce

Serves 6 to 8

ANNE GREER, Nana Grill at the Anatole Hotel   The fresh flavor of cilantro, blending with the tart tomatillos and slightly spicy chili, make this one of the most interesting ways to sauce grilled salmon, as well as one of the easiest. The pink fish looks very attractive on a bed of green sauce, and the sauce is bright enough in flavor so that the steaks do not suffer from being cooked in the oven broiler, although it does not compare with grilling with mesquite.

Wine choice: French Pouilly Fumé.

4 garlic cloves

1¼ pounds tomatillos, chopped

2 tablespoons white-wine vinegar

2 tablespoons white wine

1 teaspoon sugar

1 serrano or jalapeño pepper

¼ cup cilantro leaves (no stems), tightly packed

2 tablespoons unsalted butter

6 to 8 salmon steaks, ¾ to 1 inch thick

Salt and pepper to taste

Garnish: Sautéed chopped tomatillos (optional) and cilantro sprigs

In a 350-degree oven, roast the unpeeled garlic cloves on a baking sheet for 10 minutes. Pop them out of the skins, and place them in a 12-inch skillet with the chopped fresh tomatillos, vinegar, wine, and sugar. Sauté the mixture for 5 minutes. Add the tip of the hot pepper, about ¼-inch slice. The tip is less hot than the stem end. Continue to sauté until the tomatillos are soft.

Pour the mixture into a blender or a food processor fitted with a steel blade. Purée with the cilantro leaves to cook them slightly. Pour the mixture back into the skillet and whisk in the butter. Keep the sauce warm.

If you are grilling the salmon, rub the grill with melted margarine so it will not stick. Greer grills over mesquite logs, but an ordinary charcoal fire into which soaked mesquite chips are placed before grilling will impart the same flavor. Grill the fish for about 5 minutes to a side. The edges should be opaque, but the center should still be slightly translucent, since the fish continues to cook after being removed from the grill.

Season the fish with salt and pepper after removing it from the grill. Ladle some sauce onto each plate, and place the salmon steaks on top. The salmon can be garnished with some additional sauce, or with sautéed chopped tomatillos. Place a sprig of cilantro on top.

Note: Tomatillos are the small Mexican tomatoes found in the specialty produce departments of supermarkets. They are usually covered by a paper-thin husk, and should be firm and bright green when bought. If you can't find fresh tomatillos, use hard green tomatoes rather than canned tomatillos.

The sauce can be prepared up to 4 hours in advance and lightly reheated.

Salmon in Ginger Vinaigrette

Serves 6

WOLFGANG PUCK, Spago   This dressing is as versatile as it is flavorful with the salmon. I've used it with both fillets and steaks, as well as with swordfish, and assume it would be equally exciting with any firm-fleshed fish. It is Oriental in inspiration, and the flavors of the cilantro, ginger, and sesame oil blend for a taste that is bright and clear, while not overly spicy.

Wine choice: Alsatian Gewürztraminer.

1 ounce fresh ginger, peeled and minced (about 1½ tablespoons)

3 medium shallots, minced

½ cup rice-wine vinegar

Juice of 2 limes

2 tablespoons soy sauce

Salt and pepper to taste

Sesame oil to taste (less than 1 tablespoon)

1 cup olive oil

6 pieces of salmon (any of the species, including salmon trout) (6 ounces each)

1 bunch parsley or cilantro, chopped

⅓ cup sesame seeds, toasted in a 350-degree oven for 10 minutes

Combine the ginger, shallots, vinegar, lime juice, soy sauce, salt, and pepper. Whisk in the sesame and olive oils, beating until thick. Grill or sauté the salmon. Add parsley or cilantro to the dressing. Serve the salmon on 3 tablespoons of the dressing, and garnish with the toasted sesame seeds.

Note: The dressing can be made in advance, but do not add the parsley or cilantro until the last minute or it will discolor. While the fish can be grilled or sautéed, do not sauté steaks more than ¾ inch thick.

Broiled Salmon
with Sorrel

Serves 6

ROBERT ROSELLINI, Rosellini's Other Place   The fine slivers of bright green sorrel, along with their fresh taste, make this delicious dish as appealing to the eye as to the palate. The sauce is a simple beurre blanc made marvelous with the sorrel, and the additional sorrel used as a garnish reinforces the clean flavor.

Wine choice: French white Burgundy or California Chardonnay.

¼ cup white-wine vinegar

4 shallots, minced

¼ cup lemon juice

3 sticks (¾ pound) unsalted butter, cut into tablespoons, at room temperature

½ cup fresh sorrel, washed and cut into a fine julienne

Salt and pepper

6 salmon fillets (6 ounces each)

2 tablespoons vegetable oil

Garnish:

Additional julienned sorrel

For the sauce, in a small heavy-bottomed saucepan, simmer the vinegar, shallots, and lemon juice until the liquid is reduced to 1 tablespoon. With a whisk, beat in the butter bit by bit, adding additional butter when the preceding bit has melted and never letting the sauce come to a boil, or it will thin out and separate. Stir in the ½ cup sorrel, add salt and pepper to taste, and set aside.

Brush the salmon with oil, and sprinkle with salt and pepper. Place on a rack in a preheated broiler for 4 to 6 minutes on a side, depending on the thickness of the fillets. Be careful not to overcook them.

To serve, spoon sauce over fillets. Top with garnish.

Note: The sauce can be made up to 4 hours in advance, and kept at room temperature or stored in a Thermos bottle. Be careful, if holding it over hot water, not to let the water become too hot or the sauce will separate.

Fish Fillets with Orange, Tomato, and Cilantro Sauce

Serves 6

AMY FERGUSON, Charley's 517   The sweetness of the orange complements the flavors of the tomato and cilantro. The sauce is light and zesty, but still delicate enough not to mask the flavor of the fish. I've also used it to top poached eggs as a variation on eggs Benedict.

Wine choice: Alsatian Riesling or Pinot Blanc.

2½ to 3 pounds John Dory fillets, or red snapper, perch, or cod

Salt and pepper

⅔ cup orange juice, freshly squeezed

½ cup peeled, seeded, and finely diced tomato

2 teaspoons minced garlic

½ teaspoon minced shallot

1 tablespoon minced cilantro

¼ cup white wine

8 tablespoons (1 stick) unsalted butter

Build a fire with charcoal and, when hot, add mesquite chips that have been soaked in water for 15 minutes. Sprinkle the fish with salt and pepper, and grill it for about 3 minutes. Turn and cook 3 to 5 minutes longer, depending on thickness.

To make the sauce: Simmer the remaining ingredients, except the butter, for 5 minutes over medium heat to reduce slightly. Add salt and pepper to taste. Add the butter, 1 tablespoon at a time, beating in each tablespoon before adding the next one.

Note: The sauce can be made 4 hours in advance, and kept over hot water or in a Thermos bottle. If holding over water, make sure the water does not become too hot or the sauce will separate.

Yellowfin Tuna Grilled Rare, in Zinfandel Sauce with Beef Marrow

Serves 6

BRUCE LEFAVOUR, Rose et LeFavour Finding fresh tuna in the supermarkets in the past few years has gone from a surprise to a commonplace. What I love about it is the rich texture and flavor; that's why this recipe is so successful. Tuna has many of the same properties as a buttery filet mignon, and this red-wine sauce and enrichment with beef marrow intensify all the richness.

Wine choice: California Zinfandel.

6 yellowfin tuna steaks, about 1¼ to 1½ inches thick

Salt and pepper

1 bottle full-bodied California Zinfandel

3 shallots, chopped

5 sprigs fresh thyme

1 sprig fresh rosemary

½ bunch parsley

3 carrots, chopped

½ cup celery leaves

2 cloves garlic, unpeeled

18 slices beef marrow

18 pods fresh lima beans, shelled (fava beans, black-eyed peas or flageolets can be substituted)

3 tablespoons unsalted butter

1 teaspoon glacé de viande (page 160)

Trim the steaks of any dark meat. They should be taken from the refrigerator 1½ hours before cooking, and kept covered at room temperature. Just before cooking sprinkle them generously with salt and pepper.

In a stainless-steel or enameled pot, bring the wine, shallots, thyme, rosemary, parsley, carrots, celery leaves, and garlic to a boil. Simmer the wine until reduced by two-thirds. Strain and reserve.

Poach the marrow quickly in simmering salted water and keep it warm while cooking the tuna and finishing the sauce. Blanch the beans in boiling salted water and cook them until done but not mushy. Keep them warm.

Melt 2 tablespoons of the butter in a heavy sauté pan or skillet and roll the tuna steaks in it. Remove the steaks to a plate, pour off the butter and add the Zinfandel reduction. Bring it to a boil, and add the glacé de viande and the remaining butter. Swirl the mixture to combine over high heat and set it aside.

Place the tuna on a hot grill or in a preheated broiler. Depending on the heat, it can be ready to turn in as little as 1½ minutes and fully cooked in 2½ minutes to remain rare. Be careful not to overcook.

Pour a little of the sauce onto each plate and place a tuna steak on top of it. Garnish the tuna with slices of beef marrow, and place the lima beans in a circle around the steak on top of the sauce.

Grilled Tuna with Mint Vinaigrette

Serves 6

WOLFGANG PUCK, Spago Both the scent and fresh, clean taste of mint are wonderful additions to this dish, which is very simple to prepare and gives such a surprise when people take the first bite. Tuna is one of my favorite fish because of its richness, and the mint enhances that. The tomatoes make the dish look even prettier, and the flavors are similar to those in a taboulleh salad.

Wine choice: California Sauvignon Blanc or Alsatian Gewürztraminer.

6 tuna fillets or steaks (6 ounces each)

Freshly ground white pepper

½ cup extra-virgin olive oil

2 to 3 tablespoons chopped fresh mint

1 tablespoon lime juice

1 tablespoon minced fresh parsley

2 medium shallots, minced

6 ripe Italian plum tomatoes, peeled, seeded, and chopped

2 cloves garlic, peeled, blanched for 5 minutes in salted water and minced

Season tuna with pepper and brush with 1 tablespoon of the oil. Cover with plastic wrap and refrigerate for 2 to 3 hours. Combine the remaining ingredients; season with salt and pepper to taste.

Season tuna with salt and grill over charcoal for 4 minutes per side or until medium rare. Top with sauce, and garnish with sprigs of fresh mint.

Note: The tuna can also be broiled or sautéed in a little butter rather than grilled, and if the slices are less than ¼ inch thick, cook only on one side or the fish will be overcooked.

Grilled Rib Steak with Ladies' Cabbage

Serves 6

LAWRENCE FORGIONE, An American Place What makes this recipe so special is the side dishes, ones that I've also served with grilled lamb chops and pork chops. Ladies' Cabbage is an idea Forgione found in a nineteenth-century cookbook. The cabbage is blanched twice to take the "skunk" out of it, so it is rendered almost as delicate as the custard. Part of the appeal of this entrée is the appearance of the dish, with the light green cabbage almost the same color as the sweet buttered scallions.

Wine choice: California Cabernet.

LADIES' CABBAGE

4½ cups chopped green cabbage (1 medium head, core and outer leaves removed)

3 tablespoons unsalted butter

⅓ cup minced onions

½ teaspoon salt

Pinch of freshly ground pepper

1½ cups heavy cream

6 egg yolks

1 whole egg

A few drops of Tabasco

Bring 6 quarts of lightly salted water to a boil, and add the cabbage. Bring it to a boil for 5 minutes, drain, and repeat the procedure with fresh water. Drain well, pressing to extract the water.

Melt the butter in a 2-quart saucepan, and "sweat" the onions, covered, over low heat until transparent, about 10 minutes. Add the cabbage, tossing to make sure it is covered with butter, and cook an additional 2 to 3 minutes. Season with salt and pepper, and place the cabbage in a mixing bowl to cool.

In another mixing bowl, beat the cream, yolks, egg, and Tabasco with an electric mixer or large whisk. Pour the custard over the cabbage and stir so the vegetables are evenly distributed.

Lightly butter 6 custard cups, ramekins, or a 1½-quart soufflé dish. Ladle the mixture into the containers and place them in a water bath coming halfway up the sides in a 350-degree oven. For small cups, bake 30 to 35 minutes, or bake 1 hour to 1 hour and 20 minutes for a large mold, depending on the circumference. A knife or cake tester inserted in the middle should come out clean when the custard is done.

Note: The custard can be made a day in advance, and kept tightly covered in the refrigerator, but it should be baked right before serving.

BUTTERED SCALLIONS

30 scallions

3 tablespoons unsalted butter

3 tablespoons cold water

Salt and pepper to taste

2 tablespoons chopped parsley

Trim the root ends from the scallions, and top each ½ inch above the white part. Place the scallions, butter, and water in a sauté pan over high heat, shaking as the butter melts to distribute it evenly. As the water evaporates, lower the heat, season with salt and pepper, and cook for an additional 2 minutes, until the scallions are tender. Sprinkle with the chopped parsley.

THE STEAKS

6 rib steaks (about ¾ pound each with bone) or any cut of steak

Grill the steaks on a charcoal grill or in a preheated broiler until they reach the desired doneness. Serve with the buttered scallions and cabbage.

New York Steak with Shiitake Mushrooms and Cognac

Serves 6

WOLFGANG PUCK, Spago   This is an elegant way to serve steak, and the sauce can be cooked in the time it takes to heat the grill or broiler for the meat. Fresh shiitake mushrooms have a wonderfully rich flavor, which melds with the cognac and red wine. This is far more interesting than the classic French red-wine sauces. The enoki mushrooms and scallions give the dish additional textural variation.

Wine choice: California Cabernet Sauvignon or French red Bordeaux or Burgundy.

6 New York strip steaks, ⅜ to ½ inch thick

Salt and freshly ground pepper

8 tablespoons (1 stick) unsalted butter

1½ pounds fresh shiitake mushrooms, sliced ¼ inch thick

½ cup cognac

1½ cups dry red wine

2 packages fresh enoki mushrooms, trimmed from their bases

18 scallions, trimmed 1 inch above the white part

4 tablespoons water

Season the steaks with salt and pepper on both sides, and reserve at room temperature.

In a heavy sauté pan or 12-inch skillet, heat 3 tablespoons of the butter until bubbly. Add the shiitake mushrooms, and sauté them over high heat until they begin to brown slightly. Then season them lightly with salt and pepper and continue to cook until they are soft and the liquid has evaporated. Remove them from the pan with a slotted spoon and deglaze the pan with the cognac. Ignite carefully, and let the flame die out naturally. Reduce the cognac to a few tablespoons, add the red wine, and continue to reduce until the liquid is ¾ cup.

In another sauté pan or skillet, melt 3 tablespoons of butter and carefully sauté the enoki mushrooms, being careful that they do not break apart. Season with salt and pepper, remove them from the pan, and set them aside to keep warm. In that skillet, melt the remaining 2 tablespoons of butter and add the scallions and water. Cook them over high heat until the mixture comes to a boil, shaking the pan to distribute the butter. Lower the heat to medium, and continue to cook until the water has evaporated and the scallions are glazed. Set aside.

Grill the steaks over a hot charcoal fire or sauté in a very hot sauté pan with a little oil until they have reached the desired doneness. Remove them from the heat.

To serve: Place 3 braised scallions on each dinner plate and spoon some mushroom sauce over the onions. Center a steak atop, or arrange as you will.

Chili Corn Sauce for Charred Buffalo

Serves 6

LAWRENCE FORGIONE, An American Place   I've used this sauce with equal success on grilled beefsteaks and roasts. Its character comes from the way the chili flavor is made smoother by the cream and wine, and how the bits of corn and pepper look like colorful confetti on the meat. Even with the pepper and chili powder, the sauce is more piquant than spicy.

Wine choice: California Zinfandel, Italian Barolo, or French Rhône.

4 ears fresh corn (1½ cups frozen can be substituted, but do not use canned corn)

1 onion, minced

1 red bell pepper, finely diced

1 green bell pepper, finely diced

¼ teaspoon minced garlic

2 tablespoons vegetable oil

2½ tablespoons chili powder

Pinch of cayenne pepper

Pinch of freshly ground black pepper

4 tablespoons dry white vermouth or wine

1 quart beef or veal stock (page 160)

3 cups heavy cream

Salt to taste

6 buffalo steaks (10 to 12 ounces each)

With a sharp knife, remove the kernels of corn from the cobs, reserving both kernels and cobs for the sauce. Set aside.

In a heavy 2-quart saucepan, heat the onion, pepper, and garlic in the oil, covered, for 2 to 3 minutes over low heat. Add the chili powder and ground peppers, and stir over low heat for 3 minutes to cook the powder. Add the wine and stir until smooth. Add the stock and reserved corn cobs and bring to a boil. Cook uncovered over moderate heat, stirring occasionally, until the volume is reduced by half, and the sauce has a syrupy consistency, about 20 minutes.

Add the cream and simmer for 5 to 7 minutes over low heat. Remove and discard the corn cobs, scraping off the sauce clinging to them, and add the kernels. Simmer for an additional 3 minutes. Adjust the seasoning with salt and pepper, and serve with the steaks.

Grill the steaks over a hot charcoal fire until they reach the desired doneness.

Forgione suggests garnishing the plate with buttered scallions (page 221).

Note: The sauce can be made up to 2 days in advance, and reheated over a low flame, stirring occasionally. If using frozen corn instead of fresh, purée ¼ cup of it and add to the sauce to approximate the texture.

Grilled Rabbit

Serves 4 to 6

AMY FERGUSON, Charley's 517 It's only in the past few years that I've overcome a phobia from childhood about eating rabbit, and discovered its wonderful flavor, lighter than red meat but heartier than chicken. This is the best and simplest way I've ever prepared it. The herbs in the marinade complement it perfectly. This is one recipe that really suffers if not grilled, and I love Ferguson's combination of charcoal to which mesquite, pecan, hickory, and grapevines are added, after the chips have soaked for 15 minutes. But, if you can't find all those woods, use some mixture of mesquite with a fruitwood.

Wine choice: California Chardonnay.

1 cup olive oil

2 cloves minced garlic

2 chopped shallots

Juice of ½ lemon

2 sprigs fresh sage

2 sprigs fresh thyme

1 bay leaf

½ cup white wine

Salt and white pepper to taste

1 domestic rabbit, cut into serving pieces

Mix all the ingredients except the rabbit together, then add the rabbit. Marinate for 1 to 2 days, no longer, covered with plastic wrap in the refrigerator, turning the pieces occasionally.

Grill, covered, by placing the cover on the grill or creating a cover with a double layer of heavy-duty foil, for about 7 minutes per side for the thicker pieces and 5 minutes for the smaller, or until the juices run clear when it is pierced with a fork.

Veal Chops with Papaya Purée

Serves 6

ANNE GREER, Nana Grill at the Anatole Hotel   Sweet papaya tastes delicious with the delicate veal chops, and the orange color of the sauce makes the plate look so attractive. Since the chops are marinated, the oven broiler can be used, but when I cooked the dish that way I missed the aromatic flavor of the mesquite. Another benefit of papaya is that it contains pepsin, a natural meat tenderizer, so the skins can be added to the marinade if you think the chops might need it.

Wine choice: California Riesling or Gewürztraminer.

6 veal chops cut from the loin (about 12 ounces each)

2 cups olive oil

Juice of 2 limes

2 sprigs fresh thyme, minced, or ½ teaspoon dried

2 sprigs fresh basil, minced, or ½ teaspoon dried

2 ripe papayas

1 teaspoon honey

2 teaspoons lime juice

2 tablespoons sugar

3 tablespoons water

1 cup reduced veal stock (page 160), or ½ cup each of canned beef consommé and canned beef stock

3 tablespoons orange juice

1½ teaspoons red-wine vinegar

1 teaspoon cornstarch dissolved in ¼ cup cold water

2 tablespoons Grand Marnier

2 tablespoons unsalted butter

Salt and pepper

Place the veal chops in a low-sided glass baking dish. Mix the olive oil, juice of 2 limes, and herbs together. Pour the mixture over the chops and marinate them in the refrigerator, covered with plastic wrap, for 4 hours, turning the chops periodically.

While the chops are marinating, purée the papayas, which have been peeled and seeded, in a food processor fitted with a steel blade. Add the honey and 2 teaspoons lime juice and set aside at room temperature until you are ready to serve.

In a small heavy saucepan, caramelize the sugar by placing it over low heat until it melts and then turns an amber color. Watch carefully to make sure it doesn't burn. Add the water, stirring with a long wooden spoon since the sugar will bubble furiously. Then add the stock, orange juice, and vinegar. Simmer the mixture for 3 minutes, stirring to dissolve any remaining lumps of caramel. Add the cornstarch mixture and simmer for 5 minutes. Then add the Grand Marnier and whisk in the butter. Set the sauce aside.

Light your grill with mesquite wood, or charcoal to which soaked mesquite chips will be added before the chops are broiled. Or preheat your oven broiler. On the grill, sear the chops over the hottest part of the fire, and then move them to a cooler section of the grill. Grill or broil them for a total of 9 minutes, or until they are medium rare. Season them with salt and pepper after grilling. Divide the papaya among the plates, put a chop on each, and spoon the sauce around the edge.

Note: The sauce and papaya can be prepared a day in advance, and kept tightly covered in the refrigerator. They should be brought to room temperature or slightly heated over a low flame before serving.

Smoked Wild Boar with Currant Sauce

Serves 6 to 8

AMY FERGUSON, Charley's 517 I adored this dish when I ate it at Charley's 517, and was frustrated when all attempts at home were unsuccessful in finding wild boar. A loin from its first cousin, the domestic pig, was substituted, and the results were delicious with the savory sauce, if slightly less intensely flavored than the boar. Ferguson serves the dish with a corn custard made from fresh corn, red and green peppers, and wild rice. This makes the plates look very pretty.

Wine choice: California Zinfandel or French red Rhône, such as Hermitage or Côte Rôtie.

1 saddle of young boar, or pork loin (6 to 8 pounds)
Salt and pepper

Build a charcoal fire in a grill with a cover (or smoker), and then to the hot coals add hickory, pecan, and grapevine chips, all of which have been soaked in water for 20 minutes. Season the boar or pork with salt and pepper and place it on the grill. Cover the grill or smoker and smoke for 1½ to 2 hours, until the meat is cooked through. Serve with the sauce that follows.

CURRANT SAUCE
½ cup dried currants
½ cup cassis liqueur
½ cup white wine
2 cups veal stock (page 160)
3 shallots, chopped
2 teaspoons lemon juice
2 tablespoons unsalted butter
Salt and pepper to taste

Soak the currants in cassis and white wine for 1 hour. Over high heat, reduce the veal stock by two-thirds, and add the remaining ingredients. Simmer for 5 minutes to blend the flavors.

Grilled Chicken with Garlic and Italian Parsley

Serves 6

WOLFGANG PUCK, Spago The flavors from the garlic and parsley tucked under the skin penetrate the chicken the same way they would if used in marinating. And using the same ingredients for the sauce topping it reinforces and adds to the delicious flavor. Do not be put off by the amount of garlic called for. Once it's blanched, it loses its pungency but retains a sweet, almost nutlike flavor. This is a very easy dish, and I've done it in the oven broiler with good results.

Wine choice: California Chardonnay or Sauvignon Blanc.

3 whole small chickens, approximately 2 pounds each

3 small heads garlic, separated into cloves and peeled

⅓ cup Italian parsley leaves (regular parsley or a combination of parsley and cilantro can be substituted)

Salt

Freshly ground white pepper

3 tablespoons unsalted butter

Juice of 1½ large lemons

Bone the chickens completely, leaving the first wing joint intact. I find this is easier to do while the chickens are still whole. Make an incision down the breast bone, and, keeping your knife blade on the carcass, cut away the meat and tendons until the carcass is freed. Then cut the chicken in half, and from the underside remove the thigh and leg bones and the large wing bone, making sure not to cut through the skin. Save the bones and the wing tips for stock.

Place the garlic cloves in boiling water and boil for 2 to 4 minutes, depending on the size of the cloves. Drain and cut into paper-thin slices. Toss the garlic with the parsley and a little salt and pepper.

Stuff 2 teaspoons of the mixture between the skin and the breast and thigh meat. To this point, the recipe can be done in advance and the chickens can be refrigerated, tightly covered with plastic wrap, for a day.

Heat a charcoal or gas grill or oven broiler until moderately hot, and grill the chickens for 7 to 10 minutes per side, or until they are cooked but not dry and the juices run clear when the flesh is pierced with a fork.

While the chickens are grilling, heat the butter in a sauté pan until bubbly and add the remaining garlic-parsley mixture. Add the lemon juice and season to taste with salt and pepper. Simmer for 1 to 2 minutes.

To serve: Place the chicken halves on dinner plates or a large platter. Top with the sauce.

Grilled Rare Duck Breast with Date and Port Sauce

Serves 4

RICHARD PERRY, Richard Perry Restaurant   The sweetness of dates and port are wonderful accents with rich duck, but the meat is totally devoid of fat, so the dish remains light. Since the recipe calls for only the breasts, save the legs for Wolfgang Puck's Duck Legs with Napa Cabbage (page 248), or you can now find duck breasts alone in many supermarkets. The recipe is foolproof, and draws raves at dinner parties.

Wine choice: California Zinfandel, or French red Rhône, such as Côte Rôtie or Hermitage.

4 Muscovy or Long Island ducks (5 or 6 pounds each)

Stock:

Bones from the duck breasts

1 large onion, halved

2 carrots, peeled and chopped

1½ cups chopped leeks, white part only

2 stalks celery, with leaves

1 large tomato, halved

½ cup red-wine vinegar

½ cup red wine

6 peppercorns

2 cloves garlic, peeled

1 bay leaf

3 sprigs parsley

½ teaspoon thyme

Place the ducks with the legs down on a carving board and slice along the breast bone. Remove the skin and fat from the breast with a fillet knife, and cut the breast meat from the bone, keeping the knife running along the breast bone. Remove all tendons from the meat, cut away any remaining fat, and refrigerate the breasts, covered with plastic wrap. Discard the fatty skin, and cut off the duck legs, reserving them for another use.

Break up the duck bones and place them in a 425-degree oven for 45 minutes, or until brown. Pour off any accumulated fat, and add the onion, carrots, leeks, celery, and tomato. Roast for 20 minutes longer, then place the solid contents of the roasting pan in a large stockpot. Pour off any fat and deglaze the pan with red-wine vinegar and red wine. Add to the stockpot along with remaining stock ingredients and add cold water to cover the ingredients. Bring the liquid to a boil, and simmer uncovered for 4 hours. Strain, pressing all the liquid from the vegetables. Discard the vegetables.

Sauce:

8 dried dates

¼ cup port wine

¼ cup duck stock

½ cup water

4 tablespoons unsalted butter

4 tablespoons raspberry vinegar

4 tablespoons minced shallots

2 cups heavy cream

Salt and pepper to taste

Marinade:

½ cup molasses

¼ cup pure maple syrup

½ cup honey

1 cup dark-brown sugar, packed

2 tablespoons unsalted butter

¼ cup water

2 tablespoons port wine

For the sauce: Marinate the dates in port wine and duck stock for 3 hours at room temperature, or overnight in the refrigerator. Place the mixture and the water, butter, vinegar, and shallots in a heavy 1-quart saucepan. Cover and simmer for 15 minutes, stirring occasionally. The dates should be tender and should have absorbed almost all the liquid. Purée them in a food processor fitted with a steel blade or in a blender. Pour the cream into another saucepan and reduce it by half, then add the date mixture, simmer for 5 minutes, and adjust the seasoning with salt and pepper.

For the marinade, combine all the ingredients in a 2-quart saucepan and stir over low heat until the ingredients are well combined and the brown sugar and butter are melted.

The recipe can be done to this point, with the sauce and marinade refrigerated, tightly covered, overnight.

To finish the dish, marinate the breast meat for 15 to 30 minutes at room temperature. Any longer may result in the edges of the breasts becoming burnt owing to the sugar content of the marinade.

Light a fire of mesquite wood, and when it is very hot, place the still moist breasts on the fire. Grill for 1 minute, turn, and grill for an additional 1 minute. The duck should be charred on the outside, but still rare on the inside. Slice the cooked breasts across the grain.

To serve, arrange slices of the breast meat on plates or a large platter. Pass the sauce separately.

Note: Although the duck stock called for in the recipe adds to the sauce, the recipe can be made in much less time if some canned chicken stock (simmered with vegetables; see page 158) is used. If you do make duck stock, freeze the rest for future use. And, while the recipe calls for grilling on very hot mesquite, the breasts can be broiled in the oven broiler, but preheat it for at least 15 minutes.

ROASTS AND BRAISES

I think of most dishes in this chapter as winter more than summer food, perhaps because I hate lighting the oven in the summer and adore lighting charcoal for my grill. Dishes such as Barbara Tropp's Spicy Stewed Spareribs or Marcel Desaulniers's Braised Tenderloin with Black Beans, Tomatoes, and Jalapeño Chilies conjure up images of snow falling.

But there are roasted meats included, such as Wolfgang Puck's Duck Legs with Napa Cabbage and Richard Perry's Pork with Blue-cheese Sauce, that do not take all that much time to roast. When evaluating the time required to complete a recipe, think of the other parts of the dinner and the order in which they can be prepared. With a quick sauté, you would do the entrée last, having completed the appetizer and dessert. But, with the recipes in this chapter, think about starting the roast and then the other courses, and you may find the total dinner requires little more time.

I always think of slow-cooked dishes as "comfort foods," and have a tendency to serve them with others of the genre—such as soups as appetizers and hearty desserts. ∎

Rack of Lamb with Chive Cream Sauce

Serves 2

SUSUMU FUKUI, La Petite Chaya The fresh flavor of the chives and the shiitake mushrooms go well with the richness of lamb, and it's unusual to find a lamb recipe that works this successfully with a cream sauce. All of the ingredients in this dish form a perfect blend.

Wine choice: California Cabernet Sauvignon or French red Bordeaux.

1 tablespoon olive oil

6 tablespoons unsalted butter

1 rack of lamb (6 or 7 chops)

Salt and pepper to taste

1 large shallot, chopped

1 bunch chives

¼ cup white wine

½ cup veal stock (page 160)

½ cup heavy cream

½ pound shiitake mushrooms (or ¼ pound shiitake and ¼ pound shimeji)

1 small clove garlic, crushed

Heat the oil and 1 tablespoon of the butter in a sauté pan or baking pan over high heat. Add the lamb and brown it on all sides. Sprinkle it with salt and pepper and place it in a preheated 350-degree oven for 10 minutes for rare lamb and 15 minutes for medium rare. Remove the lamb from the oven and keep it warm, allowing it to rest for 15 minutes.

In a sauté pan or skillet, heat 3 tablespoons of the butter. When hot add the shallot and sauté it over low heat for 3 minutes. Add the chives and white wine, and cook until the wine is reduced to a few tablespoons. Add the veal stock and reduce the mixture by half. Purée in a blender or food processor fitted with a steel blade. Return the purée to the pan, add the cream, season with salt and pepper, and simmer for 5 minutes.

In another pan, heat the remaining butter and slice the mushrooms. Add the garlic to the pan and sauté for 2 minutes, then add the mushrooms and sauté until they are cooked and brown.

To serve: Remove the cylinder of meat from the bones and save the bones for the presentation. Carve the meat into 4 or 5 slices lengthwise. Place the rack on a platter, and lay the strips across the bones. Garnish with the mushrooms and top with the sauce.

Note: The sauce can be prepared up to 6 hours in advance, and reheated slowly.

Roast Lamb with Greens, Turnips, and Glazed Onions

Serves 6 to 8

BRADLEY OGDEN, The Campton Place Hotel This dish is a knockout for dinner parties, with all the colorful vegetables surrounding the lamb, and the lowly greens are flavorful and elevated to a new definition once you've tasted them this way. Admittedly this dish is a lot of work, but none of the steps are very complicated and some can be done in advance. You'll find the end result worth it—both for the drama and the flavor.

Wine choice: French red Bordeaux.

2 boned lamb loins, trimmed of fat, bones and trimmings reserved, each loin cut into 4 servings (approximately 6 ounces each)

Marinade:

6 cloves garlic, crushed

½ cup olive oil

4 tablespoons chopped fresh rosemary

1 tablespoon black peppercorns

Lamb sauce:

5 pounds lamb bones and trimmings

3 pounds veal bones

3 cups coarsely chopped carrots

3 cups coarsely chopped celery

3 cups coarsely chopped onions

8 cloves garlic, peeled, left whole

¼ cup chopped fresh rosemary

3 tablespoons chopped fresh thyme

4 bay leaves

8 sprigs parsley

1 teaspoon black peppercorns

1 gallon cold water

Combine the marinade ingredients. Marinate the lamb overnight in the refrigerator, turning occasionally, or marinate it for 8 hours at room temperature.

For the sauce, preheat the oven to 425 degrees. Place the lamb and veal bones in a large roasting pan, and place the pan in the oven to brown the bones, stirring often. This will take about 35 to 50 minutes. Add the vegetables to the pan and cook for 10 additional minutes, stirring often. Remove the pan from the oven, and add the garlic, herbs, peppercorns, and enough water to deglaze the pan. Transfer the bones and vegetables to a deep stockpot, add the remaining water to the pot, and bring it to a boil. Skim off the scum that rises, and lower the heat, simmering slowly and skimming for 3 hours. Strain the stock and reduce the liquid to 1 quart. Strain it through cheesecloth or a coffee filter, and keep warm.

Note: The 1 quart will serve for a few meals of this recipe. The remainder can be frozen, at which time repeating the dish is hardly as time-consuming.

Vegetables:

24 baby carrots

24 baby turnips

40 pearl onions

2 cups turnip greens, stems removed, washed, and broken into small pieces

2 cups collard greens, stems removed, washed and broken into small pieces

6 tablespoons minced shallots

1 teaspoon minced garlic

3 tablespoons malt vinegar

1 cup bacon fat

2 tablespoons butter

Salt and freshly ground white pepper

For the vegetables: Peel the carrots, leaving 1 inch of stem attached. Do the same with the turnips. If baby vegetables are not available, larger carrots and turnips can be cut into 3 or 4 sections, although they are not as attractive. Bring salted water to a boil and blanch the carrots and turnips for 5 to 7 minutes, and drain. Drop the unpeeled pearl onions into boiling water and boil for 1 minute. Drain and let them sit in a strainer until cool enough to handle. Then cut off the root ends and squeeze the onions out of their skin. Set aside.

In a large baking pan, place enough of the olive oil strained from the marinade to cover the bottom of the pan. Heat at medium heat on top of the stove. Pat the lamb dry and sear it in the hot olive oil to brown. Place the pan in a 450-degree oven and cook it for 10 minutes, or until the lamb is medium rare. Remove the lamb from the pan and let it rest at room temperature.

Discard the excess fat from the pan and add the greens, shallots, and garlic. Sauté for 2 to 3 minutes, until the greens are wilted. Add the malt vinegar and mix will. Remove the greens and arrange them in the center of each plate.

In a skillet, heat the bacon fat and sauté the carrots, turnips, and onions, adding the onions last since they need only 1 minute to finish cooking. With a slotted spoon, place the vegetables in the roasting pan, and add 1¾ cups of lamb stock. Heat the mixture on high heat to reduce the stock and glaze the vegetables. Finish the sauce by whisking in 2 tablespoons of butter. Season to taste with salt and ground white pepper.

To assemble: Arrange the carrots, onions, and turnips around the greens. Cut 3 medallions from each piece of lamb loin and place these on top of the greens. Ladle ¼ cup of sauce around the vegetables and serve. Or arrange them all on a large platter.

Note: The stock and initial cooking of the vegetables can be done the day before. The only last-minute procedures are roasting the lamb and cooking the greens in the pan once the thick chops have been removed, and heating the baby vegetables.

Roast Pork with Cabbage, Potatoes, and Burgundy Sauerkraut

Serves 6 to 8

JIM HALLER, The Blue Strawbery   This dish reminds me of Alsatian choucroute garni, and it's one of those hearty winter dishes that fill the house with anticipatory aromas. It not only tastes delicious, it looks attractive when arranged on a platter.

Wine choice: California Zinfandel or French red Rhône.

1 boned and butterflied pork loin (you should have about 3 to 4 pounds of boned meat)

2 cups thinly sliced cabbage

2 cups thinly sliced or diced potatoes

1 cup chopped onions

2 cloves garlic, minced

Salt and pepper to taste

2 tablespoons flour

¼ cup butter

1 pound mushrooms, sliced thick or quartered

4 cups red Burgundy

½ cup sauerkraut, rinsed well and drained

Have your butcher bone and butterfly a pork loin, or bone the eye from the loin so you have a cylinder of meat, and then slice it down the middle. While many pork recipes work equally well with pork tenderloin, it falls apart when braised in this fashion.

Bring 3 quarts of salted water to a boil and add the cabbage. Simmer for 2 minutes. Drain, pressing down to extract all the water. Mix the cabbage with the potatoes, onions, garlic, salt, and pepper. Place the cabbage-potato stuffing in the center of the pork, and tightly roll the loin lengthwise, tying it at 2-inch intervals with heavy kitchen string. Sprinkle the pork with additional salt and pepper, and rub the flour evenly all over it.

Place the pork in a roasting pan, uncovered, in a 500-degree oven, turning it occasionally so it is evenly brown, about 15 minutes. Remove it from the oven, turn the temperature down to 400 degrees, and pour off any grease that has accumulated in the pan.

Melt the butter in a sauté pan or skillet until sizzling, and add the mushrooms. Sauté them until golden, and add to the roasting pan with the wine and sauerkraut.

Cover the roasting pan tightly, and braise the pork for 1¼ to 1½ hours, or until a meat fork pierces it easily. Remove the meat from the pan, hooking two forks under the string, and place it on a warm platter. Allow the roast to rest 15 minutes before slicing. Arrange the slices on a platter.

If the pan juices are thin, reduce by bringing the liquid to a boil on top of the stove.

As with choucroute garni, steamed potatoes and a salad are the best accompaniments for this dish.

Roast Pork Tenderloin with Sauce of Maytag Blue Cheese

Serves 6 to 8

RICHARD PERRY, Richard Perry Restaurant   This is one of the most unusual combinations of flavors. The sharpness from the blue cheese cuts the sweetness of the port, and the green peppercorns add just the zip needed to make the pork sparkle even more. Maytag is a wonderful domestic blue cheese that's been made since the 1920s, by the same family that started the washing-machine company, but any imported blue cheese will work equally well.

Wine choice: California Zinfandel, Italian Barolo, or French red Rhône.

3 pounds fresh pork tenderloin

Salt and pepper

½ pound fresh pork fat, sliced thin, or bacon blanched in 4 quarts of water for 10 minutes, then rinsed

2 cups port wine

½ cup demi-glace, or concentrated canned beef bouillon

2 cups heavy cream

2 tablespoons green peppercorns packed in vinegar, drained

1½ cups crumbled Maytag blue cheese

Trim the white membranes and fat off the tenderloin, or have your butcher do it. Preheat the oven to 375 degrees, and place the tenderloins in a roasting pan with the tails tucked under so they are of a uniform thickness. Season with salt and pepper, and place the pork fat or blanched bacon on top. Bake in the center of the oven for 45 minutes, or until the meat reaches an internal temperature of 140 degrees. Remove the tenderloins from the oven and keep warm.

Pour out the accumulated fat, and deglaze the roasting pan with the port. Pour it into a saucepan, and reduce the liquid by half. Add the demi-glace, cream, green peppercorns, and cheese. Stir until the cheese has melted in, and then simmer until the mixture is reduced by half.

Slice the tenderloins, and place a ladle of sauce on each serving plate. Arrange the slices of tenderloin in a fan shape on top of the sauce, and pass extra sauce separately.

Red Beans and Rice with Ham Hocks and Andouille Smoked Sausage

Serves 8

PAUL PRUDHOMME, K-Paul's Louisiana Kitchen   I can't eat this dish without feeling the warm air off the Mississippi and the sound of jazz. It is quintessentially New Orleans to me, as it must have been to the late Louis Armstrong, who sometimes signed his letters "red beans and ricely yours." I've tried various recipes for years, and Prudhomme's is by far the best. The spicing from the ham hocks, vegetables, and sausage imparts a deep flavor to the beans. This makes a wonderful casual buffet-supper dish, since it can be multiplied into a huge quantity with little additional work.

Wine choice: I prefer a mug of chilled beer, or a Côtes du Rhône Villages.

1 pound dry red kidney beans

Water to cover the beans

6 large ham hocks (about 4 pounds)

16 cups (1 gallon) water

2½ cups finely chopped celery

2 cups finely chopped onions

2 cups finely chopped green bell peppers

5 bay leaves

2 teaspoons white pepper

2 teaspoons dried thyme leaves

1½ teaspoons garlic powder

1½ teaspoons dried oregano leaves

1 teaspoon ground red pepper, preferably cayenne

½ teaspoon freshly ground black pepper

1 tablespoon Tabasco

1 pound andouille, or any pure smoked pork sausage, such as Polish kielbasa, cut diagonally into ¾-inch slices

4½ cups hot cooked long-grain rice

Wash the beans well in a sieve, picking through to remove any pebbles. Place them in a deep pan and cover with water to a level 2 inches above the beans. Cover and let them stand overnight. Or bring them to a boil, simmer 1 minute, turn off the heat and allow them to sit, covered, for 1 hour before proceeding with the recipe.

Place the ham hocks, 10 cups of water, celery, onions, green pepper, bay leaves, and seasonings in a 6-quart saucepan or large Dutch oven. Stir them well, cover, and bring to a boil over high heat. Reduce the heat to a simmer and cook until the meat is fork tender, about 1 hour. Remove the ham from the pan with a slotted spoon and set it aside. Add the drained beans and 4 cups of water to the pan, bring to a boil, reduce the heat to a simmer, and cook for 30 minutes, stirring occasionally. Add the remaining 2 cups of water and continue to simmer for 30 minutes, stirring often. Add the andouille and continue to simmer until the beans start breaking apart, about 35 to 45 minutes. Scrape the bottom often. (If the beans start to scorch, do not stir. Immediately remove the pan from the heat and change to another without scraping any scorched beans into the mixture.)

Either add the ham hocks whole, or pick the meat from them and add. Simmer an additional 10 minutes and serve, placing the ham hocks at one end of the plate, some slices of andouille at the other, and a mound of red beans and rice in the center.

Note: This can be prepared up to 3 days in advance and kept tightly covered in the refrigerator. Reheat over a low flame or in a 275-degree oven, stirring gently so as not to break the beans.

Spicy Stewed Spareribs with Garlic

Serves 4 as an entrée, 6 to 8 as part of a multi-course meal

BARBARA TROPP, China Moon   After eating these spareribs, anything I've cooked on a grill pales by comparison. They are spicy and savory, and the meat is so tender it falls off the bones. Even with skimming, it's best to make them a day before and reheat. The fat all rises to the surface so you can take it off in a neat layer, and the flavor, as with most stews, improves with reheating.

Wine choice: California Zinfandel, Italian Barolo, or French Burgundy.

3½ pounds meaty spareribs, cut crosswise through the bone into strips about 1¼ inches wide

5 tablespoons Chinese salted black beans (sold in Oriental markets in plastic pouches, and preserved with ginger as well as salt. Do not wash before using.)

10 large cloves garlic, peeled and smashed

3 tablespoons soy sauce

1 tablespoon light-brown or white sugar

3 peppercorns

1½ cups hot water

3 tablespoons corn or peanut oil

1 teaspoon dried red-pepper flakes

6 tablespoons sliced scallions, both green and white parts

Trim the ribs of excess fat and cut between the bones, making small nuggets.

Combine the beans, garlic, soy sauce, sugar, peppercorns, and hot water, stirring to dissolve the sugar and the salt from the beans.

Heat a heavy, large non-aluminum stockpot over high heat and add the oil, swirling to glaze the pot. Reduce the heat to medium high, and when it is hot enough to foam a pepper flake, add the flakes and scallion rings. Stir until fragrant, about 20 seconds, adjusting the heat so the mixture foams without scorching. Add the ribs and toss until the meat is no longer red, about 5 minutes. Stir in the liquids and bring to a simmer. Cover the pot and simmer the stew until the ribs are very tender, which can take between 45 minutes and 1½ hours, depending on the quality of the meat. Stir a few times while the ribs are braising.

Remove the meat and decant the sauce into a fat separator. If you do not have one, refrigerate or freeze the sauce until it congeals, then scoop off the fat. Return the sauce to the pot with the ribs.

For the best flavor, make the stew up to several days in advance. Before serving, bring it to room temperature, then reheat over medium-low heat. Serve in bowls, and garnish with red pepper flakes and scallion rings.

Braised Tenderloin of Beef with Black Beans, Tomatoes, and Jalapeño Chilies

Serves 8 as an appetizer, 6 as an entrée

MARCEL DESAULNIERS, The Trellis Desaulniers serves this as an appetizer, ladled into hollowed-out brioches, but I've served it as the main course for large buffet dinners, with some yellow rice and a tossed salad. The stew looks so pretty, with black beans and chunks of fresh tomato, and the combination of spices with the zip of hot peppers makes it one of the most delicious braised-beef dishes I've ever eaten. It is not overly hot for sensitive palates.

Wine choice: California Zinfandel, French Rhône or Italian Barolo.

1 pound dried black beans, rinsed well and picked over

2 quarts water

1 tablespoon salt

1 cup finely chopped onions

1 cup finely chopped leeks, white part only

½ cup finely chopped carrots

2 finely chopped jalapeño chilies, deseeded under cold running water

½ cup finely chopped cooked black beans

2 ounces finely chopped smoked sausage, such as kielbasa

4 cups fresh tomatoes, peeled, seeded, and chopped

4 cups tomato juice

1 tablespoon dark-brown sugar

½ teaspoon cinnamon

¼ teaspoon ground cloves

1½ to 2 teaspoons salt

1 teaspoon freshly ground pepper

1 tablespoon butter

1 tablespoon vegetable oil

2 pounds beef tenderloin, cut into 1½-inch cubes

2 tablespoons finely minced garlic

1 tablespoon red-wine vinegar

¾ cup brewed coffee

6 to 8 fresh brioches (page 292)

Place the beans in a heavy pot with a cover, and add 2 quarts of water. Either soak overnight, then begin cooking, or bring to a boil and simmer 1 minute, and allow to sit covered for 1 hour before resuming cooking. If the latter method is used, the beans should then be cooked as soon as possible. Cook the beans with 1 tablespoon of salt, covered, on low heat for approximately 1½ hours, or until the beans are tender but not mushy. Stir occasionally.

In a heavy saucepan, combine the onions, leeks, carrots, chilies, ½ cup of beans, sausage, 2 cups of chopped tomatoes, tomato juice, brown sugar, cinnamon, cloves, salt, and pepper. (All the chopped ingredients can be done together in a food processor fitted with a steel blade. Be careful not to chop too fine.)

Bring the mixture to a boil, then reduce the heat and simmer uncovered for 1 hour, stirring frequently, until reduced and thickened.

In a 12-inch skillet, heat the butter and oil until they are very hot. Add enough beef cubes to fit in one layer without crowding. Sauté the cubes on all sides to brown, and remove them with a slotted spoon. Repeat with the remaining beef. Return all the beef to the pan, add the garlic, vinegar, and coffee, and allow the mixture to simmer until reduced by half. Add the reduction and meat to the vegetable mixture with 4 cups of the cooked and drained black beans and the remaining 2 cups of tomatoes. Simmer for 10 minutes, and serve the mixture in the hollowed-out brioches.

Follow the dish with small servings of Budweiser Beer Sorbet (page 311).

Note: The stew can be prepared up to 2 days in advance and slowly reheated, stirring occasionally, on top of the stove or in a 300-degree oven. It also freezes well for up to two months, and I've used less tender cuts of beef—such as round—and added time to the braising process before adding to the remaining ingredients.

Veal Medallions with Apple-Vinegar Sauce

Serves 8

ROBERT ROSELLINI, Rosellini's Other Place   Veal and apples always remind me of traveling through Normandy, and this dish pairs them beautifully in a silky sauce with a deep flavor from the stock and fruit. One of the nice things about this dish, I've found, is that the time-consuming part is making the sauce, and one batch can be used for at least 4 dinners for 8, so freeze the leftovers accordingly.

Wine choice: French white Burgundy or California Chardonnay, red Bordeaux or Beaujolais.

APPLE-VINEGAR SAUCE

4 pounds veal and chicken bones, cracked

2 pounds veal and chicken meat

2 quarts water

1 cup dry red wine

1 cup dry white wine

2 onions, quartered

2 carrots, diced

2 stalks celery, diced

6 sprigs parsley

4 sprigs fresh thyme

1 bay leaf

2 whole cloves

2 Granny Smith apples, cored and sliced

2 tablespoons cider vinegar

Salt and pepper to taste

2 tablespoons unsalted butter

THE VEAL

Salt and white pepper to taste

3 pounds veal leg, cut into 6 thick slices

1 onion, chopped

2 carrots, chopped

½ cup chopped parsley

1 cup minced celery and celery leaves

2 cloves minced garlic

In a large stockpot, bring the bones, meat, water, wines, vegetables, and seasonings to a boil, skimming off the scum as it rises. Simmer, uncovered, for 3 hours, skimming as necessary. Pour through a strainer lined with cheesecloth into another saucepan, pressing to extract the liquid from the vegetables. Discard the meat and vegetables. Skim off the fat, and boil again until the mixture is reduced to 1 quart.

Add the apples and vinegar, and simmer for 30 minutes, until the apples are mushy. Run the sauce through a food mill, or purée the apples in a food processor fitted with a steel blade and return them to the sauce. Simmer the sauce again until thickened, season with salt and pepper, and whisk in the butter, a small piece at a time.

Salt and pepper the veal slices. In a roasting pan, mix the remaining ingredients together, and place the veal slices among the vegetables so some are on the bottom and others are on the top.

Roast the veal in a 350-degree oven for 1 hour. Remove the veal, saving the vegetables and any juices that have accumulated for future stocks, and let the veal rest for 10 minutes before carving. Cut the veal slices into thinner slices.

To serve, spoon the sauce onto the plate, and top with the veal. Or arrange the veal on a platter and pass the sauce separately.

Note: Taste the sauce before serving and add a teaspoon or so of sugar if it seems a bit tart. That will depend on the innate sweetness of the apples.

Loin of Veal Roasted with Garlic and Candied Lemon Peel

Serve 6 to 8

MICHAEL ROBERTS, Trumps   Every time I make this recipe, I can't believe how good it is and how little work it takes. The two secrets are browning the roast and garlic sufficiently to smooth out the taste of the garlic, and using a good, homemade chicken stock to add richness to the sauce. The sweet tartness of the candied lemon peel is a perfect foil and garnish.

Wine choice: California Sauvignon Blanc or Fumé Blanc or French red Beaujolais.

4 lemons

3 tablespoons sugar

½ cup water

¼ cup olive oil

1 loin of veal, boned and tied (3 pounds of boned meat)

2 or 3 heads garlic, separated into cloves but not peeled

2 cups chicken stock (page 160)

Salt and pepper to taste

Remove the yellow zest from the lemons with a zester or vegetable peeler. Cut it into fine strips, and place it in a small saucepan with the sugar and ½ cup water. Cook, uncovered, over medium heat, until the peel is translucent and sticky, about 10 to 15 minutes. Remove it to a plate and let it cool.

Juice the lemons and reserve the juice for the sauce. These steps can be done well in advance.

Choose a heavy roasting pan just large enough to accommodate the veal. Heat the olive oil, and brown the veal well with the unpeeled garlic cloves. Do not be afraid to burn the garlic skins slightly, as this adds to the flavor of the sauce.

When the veal and garlic are brown, add the chicken stock and lemon juice. Bring the mixture to a boil on top of the stove, and place the pan in a 450-degree oven. Roast until the meat is medium rare to medium, about 30 minutes.

Remove the meat from the oven, and place it on a heated platter to rest for 15 minutes before carving, so the juices will remain in the meat. At this point, the liquid should be thick enough to coat a spoon and will be shiny. If not, reduce it slowly on top of the stove.

Carve the veal, and arrange it on a platter or plates with the unpeeled garlic cloves around it. Ladle the sauce on top, and garnish with the candied lemon peel.

Variations: Use chicken breasts, but remove the bone, keeping the skin on. The breasts will finish in 15 minutes, and should be kept warm while you reduce the sauce on top of the stove.

For whole boned chickens, tied in a cylinder similar in thickness to the veal, the timing remains the same as for the veal.

Chinese Duck with Endive and Lime Juice

Serves 4 to 8

JONATHAN WAXMAN, Jams The sauce is what elevates this simple roast duck to elegance, and there is an interesting combination of Western and Eastern flavors, with herbs, soy sauce, and ginger in the same recipe. Adding Belgian endive introduces yet another flavor, as well as a crunchy texture.

Wine choice: French red Rhône, such as an Hermitage or Côte Rôtie, or a California Cabernet Sauvignon.

2 Long Island ducks (5 to 6 pounds each)

4 cups dry red wine

4 shallots, chopped

1 sprig parsley

1 sprig tarragon

2 bay leaves

4 cloves garlic, peeled

2 teaspoons sugar

¼ cup rice vinegar

¼ cup soy sauce

4 tablespoons grated ginger

¼ cup freshly squeezed lime juice

Salt and freshly ground black pepper

4 spears Belgian endive

Debone the ducks by cutting along the breast bone, and holding the edge of your boning knife next to the carcass, cutting away the carcass so the wings remained attached to the breast and the thigh and leg bones are still intact. Remove the thigh bone, but removing the leg bone is not necessary. Place the meat, covered, in the refrigerator until you are ready to cook.

To prepare the sauce: Break apart the duck carcasses and place them in a large stockpot with the wine, shallots, parsley, tarragon, bay leaves, and garlic. Bring the mixture to a boil, reduce the heat, and simmer uncovered, skimming as necessary, for 1½ to 2 hours, or until the liquid is reduced to 2 cups when strained. Set it aside.

In a saucepan, cook the sugar and vinegar until caramelized. Deglaze the pan with the soy sauce, and then add the grated ginger and lime juice. Add the stock and reduce the liquid over high heat for 15 to 20 minutes, or until it is slightly thickened. Strain the sauce, and set it aside.

To roast the duck: Take a knife and remove as much fat as possible from the duck skin without removing the skin from the meat. Cut the duck into quarters. Sprinkle the pieces with salt and pepper. Place the legs in a 400-degree oven and roast for 35 minutes. Pour off any grease that accumulates and then place the breasts in the pan and roast for an additional 15 to 20 minutes. Remove the duck to a platter.

Julienne the endive and add it to the sauce. Adjust the seasoning with salt and pepper and spoon the sauce over the duck.

Duck Etouffée

Serves 8

PAUL PRUDHOMME, K-Paul's Louisiana Kitchen *Etouffée* literally means smothered, and in the Cajun cooking of Louisiana, it is used of any dish cooked in liquid with roux. The duck itself is moist and flavorful when you use Prudhomme's method of slow roasting after rubbing with spices. The vegetable sauce "smothering" the duck is rich and luscious, as only Cajun cooking can be.

Wine choice: French red Rhône or red Burgundy.

2 fresh Long Island ducks (5 to 6 pounds each)

First seasoning mix

   1 tablespoon salt

   2 teaspoons sweet paprika

   1 teaspoon garlic powder

   1 teaspoon ground red pepper, preferably cayenne

   ¾ teaspoon onion powder

   ¾ teaspoon ground sage

   ½ teaspoon black pepper

   ½ teaspoon dried thyme leaves

   ½ teaspoon filé powder (optional)

10 cups cold water

2 cups finely chopped onions

1½ cups finely chopped celery

1½ cups finely chopped green bell peppers

2 bay leaves

Wash the ducks under cold running water and pull off any visible fat. Fold the wings underneath the backs.

Combine the first seasoning mix in a small bowl and mix well. Sprinkle the seasoning mix on the inside and outside of the ducks, and on the necks and giblets, rubbing it in with your hands. Place the necks and giblets inside the ducks and put the ducks on a rack in a large roasting pan, breast side up. Bake at 250 degrees until the drumsticks turn easily, about 5 to 5½ hours. Allow ducks to become cool enough to handle, and reserve 1 cup of the drippings. Remove the necks and giblets.

Partially bone the ducks and cut each into 4 sections as follows: Slice the ducks in half lengthwise, and carefully remove the wings, breast bones, and backbones, leaving the skin attached to the meat. Reserve the bones and giblets (except the livers) for the stock. Cut the 2 halves of each duck in half so each has 4 quarters. Refrigerate the meat.

In a 4-quart saucepan, cover the duck bones, wings, necks, and giblets with the cold water. Bring the water to a boil over high heat, reduce the heat to a simmer, and cook for 1 hour, adding water if necessary to maintain about 7 cups of liquid. Strain the stock, discard the bones, and refrigerate the stock. Remove fat when cold.

Combine 1 cup each of the onions, celery, and bell peppers with the bay leaves in a small bowl. In a second bowl, combine the second seasoning mix.

Second seasoning mix

　　1¼ teaspoons garlic
　　powder

　　1½ teaspoons ground red
　　pepper, preferably cayenne

　　1 teaspoon salt

　　1 teaspoon onion powder

　　¾ teaspoon ground white
　　pepper

　　½ teaspoon black pepper

1 cup all-purpose flour

½ teaspoon minced garlic

⅓ cup finely chopped
scallions

6 cups cooked rice

Bring the stock to a boil before making the sauce.

In a large skillet, heat the reserved duck drippings over high heat until they begin to smoke, about 5 minutes. Gradually add the flour, stirring with a long-handled metal whisk, until smooth. Continue cooking, whisking or stirring constantly, until the roux is dark red-brown to black, about 4 to 6 minutes. Immediately add the vegetable mixture and stir well. Then stir in the seasoning mix. Remove the roux from the heat and add it by spoonfuls to the boiling stock, stirring until the roux is dissolved between additions. Reduce the heat to medium low and cook about 30 minutes, stirring occasionally. Remove the stock from the heat and strain it into a 2-quart saucepan. Return it to high heat and add the remaining vegetables and the garlic. Bring the mixture to a boil, reduce the heat, and simmer for 15 minutes to reduce. Stir in the scallions and cook about 1 minute more. Set the sauce aside and skim off any fat that rises to the surface.

With a small sharp knife, scrape off as much fat as possible from under the duck skin without completely detaching the skin. Place the duck in a baking pan and spoon the étouffée sauce over it. Bake the duck at 350 degrees until the meat is heated through, about 30 minutes. Serve on heated serving plates with the sauce spooned over rice.

Note: The ducks can be roasted and boned a day in advance and refrigerated, and the stock can be made at the same time, but should not be strained until you are ready to proceed.

Crisp Peppered Duck with Natural Juices

Serves 6

BRADLEY OGDEN, The Campton Place Hotel This is hardly a spur-of-the-moment dish—the ducks have to sit in the refrigerator for two days and then the roasting and sauce making take most of a day. But the recipe is delicious and foolproof, and all of these procedures only require the cook to be in the house, not tending the pots. The taste is sublime, and if you love steak au poivre, you'll adore the way the pepper cuts the richness of the duck and gives it an unparalleled flavor. Ogden serves it with Wild Rice and Pine Nuts (page 297) and Braised Red Swiss Chard (page 304).

Wine choice: Italian red, such as a Chianti or red from the Piedmont region.

3 Long Island ducks (4½ to 5 pounds each)

¾ cup coarsely cracked black pepper

3 cloves garlic, peeled and left whole

5 tablespoons kosher salt

2 tablespoons chopped fresh rosemary leaves

2 tablespoons paprika

If you are using frozen ducks, thaw them in the refrigerator overnight. Remove the wrappings, reserving the necks and giblets, and wash the ducks inside and out under cold running water. Dry well.

Spread the cracked pepper on a cookie sheet and roll the ducks in the pepper until they are well coated. Place them on wire racks on the cookie sheet and leave them uncovered in the refrigerator for 2 days. The drying ensures a crisp skin.

Crush the garlic with the flat side of a carving knife or cleaver. Combine with the salt in a bowl, and rub the mixture with your fingers to press the oils out of the garlic. Continue to rub until the salt is moist. Discard the garlic and add the rosemary and paprika. Season the ducks' cavities with the mixture, using your fingers.

Preheat the oven to 350 degrees and roast the ducks for 2 hours, until they are cooked and have rendered their fat. Remove them from the oven and let them cool. Bone the ducks by cutting along the breast bone, and then forcing the ducks flat so the backbone splits. With your fingers, remove the bones from the carcass. You should remove the thigh bone, but I leave on the legs and wings since I think they make the ducks look more attractive on the plates.

Set the ducks aside, pouring off the grease, but keeping the pan for making the sauce.

Sauce:

Bones, necks, and carcasses from the ducks

2 cups carrots, coarsely chopped

2 cups celery, coarsely chopped

2 cups onions, coarsely chopped

1 quart cold water

8 cloves garlic, peeled and left whole

¼ cup fresh rosemary, chopped

4 parsley stems

4 bay leaves

3 quarts unsalted chicken stock (page 160)

2 tablespoons white-wine vinegar

1 cup dry white wine

Note that the recipe calls for unsalted chicken stock. All the salt you need is part of the spice mixture still clinging to the duck carcasses. If additional salt is added the juice will be too salty once reduced.

Place the duck bones in the roasting pan in which the ducks were cooked, and roast them in a 325-degree oven, stirring often, until the bones are browned, about 1 hour. Add the carrots, celery, and onions to the pan and cook about 10 minutes, stirring often. Remove the pan from the oven and place the contents in a tall stockpot.

Pour the water into the roasting pan and deglaze the pan, scraping up the browned bits on the bottom. Pour the liquid into the stockpot, along with the rest of the ingredients. Bring it to a boil, skimming off the scum that rises to the surface, and simmer uncovered for 2 hours, skimming as necessary. Strain the broth into another heavy saucepan, and reduce it by simmering for 30 to 45 minutes over medium heat. Then strain it through cheesecloth or a very fine sieve. Pour into a sauce boat and serve with the ducks.

To serve, reheat the ducks in a 450-degree oven for 10 minutes to render any remaining fat. Then place them in a preheated broiler for 2 minutes if the skin is not totally crisp.

Note: The duck and sauce can be made the day before serving, or both can be frozen in advance. If the ducks are cold, reheat them in a 300-degree oven for 10 minutes, then increase the heat to 450 for 10 minutes. If they are frozen, allow them to totally defrost before crisping.

Roast Duck Legs with Napa Cabbage and Pancetta

Serves 6

WOLFGANG PUCK, Spago I firmly believe a duck should be two separate animals, since the breast meat and leg meat are rarely done justice together, and this dish is one of my favorites. The rich duck, enhanced by thyme, is combined with the smoky-tasting pancetta (an Italian smoked bacon), and then there's the contrast of the crispy cabbage and the sauce, in which the acidity of the vinegar adds additional zest. It's very little work, and can be started an hour before you want to serve it.

Wine choice: French red Burgundy or Bordeaux.

6 duck leg quarters, trimmed of excess fat

Salt and freshly ground pepper

5 sprigs fresh thyme, chopped (or 1½ teaspoons dried thyme)

1 head Napa cabbage, about 1 pound

6 ounces pancetta or bacon, cut into ¼-inch dice

3 tablespoons red-wine vinegar

3 tablespoons red wine, such as Zinfandel

2 tablespoons olive oil

Season the duck legs with salt, pepper, and thyme. Heat a sauté pan or skillet over high heat and brown the duck on both sides, skin side down first, until golden. You will not need additional grease since the skin instantly begins to render fat. Place the legs in a 400-degree oven and roast them for 50 to 60 minutes, or until tender. Halfway through the baking, remove the pan from the oven and pour off the accumulated duck fat.

Reserve 6 nice leaves from the cabbage, and cut the remaining cabbage into ¼-inch slices.

In a sauté pan, cook the pancetta or bacon over medium heat for 8 to 10 minutes, or until it is crisp on the outside. Pour half the fat out of the pan and sauté the sliced cabbage until it is hot, but still remains crisp. Add half the vinegar and wine to the pan and season with salt and pepper. Stir over high heat for 1 minute to deglaze the pan. Take off heat.

Remove the duck legs from the oven when they are done. Pour off the fat and deglaze the pan with the remaining wine and vinegar. Add the olive oil and bring the liquid to a boil. Adjust the seasoning with salt and pepper.

To serve: Place the uncooked cabbage leaves around the edges of a platter or on individual plates. Top with the sautéed cabbage, and place the duck legs on top. Spoon a little sauce onto each leg.

Chicken Breast with Coconut

Serves 6

SUSUMU FUKUI, La Petite Chaya Curry and coconut are a traditional and wonderful pairing, and the only difficult part of this recipe, at least for me, was breaking open the coconut without hammering my hand. It is a very easy and quick preparation, and the vegetables add some color and textural variation to the dish.

Wine choice: French white Burgundy, such as Mâcon Villages, or California Chardonnay.

3 tablespoons unsalted butter

2 tablespoons oil

3 whole chicken breasts, split

Flour

Salt and pepper to taste

3 carrots

4 stalks celery

2 onions

2 cloves garlic, peeled and minced

1 to 2 tablespoons curry powder

1 cup white wine

1 cup chicken stock

2 cups heavy cream

½ cup fresh coconut, grated

Heat the butter and oil in a large skillet. Lightly flour the chicken and season it with salt and pepper. When the butter foam starts to subside, add the chicken and brown it well. Remove it from the pan.

Chop all the vegetables into ½-inch pieces. Add them, along with the garlic and curry powder, to the pan in which the chicken was browned, and sauté them for 2 minutes. Deglaze the pan with the wine, add the stock and cream, and return the chicken to the pan.

Bake it covered in a 350-degree oven for 20 minutes. Remove the chicken and vegetables from the pan with a slotted spoon, and reduce the sauce over medium heat until it thickens and coats the back of a spoon. Adjust the seasoning with salt and pepper and add the coconut. Return the chicken and vegetables to the pan, and simmer for 3 minutes.

Serve by placing the vegetables around the chicken breasts and spoon sauce on top.

Note: While best if served immediately, this can be reheated in a 275-degree oven for 15 minutes.

Chicken and Seafood Jambalaya

Serves 8 as an appetizer, 4 as an entrée

PAUL PRUDHOMME, K-Paul's Louisiana Kitchen   This dish has long been the backbone of my large-party repertoire, although the recipes I used until I found Prudhomme's were never as good. It does not require a knife; a tossed salad and some garlic bread complete the dinner, and everyone loves it. In this case, the oysters are part of what makes it special, and the flavoring of the rice is perfection, both from the seasonings and the spicy sausage.

Wine choice: California Chardonnay or Sauvignon Blanc, or French white Rhône or red Beaujolais Villages.

2 bay leaves

1½ teaspoons salt

1½ teaspoons ground red pepper, preferably cayenne

1½ teaspoons dried oregano leaves

1¼ teaspoons freshly ground white pepper

1 teaspoon freshly ground black pepper

¾ teaspoon dried thyme leaves

2½ tablespoons chicken fat, lard, or beef fat

⅔ cup chopped tasso or other smoked ham, preferably Cure 81 (about 3 ounces)

½ cup chopped andouille or any good smoked pork sausage, such as Polish kielbasa

1½ cups chopped onions

1 cup chopped celery

¾ cup chopped green peppers

½ cup raw chicken meat, cut into bite-size pieces

1½ teaspoons minced garlic

4 medium tomatoes, peeled, seeded, and chopped

¾ cup canned tomato sauce

2 cups fish stock (page 160)

½ cup chopped scallions

2 cups uncooked long-grain rice

18 to 24 medium shrimp

18 to 24 oysters with their liquor (about 10 ounces)

Combine all the seasoning ingredients and set aside.

In a 4-quart heavy saucepan, melt the fat over medium heat. Add the tasso and andouille, and sauté until crisp, about 5 to 8 minutes, stirring frequently. Add the onions, celery, and green peppers, and sauté until tender but still firm, about 5 minutes, stirring often.

Add the chicken, and raise the heat to high. Cook for 1 minute, stirring constantly. Reduce the heat to medium, and add the seasoning mix and the minced garlic. Cook for 3 minutes, stirring, then add the tomatoes, and cook until the chicken is tender, about 8 minutes. Add the tomato sauce and stock and bring the mixture back to a boil. Reduce the heat to a simmer, and simmer for 8 minutes. Add the scallions and continue to cook for 2 minutes. Then add the rice, shrimp, and oysters with their liquor. Stir the mixture and remove it from the heat.

Transfer it to a baking pan or casserole, cover the pan snugly with heavy-duty aluminum foil, and bake at 350 degrees until the rice is tender but still a bit resilient, about 20 minutes. Make sure to remove the bay leaves before serving.

Note: While best served immediately, the dish can be prepared a day in advance and reheated in a 300-degree oven, covered. Stir occasionally and gently.

Boston Lettuce Custard with Medallions of Chicken, Prosciutto, and Sweetbreads

Serves 6 as an appetizer, 4 as an entrée

RICHARD PERRY, Richard Perry Restaurant   This dish looks exquisite when served. The swirling medallions of chicken, prosciutto, and sweetbread purée are perched atop a bright green cushion of spinach and Boston lettuce. The flavors are delicate, and enlivened greatly by the sweetened béarnaise. This is a very impressive party dish, or could be a sophisticated lunch.

Wine choice: California Chardonnay or French white Burgundy.

½ pound sweetbreads

2 chicken breasts, split

¼ pound thinly sliced proscuitto

2 tablespoons unsalted butter

1 egg yolk

1 teaspoon salt

¼ teaspoon freshly ground white pepper

Spinach-Lettuce Mixture:

1 cup chopped fresh spinach, packed

1½ heads Boston lettuce, chopped fine

1 tablespoon unsalted butter

2 tablespoons finely diced onion

1 egg

¼ cup heavy cream

2 teaspoons fresh tarragon, or ½ teaspoon dried

½ teaspoon salt

¼ teaspoon white pepper

Sweetbreads, which are the thymus gland of a calf, need soaking before they can be sautéed. Wash the sweetbreads and place them in a bowl with cold water for 2 hours, changing the water several times during the initial soaking. Or soak overnight in the refrigerator, covered with plastic wrap. Drain and delicately pull off as much of the filament encasing them as possible.

While the sweetbreads are soaking, bone and skin the chicken breasts, removing all fat and tendons. Place the chicken breasts 3 inches apart between two sheets of wax paper. Pound them with a meat mallet or the bottom of a heavy skillet until ¼ inch thick. Place 2 breast halves adjoining, and cover with a layer of prosciutto.

When the filament has been removed from the sweetbreads, cut them into slices ¾ inch thick. Melt the butter in a 10-inch frying pan, and when the butter foam begins to subside, quickly sauté the sweetbreads for 2 minutes, until cooked through. Place them in the bowl of a food processor fitted with a steel blade and purée with the egg yolk, salt, and pepper. Spread the sweetbread purée over the ham layer and roll the chicken breasts jelly-roll style. Put the rolls in the freezer for 30 minutes, or until they are firm enough to slice.

Wash and dry the spinach and Boston lettuce. Melt the butter in a large frying pan or Dutch oven, and sauté the onion for 5 minutes, or until translucent. Add the spinach and lettuce and simmer until they are wilted, tossing frequently so they don't burn. The quantity will become much smaller as the leaves wilt. Purée the mixture in the food processor with the egg, cream, tarragon, salt, and pepper.

Butter 12 custard cups, ramekins, or a 1½-quart soufflé dish. Cut the chicken rolls into 12 slices and arrange a slice in the center of each cup, or place slices around the bottom of the soufflé dish. Add the purée on top of the slice or slices. Place the cups, ramekins, or dish in a baking pan in a 350-degree oven. Pour hot water into the baking pan halfway up the sides of the dish or cups. For individual cups, bake for 30 minutes, and for a large mold bake for 1½ hours, or until the center of the custard is set. Let sit for 10 minutes before unmolding. Unmold and serve with Orange Béarnaise Sauce.

ORANGE BÉARNAISE SAUCE

½ cup red-wine vinegar

¾ cup white wine

1 teaspoon fresh tarragon, or ½ tablespoon dried

¼ cup minced onion

1 tablespoon dried chervil

¾ teaspoon freshly ground white pepper

1½ tablespoons chopped parsley

½ cup orange juice

¼ cup dry white wine

¼ cup sugar

1 tablespoon grated orange peel

2 egg yolks

½ pound (2 sticks) unsalted butter, melted

Combine the vinegar, wine, tarragon, onion, chervil, pepper, and parsley in a stainless-steel pan. Heat to the boiling point, and simmer until the mixture is reduced to ¼ cup. Strain through layers of cheesecloth or a paper coffee filter into a cup. Discard the solids.

In another pan, combine the orange juice, wine, sugar, and orange peel. Reduce to 2 tablespoons of liquid.

Put the egg yolks in a food processor fitted with a steel blade, and add the hot melted butter in a slow stream of driblets, beating until the mixture is thick and rich. Add the vinegar and orange-juice reductions.

Note: The molds can be prepared a day in advance and refrigerated, tightly covered, until you are ready to bake. Allow them to sit at room temperature for 30 minutes before baking. And the sauce can be prepared up to 4 hours in advance and held over hot water or in a Thermos bottle.

Stuffed Pheasant with Pistachio Nuts, Sweetbreads, and Spinach

Serves 4

JACKIE ETCHEBER, Jackie's I think every cook should learn how to bone poultry. Once you've done a chicken, you can do any bird from a 5-ounce quail to a 25-pound turkey. The first attempts may lead to batches of stir-fries or chicken salad, but it's worth a rainy afternoon of learning to be able to make a divine dish like this one. It looks as beautiful as it tastes delicious, with swirls of green spinach and delicate sweetbreads punctuated by pistachio nuts in the center of the slices. The mushroom sauce is the perfect contrast of flavors, and this dish creates one of the most elegant plates I've ever placed before guests.

Wine choice: California Chardonnay.

2 two-pound pheasants

½ pound sweetbreads

Salt and pepper

1 ten-ounce box frozen chopped spinach, defrosted and squeezed dry

½ cup carrots cut into a fine julienne or coarsely grated

¼ pound pistachio nuts, shelled, with skins removed

¼ cup olive oil

Sauce:

1 ounce dried morels

½ pound fresh mushrooms, sliced

3 tablespoons unsalted butter

3 shallots, chopped fine

½ cup brandy

¼ cup white wine

2 cups heavy cream

To bone the pheasants: With a very sharp boning knife, slice along the breast bone. Keeping the knife blade on the carcass, scrape down the carcass, freeing it by cutting through the wing and thigh joints. Once the carcass has been removed, bone the first joints of the wings and then remove the remaining parts of the wings. Scrape to free the thigh and leg bones and remove. The trick is always to keep the blade of the knife on the bone and not toward the skin, which could be pierced.

Once the pheasant is boned, cut the meat in half, and pound each half between two sheets of waxed paper to an even thickness, moving some meat from the thigh and breast toward the center of the skin if necessary.

Cook and prepare the sweetbreads as for Sweetbreads in Puff Pastry (page 150). Cut them into ½-inch dice.

Sprinkle the pheasants with salt and pepper on both sides. Spread over the halves the spinach, morsels of sweetbread, carrots, and nuts. Roll lengthwise, and tie with butcher twine every 2 inches. Heat the oil in a sauté pan or skillet and brown the rolls on all sides. Bake them in a 450-degree oven for 10 to 15 minutes. Allow them to rest for 10 minutes; then remove the twine and slice them into 2-inch-thick sections.

For the sauce: Pour hot water over the morels and soak them for 3 hours. Then drain them and wash under running water to remove any remaining grit. Squeeze them dry and chop. Sauté the morels and fresh mushrooms in the butter, along with the shallots. Add the brandy and wine and reduce the liquid until only 1 tablespoon remains. Add the cream and reduce by half, or until the mixture is thick enough to coat the back of a spoon. Add salt and pepper to taste, and serve with the slices of pheasant.

Note: The rolls can be prepared a day in advance and kept covered in the refrigerator, and the sauce can be made at the same time. But the rolls should be cooked just prior to serving, and the sauce reheated.

QUICK SAUTES AND OTHER FAST FOODS

The vast majority of the cooking done by the new American chefs is completed by a quick sauté on the stove, a trip through the steamer, or a few minutes in the poacher. Barbara Tropp may call it stir-frying while Lawrence Forgione calls it quick searing, but the end result is the same—on the plate in a matter of a few minutes.

The key words to understanding the chefs' philosophies of cooking are "finishing the dish." While Forgione's Picnic-Inspired Quail is finished in about three minutes, it can take hours to bone the birds, and they must marinate for a while. In the same way, Patrick O'Connell's Sweetbreads with Three-Mustard sauce needs a few seconds in the sauté pan, but it takes far longer to prepare the sweetbreads to get them to that point, and make the sauce.

On the other hand, Michael Roberts's Scallops Sautéed with Pine Nuts or Paul Prudhomme's Blackened Redfish go from start to finish faster than an inning of a baseball game.

It's a good idea to read through a recipe thoroughly before setting a menu. One generalization is that everything in this chapter is perfect for all who have to serve dinner a few minutes after getting home from the office. If a recipe is more detailed and requires advance preparation work, such as sauces or marinades, they can be done in advance. ∎

Lobster with Thai Sauce and Noodles

Serves 4

LYDIA SHIRE, Seasons   This dish is one of the liveliest I've eaten, and it draws the best from two cuisines—the hot spiciness of the ingredients used in Thai cooking with the sweetness and delicacy of New England lobster. It looks beautiful when presented on the plate, with bright red lobster-tail sections around the bed of spicy noodles given some crunch from the bok choy and peanuts.

Wine choice: California Sauvignon Blanc or French Pouilly Fumé or Sancerre.

4 live lobsters (1¼ to 1½ pounds each)

2 tablespoons vegetable oil

3 large fresh shiitake mushrooms

1 cup sliced bok choy

¼ cup peanuts

2 tablespoons unsalted butter

1 teaspoon chili oil (available in most supermarkets)

Sauce:

4 sprigs mint

2 sprigs cilantro

2 cloves garlic

1 teaspoon grated ginger

3 tablespoons nam pla (Thai fish sauce available in Oriental groceries)

2 tablespoons chili oil

1 cup olive oil

¾ cup champagne vinegar

Pinch of black pepper

Grated zest of ½ lemon

2 cups cooked Chinese noodles or very fine egg noodles

Bring a large pot of salted water to a boil and plunge the lobsters in head first. Boil them for 7 minutes, beginning the timing when the water returns to a boil. Remove them and plunge into ice water to stop the cooking action. When they are cool enough to handle, twist off the tails and set them aside. Crack the claws and leg joints and remove the meat. Save the bodies for lobster stock.

Place the tails in a sauté pan or baking dish and brush them with oil. Place them in a 450-degree oven for 5 minutes.

Slice the shiitake and bok choy and combine them with the peanuts. Heat the butter and chili oil in a sauté pan or skillet and sauté the vegetables until they are cooked, but the bok choy should remain crisp.

Chop the mint, cilantro, and garlic, and whisk them together with the rest of the sauce ingredients. Add the noodles and ½ cup of the sauce to the pan with the vegetables. Sauté until the noodles are hot, then add the lobster meat from the leg joints. Set the mixture aside.

To serve: Cut each lobster tail into 4 pieces, leaving the shells on. Place some noodles in the center of each plate, and place the lobster-tail sections and claws around it.

Note: The recipe can be prepared in advance up to baking the lobster and sautéing the noodles. Keep all ingredients tightly covered in the refrigerator, and reheat the claws and legs in a steamer for a few minutes to warm.

The sauce makes an excellent marinade or basting sauce for any grilled meat or fish.

Chinese Crab

*Serves 2 as a main dish, 4 to 6 as
part of a multi-course meal*

WOLFGANG PUCK, Chinois on Main   Crab with black bean sauce is one of my favorite listings on a Chinese menu, and this is a fresher and more flavorful rendition of the dish, since the flavors are concentrated by using the French method of deglazing. It's quick, easy, and delicious.

Wine choice: Alsatian Gewürztraminer or French Sancerre or Pouilly Fumé.

2 tablespoons Chinese fermented black beans

⅔ cup sake

⅔ cup chicken stock (page 160)

2 tablespoons soy sauce

1½ tablespoons minced fresh ginger

2 tablespoons sesame oil

2 fresh crabs (2 pounds each), rinsed in cold water

4 scallions, green and white portions sliced paper-thin

1 bunch minced garlic chives (Chinese chives)

2 teaspoons cornstarch, dissolved in 2 tablespoons sake

Soak the black beans in the sake, stock, soy sauce, and ginger for 1 hour.

Heat the sesame oil in a large sauté pan, and when the oil is hot and begins to smoke, sauté the crabs briefly on both sides to coat with the oil. Place the pan, uncovered, in a 400-degree oven for 10 to 12 minutes, or until the crabs are bright red. Remove them from the sauté pan, and set them aside until they are cool enough to handle. Remove the top shells in one piece and reserve them. Cut the undersides into quarters, leaving the legs attached.

Deglaze the sauté pan with the sake mixture, reducing slightly. Add the scallions and garlic chives. Remix the cornstarch and add, stirring until thickened. Add the quartered crabs and toss them over moderate heat until they are hot and the sauce adheres to them.

To serve: Reassemble the crab quarters and place the upper shell on top. Spoon any remaining sauce over the crab.

Sea Scallops with Their Roe Poached in Hot Citrus Sauce

*Serves 6 as an appetizer, 4 as an
entrée*

RICHARD PERRY, Richard Perry Restaurant   This dish has an unexpected flavor, and the oils from the citrus rind give the scallops sparkle without detracting from their delicacy. I serve it with rice pilaf to soak up the sauce. This makes a wonderful centerpiece for a buffet supper since it doesn't require a knife.

1 cup water

½ cup sugar

½ cup Johannisberg Riesling

1 tablespoon Calvados, or apple brandy

Grated rind of 1 orange

Grated rind of ½ grapefruit

Grated rind of ½ lemon

Juice of 1½ oranges

Juice of ½ grapefruit

Juice of 1 lemon

1½ pounds sea scallops, with their roe attached (see note)

½ pound (2 sticks) unsalted butter, cut into small pieces

Combine the water and sugar in a saucepan, and bring to a boil over medium heat, washing down any crystals clinging to the sides of the pan with a brush dipped in cold water. Simmer for 5 minutes, and add the wine, Calvados, citrus rinds and juices. Simmer for 5 minutes, then add the scallops and poach them until just cooked through, about 3 minutes, depending on their size. Remove them with a slotted spoon and keep them warm.

Increase the heat to high, and reduce the liquid in the pan to 3 tablespoons. Over low heat, whisking constantly, add bits of butter, allowing the bits to melt, but not letting the sauce come to a boil or it will separate and thin out. Beat until the sauce is thick and creamy. Pour it over the scallops and serve them immediately.

Note: Scallops without the roe attached work equally well, as do bay scallops. If you are using bay scallops, poach them less than a minute, watching them carefully so they do not overcook.

The poaching liquid can be prepared a day in advance and kept in the refrigerator, but poach the scallops and make the sauce at the last minute.

Scallops Sauteed with Pine Nuts

Serves 6 as an appetizer, 4 as an entrée

MICHAEL ROBERTS, Trumps   This is one of those very quick meals with a rich flavor that belies how easy it is to make. Garlic and shallots flavor a simple beurre blanc sauce, and what increases the excitement is the contrast of textures between the tender scallops and the crunchy pine nuts.

Wine choice: California Sauvignon Blanc or Fumé Blanc.

2 tablespoons clarified butter

1½ pounds fresh bay scallops

½ cup pine nuts

1 tablespoon minced garlic

4 tablespoons minced shallots

1 cup dry white wine

¼ cup freshly squeezed lemon juice

8 tablespoons (1 stick) unsalted butter

Salt and pepper to taste

Melt the clarified butter in a sauté pan or 12-inch skillet and heat until it is hot and a bead of water will sizzle. Add the scallops and pine nuts and sauté them, stirring constantly, for 1 minute, or until they are golden.

Remove the scallops and nuts from the pan with a slotted spoon and reserve. Add the garlic and shallots to the pan and sauté for 30 seconds. Add wine and lemon juice, and continue cooking until the liquid is reduced to ¼ cup. Add any juice that has rendered from the scallops. Over low heat, whisking constantly, add bits of butter, allowing the bits to melt, but not letting the sauce come to a boil or it will separate and thin out. Add the scallops and pine nuts to briefly reheat, season with salt and pepper to taste, and serve immediately.

Halibut Sauté
with Pistachios

Serves 4

SUSUMU FUKUI, La Petite Chaya   This dish looks so pretty when placed on the plate—the fillets topped by a browned crust with the nutty flavor of pistachios, and small cubes of vegetables adding color and texture as well as flavors. The most time-consuming part is shelling the nuts, and that can be done at any time in advance.

Wine choice: California Chardonnay.

4 halibut fillets, or swordfish, snapper, or any firm-fleshed white fillets (5 to 6 ounces each)

Salt and pepper

Flour

¼ pound shelled pistachio nuts, skins removed

¼ pound (1 stick) unsalted butter

3 slices white bread

4 small zucchini

½ medium onion

¼ pound mushrooms

1 clove garlic

1 large shallot

½ cup olive oil

2 tomatoes, chopped

Juice of 2 lemons

Wash the fillets, pat them dry, season them with salt and pepper, and dust with flour just before cooking. Grind the pistachios, butter and bread in a food processor fitted with a steel blade. Blend the mixture until smooth, and season it with salt and pepper.

Cut the zucchini, onions, and mushrooms into ½-inch pieces. Chop the garlic and shallot.

In a sauté pan, heat 1 tablespoon of the olive oil over high heat. Add the fillets and sauté them over high heat for 1 minute on each side, to slightly brown and cook the flour. Spread the tops of the fillets with the pistachio butter, and place the pan in a 450-degree oven for 8 to 10 minutes, or until the fillets are cooked and the tops are brown. Remove them from the oven and set aside.

While the fish is cooking, heat the remaining olive oil in a large skillet or sauté pan and add the vegetables, except the tomatoes. Sauté them until cooked but still crisp, add the tomatoes, and season to taste with salt and pepper. Add the lemon juice.

To serve, place a fillet on each plate, top with the pan juices from the baking pan, and spoon the vegetables around the fillet.

Note: The vegetables can be cut up a few hours in advance and kept in plastic bags in the refrigerator, and the nut butter can also be done in advance.

Blackened Redfish

Serves 6

PAUL PRUDHOMME, K-Paul's Louisiana Kitchen   I'll never forget my first taste of this dish at K-Paul's. With the first bite one tastes the charred spices, and then the heat is cooled by the buttery sweetness of the fish. This is perhaps Prudhomme's most famous dish, and after attempts with different types of skillets, I have decided the cast-iron one is essential to reach the proper temperature to "blacken" the fish. It's worth buying one just to make this dish if you didn't inherit one from grandma.

Wine choice: Alsatian Gewürztraminer or California Sauvignon Blanc.

1 tablespoon sweet paprika

2½ teaspoons salt

1 teaspoon onion powder

1 teaspoon garlic powder

1 teaspoon cayenne pepper

¾ teaspoon ground white pepper

¾ teaspoon ground black pepper

½ teaspoon dried thyme

½ teaspoon dried oregano

½ pound (2 sticks) unsalted butter, melted

6 fillets redfish, pompano, tilefish, or snapper (not more than ¾ inch thick, 8 to 10 ounces each)

Heat a large cast-iron skillet over the highest heat possible for at least 10 minutes, until it is beyond the smoking stage and white ash begins to form in the bottom.

While the pan is heating, mix the seasoning ingredients together well. Pour 2 tablespoons of the butter on each of the fillets, turning to coat both sides, and sprinkle generously and evenly with the seasoning mix on both sides, patting it in by hand.

Place the fillets in the skillet and pour 1 teaspoon of butter on top of each. Be careful, as the butter may flame up. Cook uncovered until the underside is charred, about 2 minutes. Turn the fish over, top with another teaspoon of butter, and cook another 2 minutes.

Repeat with the remaining fillets, if all could not fit in the skillet at one time.

Cape Scallops with Garlic and Herbs

Serves 4

LYDIA SHIRE, Seasons This is one of my favorite and quickest preparations for tiny East Coast scallops. The sauce has a richness and appealing light green tone from the pesto sauce, and the sun-dried tomatoes add a brightness along with their color. I've used commercial pesto sauce found in the supermarket freezer case, and it works quite well.

Wine choice: California Sauvignon Blanc.

2 cloves finely chopped garlic

1 tablespoon olive oil

1½ cups heavy cream

2 tablespoons Pesto Sauce (see recipe below)

Juice of ½ lemon

4 sun-dried tomatoes, cut into fine julienne strips

Salt and pepper

1½ pounds fresh bay scallops

⅓ cup dry white vermouth

½ cup toasted pine nuts

BASIL PESTO SAUCE

1 cup fresh basil leaves

1 clove garlic

2 ounces freshly grated Parmesan cheese

¼ cup pine nuts

½ cup olive oil

Salt and pepper

Sauté the garlic in olive oil over medium heat until it is lightly browned. Add the cream and reduce until the mixture is quite thick and only about ½ cup remains. Add the pesto, lemon juice, and tomatoes. Set the sauce aside.

Salt and pepper the scallops and place them in another pan with the vermouth. Set the pan over high heat and cook until the scallops turn opaque, about 1 minute, then remove them with a slotted spoon. Place them in the sauce and heat briefly, adding some of the poaching liquid if the sauce is too thick. Sprinkle with the pine nuts.

While pesto can have some spinach added to it for additional color, or walnuts in addition to the pine nuts, I am rather a purist and like this recipe. Since the scallops call for only 2 tablespoons, freeze the leftovers. Or toss it with some pasta and give yourself a treat.

Grind the basil leaves, garlic, Parmesan cheese, and pine nuts in a food processor fitted with a steel blade. Slowly add the olive oil through the feed tube with the motor running, and then season with salt and pepper. If you are making pesto in a blender, start with the oil and then add the other ingredients.

Poached Fish with Tomatoes and Purple Basil

Serves 6

JEREMIAH TOWER, Santa Fe Bar and Grill   This way of preparing fish is very light and flavorful, and fresh green basil, easier to find for most of us, works just as well as the smaller-leafed purple variety. The tomatoes and herbs enhance the flavor of the fish while not in any way masking it. The total cooking time is less than 10 minutes, so this is an elegant and quick dinner.

Wine choice: French white Burgundy, such as Meursault or Puligny-Montrachet.

6 halibut fillets (6 ounces each)

½ pound unsalted butter

1½ cups fish stock (page 160)

1½ cups skinned, seeded, and chopped fresh tomatoes

1 cup purple basil leaves, chopped

Salt and pepper to taste

Remove the skin from the fillets. Wash and pat dry.
In a sauté pan or large skillet, melt 3 tablespoons of the butter over low heat. Add the fish and enough fish stock to cover the fillets. Cover with buttered parchment paper, bring the liquid to a boil over high heat, then turn down the flame and simmer for 2 minutes. Turn the fish with a spatula and cook it an additional 2 minutes. Remove the pan from the heat, discard the paper, and allow the fish to sit for 1 minute. Remove the fish and drain it on paper toweling.

Strain the stock into another sauté pan or skillet. Bring it to a boil over high heat and boil until the liquid is reduced by one-third. Add the tomatoes and basil, heat through, then add the remaining butter, cut into 1-tablespoon pieces. Whisk the mixture until smooth, and adjust the seasoning with salt and pepper.

Place the fish on plates or a platter, spoon the sauce over it, and garnish with additional basil leaves.

Poached Salmon with Fettuccini

Serves 4

JACKIE ETCHEBER, Jackie's The spears of bright green asparagus atop the delicate pink salmon fillets make this most attractive to put on the table, and the slight hint of lemon in the sauce is sublime. It's the perfect complement to the other flavors, and is set off by the creaminess of the fettuccine.

Wine choice: French white Burgundy or California Sauvignon Blanc.

4 salmon fillets (6 to 8 ounces each)

1 cup white wine

1 pound fettuccine

½ cup heavy cream

Salt and freshly ground black pepper

Sauce:

2½ cups white wine

6 shallots, finely chopped

½ pound (2 sticks) unsalted butter, cut into 1-tablespoon pieces, at room temperature

Juice and zest of ½ lemon

2 tablespoons chopped chives

3 tablespoons heavy cream

½ pound asparagus, peeled and blanched

Wash the salmon and place it in a sauté pan or skillet just large enough to hold the fillets. Add the wine and bring it to a boil. When the wine reaches a boil, turn the fish over gently with a spatula, cover the pan with parchment paper, and place it in a 450-degree oven. Check after 5 minutes. Depending on thickness, the fish will be ready in 5 to 8 minutes. Remove it and keep warm.

Cook the fettuccine al dente, drain, and add ½ cup cream. Season with salt and pepper to taste.

To make the sauce: Combine the white wine and shallots in a small saucepan; reduce to ¼ cup liquid. Turn the heat to very low and add the butter, 2 tablespoons at a time, whisking so each addition is melted before the next one is added. Do not let the sauce come to a boil or it will separate and thin out. When all the butter is added, add the lemon juice and zest, chives, and cream. Season with salt and pepper to taste.

To assemble: Place a salmon fillet in the center of each plate with a cross of asparagus on top of each. Place noodles to either side, and top the fish with the sauce.

Salmon with Asparagus Sauce

Serves 6 to 8

BRUCE LEFAVOUR, Rose et LeFavour   What could signify the epitome of spring more than the light green tint from this asparagus cream sauce, topped with a steak of bright orange salmon. This is an easy dish, and is elegant when served. The flavors of the salmon and asparagus work in total harmony, with neither dominating and the combination bringing out the best qualities of both.

Wine choice: French Pouilly Fumé or Sancerre.

1½ pounds fresh asparagus

8 tablespoons (1 stick) unsalted butter

2 cups heavy cream

Salt and freshly ground white pepper to taste

6 to 8 salmon steaks, ¾ inch thick

Wash the asparagus well and snap off and discard the white root ends. Cut the stalks in half and plunge the top halves into a pot of boiling salted water. Cook the asparagus until limp, and drain well. Place it in a food processor fitted with a steel blade, and purée with half the butter for 2 to 3 minutes, scraping the sides of the bowl from time to time.

Chop half the bottom halves into ½-inch pieces, saving the remainder for another use. Simmer them slowly with the cream in a small heavy saucepan for 20 minutes. Strain, pressing gently to extract the liquid. Just before serving, whisk together the asparagus butter and cream. Heat slowly to just below the boiling point and correct the seasoning.

Salt and pepper the salmon steaks. Melt the remaining butter in a heavy skillet, and when the butter begins to brown, add the salmon and cook it for 30 seconds to 1 minute, depending on its thickness. Turn for another minute for rare salmon. If you wish to cook the salmon more thoroughly, reduce the heat and sauté longer. Serve the steaks on top of the sauce, and garnish with additional asparagus spears.

Note: The sauce can be prepared up to 4 or 5 hours in advance, and then reheated just before serving. LeFavour likes his steaks to remain rare, but I think that's a matter of personal taste.

Red Snapper with Black Pepper

Serves 6

LYDIA SHIRE, Seasons   We know steak can be pounded with coarsely crushed black pepper; the same method adds tremendous flavor to fish. The dish then can become more complex, with some tropical overtones, if lively lime juice is added to the sauce to cool down the pepper, and a garnish is prepared of plantains and avocado for a contrasting sweet flavor with the fish.

Wine choice: French white Rhône such as Hermitage Blanc, or California Chardonnay.

6 red-snapper fillets (8 to 10 ounces each)

Salt

2 cloves crushed garlic

3 tablespoons fresh thyme

4 tablespoons coarsely crushed black peppercorns

3 sticks unsalted butter

Sauce:

2 cups dry white wine

1 tablespoon peppercorns

3 chopped shallots

2 sprigs thyme

½ teaspoon champagne vinegar

Juice from 3 limes

Salt and white pepper

Garnish:

1 plantain or 2 green bananas

1 tablespoon unsalted butter

2 ripe avocados

Sprinkle both sides of the fillets with salt and rub the skin side with garlic and thyme. Dredge the skin side of the fillets with the pepper, pressing so the peppercorns adhere to the skin. ·

Heat 3 tablespoons of the butter in a large skillet over high heat, and when it starts to smoke sear the fillets, skin side down. Turn over onto the flesh side and place the skillet in a preheated 450-degree oven for 5 minutes, with a pat of fresh butter on top of each. Remove and keep warm.

For the sauce: Bring the wine, peppercorns, shallots, and thyme to a boil, and reduce the mixture over high heat until it is a syrupy consistency and only about 3 tablespoons of liquid remain. Beat in the remaining butter, about 2 tablespoons at a time, whisking constantly and never letting the sauce reach a boil. Add the vinegar and lime juice, and adjust the seasoning with salt and white pepper. Strain the sauce and keep it warm over hot water or in a Thermos bottle.

Peel and slice the plantain or bananas into ¼-inch slices and sauté them in hot butter until golden. Peel and slice the avocado into 12 wedges.

Place the fish on the plates skin side up and garnish with plantain and avocado. Spoon sauce around it.

Red Snapper en Papillote

Serves 4

SUSUMU FUKUI, La Petite Chaya   When guests open up these puffed packages and find the surprise of savory wild mushrooms, bacon, and potatoes, the response is first surprise and then delight. The flavor is enhanced by the rich beurre blanc sauce.

Wine choice: French white Burgundy.

4 red snapper fillets (6 ounces each)

Salt and pepper

6 tablespoons unsalted butter

1 tablespoon salad oil

1 cup ½-inch potato cubes (potatoes peeled)

4 strips bacon, cut into julienne slices

1 teaspoon minced garlic

¼ pound fresh shiitake mushrooms, stemmed and sliced

¼ pound shimeji mushrooms, stemmed and left whole (or more shiitake)

6 mushrooms, stemmed and quartered

2 teaspoons chopped shallots

½ cup white wine

Pinch of cayenne pepper

4 heart-shaped pieces of parchment paper, large enough to enclose the fish

Sprinkle the fillets with salt and pepper. Heat 2 tablespoons of the butter with the oil in a sauté pan or large skillet over medium heat. Sauté the fillets for 2 minutes on a side, and carefully remove them from the pan with a spatula. Pour off any accumulated liquid.

Add the potatoes and bacon to the pan, and sauté them until the bacon is crisp. Remove the potatoes and bacon with a slotted spoon, and add the garlic and all the mushrooms to the pan. Sauté over medium heat until the mushrooms are cooked and brown.

In a small saucepan, cook the shallots in white wine, and reduce until almost completely dry. Add a few drops of water, and then beat in the remaining butter, a few teaspoons at a time. Season with salt, pepper, and cayenne.

Cut heart shapes of parchment paper large enough so a fillet will fit on half a heart, with ½-inch edge uncovered. Place a piece of fish on each. Spoon some of the vegetables onto each, and top with the sauce. Fold over the parchment, and beginning at the point of the heart, crimp the edges together, twisting as you go around so it is tightly closed.

Place the packages on a cookie sheet and put in a 450-degree oven until they are puffed and brown, about 7 minutes. Serve immediately while still puffed up.

Note: The packages can be prepared up to 8 hours in advance and stored in the refrigerator. Let them sit for 30 minutes at room temperature before baking.

Hot and Sour Squid

Serves 3 or 4 as an entrée, 5 or 6
as part of a multi-course meal

BARBARA TROPP, China Moon The tender squid, crunchy vegetables, and savory sauce make this a dish of exquisite combinations, and the vegetables also add pretty color accents. The sauce is spicy, but the combination of garlic, ginger, and black beans with the pepper give it a complex and extremely interesting taste, in which no one flavor dominates.

Wine choice: California Zinfandel or French Beaujolais Villages.

1 pound squid

Aromatics:

1 tablespoon finely minced fresh ginger

1 tablespoon finely minced garlic

2 tablespoons Chinese salted black beans

¼ teaspoon dried red-pepper flakes

Liquids:

½ cup rich unsalted chicken stock (page 160)

2½ tablespoons soy sauce

2 tablespoons Chinese rice wine or dry sherry

2½ tablespoons white vinegar

¼ teaspoon sugar

2½ cups water

3 or 4 tablespoons corn or peanut oil

½ pound trimmed and peeled carrots, cut into thin diagonal slices a scant ⅛ inch thick

¾ pound slender zucchini, cut into coins ¼ inch thick

1 cup red bell pepper squares (¾ inch)

1 tablespoon cornstarch dissolved in 1½ tablespoons cold stock

Cut the cluster of squid tentacles above the eyes, then squeeze to remove, and discard, the pealike brain. Reserve the tentacles. Pin the tail end on your cutting board, and draw the back of your cleaver or chef's knife along the body of the squid from the tail to the head, squeezing out the innards.

Reach inside the body and pull the quill free, then pull off the outer membrane. Cut the cleaned body sac into even rings ½ inch wide, then flush the rings and tentacles clean with cool water and drain.

Combine the aromatics on a saucer, and combine the liquids in a small bowl. In a 1-quart saucepan bring 2½ cups of water to a simmer.

Heat a wok or large, heavy skillet over high heat until it is hot enough to evaporate a bead of water on contact. Reduce the heat to medium-high, add the oil and swirl to glaze the pan. When it is hot enough to sizzle a pinch of ginger, add the aromatics and stir-fry them until fragrant, about 30 seconds, adjusting the heat so they foam without scorching. Add the carrots, toss to combine, and cook halfway through, about 1 minute. Add the zucchini, toss well to glaze, then add the bell pepper and toss to combine, drizzling a bit more oil into the side of the pan if it seems dry. Give the liquids a stir, add them to the pot, and bring the contents to a simmer, tossing to blend. Cover and simmer to complete cooking the vegetables, about 1 minute. They should remain crisp.

While the vegetables simmer, blanch the squid until the flesh turns white and the tentacles curl, about 5 seconds. Drain. When the vegetables are nearly done, turn off the heat. Stir the cornstarch mixture to recombine, add it to the pan, and stir until the sauce turns glossy, about 20 seconds. Fold in the drained squid and serve at once.

Brook Trout Pan-Fried with Black Walnuts

Serves 6

BRADLEY OGDEN, The Campton Place Hotel   There's an earthy heartiness to the flavor of black walnuts that goes beautifully with the fish, adding even more crunch to the cornmeal coating, and coming through in each bite with the sauce. The fish is crispy and light, with the hint of nut flavor, and the sauce is rich and thoroughly delicious.

Wine choice: California Chardonnay.

12 fresh brook trout (4 to 6 ounces each)

4 cups milk

3 tablespoons kosher salt

2 tablespoons white pepper

1 teaspoon Tabasco

Black-walnut flour:

2 cups black-walnut pieces, ground fine in a food processor fitted with a steel blade

1½ cups yellow cornmeal

½ cup all-purpose flour

2 tablespoons kosher salt

1 teaspoon freshly ground black pepper

For frying:

1½ cups clarified butter or cooking oil

Sauce:

2 sticks unsalted butter, cut into chunks

2 cups black-walnut pieces

Juice of 3 lemons

1 cup fresh parsley, chopped

2 tablespoons kosher salt

1 teaspoon freshly ground black pepper

Clean the trout and remove the head, fins, tails, and back-bones. Soak the fish overnight in milk mixed with salt, white pepper, and Tabasco.

Combine the ground nuts, cornmeal, flour, salt, and pepper, and mix well.

Place the clarified butter or cooking oil in 2 large skillets. Heat until it is very hot and then turn down to a medium flame. Dredge the trout with the black-walnut flour and coat them evenly. Place in the skillets and cook until golden brown on both sides. Remove and drain on paper toweling. Keep warm.

For the sauce: Remove the excess grease from one of the pans. Add the butter and brown the black walnuts in it. Add the lemon juice, parsley, salt, and pepper, and whisk until all are well combined.

To serve, arrange 2 trout on each plate, and spoon the sauce across the center of each fish.

Whitefish with Ginger and Oriental Vegetables

Serves 4

JACKIE ETCHEBER, Jackie's   This way of preparing whitefish combines the use of Chinese ingredients and flavors in a very Western method. The result is a subtle blend of crunchy Chinese vegetables and ginger with a very delicate overall taste from the fish. It also has a beautiful appearance, with tiny baby corn and green snow peas making it colorful.

Wine choice: Alsatian Gewürztraminer or French Pouilly Fumé or Sancerre.

4 whitefish fillets (8 ounces each)

1 can water chestnuts (10 ounces)

1 can baby corn (10 ounces) (available at Oriental groceries)

1 can bamboo shoots (10 ounces)

6 scallions, white and green parts sliced thin

4 ounces fresh ginger, peeled and cut into a fine julienne

½ cup sesame oil

¼ cup soy sauce

6 tablespoons dry white wine

½ pound snow peas

Place the fish fillets in a buttered baking dish. Boil the water chestnuts, baby corn, and bamboo shoots in boiling water for 30 seconds to remove the canned taste. Drain and slice the water chestnuts and bamboo shoots, if whole.

Top the fish with the water chestnuts, bamboo shoots, corn, scallions, ginger, and a mixture of ¼ cup of the sesame oil, the soy sauce, and the white wine.

Cut the snow peas into a fine julienne and blanch them in a pot of boiling salted water for 30 seconds. Drain them and immediately put them in ice water to stop the cooking action. Drain them again and set aside.

Place the fish in a preheated 450-degree oven, and check after 5 minutes. The fish should be cooked but still moist. Remove it from the oven, divide the vegetables onto the plates, along with the fish, and top with julienned snow peas. Heat the remaining sesame oil, and drizzle it over the fish.

Note: The dish can be assembled 4 or 5 hours in advance and refrigerated. Add a few minutes of cooking time to compensate for the coldness of the pan and ingredients.

Chicken Breasts with Sweet Garlic Sauce and Garlic Flan

Serves 6

JEAN-LOUIS PALLADIN, Jean-Louis at Watergate When poached to remove its pungency, garlic becomes sweet and almost nutlike, and those are the flavors that come through. The addition of poached garlic to the flan, as well as in the sauce, unifies the meal and shows how the garlic complements the creamy texture of a custard. There's a richness to the dish that elevates the simple chicken breasts to elegant dinner-party fare.

Wine choice: California Sauvignon Blanc.

6 whole chicken breasts

2 heads garlic, cloves peeled

1½ cups consommé, beef stock, or veal stock (pages 160 and 161)

½ cup heavy cream

1 egg

Salt and pepper to taste

4 tablespoons unsalted butter

6 tablespoons fond de veau (see note)

Bone and skin the chicken breasts, removing all visible fat and tendons. Pound them to a uniform thickness and set aside.

In a 2-quart saucepan, bring a large quantity of salted water to a boil. Add the peeled garlic cloves and simmer for 20 minutes. Drain them and set aside.

Then place the garlic in the consommé and simmer for an additional 10 minutes. Remove garlic from consommé.

For the flan, purée half the garlic with ½ cup of the consommé, the cream, egg, salt, and pepper. Divide the mixture among buttered individual ramekins, and set them in a pan with 1 to 2 inches of hot water. Cook for 15 minutes at 325 degrees, then reduce the temperature to 225 degrees for 20 minutes, or until a knife or cake tester inserted in the center comes out clean.

In a large sauté pan or skillet, melt the butter until sizzling. Add the chicken breasts and sauté them quickly until slightly brown but not overcooked. Remove them from the pan and keep them warm. Deglaze the pan with the remaining consommé. Purée the remaining garlic, add it to the pan with the fond de veau, and simmer for 15 minutes to reduce the liquid.

Serve the chicken breasts with a small flan in the center of the plate and the chicken breast halves on either side. Spoon the sauce over both the chicken and the flan.

Note: Fond de veau is a reduction of unsalted veal stock, which gives sauces a great intensity of flavor. Once made, cubes of it keep almost indefinitely in the freezer, and once you've tasted how it enhances a sauce or soup you'll think it's worth the trouble to make it.

The sauce and flan can be prepared a day in advance and kept covered with plastic wrap in the refrigerator. The flan should be reheated, covered, in a 275-degree oven, and the sauce will reheat as it deglazes the pan after the chicken breasts are sautéed.

Chicken Sauté

Serves 8 as an appetizer, 4 to 6 as an entrée

ANNE GREER, Verandah at the Anatole Hotel   This is either a fresher and lighter version of creamed chicken, or a Westernized version of a Chinese stir-fry. However you view it, it's delicious. The chicken has a wonderful flavor from being marinated in the dressing, and the vegetables add beautiful color as well as crunchy texture. It can be done in a matter of minutes, and the final sprinkling of dill is a crowning glory.

Wine choice: French Pouilly Fumé or Alsatian Gewürztraminer.

4 whole chicken breasts

2 tablespoons chopped fresh ginger

3 tablespoons white-wine vinegar

½ cup vegetable oil

Salt and pepper to taste

1 tablespoon Dijon mustard

1 teaspoon sugar

1 tablespoon minced fresh herbs, such as a mixture of thyme, oregano, basil, and tarragon (optional)

2 red bell peppers, roasted

3 tablespoons unsalted butter

1 clove garlic, peeled

2 cups snow peas, washed and stringed

1 English cucumber, peeled and cut into julienne strips, or 2 regular cucumbers, peeled, seeded, and julienned

Juice of 1 lemon

2 tablespoons snipped fresh dill

Salt and pepper to taste

2 to 4 tablespoons heavy cream

Skin and bone the chicken breasts, removing all fat and tendons. Pound them lightly to an even thickness, and cut them into strips. Combine with the ginger and a vinaigrette dressing made by whisking together the vinegar, oil, salt, pepper, mustard, sugar, and herbs, if used. Marinate the chicken in the dressing for 2 hours, covered, in the refrigerator.

To roast the peppers, place them in a 500-degree oven, turning frequently, until the skin is black and charred, about 15 minutes. Remove them from the oven, wrap them in a kitchen towel, and allow them to sit for 15 minutes or until cool enough to handle. Peel away the skin and wash away the seeds. Cut the peppers into strips.

Heat 2 tablespoons of the butter in a large sauté pan or wok. Drain the chicken on paper towels and pat it dry or it will not brown. Pick off any pieces of ginger clinging to the chicken pieces. Sauté the chicken and whole garlic clove in the hot butter for 2 minutes, or until it is cooked but still very tender. Remove it with a slotted spoon and place it in a bowl. Discard the garlic. Melt the remaining 1 tablespoon of butter in the pan and add the vegetables. Sauté them for 1 to 2 minutes, making sure the snow peas and cucumbers remain crisp.

Return the chicken to the pan, add the lemon juice, dill, salt and pepper to taste, and enough cream to make a light sauce. Heat through and serve immediately.

Chicken Stir-Fry with Raisins and Sambuca Mayonnaise

Serves 6

JIM HALLER, The Blue Strawbery The flavors in this quick and easy stir-fry, with the slightly sweet raisins balanced by the heady Sambuca in the simple mayonnaise sauce, make this one of my favorites. In addition to serving it as an entrée, I've also done it as a warm salad, mounding the chicken on a bed of mixed greens, and garnishing it with fruit.

Wine choice: California Chardonnay.

3 whole large chicken breasts

1 cup raisins

4 tablespoons olive oil

½ cup chopped scallions, both green and white portions

¼ cup white wine

Hot Sambuca mayonnaise:

1 cup homemade or good-quality commercial mayonnaise

¼ cup minced scallions, green and white portions

1 egg yolk

Juice of 1 lemon

4 tablespoons Sambuca

1 tablespoon olive oil

1 teaspoon minced tarragon

Salt and pepper to taste

Garnish:

Chopped herbs or strips of roasted red bell peppers

Bone and skin the chicken breasts, removing all fat and tendons. Pound them lightly to an even thickness, and cut them into slices or squares. Set them aside.

Cover the raisins with hot water and soak for 30 minutes to soften, then drain.

Heat the olive oil in a sauté pan, skillet, or wok until a round of scallion will sizzle. Add the chicken and scallions and stir-fry for 30 seconds over high heat, stirring constantly. Add the raisins and white wine and continue to cook for 1 minute over high heat. Scoop the mixture into a serving dish and set aside.

In a small saucepan, combine all the sauce ingredients. Whisk them until well blended, and set the pan over low heat to warm, stirring constantly. Do not let the sauce come to a boil or it will separate. If it does, pour it slowly into a blender or food processor fitted with a steel blade, motor running, until smooth.

Stir the sauce into the chicken, and garnish with chopped herbs or strips of roasted red pepper.

Breast of Chicken in Lemon Sauce

Serves 6

JEAN-LOUIS PALLADIN, Jean-Louis at Watergate Put aside any preconceptions about lemon chicken; this is rich and intensely flavored from the stock, and tomatoes are an unexpected ingredient. While there's nothing difficult about any of the procedures in this dish, the stock does have to cook for hours. But one batch yields enough to serve the entrée at least three times, so freeze the remainder, and subsequent servings can be on the table in a matter of minutes.

Wine choice: California Sauvignon Blanc or Chardonnay.

3 chickens (about 4 pounds each)

2 onions, unpeeled and quartered

2 cloves garlic, unpeeled

4 calves' feet

5½ quarts water

2 leeks, washed well under cold running water, with white part cut into 2-inch sections

1 stalk celery, cut into 2-inch pieces

6 carrots, scrubbed and cut into 2-inch pieces

10 ripe Italian plum tomatoes, cut into quarters

1¼ cups freshly squeezed lemon juice (about 8 lemons)

⅓ cup sugar

Salt and freshly ground black pepper

1 tablespoon peanut oil

Wash and dry the chickens inside and out. With a boning knife, cut along the breast bone, pull away the skin, and remove the breast meat. Pull out the tendons, and set the meat aside.

In a large roasting pan, place the chicken carcasses, including the legs and wings, with the onions, garlic, and calves' feet. Roast in a preheated 350-degree oven for 1 hour. Remove the thighs and drumsticks, reserving the meat for another use, and return the remainder to the oven for 1 hour more.

Remove the pan from the oven, pour off any fat that has accumulated, crack the bones, and place the meat and bones in a stockpot. Deglaze the roasting pan with 1 quart of water. Pour it into the stockpot and add 4½ more quarts of water. Add the leeks, celery, carrots, and tomatoes, and simmer the mixture over low heat for 4 to 6 hours. Strain and return the stock to the heat and reduce for another hour. You should have about 3 cups of liquid remaining.

In a saucepan, combine the lemon juice and sugar, and boil until the liquid is reduced to ½ cup. Add the stock reduction to the lemon-caramel sauce and simmer for 15 minutes. Season with salt and pepper to taste and strain.

Season the chicken breasts with salt and pepper. Heat the peanut oil in a sauté pan or skillet and add the breasts, sautéing over medium heat for about 5 minutes to a side. Cover with 1 cup of the hot sauce and serve.

Note: The sauce can be prepared up to 2 days in advance and refrigerated. Freeze the remaining sauce.

Breast of Duck with Savory Olive Tarts

Serves 4

LYDIA SHIRE, Seasons   Oriental ingredients are now becoming part of every cook's larder, since so many of them are called for in distinctly non-Chinese meals. The flavors from the garlic, ginger, and sesame penetrate the flesh of the duck, and the crisp pastry filled with succulent olives pairs well with the rich duck breast.

Wine choice: French red Rhône, such as Hermitage or Côte Rôtie, California Zinfandel, or Italian Barolo or Barbera.

1 cup imported soy sauce

1 head garlic, with the cloves left unpeeled and crushed

2 tablespoons grated ginger root

¼ cup sherry

¼ cup sesame oil

4 duck breasts (8 ounces each)

1 tablespoon vegetable oil

The tarts:

1 cup assorted ripe olives, such as oil cured, Greek, etc. (do not use canned olives)

⅓ cup extra-virgin olive oil

Juice of 1 lemon

1 tablespoon chopped fresh oregano

3 cloves garlic

1 small onion

¼ pound puff pastry (frozen can be used)

1 tomato, peeled, seeded, and chopped

Make a marinade of the soy sauce, garlic, ginger, sherry, and sesame oil. Leave the skin on the duck breasts, and slash it in 3 or 4 places. Put the breasts in the marinade for 2 hours. Do not marinate longer. To a heavy sauté pan add 1 tablespoon oil and put it over medium-high heat. Lay the duck breasts in the pan, skin side down, and cook until the fat has been rendered from the skin and the skin is black and crispy, about 5 to 7 minutes. Turn the breasts over for 30 seconds and remove them from the pan. Allow them to rest, and keep warm.

To make the tarts: Marinate the olives, sliced and pitted, in olive oil, lemon juice, and oregano for at least 1 hour. Chop the garlic and onion fine, and sauté them briefly in a few tablespoons of the oil from the marinade.

Roll the pastry ¼ inch thick. (Allow it to defrost well first if frozen.) Make 4 rectangles of puff pastry 2½ inches by 4 inches, building up a ½-inch border. Bake them in a 350-degree oven for 25 to 30 minutes, or until golden and flaky.

Add the garlic and onions to the olives and divide them among the shells. Top them with a little chopped tomato and return them to the oven to warm through, along with the duck breasts if they have cooled.

To serve: Slice the duck breasts on the diagonal into 5 slices each. Strain the marinade and heat it, simmering for 2 minutes, to use as a sauce around the meat. Serve the duck with the olive tarts, and garnish the plates with some fresh herbs.

Note: The puff-pastry shells can be done a day in advance and kept in a dry place.

Fried Corncakes with Duck Breasts and Broccoli in Pinot Noir Sauce

Serves 6 as an appetizer or 4 as an entrée

MICHAEL ROBERTS, Trumps   In this recipe, the flavor lives up to the dramatic presentation, with bright green broccoli and rich red duck and sauce perched on pale yellow corncakes. It's very easy to prepare, and most of the work can be done well in advance. The result is a hearty combination, while not overly heavy.

Wine choice: French red Burgundy or Bordeaux, or California Cabernet Sauvignon.

Corncakes:

2 cups yellow cornmeal

5 to 6 cups water

1 teaspoon salt

¼ teaspoon black pepper

Sauce:

1 cup California Pinot Noir

4 cups clear duck or chicken stock (page 160)

1 cup heavy cream

Salt and pepper

6 to 8 stalks broccoli

3 whole duck breasts (many supermarkets now sell the breasts frozen)

½ cup clarified butter

For the corncakes: In a tall-sided pot, slowly whisk the cornmeal into the cold water. Cook over a low flame, stirring constantly, until the mixture thickens and pulls away from the sides of the pot. It should take at least 20 minutes, and the longer it cooks the better. Add salt and pepper, and turn the mush out onto a buttered 9-by-13-inch sheet pan or baking pan. Chill, and cut out the corncakes with a 3-inch cookie cutter. You should have 12.

For the sauce: In a saucepan, reduce the Pinot Noir by half. Add the stock and reduce the total by two-thirds. Add the cream and reduce until the sauce is thick enough to coat the back of a spoon. Add salt and pepper to taste, depending on how salty the stock was.

Remove the breasts from 3 ducks, if the entire birds were purchased. Remove the skin from the breasts and cut it into small strips. Fry the strips in a skillet until they have rendered their fat and the skin is crisp. Drain the cracklings on paper towels and reserve. Reserve the fat for another use, or for frying the corncakes in place of the clarified butter. Cut the duck breasts into strips, and sauté them briefly in a little butter. Set aside.

Cut the broccoli flowerets off the stalks, separating them into bite-size pieces. Reserve the stalks for another use. Blanch the flowerets for 1 minute in boiling salted water, and place them immediately in ice water to keep their color bright green. Drain them on paper towels.

To assemble: Fry the corncakes in clarified butter or duck fat until crisp and golden brown on the outside. Arrange 2 in the center of each plate. Heat the strips of duck breast in the finished sauce, and arrange them in a circle around the corncakes. Repeat this procedure with the broccoli. Bring the sauce to a boil and spoon it onto the plates. Garnish with the crispy duck skin.

Note: Down to the assembly of the dish, all procedures can be done up to a day in advance and the ingredients kept refrigerated.

Picnic-Inspired Quails

Serves 4

LAWRENCE FORGIONE, An American Place   When I ordered this at An American Place, the elegant plate placed before me bore no resemblance to picnic fare I'd prepared, but eating it provided the answer to the curious name. The quail breasts were breaded with crunchy potato chips, and the nest in the center topped with tiny quail eggs was a mélange of pickled vegetables. The dish was exquisite, with sections of fried quail breast and sweetly marinated grilled legs alternating around the vegetables. The flavors more than live up to the dramatic appearance.

Wine choice: California Sauvignon Blanc or French Bordeaux or Beaujolais.

8 fresh quails (5 ounces each)

¼ cup honey

2 tablespoons cider vinegar

4 ounces salted potato chips

½ cup white breadcrumbs

Salt and pepper

Flour

2 eggs

½ cup light cream

Sauce:

¼ cup oil

Reserved quail carcasses

½ cup chopped onions

½ cup Hudson Valley apple wine

1 tablespoon stoneground mustard

3 cups quail stock, or dark poultry stock (a mixture of duck and chicken stock), or just chicken stock (page 160)

1 teaspoon lemon juice

2 tablespoons unsalted butter

The vegetables:

1 half-sour pickle

1 garlic pickle

4 pickled green tomatoes

2 pickled red peppers (or 1 jar pimentos)

4 teaspoons chopped parsley

1 cup sauerkraut, drained well

2 tablespoons vegetable oil

2 teaspoons white-wine vinegar

4 to 32 quail eggs, hard-cooked and peeled (optional)

1 cup oil

Remove the leg and thigh sections from each quail with a pair of small scissors, and marinate the quarters in the honey and vinegar.

Bone the quail breasts by slitting along the breast bone and removing the wings. Pull off the 2 breast sections, and chop the bones for the sauce.

Finely grind the potato chips in a food processor fitted with a steel blade, and mix them with the bread crumbs. Season each quail breast with salt and pepper, then dust with flour. Mix the eggs and cream, and dip each breast section into the mixture, then roll in the crumbs, patting them on evenly. Until you are ready to use them, refrigerate, covered with plastic wrap.

For the sauce: In a heavy 2-quart saucepan, heat the oil to smoky hot. Add the chopped quail carcasses and brown them evenly, stirring frequently. Lower the heat to medium, add the onions, and sauté them for 5 minutes. Pour the grease out of the pan, and add the apple wine and mustard. Add the stock and cook over medium heat until the mixture has reduced by half and has a light, syrupy consistency. Strain through a fine strainer, add the lemon juice, and whisk in the butter.

For the garnish: Cut the pickles, green tomatoes, and red peppers into fine julienne strips. Add the remaining ingredients except the quail eggs (which are a lovely touch but rather expensive) and toss to warm them in a sauté pan over medium heat.

To finish the dish: Drain the leg sections from the marinade and grill them over a fire or under a broiler until golden brown. Heat 1 cup oil to 350 degrees and fry the pieces of breaded quail breast. Remove them with a slotted spoon and drain them on paper toweling.

Arrange a mound of warmed pickled vegetables in the center of each plate, and in each nestle quail eggs, if used. Spoon the sauce around the vegetables and place alternating pieces of breast and leg, 4 each, in a circle around the vegetables.

Note: Everything up to the final cooking of the quail can be done a day in advance.

Squab with Oysters and Zinfandel

Serves 4

JASPER WHITE, Restaurant Jasper   The richness of the squab and oysters tie the two together, and the nest of greens holding the squab legs makes a perfect foil for the other half of the dish. The red Zinfandel sauce is delicious, and tastes very different when eaten with the squab than with the oysters.

Wine choice: California Zinfandel or Cabernet Sauvignon.

4 small Belgian endives

1 cup wild rice

2½ cups water

Salt

4 squabs, about 1 pound each

½ cup vegetable oil

1 onion, roughly chopped

1 carrot, roughly chopped

1 stalk celery, roughly diced

2 cloves garlic, peeled

1 bottle Zinfandel

2 cups veal or chicken stock (page 160)

½ cup clarified unsalted butter

Freshly ground black pepper

12 fresh oysters, shucked

1 cup fresh breadcrumbs

2 tablespoons chopped parsley or chives

Melted butter

2 tablespoons unsalted butter

Vinaigrette dressing (page 183)

Separate the endives into spears and set them aside.

To cook the wild rice: Wash it in a strainer under cold running water for 3 minutes, or until the water runs clear. Place it in a heavy 1-quart saucepan and add 2½ cups water and ½ teaspoon salt. Bring the water to a boil and simmer the rice, covered, for 45 minutes to 1 hour, stirring occasionally. Turn off the heat and leave the pan covered for 30 minutes. Fluff the rice with a fork, and if it is still hard, place it in a preheated 300-degree oven for 15 minutes, adding water if dry. Set it aside and keep warm.

Cut the leg and thigh sections off the squabs, leaving the bones in. Peel the skin off the body and carefully remove the breasts, leaving no skin or bones attached. Chop the carcasses for the sauce.

Brown the bones in ¼ cup of the vegetable oil for 5 minutes, then add the onion, carrot, celery, and garlic, and sauté them until browned, about 10 minutes. Add 2 cups of Zinfandel and the stock. Simmer slowly, uncovered, for 1 hour. Strain, pressing to extract all the liquid, and set the liquid aside. You should have about 1½ cups of sauce.

Heat the clarified butter in a sauté pan or 14-inch skillet and sauté the squab pieces, seasoning them with salt and pepper. Start with the skin side down, and after 1 minute turn the breasts over. After another minute, remove the breasts and turn the legs over. Allow the breasts to rest while the legs finish cooking. Remove the legs, set all the pieces aside, and keep warm.

Dredge the shucked oysters in the remaining oil, then roll them in breadcrumbs seasoned with salt, pepper, and parsley. Drizzle them with a little melted butter and broil them in a pan in a preheated broiler until they are golden, about 2 minutes. Be careful not to overcook. Set them aside.

Deglaze the sauté pan with ½ cup of the Zinfandel, add the sauce, and bring it to a boil. Remove from the heat and stir in a 2-tablespoon lump of unsalted butter.

Carve the squab breasts into slices across the grain, and get all the ingredients ready.

To serve: Put a few spoonfuls of sauce in the center of each plate, and spoon the wild rice at the top of the plate. Alternate squab breast slices and oysters over the sauce. Serve the endive, dressed with vinaigrette, on side plates with the squab legs on top of the salads.

Note: Up to sautéing the squab and broiling the oysters, this dish can be done as long as a day in advance, with the components kept covered separately in the refrigerator. Reheat the rice and sauce over low heat.

Lamb with Fennel and Young Vegetables

Serves 6

BRUCE LEFAVOUR, Rose et LeFavour The baby vegetables scattered around rare slices of lamb, and the fresh flavor of fennel in the sauce, make this a very special lamb dish. I love cooking with baby vegetables, and if you can't find them, carve their larger versions into smaller pieces of the same shape.

Wine choice: French Bordeaux or California Cabernet Sauvignon.

3 racks of lamb (6 or 7 chops each)

Fennel Reduction:

⅓ cup white wine

⅓ cup white-wine vinegar

½ teaspoon freshly ground black pepper

3 medium shallots, chopped

¾ fennel bulb, chopped

1½ tablespoons Pernod or Ricard

Vegetables:

18 baby carrots

18 baby turnips

6 to 10 very small red potatoes

6 baby leeks

12 sugar snap peas or snow peas

18 red or white pearl onions

Carefully bone the racks, and trim all fat and sinews from the cylinders of meat. Reserve them at room temperature, and save the bones and scraps for other lamb recipes requiring a lamb-reduction sauce.

In a heavy saucepan, combine the wine, vinegar, pepper, shallots, chopped fennel, and Pernod. Reduce over high heat until almost all the liquid has evaporated. Set aside.

Peel the carrots and turnips, leaving 1 inch of the stems attached. Wash but do not peel the potatoes (but cut them in half if more than 1½ inches in diameter). Cut the leeks to 4 inches, and make one cut in each from the base to the top. Pull the leeks apart and wash them well under running water. Then trim the bases, but not so much that the leeks fall apart. String the sugar snap or snow peas.

Plunge the onions, without peeling, into a quart of boiling water and boil 1 minute. Drain the onions, and leave them in the strainer until they are cool enough to handle. Trim off the root ends, and squeeze the onions so they pop out. Set aside.

Steam the potatoes in a vegetable steamer until tender, and set aside. Bring 1 quart of salted water or vegetable stock (the water in which other vegetables have been cooked) to a boil. Add the carrots, turnips, and leeks, and simmer for about 8 to 12 minutes, depending on the sizes of the vegetables, until they are just tender. Scoop out with a slotted spoon, and set them aside, tossing them with salt, pepper, and 1 tablespoon of the butter. Reserve the water or stock.

Blanch the sugar snap peas or snow peas in boiling water for 45 seconds, and refresh them by plunging them into ice water to stop the cooking action. Set aside.

Salt and freshly ground white pepper

2 sticks (½ pound) unsalted butter, at room temperature

¼ fennel bulb, trimmed and finely chopped

3 egg yolks

1½ tablespoons chopped fennel leaves

Dash of cayenne pepper

2 tablespoons unsalted butter

Chop the remaining portion of the fennel, and drop it into the water in which the vegetables were cooked. As soon as the water returns to a boil, strain out the fennel and set it aside.

Place the fennel reduction in the top of a double boiler. Whisk in the egg yolks, and then gradually add the remaining butter, whisking constantly, as you would for a hollandaise. When all the butter is incorporated, strain the sauce into a bowl, pushing on the solids to extract all the liquid. Add salt, pepper, fennel leaves, and cayenne. Add the blanched chopped fennel and keep the sauce warm.

In a heavy sauté pan, heat 2 tablespoons unsalted butter until it gets very hot and starts to brown. Salt and pepper the lamb and quickly sauté it, rolling and turning it so that it browns. Three to 4 minutes should be sufficient. Place the meat on a carving board and allow it to rest for 5 minutes. Use the time to reheat any vegetables that might have gotten cold. Slice each piece of lamb lengthwise, with the grain, into 6 long slices. Divide the slices on the plates, scatter the vegetables around them, and serve the sauce separately.

Note: The sauce and lamb must be done immediately before serving, but the vegetables can be prepared a day in advance, and kept in plastic bags in the refrigerator. If you are cooking in advance, leave them slightly undercooked, and then reheat them briefly in a vegetable steamer.

Curried Rice Noodles with Minced Pork

Serves 3 or 4 as a main dish, 5 or 6 as part of a multi-course meal

BARBARA TROPP, China Moon   Curry paste, the "secret" to this dish, has a sweet-hot flavor, and it's delicious with the colorful vegetables and other ingredients. This dish is more savory than hot, with the scallion and onion adding additional zip. It's also very easy and quick to prepare, and is an entire meal in itself.

Wine choice: California Zinfandel.

2 tablespoons soy sauce

2 tablespoons Chinese rice wine or dry sherry

1 teaspoon cornstarch

Several grinds of freshly ground black pepper

½ pound freshly ground pork butt

6 ounces wire-thin, dry rice noodles (sold in 4 rectangular "pads" to a package in Chinese markets)

5 tablespoons corn or peanut oil

⅓ cup green and white scallion rounds

⅓ cup thin-sliced arcs of sweet red onions, or ½ cup rounds from bulbs of red scallions

1 tablespoon Chinese rice wine or dry sherry

½ cup tiny-diced carrots

½ cup diced red bell peppers

Liquids:

⅔ cup rich, unsalted chicken stock

1 tablespoon soy sauce

1½ tablespoons Chinese rice wine or dry sherry

2½ tablespoons DawSen's curry paste (an oil-based curry blend, sold bottled in Chinese groceries)

⅛ teaspoon sugar

1 teaspoon Chinese or Japanese sesame oil

Freshly ground black pepper

Fresh cilantro sprigs for garnish

In a food processor fitted with a steel blade, blend the soy sauce, wine, cornstarch, and pepper until smooth. Distribute the pork around the blade, and pulse to combine the marinade with the meat and polish it to a fine consistency. Scrape the meat into a small bowl, seal with plastic wrap pressed directly onto the surface, and set it aside for a few hours at room temperature or overnight in the refrigerator. If it is chilled, bring it to room temperature before cooking.

Cover the noodles with warm water and soak them about 10 minutes, or until supple. Drain in a colander and rinse.

Heat a wok or large, heavy skillet over high heat, until hot enough to evaporate a bead of water. Add 5 tablespoons of oil, reduce the heat to medium-high, and swirl to glaze the pan. When it is hot enough to foam a round of scallion, add the scallions and onions, tossing about 30 seconds, until fragrant. Adjust the heat so they foam without browning. Splash with the wine, tossing to evaporate the alcohol, then add the carrots. Toss 15 seconds, then add the red peppers and toss to mix. Add the pork and toss until it is almost all gray, breaking the meat into small bits. Stir the liquids and sugar and add to the pan; bring to a simmer. Add the noodles, stir to combine, and reduce the heat to low. Cover and cook for 2 minutes, until the liquids are absorbed. Turn off the heat and sprinkle with sesame oil and pepper. Stir and adjust with more pepper if needed. Serve immediately in heated pasta bowls, garnished with fresh coriander.

Steak with Garlic Cream Sauce

Serves 6

SUSUMU FUKUI, La Petite Chaya   This is one of the best sauces I've ever eaten with beef, and I've served it with broiled lamb chops as well. Its flavors from wine and cognac are smoothed out by the garlicky cream, more sweet than sharp since the garlic is roasted. The potatoes are very simple to prepare, and are the perfect creamy balance with the steak.

Wine choice: French red Burgundy.

6 New York strip steaks (10 ounces each)

Salt and freshly ground black pepper to taste

8 cloves garlic, unpeeled

1¼ cups heavy cream

2 pounds boiling potatoes

¼ cup milk

1 clove garlic, minced

6 tablespoons unsalted butter

¼ pound Gruyère cheese, grated

2 tablespoons cognac

¼ cup dry white wine

1½ cups veal stock (page 160)

Sprinkle the steaks with salt and pepper and set them aside at room temperature. Place the garlic cloves on a baking sheet and place them in a 350-degree oven for 10 minutes. When they are cool enough to handle, pop the cloves out of their skins and purée them with ½ cup of the cream. Set aside.

Peel the potatoes and slice them very thin. Cook the potatoes in the milk, the remaining cream, the minced garlic, and 2 tablespoons of the butter for 8 minutes, or until they are tender. Place them in a buttered gratin dish and sprinkle with the cheese. Place the dish under a broiler, about 6 inches from the heat, until the top is brown.

In a sauté pan, heat 4 tablespoons of the butter, and when it is hot add the steaks. Sear them over high heat and cook until medium rare, or to your liking.

Remove the steaks from the pan and keep them warm. Flambé the pan with the cognac, and then deglaze with the wine. Add the veal stock and reduce the mixture by half. Add the garlic cream, simmer for 5 minutes, and adjust the seasoning with salt and pepper.

Serve the steaks with the potatoes and top the steaks with the sauce.

Note: The potatoes can be done a day in advance and reheated in a 300-degree oven, and the garlic can be roasted in advance. The sauce should be done at the last minute.

Peacock Beef

Serves 6

PATRICK O'CONNELL, The Inn at Little Washington One of my favorite Japanese meals is negimaki, rolls of beef around scallions. O'Connell's dish is related to that in appearance, but the flavor is far superior, with an interesting blend of spices in the sauce, which is quite light since the thickness comes from reducing the stock. The medallions look beautiful on the plate, with bright green centers surrounded by the tender beef.

Wine choice: French Côte Rôtie or Hermitage, or a California Cabernet Sauvignon or Zinfandel.

2 pounds beef tenderloin, well trimmed

18 to 24 scallions

½ cup light soy sauce

1 tablespoon finely minced ginger

2 cloves garlic, crushed

¼ teaspoon five-spice powder

2 tablespoons sesame oil

1 cup beef stock (page 160)

2 tablespoons vegetable oil

1 small piece star anise

Slice the beef into 12 ½-inch-thick slices, and place them well apart between 2 slices of waxed paper. With a meat mallet or the bottom of a heavy skillet, pound the beef into thin ovals. Trim the root ends off the scallions and trim the scallions 1 inch above the top of the white part. Place 1½ to 2 scallions along the edge of each slice of beef and roll it up tightly. Secure the rolls with toothpicks or tie them with string, and chill them for at least 1 hour, covered with plastic wrap, in the refrigerator. This may be done up to one day before you proceed with the recipe.

Mix the soy sauce, ginger, garlic, five-spice powder, and sesame oil. Set the mixture aside.

In a small saucepan, bring the stock to a boil and simmer until it is reduced by half. Set aside.

Heat the oil over high heat in a sauté pan or 12-inch skillet. Brush the beef rolls with the soy mixture and sear them, turning with tongs, until they are brown on all sides. Lower the heat to medium and continue to cook and turn for 5 minutes. Remove and repeat with the remainder of the beef. Place the rolls on a heated platter to keep warm. Add the reduced stock, the star anise, and the remaining brushing sauce to the pan, and deglaze.

Slice the beef rolls into medallions on a diagonal and arrange them in a circle on a platter or on plates with some sautéed cucumbers or flowerets of steamed broccoli in the center. Spoon a little of the sauce over the medallions.

Sautéed Veal Steaks with Montana Beef Jerky Sauce

Serves 4

LAWRENCE FORGIONE, An American Place Little did the Indians using beef jerky as a trail food imagine it would become so sophisticated. It has a flavor similar to prosciutto, frequently paired with veal in Italian dishes, and permeates the creamy sauce. The diced red and green peppers add touches of color.

Wine choice: French white Burgundy, such as a Meursault or Montrachet, or a California Chardonnay.

4 veal loin eye steaks (5 ounces each)

Salt and pepper

2 ounces beef jerky, cut into a fine julienne

3 cups rich veal stock (page 160)

4 tablespoons vegetable oil

1 medium onion, sliced

1 teaspoon coarsely ground black pepper

¼ cup white-wine vinegar

½ cup dry white wine

2 cups heavy cream

1 cup cooked chickpeas, drained

1 red pepper, cut into small pieces

1 green pepper, cut into small pieces

Sprinkle the veal steaks with a little salt and pepper on both sides and set them aside. Soak the jerky julienne for 1 hour in 2 cups of the veal stock.

In a sauté pan or 12-inch skillet, heat the oil until smoking hot. Add the veal steaks and cook them until they are evenly browned, about 3 minutes. Turn them over to brown on the other side. When they are brown, remove the steaks to a lightly buttered baking dish and bake them for 5 minutes, or until medium rare, in a preheated 350-degree oven.

Pour off the grease from the sauté pan and add the onion. Sauté until lightly brown, about 5 minutes. Add the black pepper and continue to sauté another minute. Deglaze the pan with the vinegar and reduce it by two-thirds. Add the white wine and the 2 cups of veal stock in which the jerky soaked, reserving the jerky for a garnish. Boil the mixture over high heat until it has reduced to a syrupy consistency, then add the cream and simmer until reduced by one-quarter. The sauce should be thick enough to coat the back of a spoon.

In a small saucepan, simmer the cooked chickpeas in the remaining 1 cup of stock until the stock thickens, about 10 minutes.

Strain the creamy veal sauce into another pan and add the red and green peppers and chickpeas. Bring the sauce to a boil and simmer for 5 minutes, skimming as necessary to remove any foam.

Place a veal steak in the center of each plate, spoon the sauce over it, and garnish with the julienne of jerky.

Note: The dish can be started a few hours in advance, at which time the sauce can be finished and reheated. The chops can be kept at room temperature and placed in the oven for their final baking just prior to serving.

Sweetbreads with Three-Mustard Sauce

Serves 6

PATRICK O'CONNELL, The Inn at Little Washington After serving this recipe to rave reviews from friends who swore they would never eat sweetbreads, it turns out that what they objected to, or thought they did, was the texture. If you weight them, the "lobey" look disappears, but the delicate flavor remains. What makes the dish special is the delicate mustard-laced sauce, and how pretty it looks on the plate, with slices of sweetbread alternating with bright green snow peas like a big flower.

Wine choice: California Chardonnay or Sauvignon Blanc or Alsatian Gewürztraminer.

3 pairs veal sweetbreads (about 3 pounds)

2 quarts chicken stock (page 160)

Salt and pepper

Flour

2 sticks (½ pound) unsalted butter

¾ teaspoon lemon juice

36 snow peas, washed and stringed

Pinch of sugar

12 large fresh mushrooms, sliced

Rinse the sweetbreads and cover them with cold water. Place them in the refrigerator overnight, covered with plastic wrap. The next day, pull off the white membrane encasing the sweetbreads, and the tube connecting the two lobes.

Place the chicken stock in a 2-quart saucepan and bring it to a boil. Add the sweetbreads, turn the heat down to a simmer, and poach them about 10 minutes over medium heat, until the lobes spring back to the touch. Remove the sweetbreads with a slotted spoon and plunge them into a bowl of ice water to stop the cooking action. Rinse them well, place in a colander over a bowl, and set a plate weighted with 2 or 3 soup cans over the sweetbreads. Refrigerate them overnight.

The next day, slice the sweetbreads into thin arcs and sprinkle them lightly with salt and pepper. Dust them with flour and set aside. In a sauté pan or 12-inch skillet, melt 3 tablespoons of the butter over high heat. Add the sweetbreads and sauté them on both sides until golden brown. Repeat until all slices are fried, adding more butter as necessary. Remove them to a warm platter, sprinkle lightly with lemon juice, and keep them warm in a low oven.

Melt 2 tablespoons of the butter in another sauté pan. When the foam starts to subside, add the snow peas and season with a pinch of sugar, ½ teaspoon of salt, and a pinch of pepper. Sauté the peas about 2 minutes over high heat, or until they are glazed and still crisp. Remove them with a slotted spoon and set aside.

Wipe the mushrooms with a damp cloth and slice them thin. Melt 3 tablespoons of the butter in a sauté pan over high heat. Add the mushrooms and season with ½ teaspoon salt and a pinch of pepper. Sauté them about 3 minutes, until they are cooked but still firm. Remove them and set aside.

Mustard sauce:

1 cup Chablis, or other dry white wine

1 shallot, finely minced

1 teaspoon Dijon mustard

1 teaspoon whole-grain mustard

1 teaspoon tarragon mustard

1 cup heavy cream

1 teaspoon cornstarch, dissolved in ¼ cup cold water

½ teaspoon minced garlic

2 tablespoons white-wine vinegar

2 tablespoons white vermouth

2 teaspoons minced scallions

2 teaspoons minced fresh tarragon, or ½ teaspoon dried

1 egg yolk

1 to 2 tablespoons tomato paste

¼ to ½ cup melted butter

Salt and pepper

Pinch of sugar

To make the sauce: In a small saucepan, combine the wine and shallot, and cook over high heat until the liquid has reduced to 2 tablespoons. Stir in the mustards and cream, and bring the mixture to a boil, reducing for 5 minutes over low heat. Add the cornstarch mixture and garlic and return the sauce to a boil, stirring until thickened, and simmer 5 minutes. Set aside.

In another small saucepan, bring the vinegar, vermouth, scallions, and tarragon to a boil, and reduce until 1 tablespoon of liquid remains. Cool it slightly and place with the egg yolk and tomato paste in a blender or food processor fitted with a steel blade. With the motor running, add the hot butter in a very slow stream until the sauce has the consistency of a hollandaise. Mix this sauce with the mustard sauce, whisking until smooth, and season to taste with salt, pepper, and a pinch of sugar.

To assemble: Fan slices of sweetbreads and snow peas like a flower and place some mushrooms in the center. Ladle the sauce around the edge, and pass extra sauce separately.

Note: The sweetbreads can be sliced and seasoned for sautéing up to 6 hours in advance and refrigerated. The sauce can be prepared at the same time and reheated in the top of a double boiler.

EXTRA TOUCHES

Simple meals can be made memorable by the small touches—bacon and eggs with homemade breads and jams, or a baked chicken with an elegant starch or vegetable.

While in a French restaurant one might notice the crispness of the crust on a baguette, French bread is French bread. But many of the new American chefs consider baking bread, along with churning ice creams and sorbets, to be part of the kitchen's daily routine. These small dishes reflect their styles and philosophies of cooking as much as any part of the meal. For Paul Prudhomme, the Jalapeño Cheese Bread is an immediate statement that the meal to follow will hardly be delicate, while for Barbara Tropp, making Pan-fried Scallion breads is the only way they could be included on her menu, since nothing like them is available commercially.

The chefs' concept of vegetables is also changing. While a decade ago fine restaurants were serving fresh vegetables, it was the "du jour syndrome," and one or two were served with a wide range of entrées. Now, chefs are conceiving the starch and vegetable as part of the entrée's presentation. The side dishes are becoming an extended garnish, replacing the ubiquitous sprig of parsley or slice of twisted orange. In Bradley Ogden's kitchen, there may be up to 20 different vegetables and starches being served on a given evening. ∎

Jalapeño Cheese Bread

Makes 3 loaves or about 30 rolls

PAUL PRUDHOMME, K-Paul's Louisiana Kitchen   This is one of the most flavorful breads I've ever eaten, and it's extremely versatile. Sliced thin, it can be filled with cream cheese, cut into rectangles, and served as an hors d'oeuvre. Placing meat in it for sandwiches gives picnic fare a far better flavor than any I've tasted.

8 cups all-purpose flour

1 pound cheddar cheese, grated (about 5 cups)

½ cup sugar

1½ teaspoons salt

¾ cup minced jalapeño peppers

2 cups warm water (105 to 115 degrees)

3 packages dry yeast

2 tablespoons plus 2 teaspoons lard or vegetable oil

In a very large bowl combine 7 cups of the flour, the cheese, 7 tablespoons of the sugar, and the salt. Remove the seeds from the peppers under cold running water, being careful not to touch your eyes after handling the peppers. Chop them well and add them to the bowl.

In a separate bowl, combine the water, yeast, and remaining 1 tablespoon of sugar. Let the yeast sit for 10 minutes; stir until all yeast granules are dissolved. Add the lard or oil to the liquid mixture, stirring until the lard is melted.

Add half the liquid to the flour mixture, and mix with your hands to moisten the flour as much as possible. Add the remaining liquid and mix until it is thoroughly incorporated.

Turn the dough onto a lightly floured surface and knead for about 15 minutes, or until the dough is smooth and elastic and the peppers are evenly distributed. Add only enough flour to keep the dough from sticking.

Place the dough in a large greased bowl and invert it so the top is greased. Cover it with a dry towel and let stand in a warm place until doubled in volume, about 1 to 1½ hours.

Punch the dough down and divide it into 3 equal portions. Form each into a ball, then stretch out the dough and tuck the ends under to form a smooth surface. Pop any large air bubbles visible, and place the loaves in greased 8½-by-4½-inch loaf pans. Cover them with a towel and allow to rise until almost doubled in size, about 45 minutes to 1 hour.

Bake the loaves at 325 degrees until dark brown, about 1 hour. Rotate the pans after 25 minutes in the oven for more even browning.

Spinach and Cheese Breadsticks

Makes about 2 dozen

JASPER WHITE, Restaurant Jasper   Rather than thinking of those rocklike creations in the stores, think of long chewy rolls, flavored with spinach and Parmesan cheese.

1 package dried yeast

1 tablespoon sugar

¼ cup warm water

½ onion, finely diced

¼ cup olive oil

¼ pound spinach, washed and destemmed

4½ to 5 cups high-gluten bread flour

1 teaspoon salt

½ teaspoon freshly ground black pepper

¾ cup Parmesan cheese

1 cup warm water (about)

1 egg, lightly beaten

In a large mixing bowl, dissolve the yeast with the sugar and ¼ cup of warm water. Let the yeast sit for 10 minutes.

Sauté the onion in the olive oil over medium heat for 5 minutes, or until it is transparent. Add the spinach and stir gently until the spinach has wilted, about 4 minutes. Cool, drain, and chop roughly.

To the yeast mixture, add the spinach, flour, salt, pepper, and ½ cup of the Parmesan cheese. Add 1 cup of warm water, slowly, while incorporating it into the flour. The proper amount of water has been added when the dough does not stick to the sides of the bowl. Knead until a strong dough has been formed, about 8 minutes in a mixer with a dough hook or 15 to 20 minutes by hand.

Cover it with a damp towel and remove the bowl to a warm place in the kitchen. When the dough has doubled in volume, punch it down, and repeat the process.

Roll the dough into a large square about ¾ inch thick. With a pastry brush, brush the dough with the egg wash, and sprinkle the remaining cheese over the top. Cut the dough into strips 1 inch wide and 6 inches long, using a pizza wheel or a very sharp knife.

Place the strips on a buttered baking sheet and bake in a 350-degree oven for 15 to 20 minutes, or until they are golden brown.

Brioches

Makes 10 to 18 small brioches, depending on the container

MARCEL DESAULNIERS, The Trellis   The buttery flavor and light texture of brioches make them my favorite bread, and hollowed out they become elegant containers for hot fillings such as any stew. While they take a little time, they are not difficult to make, and the leftovers can be frozen in plastic bags for up to a month.

4½ cups sifted all-purpose flour

2 teaspoons salt

2 tablespoons granulated sugar

½ cup warm water

1¾ tablespoons granulated yeast

6 large eggs

8 tablespoons (1 stick) unsalted butter, softened to room temperature

1 egg, beaten with 1 tablespoon water

S ift the flour and salt together. Dissolve the sugar in warm water in a large mixing bowl. Add and dissolve the yeast by stirring slowly. Place the flour and salt on top of the sugar-yeast mixture, add the eggs on top of the flour, and mix slowly until all the ingredients are combined.

Knead the mixture for several minutes on a floured board until the dough becomes smooth and elastic. Then add the softened butter, 1½ tablespoons at a time, until all the butter is completely incorporated. Transfer the dough to a buttered bowl. Cover it with a dry towel and let rise until the dough is doubled in volume, preferably overnight.

Punch the dough down and refrigerate until it is firm and workable.

This recipe will make about 10 brioches if baked in oven-proof coffee cups, and about 15 to 18 if done in muffin tins. If you are using coffee cups, divide the dough into pats the size of a small orange; if using muffin tins, divide into pats the size of a lemon. Brush the cups or tins with softened butter.

Pinch one small piece of dough from each pat and reserve. Form the pats of dough into round shapes and place them in buttered cups; then take the reserved pieces and pinch them into pear shapes. Make dents in the round dough and place the pear-shaped pieces in the dents, after wetting the pointed ends in water.

Let the dough rise until doubled in size, about 2 hours. Then brush the brioches with 1 egg beaten with 1 tablespoon of water, and bake them in a 350-degree oven for 15 to 18 minutes.

Cream Biscuits

Makes about 24

LYDIA SHIRE, Seasons Long before the commercial oyster cracker, New Englanders were serving their chowders with biscuits. The cream gives them a moistness and richness not usually encountered.

2½ cups pastry flour

3 teaspoons baking powder

1 teaspoon sugar

1 teaspoon salt

¾ to 1½ cups heavy cream

4 tablespoons melted butter

¼ cup finely chopped parsley

M ix all the dry ingredients together and add as much cream as necessary to make a soft dough, but one that holds together. Knead the dough briefly, and roll it on a floured surface, using a floured rolling pin, to ½ inch thickness. Brush the dough with melted butter and sprinkle with parsley, then fold the dough in half so the parsley is in the middle and you have 2 layers, 1 inch thick.

Cut the dough into 1-inch rounds and place them on an ungreased cookie sheet. Bake them in a 375-degree oven for 12 minutes, or until they are lightly colored. Serve hot.

Note: The biscuits can be frozen for up to a month.

Irish Soda Bread with Scallions

Makes 2 loaves

MARCEL DESAULNIERS, The Trellis   The scallions add much flavor to this recipe, a very quick and easy soda bread. It goes beautifully with everything; I've used it for sandwiches as well as served it with meals.

4 cups flour
1 teaspoon baking powder
1 teaspoon baking soda
1 teaspoon salt
4 whole scallions, trimmed and cut into small slices, including the green tops
4½ tablespoons vegetable oil
1½ cups buttermilk

Combine the flour, baking powder, baking soda, salt, and scallions in a large bowl. Mix the oil and buttermilk until they are well combined. Slowly add the liquid to the flour mixture, until the dough forms a ball. Remove the dough and place it on a floured surface. Knead the dough with the heels of the hands until it is smooth.

Form the dough into 2 loaves, and place them far apart on a floured baking sheet. Bake them at 350 degrees for 40 minutes.

Pan-Fried Pepper-Scallion Bread

Makes 2 eight-inch flatbreads, serves 6 to 8

BARBARA TROPP, China Moon   There is something enticing about fried breads, with chewy insides and a crisp golden-brown crust. These are even more special, since the scallions and other seasonings add flavor to the interior, and they are quite easy to make. Tropp uses chicken fat, but sesame oil can also be used for a very different, but equally good, result.

Cold-water dough:
1 cup all-purpose flour
⅛ teaspoon freshly ground pepper
1 tablespoon baking powder
About ⅓ cup cold water

For the cold dough, combine the dry ingredients and add cold water as necessary to bring the dough together in a ball. This may be done in a food processor fitted with a steel blade. Repeat the procedure for the hot dough, then combine the two balls and knead the dough until soft and smooth, adding flour as required should the dough be sticky. Place the

Hot-water dough:

1 cup all-purpose flour

1 teaspoon kosher salt

⅛ teaspoon freshly ground pepper

About ⅓ cup boiling water

Seasonings:

2 teaspoons chicken fat or sesame oil

1½ teaspoons kosher salt

Pinch of freshly ground pepper

6 tablespoons thinly cut scallion rounds, both white and green

½ cup corn or peanut oil for pan-frying

dough in a lightly oiled bowl, and glaze it slightly with oil. Cover it with a dry towel and set it aside for 30 minutes at room temperature.

Divide the dough in half, and shape each half into a ball, setting one aside under a dry towel.

On a lightly floured board, roll the second ball into a circle ⅛ inch thick, dusting it with flour if needed to prevent sticking. With your hand, smooth half the seasoning fat or oil evenly on top, sprinkle with half the salt, several grinds of pepper, and a thick sprinkling of scallion rounds. Roll the dough up like a carpet. Then, holding one end in place on the board, grasp the loose "tail" and wrap it in a flat spiral around the stationary end, thus creating a flat, coiled bread round, flouring the board as required. Tuck the loose end under the bread; it will be 7 to 8 inches in diameter. Repeat the process with the second dough ball.

Breads should be fried as soon as rolled.

To fry, heat a well-seasoned heavy 9- or 10-inch skillet over high heat. Reduce the heat to medium, add enough oil to glaze the bottom evenly with ⅛ inch of oil, then heat until the oil is hot enough to foam a pinch of flour. Add one bread, and cook it over moderate heat until the bottom is evenly brown, about 4 minutes, adjusting the heat so the bread does not scorch. Flip the bread, dribble with a bit more oil from the sides of the pan, swirling to distribute it under the bread. Cook the bread an additional 4 minutes, then remove it to a cutting board. Repeat with the second bread.

To serve, cut the breads into wedges and garnish with freshly cut scallion rings or a scallion cut as a brush.

Note: Tropp says, "Depending upon the pan and the feel of the dough, I sometimes cover the breads about 2 minutes into the cooking, so that steam builds up inside the pan and cooks the bread through. I do this for each side, but always uncover the pan for the final minute to recrisp."

Cornbread with Chili

Makes 12 small molds or muffins

ANNE GREER, Nana Grill at the Anatole Hotel   This is the best cornbread I've ever eaten. The chilies and red pepper give it color and flavor, folding in the egg whites lightens it, and the cream and buttermilk make it moist. In addition to using the muffins as a platform for Greer's Shrimp in Tequila with Orange Butter Sauce (page 138), I've served them in place of rolls in my bread basket.

½ cup fresh white corn, scraped from the cob (or use frozen but not canned corn)

1 cup stoneground yellow cornmeal

1 tablespoon baking powder

½ teaspoon baking soda

1 teaspoon sugar

1 teaspoon salt

½ cup all-purpose flour

¼ cup melted unsalted butter

½ cup cream

1 cup buttermilk

2 eggs, separated

3 tablespoons diced green chili, either fresh or canned

3 tablespoons diced canned pimento or red bell pepper

Using a food processor fitted with the metal blade, grind the corn and cornmeal for 20 seconds. In a large mixing bowl, combine the other dry ingredients, and add the corn and cornmeal. Mix the butter, cream, buttermilk, and egg yolks, and add them to the dry ingredients, beating well.

In a separate bowl, beat the egg whites until stiff peaks form. Fold the whites into the cornmeal mixture with the green and red peppers.

Spray the inside of 12 individual bundt or savarin molds with nonstick vegetable-oil spray, or butter them. Divide the batter among the molds and place them on a cookie sheet. Bake them at 400 degrees for 10 to 15 minutes. Let them cool on a rack, and unmold.

These breads freeze very well for up to 2 weeks.

Indian Doughnuts

Makes about 36

JIM HALLER, The Blue Strawbery   These are really a cross between doughnuts and cornbread. Their texture is dense, but they're rich and flavorful from the butter. I serve them for breakfast right from the fryer, but if you're going to reheat them, don't dust them with powdered sugar until they come from the oven.

1½ cups scalded milk

2 cups stoneground yellow cornmeal

2 cups flour

1½ cups sugar

1 tablespoon baking powder

1 tablespoon cinnamon or nutmeg

1 teaspoon salt

1 cup flavored butter, melted

3 eggs, lightly beaten

3 cups safflower or peanut oil for deep frying

Powdered sugar

Pour the scalded milk over the cornmeal, whisking vigorously until smooth. Sift the dry ingredients together, and add them to the cooled cornmeal mixture. Stir well, then whisk in the butter and eggs. If necessary, add more flour to make the dough firm enough to handle.

Knead lightly on a floured board, and roll the dough ½ inch thick. Cut it with a doughnut cutter, and allow them to sit for 15 minutes before frying.

In a skillet or deep saucepan, heat the oil over medium heat to a temperature of 375 degrees. Add the doughnuts so a batch is not crowded in the pan and fry until they are golden, turning as needed. Drain well, and sprinkle with powdered sugar.

FLAVORED BUTTERS Haller makes his own butter by placing heavy cream in the food processor and leaving it on until it is butter, reserving the skim milk that's left for soups. To flavor the butter, he places 1¼ pounds butter, broken into small pieces, in the food processor with the flavoring ingredients and processes until blended. He thinks "ripe pears whipped into fresh butter, or blackberries, or maple syrup, or lobster meat" is great. For the Indian doughnuts, I suggest Haller's Sweet Curry Butter (adding 2 tablespoons of curry powder and 2 tablespoons of maple syrup) or Curried Pear Butter (1 very ripe peeled and cored pear, 1 tablespoon curry powder).

Wild Rice and Pine Nuts

Serves 6

BRADLEY OGDEN, The Campton Place Hotel   Braising the wild rice in stock with vegetables gives it a rich taste, and its natural nutty flavor is brought out by the crunchy pine nuts. This is a wonderful side dish with any roasted meat, and it can also be used as a stuffing for a whole chicken or baked chicken breasts.

1 cup wild rice

3 tablespoons vegetable oil

¼ cup yellow onions, diced

¼ cup carrots, diced

3½ cups chicken stock (page 160)

3 bay leaves

¼ teaspoon freshly ground black pepper

2 tablespoons unsalted butter

½ cup pine nuts

Wash the wild rice well in a strainer, until the water runs clear, and shake it well to dry. Heat the oil in a heavy 2-quart saucepan, add the vegetables and rice and sauté them over medium heat for 5 minutes, stirring constantly. Add the stock, bay leaves, and pepper, and bring to a boil. Cover the pan and place it in a 325-degree oven for 1½ to 2 hours, or until the rice is tender and has absorbed the liquid. Stir occasionally, and add water if the rice is becoming dry before it is tender.

Check for seasoning, and add salt if necessary. If canned broth is used, it is likely no salt will be needed.

Melt the butter in a sauté pan or skillet and toast the pine nuts over low heat until brown. Add to the rice and serve.

Apricot-Almond Bread

Makes 1 large or 2 small loaves

MARCEL DESAULNIERS, The Trellis   This bread, extremely easy and quick to make, is a variation on the classic combination of dates and walnuts. But you'll find, as I did, that dried apricots and almonds give it a far perkier and more interesting taste. I've served this for brunch and with simple baked poultry at dinner, or it's delicious with cream cheese for tea sandwiches.

1 cup sliced almonds

1½ sticks unsalted butter, softened

1½ cups sugar

3 eggs

2 teaspoons baking powder

1½ teaspoons baking soda

½ teaspoon salt

1½ teaspoons cinnamon

2 teaspoons almond extract

3½ cups all-purpose flour

½ cup sour cream

2 cups chopped dried apricots

In a 350-degree oven, toast the almonds on a baking sheet for 10 minutes. In a mixing bowl, cream together the butter and sugar until light and fluffy. Add the eggs, one at a time, and beat well after each addition. Add the baking powder, baking soda, salt, cinnamon, and almond extract. Beat until smooth, and then add the flour ½ cup at a time, alternating with the sour cream. Beat until smooth, then stir in the almonds and chopped apricots.

Place the mixture in a buttered and floured 12-inch loaf pan or two 8-inch pans, and place in the middle of a 350-degree oven. One large loaf will take 1 hour and 15 minutes, and two smaller loaves will take 45 minutes, or until a cake tester comes out clean. Allow the bread to cool in the pan on a rack before removing the loaves from the pans.

Stir-Fried Wild Rice with Chinese Greens

Serves 4 to 5 as a large bowlful, 6 to 8 in smaller portions

BARBARA TROPP, China Moon   The wild rice is enhanced immeasurably by the dried and fresh wild mushrooms, crispy greens, and leeks. Tropp uses Chinese celery for the dish, but the leaves from bok choy, much easier to find in supermarkets, work equally well. I've served this as a combination vegetable-starch with any number of simple meat recipes, and it elevates anything from a hamburger to a roast fillet of beef to a new height of elegance.

1 cup wild rice

2 cups cold water

8 medium dried shiitake mushrooms

½ cup rendered chicken fat

⅔ cup thinly sliced leeks

1½ cups sliced wild mushrooms, such as chanterelles or morels

2 cups Chinese greens, sliced

2 tablespoons Chinese rice wine or dry sherry

Roasted Szechwan Pepper-Salt (page 152) to taste

Wash the rice in several changes of cold water, stirring with the hands to dislodge any particles. Continue the process until the rinse water is clear, about 5 minutes. Drain well. Put the rice and cold water in a heavy 2-quart saucepan. Bring the water to a boil, reduce the heat to a weak simmer, then cover tightly and cook about 20 minutes. Do not remove the lid once it is in place. Turn off the heat and let the pot sit undisturbed for 20 minutes longer. If all the water is not absorbed or the rice is overly firm (in which case additional water is needed), place the covered pot in a 300-degree oven until it is light and fluffy. Spread the rice on a baking sheet and refrigerate it until thoroughly chilled. Once cold, the rice may be placed in a plastic bag for several days.

Cover the dried mushrooms with cold water and soak them until spongy, ideally overnight. Drain and rinse them, then snip off and discard the stems. Cut the caps into coarse dice.

To stir-fry, heat a wok or large, heavy skillet over medium heat until it is hot enough to sizzle a bead of water. Add 3 tablespoons of chicken fat, and swirl to glaze the pan. When it is hot enough to sizzle a slice of leek, add the leeks and toss until fragrant and supple, about 3 minutes, adjusting the heat so they foam without burning. Add the wild and dried mushrooms, and toss until the mushrooms are tender, dribbling in more fat as needed. Add the greens, tossing for a moment, then add the wine and rice. Toss to combine the ingredients and heat through. Remove from the heat and sprinkle with Szechwan Pepper-Salt to taste.

All steps up to the stir-frying can be done up to a few days in advance. The dish can be kept warm in a slow oven for 30 minutes.

Corn Spoon Bread

Serves 8 to 10

BRADLEY OGDEN, The Campton Place Hotel This is a perfect accompaniment to highly spiced dishes, since the interest comes from the grainy smoothness of the texture rather than competing flavors. Unlike traditional corn spoon breads, this one calls for a large number of eggs, so it is light and fluffy rather than heavy.

4 cups water

1 tablespoon kosher salt

8 tablespoons (1 stick) unsalted butter

¼ teaspoon ground white pepper

1½ cups stoneground yellow cornmeal

1½ cups buttermilk

7 eggs

½ cup heavy cream

1 cup corn kernels (approximately 3 ears), or defrosted frozen corn (do not used canned corn)

Simmer the water, salt, butter, and pepper in a heavy 2-quart saucepan. Slowly add the cornmeal, whisking to ensure that no lumps form. Cook over low heat for 3 minutes, whisking constantly, until very thick. Turn off the heat and add the buttermilk slowly, stirring.

Beat the eggs and add them to the cornmeal mixture, then add the cream and corn.

Butter a 10-by-14-inch baking pan and pour in the mixture. Bake it in a 400-degree oven for 35 to 45 minutes or until the spoon bread is set and the top has browned. To serve, scoop out with an ice-cream scoop or serving spoon.

Mushroom Polenta

Serves 4 to 6

LYDIA SHIRE, Seasons The sautéed onions and mushrooms add a delicate but very savory taste to the polenta, basically the Italian version of a corn spoonbread. This is a hearty starch, and goes well with any roast meat or poultry. For a brunch dish, I've placed poached eggs atop slices of this version with a mushroom sauce. It's quite easy to make, and triangles of polenta look very elegant on a plate.

8 tablespoons (1 stick) unsalted butter

1 medium onion, chopped

Melt the butter in a sauté pan or skillet and sauté the onion and mushrooms for 5 minutes, or until the onion is translucent. Set aside.

¼ pound mushrooms, preferably shiitake, sliced

2 cups water

1 teaspoon salt

1 cup yellow cornmeal

1 egg white, stiffly beaten

½ cup clarified butter

In a heavy saucepan, bring the water to a boil with the salt. Slowly add the cornmeal, whisking constantly, and beat until smooth. Bring the mixture back to a simmer and cook for 3 minutes, stirring constantly with a wooden spoon. The mixture will become very thick. Add the onion mixture and fold in the egg white.

Pour the polenta into a buttered loaf pan and let it cool.

Slice it ½ inch thick. Heat the butter over medium heat and add some of the slices. Fry until brown, then flip over with a spatula and fry the other sides. Continue until all are fried. Cut each slice in half diagonally.

Note: The polenta mixture can be made a day in advance, but should be fried just prior to serving.

Sweet Potatoes Stuffed with Bacon and Collards

Serves 6

JAMES HALLER, The Blue Strawbery   Haller's recipe is a savory combination of flavors. The crispy bits of bacon and greens accentuate the basic smoothness and creaminess of the sweet potato. I've served this with a number of poultry and pork dishes with great reception.

3 large sweet potatoes

1 pound bacon

4 cups chopped collard greens

½ cup fresh breadcrumbs

3 tablespoons melted butter

⅓ cup dried currants

Scrub the potatoes and bake them in a 400-degree oven for about 45 minutes, or until they are tender. Slice them in half lengthwise, and scoop out and mash the pulp, reserving the shells.

Slice the bacon into ½-inch pieces, and fry until crisp in a large skillet. Remove the bacon with a slotted spoon and drain it on paper toweling. Pour off all but 4 tablespoons of the grease from the skillet, and add the collard greens. Sauté them for about 6 minutes, until wilted and cooked.

Add the potato pulp and bacon bits and stir to blend. Stuff the mixture into the shells, mounding on the top. Mix the breadcrumbs and butter and sprinkle on top of the potatoes, then pat on the dried currants. Reheat the potatoes in a 350-degree oven until they are hot and the crumbs have browned, about 15 minutes.

Note: The recipe can be prepared a day in advance to the point of baking to brown the topping. Bake the next day in a 300-degree oven for 25 minutes to brown the top and reheat the potato.

Robinson Bar Potatoes

Serves 6

BRUCE LEFAVOUR, Rose et LeFavour   This version of gratin de pommes de terre, named for LeFavour's ranch in Idaho, is excellent with any simple or sauced meat entrée. I use buttery-textured Finnish yellow potatoes, but red potatoes also absorb the cream and cheese for a smooth and flavorful taste.

6 medium red potatoes, or Finnish yellow potatoes

1 clove garlic, cut in half

1 tablespoon soft unsalted butter

Salt and pepper to taste

2 ounces grated Comte cheese (about ½ cup), or Gruyère cheese

¾ cup heavy cream

Peel the potatoes and, using a mandolin or the slicing disk of a food processor, slice them thin and put them in a bowl of cold water.

Rub a 9- by-13-inch gratin or baking dish with the cut surface of the garlic, and then coat it thoroughly with the soft butter. Dry the potato slices well with paper towels.

Starting at one end of the prepared dish, place rows of potatoes, overlapping each preceding row one-third with the next row. Lightly salt and pepper the layer and sprinkle with half the cheese. Starting at the opposite end, repeat the layering, using the remainder of the potatoes. End with salt, pepper, and cheese, and pour the cream over. Bake for 20 to 30 minutes on the top shelf of a 375-degree oven. Serve immediately, or the dish may be kept in a warming oven for 15 minutes.

Freddie's Roast Potatoes

Serves 6

JASPER WHITE, Restaurant Jasper   Crusty cubes of roast potato mixed with toasted cloves of garlic, sweet rather than pungent after cooking, make this a hearty and wonderful accompaniment to roast meats. The only trick to the dish is to make sure the skins on the garlic cloves do not break while you are removing them from the bulb, or they will burn as they roast rather than browning.

6 to 8 medium potatoes, preferably Maine or Nova Scotia (about 2½ pounds of potatoes)

1 head garlic

1 stick unsalted butter or ½ cup goose or duck fat

Salt and pepper to taste

Peel the potatoes and cut them into 1½-inch cubes. The potatoes need not be totally uniform. Blanch them in boiling salted water for 7 to 8 minutes, then drain them and place in a bowl of ice water to stop the cooking action. Drain them well and pat them dry with paper toweling.

Carefully separate the cloves of garlic, keeping the skin on.

With the butter or fat grease a roasting pan large enough to hold the potatoes in one layer. Add the potatoes and garlic and season them with salt and pepper.

Bake in a 350-degree oven for 50 minutes, turning the potatoes frequently, until a golden-brown crust forms.

Richard's Favorite Potatoes

Serves 6

LAWRENCE FORGIONE, An American Place There's nothing more popular with guests than crispy oven-roasted potatoes, and these potatoes are quite easy to make. Keeping them in ovals makes them look elegant on the plate.

3 large baking potatoes
1 peeled garlic clove, cut in half
¾ cup clarified butter
Salt and pepper

Peel the potatoes, trying to keep them as smooth as possible, and cut them in half lengthwise. Place the flat sides down on a cutting board and rub the surface of the potatoes with the cut garlic clove.

With a sharp knife, slice the potato halves across as thin as possible. Brush a roasting pan with a little of the butter, and place each of the potatoes on the pan, keeping them whole. Give them a slight push to "shingle" the slices slightly, and brush them with the remaining clarified butter. Season each potato with salt and pepper.

Place them in a 375-degree oven for 35 to 45 minutes, basting them occasionally with butter. The edges of the potatoes should be golden brown and crisp. Remove them with a spatula to keep them together.

Note: The potatoes can be baked up to 4 hours in advance, and then reheated in a 350-degree oven for 10 minutes. If made in advance, they should be removed after 30 minutes and crisped when reheated, or else they will become too dry.

Grilled Leeks

Serves 6

JASPER WHITE, Restaurant Jasper Grilled vegetables are among my favorite spring and summer dishes, and leeks seem to go best with lamb and chicken. There's a sweetness to the leek that emerges on the grill, and the only trick to this dish is washing the leeks well. They can look pristine on the outside but still be filled with grit.

6 medium leeks
¼ cup vegetable oil
Salt and pepper
1 lemon
¼ cup freshly grated Parmesan or Romano cheese

Cut the leeks about 6 inches long, going about 1 inch into the green part of the leek. Make an incision the length of each leek, halfway through, to get into the center. Soak the leeks in cold water, changing the water a few times, and then hold them one at a time under cold running water to get rid of any remaining dirt.

Dip the leeks in oil, and season with salt and pepper. With the incisions facing up, put the leeks over a hot fire, about 2 inches from the coals. Cook for 5 to 7 minutes, or until they are well charred. Remove some of the outer leaves, squeeze a little fresh lemon juice over the top and sprinkle with cheese.

Braised Red Swiss Chard

Serves 6

BRADLEY OGDEN, The Campton Place Hotel Braising greens with bacon and a sweet-and-sour sauce is traditionally Southern. What makes this recipe so special is the grated ginger. It brings the greens to life, and heightens all other flavors. I've used this recipe with lowly collard greens, as well as with delicate chard, and the results were equally delicious.

3 oranges

½ cup bacon cut into ½-inch pieces

½ cup diced onions

2 bunches red Swiss chard, stems removed, and cut into thin strips 3 by ½ inch

¼ cup sugar

3 tablespoons red-wine vinegar

1 cup chicken or duck stock (page 160)

1 teaspoon kosher salt

½ teaspoon freshly ground black pepper

3 tablespoons grated fresh ginger

With a zester, vegetable peeler, or sharp knife, cut the orange zest from the oranges, trying to get as little of the white pith as possible. Cut the zest into a fine julienne and set it aside. Squeeze the oranges; you should have about 1 cup of juice. Set it aside and add to braising liquid.

In a heavy saucepan, cook the bacon over medium heat until it is golden and almost crisp. Add the onions and sauté for 2 minutes. Add the rest of the ingredients, stirring until the mixture is combined and the leaves have started to wilt. Cover and braise for 15 minutes over medium heat, stirring occasionally.

Damson-Plum Chutney

Makes 2 to 3 quarts

MARCEL DESAULNIERS, The Trellis The combination of plums, currants, and apples creates a very light and savory chutney, and it goes beautifully with any hot or cold baked or grilled meat. I've also tried it on top of grapefruit and popped them under the broiler as a first course for brunch. It can be refrigerated for a few weeks, or frozen for up to a few months.

5 pounds damson plums, washed, pitted, and coarsely chopped

2 Granny Smith apples, unpeeled, cored and coarsely chopped

½ cup orange juice

½ cup freshly squeezed lemon juice

4 cups sugar

2 cups dried currants

½ cup balsamic vinegar

1 teaspoon cinnamon

2 teaspoons ground ginger

Place all ingredients except cinnamon and ginger in a large stainless-steel or enameled saucepan. Bring the mixture to a boil over medium heat, then reduce the heat and allow it to simmer, stirring occasionally, for 1½ hours.

Remove the pan from the heat, and add the spices. Cool thoroughly and place in sterilized jars. Refrigerate or freeze.

Cranberry Relish

Makes 2 cups

BRADLEY OGDEN, The Campton Place Hotel This relish is a delicious change from cranberry sauce as an accompaniment to roast turkey, and it enhances breakfast meats like sausage and Canadian bacon. The mace and vanilla give the relish a far more interesting taste than any other flavoring I've tried.

2 oranges

1 cup granulated sugar

¾ cup water

½ teaspoon ground mace

1 teaspoon vanilla extract

1 package fresh or frozen cranberries, washed and picked over (12 ounces)

With a vegetable peeler, cut the orange zest off the oranges, and then squeeze the oranges. Cut the zest into a fine julienne with a sharp knife. Combine the orange juice, zest, sugar, and water in an enameled or stainless-steel saucepan and bring the mixture to a boil. Add the mace and vanilla, and simmer for 10 minutes. Add the berries, and simmer for 5 minutes or until they pop and the mixture thickens.

Cool and store in sterilized jars in the refrigerator.

Pumpkin Candy

Makes 2 pounds

LAWRENCE FORGIONE, An American Place   There's an innate sweetness to pumpkin that helps turn it into a delicious candy, and I've made this when pumpkin was not in season with acorn squash, a close relative. The color is not as vivid, but the flavor is just as good. Serve this after dinner with coffee, or keep some squares in a bonbon dish.

1 quart fresh pumpkin meat, cut into 1-by-1½-inch pieces

2 to 2½ cups water

1 cup brown or maple sugar

1 cup granulated maple sugar or raw sugar

Place the cubed pumpkin in a saucepan and cover it with water, about 2 to 2½ cups. Bring it to a boil and simmer for 15 to 20 minutes, uncovered, until the pumpkin is just tender. Remove the pumpkin with a slotted spoon. There should be about 1½ cups of liquid remaining.

Add the brown or maple sugar and dissolve over low heat. Place the pumpkin pieces back in the pan and bring slowly back to a boil, then lower the heat and simmer for 15 minutes. Let the pumpkin pieces stand in the syrup overnight.

The next day, bring the mixture back to a boil and simmer for 5 minutes.

Remove the pumpkin pieces from the syrup and spread them out on a wire rack so the pieces are not touching one another. Let them stand in a warm place or in a 140-degree oven for 3 to 4 hours to dry. Roll each piece in the maple or raw sugar, and store them in a dry, cool place. Do not stack or crowd the candy together.

ICE CREAMS AND SORBETS

Acknowledging our love affair with ice creams and sorbets, and the Italian fruit ices of our youth, is another reflection of culinary independence. No longer does a dessert have to be a puff-pastry construction bonded with a mortar of crème pâtissière to be deemed a fit ending for an elegant meal. Ice cream, everyone's childhood treat, has come of age.

Retail shops selling churned ice creams low in preservatives and high in butter fat are popping up around the country in the eighties the way Golden Arches did in the sixties and seventies. In 1982, Carol T. Robbins and Herbert Wolff, a Boston-based team, selected *The Very Best: Ice Creams and Where to Find Them.* They found such flavors as Indian pudding, cherry Amaretto and veggie.

In restaurants, making ice creams daily has become as standard a practice as baking bread or mixing salad dressings. In Los Angeles, Spago's fresh banana ice cream is as much a hallmark of the restaurant as its pizzas, and at The Trellis in Williamsburg, spiced pumpkin is a favorite flavor.

Chefs are not only concocting ice creams to stand alone. They are also constructing more elaborate desserts with the homemade ice cream as the base. Jimmy Schmidt at the London Chop House stuffs a honey-baked pear, which has caramelized as it baked, with his caramel ice cream, and Richard Perry fills individual baked Alaskas with a rich double chocolate laced with brandied raisins.

What initially seems at odds with our down-to-earth fondness for ice creams is the parallel trend in restaurants to import the formal European custom of the intermezzo sorbet. Traditionally the course signified the switch from white to red wine, and many chefs have taken the opportunity to invent unusual combinations, including the marriage of fruit and herbs.

Both ice creams and sorbets serve as a reflection of the chefs' styles. Barbara Tropp's ice creams are made without heavy cream, since she believes they would be cloying on the palate following the lightness of her food at China Moon. And Robert Rosellini uses no water and practically no sugar in his sorbets at The Other Place, so the impact of the flavor is from the natural fruit.

Almost all homemade ice creams and sorbets are better if eaten the day they are made, since the flavors have a tendency to diminish. They should be allowed to stand out until slightly soft before serving.

While the texture of ice creams and sorbets comes from churning, which smooths out the ice crystals as they form and keeps the mixture light by incorporating air, occasional makers may not want to invest in the necessary equipment. Here are some methods to achieve close to the end result of an ice-cream maker:

No-Freezer Ice Cream

The product is actually a frozen mousse rather than a legitimate ice cream. This method works for ice creams with a high percentage of heavy cream, but not for those made with light cream. For those mixtures, use the No-Freezer Sorbet Method.

Rather than adding all the heavy cream to the custard mixture, add only one-third the amount. Your custard will be very thick, and it should be thoroughly chilled before proceeding.

Whip the remaining cream, and fold it gently into the cold custard. Place the mixture in the freezer in a stainless-steel bowl, and freeze until the outer few inches of the ice cream are frozen, but the center is still soft. Remove the bowl from the freezer, break up the frozen section and beat well. Return the mixture to the freezer until the outer edge has frozen again. Remove, and beat the mixture again with an electric mixer. Return to the freezer and freeze until solid.

No-Freezer Sorbet—Method 1

Whenever you think you've invented the wheel, someone comes along rolling one. After I had worked with this method for a few months, Robert Rosellini's recipes arrived with the following line: "Freeze in ice-cream machine or half freeze in ice-cube trays, then whip and freeze until hard."

That about sums up all my experimentation.

For sorbets, fill ice-cube trays with the mixture and freeze until the cubes are about half set. Unmold them into a large stainless-steel bowl and beat with an electric mixer until smooth. Or empty them into the bowl of a food processor fitted with a steel blade and beat well. Then pack the mixture lightly back into the trays and repeat the process. After the second beating, place the mixture in a bowl and freeze completely.

No-Freezer Sorbet—Method 2

The first method is a one-day operation, but if you have both a day to spare and a sturdy food processor, you can try Anne Greer's alternative method, developed while she was a consultant to the Cuisinart company.

For sorbets containing fresh fruit, freeze the fruit on cookie sheets for at least 24 hours, and place the sugar syrup in ice-cube trays for the same period of time. You can save freezer space by placing the frozen fruit and juice in plastic bags once they are fully frozen.

Place half the fruit cubes in a food processor fitted with a steel blade, and pulse on and off until the cubes are finely chopped, about 10 times. Add half the syrup cubes, and pulse until the mixture is the consistency of shaved ice, about 12 times. Then continue processing, adding about ¼ cup cream through the feed tube, stopping to scrape the sides of the bowl several times. Process until you have a mixture with an ice cream–like texture. Repeat with the remaining fruit and cubes and freeze until you are ready to serve.

Apple-Basil Sorbet

Makes 1½ quarts

ROBERT ROSELLINI, Rosellini's Other Place   The combination of the sweet apples and the aromatic freshness of basil makes this the perfect intermezzo sorbet —it truly cleanses the palate, and the flavors harmonize well. For a pretty presentation of the sorbet, make cups by hollowing out shiny red apples and placing scoops in the centers just before serving. This sorbet should be eaten within a few hours to taste its best.

6 McIntosh or other cooking apples, peeled, cored, and diced

3 cups apple juice or fresh apple cider

½ cup loosely packed fresh basil leaves

¼ cup sugar, if necessary

In a heavy 2-quart saucepan, cook the apples and apple juice over medium heat until the apples are mushy. This takes between 20 and 30 minutes. Purée in a blender, food mill, or food processor fitted with a steel blade. Cool the mixture to room temperature and stir in the chopped basil leaves.

Taste the mixture for sweetness, and add sugar, 1 tablespoon at a time, if it is too tart for your taste. The addition of the sugar will depend on the sweetness of the apples. The apple juice should be enough to sweeten them.

Process the mixture in an ice-cream machine, or follow the No-Freezer Sorbet method opposite. Garnish with a fresh basil leaf.

Minted Lime Sorbet

Makes 1 quart

ANNE GREER, Nana Grill at the Anatole Hotel   I've served this sorbet both as an intermezzo and, as Greer uses it, to top grilled apples for dessert (page 336). The combination of lime and mint is one of the freshest I've ever put in my mouth, and it's not overly sweet. It also has a most appealing green color, and could top a fruit salad.

2 cups water

1 cup sugar

2 cups fresh mint leaves, loosely packed

½ cup freshly squeezed lime juice

1 tablespoon crème de menthe

Combine the water and sugar in an enameled or stainless-steel saucepan. Bring to a boil and simmer briefly until all the sugar is dissolved. Add the mint leaves and let them steep until the mixture is cool.

Drain the mint mixture, pressing to extract the juice from the leaves. Add the lime juice and crème de menthe. Process in an ice-cream freezer, or use the No-Freezer Sorbet method opposite.

Pear, Thyme, and Rosemary Sorbet

Makes 1 quart

BRUCE LEFAVOUR, Rose et LeFavour   I vividly remember that my first meal at Rose et LeFavour included this sorbet as an intermezzo, and I was astonished at how clean the taste was. The sweet pear was followed by the aftertaste of the herbs. I've made it many times since, and served it with many fruit salads dressed with an herb vinaigrette, or as part of a seafood and fruit salad. The herbs for this must be fresh, and it should be served within a few hours after it's made for the best flavor.

4 sprigs fresh thyme
4 sprigs fresh rosemary
1½ cups water
1¾ cups Comice pear juice and pulp, about 3 pears
¼ cup lemon juice
⅓ cup sugar

Boil the thyme and rosemary with the water until the "tea" is reduced to ½ cup. Strain and cool.

Peel and core 2 or 3 ripe Comice pears and process them with the lemon juice in a food processor fitted with a metal blade. Beat in the sugar and the cooled herb liquid, and freeze in an ice-cream freezer, or follow the No-Freezer Sorbet method on page 308.

Kiwi Sorbet

Makes 1 quart

BARRY WINE, The Quilted Giraffe   The flavor of Galliano, an Italian liqueur, brings out all the flavor of the kiwi fruit. I adore the interplay of the two tastes, and this is a sorbet that works well as an intermezzo or as dessert. It's light and elegant while not overly sweet, which makes it a wonderful dessert following a rich meal.

12 ripe kiwi fruit
1 cup Galliano liqueur
1 teaspoon fresh lemon juice

Peel the kiwis with a sharp knife and cut them into large pieces. Purée with the Galliano and lemon juice and chill.

Freeze in an ice-cream freezer, or follow the No-Freezer Sorbet method on page 308.

Note: For this sorbet, the fruit must be puréed in a food processor fitted with a steel blade or pushed through a food mill. If the seeds are placed in a blender, they will be pulverized and it will detract from the look of the sorbet.

Budweiser Beer Ice

Makes 1 quart

MARCEL DESAULNIERS, The Trellis This sorbet is wonderful to serve with any highly spiced foods. I prefer beer to wine with most Mexican and Chinese food, and I've served this following various things made with chili peppers. There's a sweetness to beer, and the flavor mixed with the citrus juices calms down the palate in a delicious way.

1 cup sugar
½ cup water
2 cups Budweiser beer
Juice of ½ lemon
Juice of ½ orange

Bring the sugar and water to a boil in a small saucepan, and simmer for 5 minutes. Cool the syrup to room temperature.

Combine the cooled syrup with beer, lemon juice, and orange juice.

Freeze the mixture in an ice-cream freezer, or follow the No-Freezer Sorbet method on page 308.

Green-Grape Sorbet

Makes 1 quart

ROBERT ROSELLINI, Rosellini's Other Place On a hot day there's nothing like a bunch of chilled grapes as the ending to a meal, and this is even better; the grapes are frozen. Since there is very little sugar and no other ingredients, the flavor you experience is the delicacy of grapes, made even lighter in this texture.

3 pounds seedless green grapes, stemmed and mashed
½ cup sugar

In a heavy saucepan, bring the grapes and sugar to a boil over low heat, stirring frequently. Simmer until they are pulpy, about 15 minutes.

Press the grapes through a food mill, or purée in a food processor fitted with a steel blade and then strain through a fine sieve to remove the peel. Let the mixture cool, and then process in an ice-cream freezer, or follow the No-Freezer Sorbet method on page 308.

Note: While the pale green of this sorbet is attractive, equally appealing is the pale pink from red grapes. For a sorbet sampler, you might consider making both, but do not mix green and red grapes.

Pineapple-Orange Ice with Fresh Pineapple and Oranges

Makes 1½ quarts

ANNE GREER, Nana Grill at the Anatole Hotel   The addition of cream to what is basically a purée of frozen fruit binds the two flavors together and gives the sorbet a wonderful creamy texture. Blood oranges make the mixture a faint pink, but any sweet oranges will produce a wonderful flavor. I sometimes add a touch of crème de cassis to achieve the pink tone.

Greer serves this dessert on thin slices of orange, and tops it with a tablespoon of Grand Marnier. It's both elegant and delicious.

The directions below are given for an ice-cream freezer, or you can follow Greer's ingenious No-Freezer Sorbet—Method 2 (page 308).

1 fresh pineapple, very ripe, peeled, cored, and cut into 2-inch cubes

3 tablespoons sugar

1 cup juice and sections from blood oranges (approximately 6)

½ cup pineapple juice

½ cup heavy cream, chilled

Purée the pineapple in batches in a blender or food processor fitted with a steel blade. Set it aside in a bowl, and blend the sugar with the orange and pineapple juice until the sugar is dissolved. Mix all together with the cream, and process in an ice-cream freezer according to the manufacturer's directions or use the No-Freezer Sorbet Method.

Red-Currant Sorbet

Makes 1 pint

ROBERT ROSELLINI, Rosellini's Other Place   The taste of succulent red currants explodes in your mouth, since they are the only ingredient with the exception of a little sugar to enhance their flavor. The taste is bright and fresh, and reminds me of the fresh fruit ices of Italy.

1 quart fresh red currants, washed and stemmed

½ cup sugar

In a heavy saucepan, bring the currants and sugar to a simmer, crushing some of the berries. Stir frequently, and add a few tablespoons of water if necessary. Cook until the fruit is pulpy.

Press through a food mill, or purée in a blender or food processor fitted with a steel blade and then push through a sieve. Cool, and then freeze in an ice-cream machine, or follow the No-Freezer Sorbet method on page 308.

Blueberry-Maple Sorbet

Makes 1 quart

BARRY WINE, The Quilted Giraffe   The flavor of blueberries is complemented and made more complex by sweetening this sorbet with maple syrup. The two ingredients blend in a subtle way, with one leading into the next rather than either dominating. I've served the sorbet plain, or on top of a dish of fresh blueberries with a dollop of whipped cream.

2 pints fresh blueberries

⅔ cup pure maple syrup

1 teaspoon lemon juice

Rinse the berries well, and remove any particles of stem. Purée them in a blender or food processor fitted with a steel blade. Add the maple syrup and lemon juice and purée again.

Strain the mixture through a fine strainer or a double layer of cheesecloth. Freeze in an ice-cream machine, or follow the No-Freezer Sorbet method on page 308.

Note: While fresh berries are far better than frozen, whole frozen berries can be substituted, but not those packed in syrup. If using frozen berries, allow them to defrost before making the recipe.

Pear Ice Cream with Pinot Noir Syrup

Makes 1 quart

BARBARA TROPP, China Moon   While this is a silky-textured ice cream rather than a sorbet, the use of half-and-half and the lack of eggs bring the taste of pears vividly to the fore. The snow-white ice cream is incredibly light, and the wine syrup, flavored with citrus peels and aromatic cassia bark, is a perfect topping. It has all the lightness and delicacy of frozen poached pears.

Two recipes for the syrup are given: one a reduction of the poaching liquid, and the other a syrup made expressly to top the ice cream.

PEAR ICE CREAM

6 tablespoons freshly squeezed and strained lemon juice

¼ cup water

1½ pounds ripe but firm Anjou pears (about 3 medium)

¾ cup sugar

2 cups half-and-half

1 tablespoon eau-de-vie Poire William or other high-quality white-pear liqueur

Combine 2 tablespoons of the lemon juice and the water in a non-aluminum, 2- to 2½-quart saucepan. Halve, core, and peel the pears, one by one, cubing them and quickly dropping the cubes into the acidulated water to prevent discoloration.

Add the sugar, stir to combine, and bring the pears to a simmer over moderate heat. Cover the pan and simmer 8 minutes, then turn off the heat and let the pears steep in the covered pot an additional 10 minutes.

Scrape the hot mixture into a food processor fitted with a steel blade, and purée for 60 seconds, stopping after 30 seconds to scrape down the sides of the bowl. This can also be done in a blender or the mixture can be put through a food mill.

Place the purée in a stainless-steel bowl, and add the half-and-half, stirring well to blend. Add 4 to 5 tablespoons of lemon juice, 1 tablespoon at a time, as needed to bring out the full taste of the pears. Add a bit more sugar if the pears need it, then stir in the liqueur.

Freeze in an ice-cream maker, or use the No-Freezer Sorbet Method on page 308.

Serve the ice cream with either of the following syrups. If you wish to garnish the ice cream with pear slices, use the second syrup recipe.

PINOT NOIR SYRUP

3½ cups Pinot Noir wine

1 section fresh orange peel (4 inches)

1 section fresh lemon peel (4 inches)

1 thumbnail-size piece of cassia bark, crumbled

⅓ to ½ cup sugar

The following recipe is for making a syrup to be served as a pool under the pear ice cream. If you are poaching pears as a garnish, see below.

Bring all the ingredients to a boil in a heavy 2-quart saucepan, and simmer over low heat until the liquid has reduced to 1 cup. When it has almost reduced, taste and adjust the sugar as needed. Strain to remove the solids and chill.

Pinot Noir Syrup for poaching pears

1½ cups Pinot Noir wine

1½ cups water

⅔ to ¾ cup sugar

Peel of ½ lemon

Peel of ½ orange

3-inch length Chinese cassia bark, crumbled

6 ripe pear halves

While thin slices of pears poached in this syrup are a wonderful garnish for the pear ice cream, I have started using this recipe for poaching pears for any purpose. The citrus peels and mellow cassia bark add subtle flavors to the pears.

Bring the wine, water, and ⅔ cup sugar to a simmer in a non-aluminum saucepan, stirring to dissolve the sugar. Add the citrus peels and cassia bark, cover the pot, and simmer for 10 minutes. Add the peeled and cored firm pear halves, cover, and simmer 10 to 15 minutes, or until the pears are just tender when pierced with the point of a knife.

Remove the pot from the heat and let the pears steep several hours or overnight. Remove the pears with a slotted spoon, then strain the liquid into a clean saucepan. Bring it to a boil and reduce the liquid by about half or two-thirds, until it has a syrupy consistency and coats the back of a spoon. Taste the syrup and adjust as needed with sugar and/or a bit of lemon juice.

Slice the pears crosswise into thin slices, spreading them slightly.

Meyer Lemon Ice Cream

Makes 1 quart

BARBARA TROPP, China Moon Meyer lemons are a species native to California that have an orange tinge to the juice, and until they are available across the country, regular lemons work well. This ice cream is refreshing with its only barely sweetened lemon flavor, and soothes the palate with its light creaminess. While I've served it plain with great success, I also like a little Cointreau or Grand Marnier on top of it, and a few cookies for some crunch.

4 to 6 Meyer or regular lemons with soft, unblemished skins (enough to yield 5 tablespoons of strained juice)

1 cup sugar

2 cups half-and-half

Pinch of salt

Wash the lemons, then remove the skin with a sharp vegetable peeler, taking care to get just the yellow zest and leaving behind the white pith. Squeeze as many lemons as required to yield 9 tablespoons of strained juice.

Grind the peel and sugar in a food processor fitted with a steel blade until the peel is very fine and the sugar is liquidy, about 3 to 4 minutes. Add the juice, process to combine, then add the half-and-half and salt. Process to blend.

Scrape the mixture into a bowl and set it aside for 10 to 15 minutes to allow the lemon juice to curdle the half-and-half and thicken it slightly. Stir, adjust the taste with sugar if needed, and freeze the mixture in an ice-cream freezer, or follow the No-Freezer Sorbet method on page 308.

Note: The ice cream keeps well for a week or more with a piece of plastic wrap pressed directly on the surface. For fullest flavor, serve slightly soft.

Caramel
Ice Cream

Makes 1½ quarts

JIMMY SCHMIDT, London Chop House Schmidt devised this recipe as the stuffing for poached pears (page 331). But I love to serve it plain as well. The flavor is luscious. It's much lighter than most ice creams owing to the percentage of light cream, but it still has the custardy texture from eggs we expect from ice cream. I've also served it with a caramel sauce to enrich the taste even further.

1½ cups sugar
Juice of 1 lemon
¾ cup water
2¼ cups light cream
12 egg yolks
1¼ cups cold heavy cream

In a heavy saucepan, combine the sugar, lemon juice, and water. Bring to a boil over medium heat, washing down with a brush any sugar crystals clinging to the sides of the pan. Let the syrup cook to a dark caramel color, which will take about 10 minutes. Watch carefully so it doesn't burn. Remove the pan from the heat and gradually add the light cream, stirring with a long-handled spoon, tipping the pan away from you since the cream will bubble up furiously. Stir well, and return the pan to low heat to melt any lumps of caramel.

In a large bowl beat the egg yolks until thick and light-colored. Slowly add the caramel mixture, whisking continuously. Pour the mixture into a saucepan and cook it over low heat, stirring constantly, until it thickens and coats the back of a spoon. Do not let the custard boil, or the egg yolks will curdle. Remove from the heat and add the cold heavy cream to stop any further cooking.

Strain the mixture through a fine sieve, and process in an ice-cream freezer, or use the No-Freezer Sorbet method on page 308.

Pumpkin-
Caramel
Ice Cream

Makes 1 quart

MARCEL DESAULNIERS, The Trellis The richest pumpkin pie cannot compare with this ice cream. It's highly spiced, so the flavor comes through as a contrast with the cold creaminess of the custard. While delicious alone, it is a wonderful topper for any nutty pie or cake.

Pumpkin is one of the few foods that does not suffer a great deal from being used in its canned form. For a slightly lighter texture and color, a mixture of half pumpkin and half puréed fresh acorn squash, baked whole until tender, works well. Unlike most ice creams, this one needs a day for the flavors to mellow and reach their peak.

3 cups heavy cream

1 cup sugar

2 teaspoons lemon juice

½ cup pumpkin purée

½ teaspoon ground nutmeg

½ teaspoon ground cloves

½ teaspoon ground cinnamon

5 egg yolks (reserve whites for another use)

In a heavy saucepan, bring the cream to a boil over low heat. While the cream is heating, place the sugar in another heavy 3-quart saucepan over low heat. Caramelize the sugar, stirring with a wooden spoon to break up any lumps, for 8 to 10 minutes. The syrup should be maple-syrup-colored; be careful it does not burn.

Remove the caramelized sugar from the heat, and add the hot cream, ½ cup at a time. Use a long-handled spoon and tilt the pan away from you, since it will boil up furiously at first. Place the pan back on low heat, and stir until the remaining lumps of caramel are melted.

In a large bowl, combine the lemon juice, pumpkin, spices, and egg yolks. Whisk in the warm cream, then pour through a strainer to remove any caramel lumps. Return to the saucepan or a double boiler and heat over low heat, stirring constantly, until the mixture thickens enough to coat the back of a spoon. Do not let it boil or the egg yolks will curdle.

Chill the custard in the refrigerator. Process in an ice-cream machine, or use the No-Freezer Ice Cream Method (page 308).

Coffee Ice Cream

Makes 1 quart

BARRY WINE, The Quilted Giraffe The problem with all commercial coffee ice creams is that, no matter how high the quality of the cream, they are made with a low-grade coffee, so the end flavor is not rich and intense. In this ice cream, since the coffee bean can be a known commodity, the flavor changes with the type of bean used. After trying a few varieties, I found the French roast gives a strong coffee flavor, while a Colombian bean is more delicate but just as rich. One dismal failure was a New Orleans coffee with chicory—much too bitter. I've served this ice cream alone, topped with a coffee liqueur, or as the filling for a meringue shell.

2 cups heavy cream

1 cup milk

½ cup freshly ground coffee

6 egg yolks

½ cup sugar

Pinch of salt

Heat the heavy cream and milk to a simmer in a heavy 1-quart saucepan. Turn off the flame and stir in the coffee grounds. Let the grounds steep, stirring occasionally, for 18 minutes.

While the coffee is steeping, separate the eggs, reserving the whites for another use. Add the sugar to the yolks and whisk until they are light and lemon-colored. Strain the cream mixture through a cheesecloth-lined sieve into another saucepan. Reheat the cream, but do not let it come to a simmer. Gently ladle some into the yolk-and-sugar mixture, whisking constantly so the hot liquid does not cook the yolks. Cook the mixture over low heat, stirring with a wooden spoon, until it thickens and coats the back of a spoon. Do not let it boil or the egg yolks will curdle. Strain and chill until cold.

Process in an ice-cream freezer, according to the manufacturer's directions, or use the No-Freezer Ice Cream Method (page 308).

White-Chocolate Ice Cream with Dark-Chocolate Sauce

Makes 1½ quarts

PATRICK O'CONNELL, The Inn at Little Washington   There's an elegance to white-chocolate anything, and there's a delicacy in the flavor that makes this one of the most luscious ice creams I've ever put in my mouth. The light cream and undertaste of rum enhance the chocolate.

The high-grade chocolate used is essential to the success of the ice cream. You need the imported white chocolate, and not the bits sold for baking. They'll give it a chalky, waxy taste.

3 egg yolks

⅔ cup sugar

2 cups light cream

9 ounces imported white Swiss chocolate, broken into small pieces and melted in a 200-degree oven

4 tablespoons light rum

1 tablespoon vanilla

1 cup heavy cream

DARK CHOCOLATE SAUCE

8 ounces good-quality semisweet chocolate

¼ cup strong coffee

3 tablespoons Grand Marnier

3 tablespoons heavy cream

In a stainless-steel bowl, beat the egg yolks with the sugar and light cream until light-colored. Set the bowl over a pot in which 2 inches of water is simmering. Stir until the mixture thickens and coats the back of a spoon, about 10 minutes. Do not let it come to a boil or the egg yolks will curdle. Beat in the melted chocolate and refrigerate the mixture until cold. When it is cold, add the rum, vanilla, and heavy cream.

Freeze in an ice-cream freezer, or follow the No-Freezer Ice Cream Method (page 308). Serve with Dark Chocolate Sauce.

Break the chocolate up into small pieces, and add the rest of the ingredients. Heat over low heat in a small, heavy-bottomed saucepan until the chocolate is melted, stirring occasionally. Whisk until smooth.

Chocolate Ice Cream with Brandied Raisins

Makes 1½ quarts

RICHARD PERRY, Richard Perry Restaurant   This is everyone's memory of that wonderful ice cream from childhood come true. The semisweet and unsweetened chocolate give it an incredible richness without a great deal of sugar, and the brandy undertaste makes the ice cream a more sophisticated concoction.

3½ cups heavy cream

6 ounces good-quality semisweet chocolate

1 ounce unsweetened chocolate

½ cup sugar

¼ cup water

3 egg yolks

Pinch of salt

1 teaspoon vanilla

½ cup raisins, soaked in ¼ cup brandy until liquid is absorbed

Place 1 cup of the cream in a saucepan. Break the chocolates into small pieces and add them, stirring over low heat until the chocolate is melted and the mixture is smooth.

Place the sugar and water in another saucepan, and cook until the syrup spins a thread when dropped into ice water (230 degrees on a candy thermometer). While the sugar syrup is cooking, beat the egg yolks and salt in a mixing bowl. Add the hot sugar syrup in a thin stream while beating the yolks at high speed. This can be done in a food processor fitted with a steel blade. Add the chocolate cream and beat until well mixed. Add the vanilla and the remaining heavy cream.

Freeze in an ice-cream freezer, or use the No-Freezer Ice Cream Method (page 308). When the mixture is almost frozen, stir in the raisins and continue to freeze.

DESSERTS

Sociologists maintain contemporary American society operates on the "save and splurge" principle, and this extends to the way we eat. For shopping there is a dual trend of buying staples at no-frills warehouse stores, in order to save money to splurge at the growing number of super supermarkets on the freshest and most exotic produce, a good bottle of wine, a wedge of fine imported cheese.

And the way we eat is consistent with this as well. "We'll skip the salad dressing, eat marginally at dinner, and then blow it all on dessert," said Los Angeles *Times* food editor Betsy Balsley. We are becoming a country of chocoholics, with consumption of chocolate almost doubling in the past decade and prices for imported chocolates skyrocketing. There are now two newsletters—*Chocolate News* and *Chocolatier*—devoted to nothing but chocolate, and chocolate weekends at the Hyatt Regency in Chicago and the Mohonk Mountain House in New York attract sellout crowds.

Many new American chefs recognize our passion for chocolate, and have constructed desserts accordingly. Susumu Fukui's terrine of chocolate is marbled and placed in a shell of white chocolate, while Jimmy Schmidt's options range from a light frozen mousse coated with praline to a pâté of chocolate in a Grand Marnier sauce that is the richest chocolate dessert I've ever made—and enjoyed every bite of.

In addition to satisfying our craving for chocolate, many chefs are basing desserts on the classics—from Barry Wine's Dessert Strudel to Bradley Ogden's Bread Pudding with Blueberry Sauce.

And there will always be a place for tarts and soufflés in our lives and on restaurant menus. Drawn from the repertoire of classic French and other European cuisines, such desserts as Robert Rosellini's Hazelnut Torte and Jean Louis Palladin's Fresh Fruit Soufflé are sure-fire winners. But also fitting into the European tradition are the many fruit desserts. It seems many chefs agree with Jimmy Schmidt that "the pear is the perfect fruit," because I enjoyed them from coast to coast. ■

Terrine of Dark and White Chocolate with Two Sauces

Serves 8

SUSUMU FUKUI, La Petite Chaya   The flavor and texture of this concoction are like those of a wonderful rich chocolate mousse. And the surprise comes when it is sliced: the whipped cream is barely mixed in, so there are swirls of white marbling through the deep, rich chocolate. The pan is lined with white chocolate, which makes the terrine all the more elegant, and the dual sabayon and raspberry-purée sauces add their own special and delicious flavors along with more color on the plates.

12 ounces good-quality semisweet chocolate

¾ cup milk

1¼ cups heavy cream

2 tablespoons Grand Marnier

4 tablespoons cognac

½ cup shelled pistachio nuts, coarsely chopped

1 pound white chocolate

Sabayon Sauce

Raspberry Sauce

SABAYON SAUCE

4 tablespoons sugar

¼ cup kirsch

2 tablespoons cognac

6 egg yolks

10 ounces heavy cream

RASPBERRY SAUCE

2 pints raspberries

1 tablespoon Framboise

Break the dark chocolate up into small pieces and melt it with the milk and ¼ cup of the cream in the top of a double boiler over hot water or over low heat. Beat the mixture until smooth and set aside to cool.

Whip the remaining cream, and beat in the liquors. Fold the chocolate and whipped cream together with the pistachio nuts until marbled. Do not fold to make it homogeneous.

Chill a terrine or loaf pan in the freezer. Melt the white chocolate and spread a layer evenly in the terrine, and freeze until hard. Put the dark chocolate mixture into the pan and freeze.

To serve: Dip the terrine in hot water for 30 seconds. Run a sharp knife around the sides and invert onto a platter.

Combine the sugar and liquors in a small saucepan and bring the mixture to a boil. Simmer for 2 minutes, until the sugar is dissolved. Beat the egg yolks until light and lemon-colored, and then add the hot syrup in a slow stream, beating constantly. Place in a heavy saucepan over low heat or in the top of a double boiler over hot water, and stir until the mixture thickens and coats the back of a spoon. Do not let it come to a boil or the egg yolks will curdle. Whip the cream until soft peaks form, and fold it into the cooled custard mixture.

Purée the berries and strain. Mix the purée with the liqueur.

Note: The terrine and sauces can be prepared up to 2 days in advance and kept refrigerated, covered tightly with plastic wrap.

Pâté of Bittersweet Chocolate with Grand Marnier Sauce

Serves 8

JIMMY SCHMIDT, London Chop House   This is the dessert chocoholics dream about. I've never made anything as intensely screaming chocolate, nor enjoyed eating any chocolate dessert more. The rum in the pâté, along with the coconut and Grand Marnier in the light custard sauce, makes this a sure-fire winner.

Part of the secret to this, and any other chocolate dessert, is the quality of chocolate used. Schmidt uses nothing but Tobler's Extra Bittersweet. Hershey's Special Dark is my choice, since it imparts the same flavor at about one-third the price.

15 ounces bittersweet
chocolate

1 cup heavy cream

4 tablespoons unsalted butter

4 egg yolks

¾ cup confectioners' sugar

6 tablespoons dark rum, such
as Meyer's

Break the chocolate into small pieces and place it in a stainless-steel bowl. Add the cream and butter and place the bowl over a saucepan filled with simmering water, stirring occasionally until the chocolate is melted. Beat until the mixture is homogeneous, at which time it will be glossy and dark. While this can be done in a double boiler, the mixing-bowl method is preferable, since room in the bowl is needed for beating the mixture while it melts.

Remove the bowl from the heat and whisk in the egg yolks, one at a time. Beat well after each addition.

Place the confectioners' sugar in a sifter or sieve. Sift it onto the chocolate, whisking at all times. Continue until all the sugar is added and the chocolate is thick and glossy. Add the rum and whisk it in.

Line a 4-cup loaf pan with parchment paper or waxed paper, allowing the paper to extend 2 inches beyond the top of the pan. To keep the paper in place, rub butter around the sides and bottom of the pan. Butter the paper.

Pour the pâté mixture into the mold. Cover the top with plastic wrap and refrigerate the pâté overnight. It can be made 2 days before serving.

GRAND MARNIER SAUCE

1½ cups light cream

¾ cup shredded sweetened
coconut

¼ cup sugar

Pinch of salt

¼ teaspoon vanilla

5 egg yolks

4 to 6 tablespoons Grand
Marnier or other orange
liqueur

Scald the cream by bringing it just to the boiling point over low heat. Add the coconut and allow it to steep until the cream is cool. Then reheat it to the scald point again, while beating the sugar, salt, vanilla, and egg yolks in another saucepan. Slowly stir the hot cream into the egg mixture, beating constantly with a whisk.

Place the sauce in the top of a double boiler over hot water, or in a heavy saucepan over low heat. Stir with a wooden spoon until the mixture thickens and coats the back of the spoon. Do not allow it to boil or the egg yolks will curdle. Remove the sauce from the heat and whisk for a few seconds to cool. Strain through a fine sieve to remove the coconut, and add the Grand Marnier. Cool and refrigerate.

To assemble: Remove the pâté from its mold by lifting with the paper. If the chocolate ran onto the mold, and the pâté does not easily come out, dip the mold into hot water for a few seconds to help loosen the pâté.

Remove the paper and slice the pâté ⅓ inch thick, using a very hot knife or a cheese wire. Allow it to sit at room temperature on plates for 30 minutes, then spoon sauce around the sides.

Note: Both the pâté and the sauce should be prepared a day in advance. As the sauce begins to cool, place a piece of waxed paper directly on the surface so no skin will form. Both should be kept in the refrigerator until 30 minutes before serving.

White Chocolate Mousse

Serves 6 to 8

RICHARD PERRY, Richard Perry Restaurant   There's nothing as elegant as white-chocolate desserts. They look so light, and can be embellished with pretty red berries, but the taste is rich and intensely chocolate. I love to garnish this mousse with strawberries dipped in dark chocolate, and I've also served it with a simple raspberry purée sauce like the preceding recipe. The key to the success is using a good-quality chocolate, such as Droste's. The commercial white bits give a waxy taste when chilled.

9½ ounces white chocolate

3 egg yolks

1 cup heavy cream

2 tablespoons Amaretto

1 tablespoon vanilla extract

6 egg whites

Pinch of salt

2 tablespoons sugar

Break up the chocolate into small pieces and melt it over hot water in the top of a double boiler, or place it in a bowl in a 200-degree oven for 10 minutes.

Whisk the egg yolks until they are pale yellow and thick, and then whisk in the cream. Heat the mixture in the top of a second double boiler over hot water or in a heavy saucepan over very low heat, stirring constantly, until the custard is hot and thickened enough to coat the back of the spoon. Do not let it come to a boil or the egg yolks will curdle. Beat in the Amaretto, vanilla, and chocolate. Pour the mixture into a large bowl and whisk until smooth. Then place it in the refrigerator to cool to room temperature while you are beating the egg whites.

Place the egg whites in a large bowl and add a pinch of salt. Beat at medium speed until frothy, then increase the speed to high, and beat until stiff peaks form, gradually adding the sugar to the whites.

Stir one-quarter of the whites into the chocolate mixture to lighten it, then fold in the remaining whites. Refrigerate until chilled.

Serve on chilled dessert plates.

Note: The mousse can be prepared a day in advance, and stored, covered with plastic wrap, in the refrigerator.

Barquette of Chocolate Praline

Serves 6

JIMMY SCHMIDT, London Chop House The base of this dessert is a heavenly light frozen chocolate soufflé, and using a milk container as a mold is a genius idea for this—or any other—frozen soufflé. It's very easy to make both the soufflé and the wonderfully crunchy praline topping, but it takes the patience of Job and four hands to peel off the chocolate to cover the sides and form a flower on the top of each slice. It looks beautiful, but the dessert is every bit as delicious if this step is omitted.

½ teaspoon gelatin

7 ounces Frangelico

6 ounces chocolate, such as Tobler's Extra Bittersweet or Hershey's Special Dark

6 eggs, separated

¼ cup sugar

Pinch of salt

¼ teaspoon vanilla

1¼ cups heavy cream

Praline:

2 cups sugar

Juice of ½ lemon

1 cup water

½ cup blanched almonds

For assembly:

9 ounces chocolate, such as those mentioned above

2 tablespoons unsalted butter

Wash out a 1-quart milk carton, and place it in the freezer.

Sprinkle the gelatin over 4 tablespoons of the Frangelica in a custard cup to soften for 10 minutes. Place the cup in a pan with hot water halfway up the sides, and place over low heat. Stir to dissolve and set aside.

Melt the chocolate by breaking it into small pieces and placing it in a bowl in a 200-degree oven or in the top of a double boiler.

In a large bowl, beat the egg yolks with the sugar, salt, and vanilla until thick and light yellow. Add the gelatin mixture and chocolate to the egg yolks, beating well.

Whip the egg whites into soft peaks and set aside. Whip the cream into soft peaks, and slowly add the remaining liqueur. Fold the whites and whipped cream into the yolk mixture, and pour into the container. Freeze overnight.

For the praline: Butter a cookie sheet and set it aside. Combine the sugar, lemon juice, and water, and bring to a boil over high heat. Reduce the heat to medium, and boil until the syrup begins to turn golden. Add the almonds, stir, and continue to boil until it becomes a deep amber color, about 1 minute, being careful that it does not burn. Pour the syrup onto the buttered pan and allow it to cool until hard. Break up the praline into small pieces and grind in a blender or food processor fitted with a steel blade until it becomes a powder. Place the praline powder in an airtight container in the freezer. Any leftover praline will stay for up to 3 months in the freezer to be used for other recipes.

To assemble: Melt the chocolate and butter, and beat until smooth. Allow the chocolate to cool slightly while you cut the container away from the soufflé base and cut the soufflé into 6 slices. Cover all sides of the slices with the praline powder.

Spread the chocolate on the back of a cookie sheet and refrigerate until it is firm but still pliable. Using a putty knife or scraper, peel up the chocolate in long strips, wrapping it around the sides of the slices and forming it into a flower on top. Place each slice back in the freezer until all 6 are done. Leave in the freezer until time to serve.

Quick Chocolate Soufflé

Serves 4

AMY FERGUSON, Charley's 517   The soufflé is light and delicious. The lightness is due to the absence of flour in the base, which also means it is trickier to make successfully. A few of mine have flopped, and I've served the "chocolate pancake" topped with a scoop of vanilla ice cream. No one knew it was supposed to be a soufflé, and it was a wonderful dessert.

4 ounces good-quality chocolate

¼ cup strong coffee

¼ cup heavy cream

4 eggs, separated

2 additional egg whites

2 tablespoons sugar

Prepare a 6-cup soufflé mold by rubbing it with butter and dusting it well with granulated sugar. Knock out excess sugar.

Break the chocolate into small pieces and melt with the coffee and cream in the top of a double boiler over hot water or in a bowl in a 200-degree oven. Beat until thick and glossy, and then add the egg yolks, one at a time, beating well after each addition.

Whip the egg whites at medium speed until frothy, then increase the speed to high, and whip until stiff peaks form, gradually adding the sugar. Fold into the chocolate mixture and place in the soufflé dish. Place the dish in the center of a preheated 400-degree oven, and immediately turn the oven down to 375 degrees. Bake 30 minutes and serve immediately.

Chocolate
Marquise Torte

Serves 8 to 10

ANN-KATHLEEN MCKAY, pastry chef at Rose et LeFavour   In this torte the chocolate in the meringue reinforces the same flavor in the filling, but the textural variation between the two adds so much. This is really an easy dessert to make, and the result is elegant. If you can beat an egg white, you'll do it perfectly.

The flavor of the torte is definitely chocolate, but you'll find it's not overly sweet, so it makes a lovely end to a rich dinner.

Meringue:

4 tablespoons cocoa

1 cup confectioners' sugar

¾ cup egg whites (about 6 to 8 eggs)

⅔ cup sugar

Chocolate butter cream:

¼ pound bittersweet chocolate

6 tablespoons unsalted butter

½ cup confectioners' sugar

3 eggs, separated

6 tablespoons cocoa

1½ cups heavy cream

For the meringue: Sift the cocoa and powdered sugar together twice and set aside. In a large bowl, totally devoid of grease, beat the egg whites on medium speed with a mixer. Beat until soft peaks are formed, then raise the speed to high, and slowly begin to add the granulated sugar, a few tablespoons at a time. Beat until the meringue is stiff and glossy, and no sugar remains undissolved. By hand, fold in the cocoa mixture in thirds, working quickly but gently.

Draw two 9-inch circles on a piece of parchment paper set on a cookie sheet. Spread the meringue evenly in the two circles, smoothing the tops with a spatula. Bake at 300 degrees for 50 to 60 minutes, until the circles are firm. Turn off the oven and leave the door ajar until the meringues cool to room temperature. Remove them from the parchment and set aside.

For the butter cream: Coarsely chop the chocolate, and melt it in a large bowl over simmering water, whisking until smooth. Remove the bowl from the heat and add the butter, cut into ½-tablespoon pieces, and the powdered sugar. Beat until smooth, and add the egg yolks, one by one. Sift the cocoa over the mixture and whisk well. Let cool to room temperature.

Beat 6 tablespoons of the cream until soft peaks form, and set aside. Beat the 3 egg whites until stiff, and fold along with the whipped cream into the chocolate mixture until thoroughly incorporated.

Whip the remaining cream until stiff, and set aside.

To assemble: Place 1 meringue layer on a tray with overlapping sheets of waxed paper underneath. Spread with one-third of the chocolate mixture, top with two-thirds of the whipped cream and the second meringue layer. Use the remaining chocolate to cover the top and sides of the torte. Place the remaining cream in a pastry bag and pipe around the edge in a shell pattern. Refrigerate, and remove from the refrigerator 30 minutes before serving.

Note: I like the way this dessert tastes if it is made a day in advance and allowed to mellow in the refrigerator overnight. The meringue is a bit less crunchy that way. This is a matter of personal preference.

My Grandma's Devil's Food Cake

Serves 10 to 12

JAMES HALLER, The Blue Strawbery   There's something about even the richest torte that doesn't compare with an old-fashioned devil's food cake. This one is dense and moist, and the walnuts add a crunch to make the chocolate even more interesting. Although Haller says icing is permissible, I've served it with a bowl of rum-flavored whipped cream and it's wonderful.

4 squares (4 ounces) unsweetened chocolate

5 tablespoons sugar

5 tablespoons milk

1 tablespoon flour

2 tablespoons vanilla

1½ sticks (¾ cup) unsalted butter, at room temperature

1 cup sugar

Pinch of salt

2 eggs

1 teaspoon baking soda

1 cup buttermilk

2 cups flour

1 cup chopped walnuts

Melt the chocolate with the sugar and milk in the top of a double boiler, whisking until smooth. Add the flour and simmer until the mixture is smooth and pudding-like. Remove it from the heat and add the vanilla. Let the chocolate mixture cool while preparing the batter.

Cream the butter with the sugar until light and fluffy. Add the salt and beat in the eggs, one at a time. Add the baking soda, and then add the buttermilk and flour alternately, beating until the batter is smooth. Fold in the walnuts and the cooled chocolate pudding.

Butter and flour a tube pan, and pour in the cake mixture. Bake at 325 degrees for 1 hour, or until a cake tester or knife comes out clean. Remove the cake from the pan to cool, and top with whipped cream or an icing of your choice.

Maple-Poached Pears with Wild Hickory Nuts

Serves 6

LAWRENCE FORGIONE, An American Place   While pears are traditionally delicate, the savory flavor of hickory nuts and maple syrup makes this a hearty dessert. Forgione stuffs the pear cavities with pastry cream, but I've done it with whipped cream and liked the results even better. Either way, the combination of flavors is delicious.

6 Comice pears, ripe but still firm

1½ cups pure maple syrup

1 cup water

Juice of 1 lemon

½ stick cinnamon

Pastry cream:

2 egg yolks

⅓ cup sugar

¼ cup boiling milk

8 tablespoons (1 stick) unsalted butter

⅓ cup ground wild hickory nuts

Warm Vanilla Cream:

1 quart heavy cream

1 vanilla bean, split lengthwise (or 1 tablespoon extract)

½ cup sugar

6 egg yolks

Garnish:

Whole hickory nuts and mint leaves

With a vegetable peeler, remove the skin from the pears, starting at the stem ends, and with a small melon scoop carefully remove the cores from the bottoms. Arrange the pears standing in a deep saucepan. Pour over the maple syrup, water, and lemon juice, and add the cinnamon stick. Cover the pears with a round of parchment paper to retain the steam, and bring to a boil over low heat. Immediately remove the pan from the heat and allow the pears to cool to room temperature. They should be cooked, yet still firm.

When the pears have cooled, remove them to an absorbent towel or paper toweling and drain. Retain the poaching liquid.

For the pastry cream: Beat the egg yolks with the sugar until thick and lemon-colored, and add the boiling milk, whisking constantly. Place the mixture in a small saucepan or in the top of a double boiler over hot water, and heat, stirring constantly, until the custard thickens and coats the back of a spoon. Do not allow it to boil or the eggs will curdle. Whisk to cool for a few moments, and then beat in the butter, a tablespoon at a time, beating until smooth. Stir in the ground hickory nuts and set aside.

For the sauce: Scald the heavy cream and vanilla. Lower the heat and allow the cream to simmer for 3 to 5 minutes, stirring from time to time. In a large stainless-steel or glass bowl, mix the sugar and egg yolks, whisking until light and smooth, and while whisking add 1 cup of the cream. Pour the mixture into the saucepan with the remaining cream, and stir over low heat until the custard thickens slightly. Do not let it boil. Strain the custard through a fine strainer, and dot the top with butter so a skin does not form.

Fill the cavity of each pear with the pastry cream, spoon the warm sauce around the pears, and sprinkle whole hickory nuts on top of the sauce. Use mint leaves at the stem of the pear as a garnish.

Note: The pears and pastry cream can be made a few days in advance and kept refrigerated, the pears in their poaching liquid, in a jar. The sauce can also be made in advance; place a sheet of waxed paper directly on the surface so a skin will not form.

Pears Poached in Red Wine and Cassis with Its Sorbet

Serves 10

JEAN-LOUIS PALLADIN, Jean-Louis at Watergate   This dessert turns the cook into an artist. The result is beautiful and complex, but it's easy to make. The pears are poached in the pretty pink syrup, then some of them are puréed and added to it, with the majority of that resulting liquid frozen as a sorbet. The plates come to the table with all three components, so they are united by flavor but the textures are very different. It's a knockout as the ending to a sophisticated dinner.

10 fresh ripe pears
2 lemons
2 bottles dry red wine
4 cups sugar
1 cup water
1 cup cassis

Peel the pears, cut each in two, and remove the cores with a melon baller. Coat all surfaces with lemon juice to prevent discoloration. Bring the wine, sugar, water, and cassis to a boil, and add the pear halves. Reduce the heat to a simmer and poach the pears for 10 to 15 minutes, or until they are tender. Remove the pears with a slotted spoon and set them aside.

Boil the cooking liquid until the volume is reduced by one-third. Purée half the pears in a food processor fitted with a steel blade or put them through a food mill, and stir the purée into the poaching liquid.

Save 1½ cups, and process the remainder in an ice cream machine, or follow the No-Freezer Sorbet Method on page 308. Reduce the remaining sauce to ¾ cup. To serve: Slice the remaining pears and fan on a plate with a scoop of sorbet and top with some sauce.

Comice Pears with Champagne Sabayon

Serves 6

JIMMY SCHMIDT, London Chop House This is one of the most delicious and lightest poached-pear desserts I've ever made. The pears taste almost caramelized from being baked with honey, and this taste is reinforced by the light caramel ice cream filling them. The champagne sauce is light and not overly sweet, and the Poire William ties it to the taste of the fruit.

6 ripe Comice pears
Juice of 4 lemons
¾ cup honey

Champagne sabayon
4 egg yolks
⅔ cup sugar
Pinch of salt
Pinch of vanilla
½ cup brut Champagne
4 to 6 tablespoons Poire William

Caramel Ice Cream (page 316)
Sprigs of mint

Peel the pears, leaving the stems intact. Apply lemon juice to all the exposed surfaces to prevent discoloration. Decore the pears through the bottom with a melon baller coated with lemon juice, and trim the bottom flat so the pear stands upright.

Place the pears in a baking dish, and squeeze the remaining lemon juice over them. Pour the honey over them, and place the dish in a 350-degree oven. Baste the pears frequently with the honey and juice that collects in the pan. Bake them for about 30 minutes, or until they are tender but a skewer still meets some resistance. Chill the pears in the refrigerator and baste occasionally as the syrup thickens.

For the sauce: In a stainless-steel mixing bowl, beat the egg yolks with sugar, salt, and vanilla until thick and light-colored, and a ribbon is formed when the beaters are lifted. Place the bowl over a saucepan of simmering water, and slowly add the champagne, whisking constantly to retain a silky texture. Add the liqueur, and continue to whisk until the custard thickens and coats the back of a spoon. Do not allow it to boil or the egg yolks will curdle. Set the custard aside at room temperature while assembling the dish.

To assemble: Fill the pear cavities with the caramel ice cream, and place the pears in chilled bowls. Form scoops of caramel ice cream and place one in front of each pear. Spoon the sabayon over the pears, and garnish with sprigs of fresh mint.

Note: The pears and ice cream can be made 2 days in advance and refrigerated; however, the sauce should not be made more than a few hours in advance.

Seckel Pears in Late-Harvest Riesling

Serves 6

JASPER WHITE, Restaurant Jasper   When I first looked at this recipe, after savoring each bite of the pears at Restaurant Jasper, I was shocked that peppercorns were listed as an ingredient. Along with the cinnamon and cloves, the pepper taste is not prominent, but all the spices bring out the sweetness of the pears. They are a delicate, elegant, and delicious dessert.

Drier and less expensive Riesling can be substituted for the late-harvest, but add honey to compensate.

18 Seckel pears (or as many as you want to poach at one time)

1 lemon

1 bottle late-harvest Riesling, such as Robert Mondavi, or dry Riesling and ½ cup honey

1 cup water

½ orange, cut into slices

2 cinnamon sticks

3 whole cloves

10 whole white peppercorns

½ cup orange juice

Peel the pears with a vegetable peeler, leaving the stems attached and core from the bottom, using the small end of a melon baller. Place the pears in a mixing bowl filled with cold water and the juice of a lemon to prevent discoloring.

Combine the remaining ingredients in a non-aluminum 2½-quart saucepan and simmer for 15 minutes. Strain out the solids and return the liquid to the pan. Add the pears, so they are barely covered with liquid, and simmer for 10 minutes over low heat, or while they are still hard in the center. Turn off the heat and allow the pears to cool in the syrup. Chill, and serve in a glass bowl with some of the poaching liquid.

Note: The pears can be done in a large batch, since they will keep for a month, tightly covered, in the refrigerator with their poaching liquid.

Raspberry and Fig Gratin

Serves 6

JEREMIAH TOWER, Santa Fe Bar and Grill   This elegant dessert takes no time at all to prepare, and the warm fruit slightly sweetened by brown sugar is totally delicious. The combination of fresh figs and raspberries cannot be beaten, and this way of preparing them lets all the natural flavors of the fruit emerge.

Although this dessert is rich while remaining light, it's even better topped with a scoop of vanilla ice cream.

1½ cups fresh raspberries, washed and drained

¾ cup sour cream

3 tablespoons milk

1½ cups fresh figs, peeled and cut into thick slices

5 tablespoons dark-brown sugar

Place the raspberries in an ovenproof gratin dish or baking dish, about 6 by 9 inches. Mix the sour cream with the milk, and spread the mixture over the raspberries. Top with the sliced figs and sprinkle generously with brown sugar.

Place in a preheated broiler, about 6 inches from the flame, to melt the sugar and warm the fruit. Serve warm.

Note: The gratin can be layered in advance and kept at room temperature for 3 or 4 hours before broiling.

Rhubarb Mousse

Serves 8

PATRICK O'CONNELL, The Inn at Little Washington   Not only does rhubarb have a wonderful pink color, the flavor is both deep and rich. While I've made rhubarb pies for years, the texture of this silky mousse is far superior. It's an easy dessert to make, and one that draws raves from guests.

1¼ pounds fresh rhubarb, diced fine

1 cup sugar

1 tablespoon unflavored gelatin

4 tablespoons cold water

2 cups heavy cream

Combine the rhubarb and sugar in a heavy saucepan and bring to a simmer. Simmer for 20 minutes, or until the rhubarb is soft, and reserve ½ cup of the mixture. Purée the remainder and set it aside.

Sprinkle the gelatin over 4 tablespoons of cold water, and allow it to soften for 10 minutes. Heat the gelatin in a small saucepan over low heat until it is dissolved and no grains remain. Stir into the rhubarb purée.

Whip the cream until stiff, and fold in the purée and cooked rhubarb. Chill well before serving, and serve with additional whipped cream or crème anglaise.

Note: The recipe makes enough for 8 individual mousses, or it can be prepared in one large bowl. The mousse can be made up to 2 days in advance and kept covered with plastic wrap in the refrigerator.

Apricot Souffle with Ginger-Nutmeg Sauce

Serves 6

JIMMY SCHMIDT, London Chop House   We think of soufflés as light, and this one is lighter than most, since it calls for neither flour nor butter in the base. At the same time, however, it has a sublime and intense flavor from the dried apricots, complemented perfectly and greatly enhanced by the ginger and nutmeg in the sauce. This is a truly elegant dessert, and I've never seen a combination quite like it.

APRICOT SOUFFLÉ

1 cup hot water

½ pound dried apricots

¾ cup sugar

Pinch of salt

½ teaspoon vanilla

4 eggs, separated

4 tablespoons Apry or Grand Marnier liqueur

2 additional egg whites

Confectioners' sugar

The night before, pour the water over the apricots and allow them to sit, covered, overnight.

Preheat the oven to 400 degrees. Butter the inside of a 6-cup soufflé mold, and roll granulated sugar around inside it. Turn the mold upside down and knock gently to remove excess sugar.

Purée the apricots and any remaining water in a blender or food processor fitted with a steel blade. Strain the purée through a fine sieve to remove the skins.

Combine the purée, sugar, salt, vanilla, and egg yolks in a large mixing bowl. Beat at high speed with an electric mixer until the mixture is light-colored and thick. Add the Apry or Grand Marnier and beat again.

In another bowl, beat the egg whites at medium speed until foamy. Increase the speed to high, and beat until soft peaks are formed.

Beat one-third of the whites into the apricot mixture to lighten it, then fold in the remaining whites and pour the mixture into the prepared soufflé dish.

Place the soufflé in the center of the oven and immediately turn the temperature down to 375 degrees. Bake for 30 to 35 minutes, until the soufflé is well risen and lightly browned on top (the center will not be firm).

Remove the soufflé from the oven; dust with confectioners' sugar placed in a sifter or sieve. Serve immediately with ginger-nutmeg sauce.

GINGER-NUTMEG SAUCE

4 ounces fresh ginger, peeled and thinly sliced

½ cup sugar

¾ cup water

2 whole nutmegs

2 cups light cream

For the sauce: Combine the ginger, sugar, and water in a saucepan. Bring to a simmer over medium heat and cook until the ginger slices are tender, about 15 minutes. Purée in a blender or food processor fitted with a steel blade, and strain through a fine sieve to remove the fibers. Set aside.

Crack the nutmegs by wrapping them in a tea towel and hitting them with a hammer a few times. Scald the cream by heating it to a boil over low heat. Add the nutmegs and allow

8 egg yolks (2 from the extra egg whites in the soufflé, plus 6 extras)

Pinch of salt

¼ teaspoon vanilla

them to steep until the cream cools, and then reheat the cream to a simmer.

In a saucepan, beat the egg yolks, salt, and vanilla. Slowly stir in the cream, pouring it through a sieve to remove the nutmeg.

Place the pan over low heat, and cook until the mixture thickens and coats the back of a spoon, stirring constantly. Do not let the mixture come to a boil, or the egg yolks will curdle. (This can be done in a double boiler.)

Remove the custard from the heat and whisk in the ginger syrup.

To serve: Poke a hole in the top of the soufflé and pour in half the sauce. Pass the remaining sauce separately.

Note: While the egg whites must be beaten at the last minute, the base and sauce can be prepared up to 3 hours in advance.

Fresh Fruit Soufflé

Serves 10

JEAN-LOUIS PALLADIN, Jean-Louis at Watergate This recipe is more a method than a specific dessert, since there is such a wide variety of fruits that work well. I've made it with strawberries, raspberries, papaya, and even pineapple. The only guideline is that the fruit be fresh, ripe, and intensely flavored. After that, it's up to you, and the results are always delicious.

5 egg whites

3 tablespoons sugar

6 egg yolks

1½ cups fruit purée, sweetened to taste (with not more than 4 tablespoons sugar)

Confectioners' sugar

2 to 4 tablespoons liqueur, chosen to complement the fruit

Butter 10 individual 5-ounce soufflé dishes. Place them in the freezer for 5 minutes, then butter again, sprinkle with sugar, and tap out the excess. Store the dishes in the freezer until you are ready to use them.

Beat the egg whites at medium speed until frothy, then increase the speed to high and beat them until stiff peaks form, adding 1 tablespoon of the sugar. Beat the yolks with the remaining 2 tablespoons of sugar until thick and light-colored. Add ½ cup of the fruit purée. Fold the whites and the yolk mixture together gently.

Fill each mold three-quarters full, and set them in a pan with 1 inch of hot water over low heat on top of the stove. After 1 minute, remove the molds from the water and place them directly on a rack in the center of a preheated 450-degree oven. Bake for 10 minutes, or until the soufflés are about 2 inches above the top of the mold. Sprinkle with powdered sugar and serve immediately.

While the soufflés are baking, warm the remaining purée and stir in the liqueur. Serve as a sauce.

Grilled Apples with Minted Lime Sorbet

Serves 6 to 8

ANNE GREER, Nana Grill at the Anatole Hotel   The combination of flavors, textures, and temperatures in this dish makes it seem far more complex than it is to make. The apples are marinated in red wine, which then becomes a syrup, with a little caramel as an additional sauce. While the aromatic smoky flavor of grilling the apples over mesquite adds to the dish, I've done it most successfully in my oven broiler. The apples remain crunchy, and their warmth is contrasted with the tangy coolness of the sorbet. The dessert is best when served after an entrée calling for red wine.

6 red Delicious or a combination of red and green Delicious apples, or any firm apples

1½ cups dry red wine

2 tablespoons honey

⅓ cup port

¾ cup sugar

2 tablespoons water

2 cups Minted Lime Sorbet (page 309)

Sprigs of fresh mint (optional)

Core the apples and cut each into 8 slices. Mix the red wine, honey, and port, and use the mixture to marinate the apples for 3 to 4 hours in the refrigerator, covered with plastic wrap.

When you are ready to cook, drain the apples and place them on a grill or in a preheated broiler until they are cooked but still slightly crisp. They should not be mushy. This takes 5 to 10 minutes, depending on the cooking method. Add ¼ cup of the sugar to the marinade, and boil until it is reduced by half and has a syrupy consistency.

Combine the remaining sugar and the water in a saucepan, and bring to a boil, cooking until the sugar caramelizes and is walnut brown. Remove it from the heat.

When you are ready to serve, place a layer of the wine reduction in the center of the dessert plate. Top with a fan of apple slices, and pour a little of the caramel sauce into the center. Top with ¼ cup of the sorbet, and garnish with a sprig of fresh mint, if desired.

Note: The sorbet can be made a few days in advance, and kept, with plastic wrap pressed directly on the surface, in the freezer.

Bread Pudding with Blueberry Sauce

Serves 12

BRADLEY OGDEN, The Campton Place Hotel   What is so exciting about this approach to bread pudding is its lightness and elegance. Rather than being broken into tiny pieces, the bread is treated almost like tea sandwiches, and baked in a light custard. The sauce is also a fresher interpretation of this American classic. Blueberries, rather than whiskey, add to the pudding without making it heavy, or heady.

BREAD PUDDING

1 loaf unsliced white bread, stale and old (1½ pounds)

8 tablespoons (1 stick) unsalted butter, melted

½ cup raisins soaked for 1 hour in bourbon or rum (optional)

4 eggs

3 egg yolks

3 cups milk

¾ cup heavy cream

¾ cup sugar

2 teaspoons vanilla

BLUEBERRY SAUCE

½ pound fresh or frozen blueberries

½ cup sugar

1 tablespoon freshly squeezed lemon juice

Cut the crusts off the bread, slice it thin, and butter each slice with a pastry brush. If the bread is not stale, cut off the crusts and place the slices in a 200-degree oven for 20 minutes so it will become dry before buttering. Place the slices overlapping in a 10-by-14-inch baking pan. If you are using the optional raisins, place them in the pan before putting in the bread.

Combine the eggs and egg yolks in a large mixing bowl, and beat them lightly. In a saucepan, heat the milk, cream, and sugar, and bring to a simmer, stirring to dissolve the sugar. Slowly add this to the egg mixture, whisking constantly. Add the vanilla, and strain the mixture over the bread slices. With a fork press down on the bread to ensure that it absorbs the custard.

Place the baking dish in a large pan with hot water about halfway up the sides, and bake in a 350-degree oven for 45 to 50 minutes, until the custard is brown on top. A knife or cake tester inserted in the center should come out clean. Remove and cool before serving with the sauce.

Combine the sauce ingredients in a small heavy saucepan, crushing some of the berries. If the berries are frozen, it will be easier to start the sauce if 1 tablespoon of water is added. Bring the berries to a boil over low heat, stirring frequently, and cook for 2 minutes. Cool before serving.

Blueberries in Crème Fraîche Tart

Serves 6 to 8

KILIAN WEIGAND, pastry chef at Seasons   The slightly tart flavor of crème fraîche seems to bring out the sweetness of the blueberries better than any sweeter custard. This dessert looks beautiful when served, with the layer of deep purple berries topped with the white cream, and it's extremely easy to make.

¾ pint fresh blueberries

3 eggs

½ cup sugar

1 teaspoon vanilla

1¼ cups crème fraîche

1 prebaked 9-inch pie crust

Wash the berries, picking them over to remove any stems. Lightly beat the eggs with the sugar and vanilla and add the mixture to the crème fraîche. Pour the mixture into a stainless-steel bowl and place over a saucepan of simmering water. Heat, stirring constantly, until the mixture is hot and starting to thicken.

Place the blueberries in the bottom of the prebaked pie shell and pour the warm custard over them. Place in the center of a preheated 350-degree oven and bake for 10 minutes, or until the custard is set. Chill well before serving.

Note: Crème fraîche is now commercially available, but if you have trouble finding it, add 1 tablespoon of buttermilk to 1 cup heavy cream and allow it to sit at room temperature for a few hours, or until thickened.

Raspberry-Blueberry Tart with Raspberry and Chocolate Sauces

Serves 8

JACKIE ETCHEBER, Jackie's   Fruit tarts are easy to make, and just arranging the fruit in concentric circles on the top makes them look dramatic and you look like a professional pastry chef. What adds to this version is the nuts in the crust and sprinkled over the filling. The sauces make it richer, and chocolate is the perfect flavor foil to the fruit. Sliced strawberries can be used in addition to or in place of one of the other berries.

For tart shell:

4 tablespoons unsalted butter

6 tablespoons sugar

3 tablespoons ground blanched almonds

1 cup all-purpose flour

Pinch of salt

1 egg, lightly beaten

Pastry cream:

1 package gelatin

½ cup cold water

1 cup milk

½ teaspoon vanilla

3 egg yolks

⅓ cup sugar

2 tablespoons flour

Assembly:

¼ pound hazelnuts, ground

1 pint raspberries

1 pint blueberries

CHOCOLATE SAUCE

9 ounces good-quality semisweet chocolate

2½ tablespoons unsalted butter

1 cup milk

3 tablespoons heavy cream

¼ cup sugar

RASPBERRY SAUCE

1 pound frozen raspberries

B eat the butter, sugar, and almonds together until light and fluffy. Add the flour and salt, making fine crumbs, and then add the egg, combining by hand to form a ball. Wrap in plastic and refrigerate, preferably overnight. Roll the dough into a circle and pat well into a 10-inch false-bottom tart pan. Bake at 425 degrees in a preheated oven for 15 minutes, until brown and crisp.

For the pastry cream: In a small bowl, sprinkle the gelatin over ½ cup of cold water to soften, and set aside.

In a large saucepan, bring the milk to a boil with the vanilla over low heat. In a mixing bowl, beat the egg yolks with the sugar until thick and lemon-colored. Add the flour and beat until well combined. Gradually pour in the heated milk, whisking constantly. Then place the mixture in the saucepan and cook over very low heat until the custard thickens and coats the back of a wooden spoon. This can be done in a double boiler. Make sure the custard does not come to a boil or the egg yolks will curdle. Add the gelatin to the hot mixture and stir until dissolved.

To assemble, spread the pastry cream evenly on the tart shell and sprinkle with the hazelnuts. Starting from the outside, arrange the berries in concentric circles, alternating the fruits.

Serve with the Chocolate Sauce on one side of the dish and the Raspberry Sauce on the other.

Melt the chocolate with the butter in the top of a double boiler over hot water or in a bowl in a 200-degree oven. Beat until smooth and glossy. Bring the milk and cream to a boil with the sugar, stirring to dissolve the sugar. Beat the milk mixture into the chocolate mixture. Set the sauce aside until it reaches room temperature.

Defrost the berries, purée in a blender or food processor fitted with a steel blade, strain to remove the seeds, and refrigerate.

Note: The pastry cream, sauces, and crust can be prepared a day in advance, but the tart should not be assembled more than a few hours in advance or the crust will become soggy.

Grapefruit Tart

Serves 6 to 8

PATRICK O'CONNELL, The Inn at Little Washington   After eating this light and luscious filling, set off by the crunchiness of the nut crust, I can't imagine why grapefruit has been a virtually ignored member of the citrus family when it comes to desserts. The contrast of the velvety and slightly tart grapefruit custard with the earthy nut crust is delicious, and very easy to make.

Crust:

2½ cups ground pecans (about ¾ pounds)

⅓ cup sugar

¼ cup unsalted butter, melted

Filling:

4 tablespoons unsalted butter

¼ cup heavy cream

¾ cup sugar

⅔ cup freshly squeezed grapefruit juice

½ cup freshly squeezed orange juice

4 eggs, lightly beaten

Grated rind of 1 grapefruit

2 teaspoons gelatin

Whipped cream

Mix the pecans, ⅓ cup sugar, and butter together and pat into a 9-inch pie shell. Chill for 30 minutes in the refrigerator, and then bake at 375 degrees for 10 minutes. Set aside to cool.

Melt the butter with the cream in a heavy 2-quart saucepan. Add the sugar, and stir until dissolved. Add ½ cup of the grapefruit juice, the orange juice, the eggs, and the grapefruit rind. Sprinkle the gelatin over the remaining grapefruit juice to soften, and set aside. Cook the cream-citrus mixture over low heat, stirring constantly, until it thickens and lightly coats the back of a spoon. Do not allow it to come to a boil or the eggs will curdle. Add the gelatin mixture and stir until the gelatin is dissolved.

Pour the custard into the pie shell and chill until it is firm and set. Decorate with whipped cream.

Kiwi Tart

Serves 6 to 8

BRUCE LEFAVOUR, Rose et LeFavour   Kiwi tarts are beautiful, with the green fruit dotted with tiny black seeds arranged around the top. This one is even more special, since the kiwis are marinated in aquavit (basically a vodka flavored with caraway seeds), which seems to bring out their flavor best, and sparkled with ginger in a number of forms. Ginger marmalade protects the crust from becoming soggy, while pale pink pickled ginger is sprinkled over the top, on which kiwis alternate with strawberries.

6 large kiwis

Salt

3 ounces dark aquavit

3 large strawberries, sliced

6 tablespoons ginger marmalade

1 prebaked 9-inch pie shell or tart shell

¾ cup heavy cream

2 tablespoons shredded pickled ginger (available in Oriental markets) for garnish

Coarse sugar for garnish

Peel the kiwis, slice them across the grain into ¼-inch slices, and salt them very lightly. Place the slices in a stainless-steel bowl with the aquavit to marinate for 10 minutes. Drain and reserve the liquor.

Slice each strawberry into 4 slices lengthwise and set aside.

Heat the ginger marmalade slowly in a small heavy saucepan, and push it through a sieve. When it is still warm, spread it over the inside of the pie shell. Set the shell aside to cool completely, while you whip the cream stiff. Add 3 tablespoons of the reserved aquavit to the whipped cream and beat again.

To assemble: Spread the whipped cream in the shell. Starting on the outside, arrange the kiwis in circles with the slices overlapping until the entire top of the tart is filled in. Place a strawberry slice in the center, and intersperse the other strawberries over the kiwis. Just before serving, sprinkle the top with the ginger and sugar.

Apple Pandowdy

Serves 4

LAWRENCE FORGIONE, An American Place   This dish, mentioned by Nathaniel Hawthorne more than a century ago, probably got its name from its "dowdy" or unstylish appearance. But Forgione's version hardly fits that image. Baked in individual soufflé molds, the apples are highly spiced and remain crisp, while the bread is crusty and a perfect foil. Forgione serves the dessert with a boat of pouring cream (very slightly whipped cream), and this is the final enhancement.

8 slices good-quality white bread

8 tablespoons (1 stick) unsalted butter, softened at room temperature

Sugar

3 baking apples such as McIntosh or Jonathan, peeled, cored, and sliced

3 tablespoons molasses

½ teaspoon ground cinnamon

¼ teaspoon ground nutmeg

2 tablespoons dark rum

⅓ cup light-brown sugar

2 tablespoons lemon juice

1 tablespoon vanilla

Cut the slices of bread into rounds to fit into individual (1-cup) soufflé dishes. Spread with 4 tablespoons of the butter, and sprinkle with a little sugar.

Cut the remaining butter into small bits, and toss with the remaining ingredients in a bowl, evenly distributing the sugar and spices.

Place one slice of bread, buttered side down, in each of the dishes. Spoon in the apple mixture to fill each dish to ½ inch from the top. Place the second slice of buttered bread, buttered side up, on top.

Place the dishes in a baking pan, and pour hot water halfway up the sides. Bake in a 375-degree oven for 25 to 30 minutes, until the tops are buttery golden brown.

Dessert Strudel

Enough for 2 strudels, each serving 12

BARRY WINE, The Quilted Giraffe   Wine's filling, with prunes steeped in red wine, ginger, and tea forming the binding for apples, pears, and candied lemon peel, is the best I've ever eaten, and makes you think of strudel as a sophisticated dessert rather than what grandma made. Phyllo dough in the frozen-food section of supermarkets makes assembling this dessert a matter of minutes.

It's worth the effort to make the candied lemon peel, since commercially prepared peels are hard and do not blend with the flavor of the other fruits.

STRUDEL FILLING

1 pound pitted dried prunes

2 cups Zinfandel

1½ cups sugar

2 tablespoons fresh ginger, finely minced

3 tea bags

3 lemons

4 Granny Smith apples

2 Bosc pears

¼ cup heavy cream

¼ cup Armagnac

¼ cup Mirabelle

Pinch of salt

Whipped cream (optional)

Soak the prunes for 2 hours in warm water to soften, drain them, and place in a saucepan with the wine, sugar, and ginger. Bring the mixture to a boil over medium heat and simmer for 1 hour, stirring frequently especially toward the end of the cooking time. Turn off the heat, drop the tea bags into the saucepan, and allow them to steep for 45 minutes. Remove the tea bags and purée the mixture in a blender or food processor fitted with a steel blade.

While the prunes are cooking, prepare the candied lemon peel. Cut the entire skin, yellow zest and white pith away from 3 lemons. If you want to save the lemon juice for another use, squeeze the lemons beforehand, and then pull out the membrane and all you will have left is the skin.

Cut the skin into fine slices, and place them in a pot of cold water. Bring to a boil, strain off the water, and add fresh cold water. Repeat this process 3 times in all, to remove all the bitterness from the lemon.

Sprinkle the lemons generously with sugar, and place them on a low flame to cook for 20 to 30 minutes, or until tender. You will not need any additional water, since water is retained in the peel from the boilings. Stir frequently.

Chop the lemon peel fine, and add ½ cup to the prune mixture. Peel the apples and pears, and cut them into small dice. Fold into the purée, along with the cream, liquors, and a pinch of salt.

Fill the strudels (see method below), and bake. The strudels are best served at room temperature on the day they are made, or they can be made up to 2 days in advance and reheated in a 325-degree oven for 15 minutes, or until warm. Serve with whipped cream, if desired.

PREPARING AND BAKING PHYLLO-DOUGH STRUDELS

1 pound phyllo dough

1½ pounds unsalted butter, melted

1 pound walnuts

3 cups ground vanilla cookie crumbs

The two pitfalls in making strudel are not properly defrosting the phyllo dough for at least 8 hours, and tearing the sheets as you separate them. With this recipe, the former is an easy task, and lifting individual sheets need not be done. Remember when working with phyllo dough always to cover the dough not being used with a damp towel, since it can dry out completely in the time it takes to assemble the first strudel.

Place the walnuts on a baking sheet in a 350-degree oven and toast them for 7 to 10 minutes, until lightly brown. Cool them, and chop them fine in a blender or food processor fitted with a steel blade. Mix the nuts with the cookie crumbs, ground from commercially packaged cookies, and set the mixture aside in a bowl.

Unfold the phyllo dough and divide it into two ½-pound units, setting one aside. Cover it with a damp towel. Place a sheet of waxed paper under the other unit of dough, and then fold the dough in half vertically with the fold on the right. Starting with the bottom sheet, which will then be on top, fold back a sheet, as if you were turning the pages of a book, brush with melted butter, and sprinkle with the nut-and-cookie-crumb mixture. Butter each sheet and sprinkle the nut–crumb mixture on every third or fourth sheet. When you get to the top sheet, give the phyllo a 180-degree turn, so the untreated sheets are again on your right. Place a piece of waxed paper on the side already coated with butter, so the untreated sheets will not stick to it, and repeat the process. Sprinkle crumbs on those sheets where crumbs are evident on the treated side.

Place the strudel filling across the bottom of the dough, tuck in the two ends, and roll, using the waxed paper underneath the strudel as a guide. Place seam side down on a jelly-roll pan or baking pan with sides. Do not use a cookie sheet, because the butter seeps out during baking and will cause spills in the oven.

Brush the top with more butter, and slice through the dough on the diagonal to create 12 slices. Brush again with butter, and set aside. Repeat with the second half of the dough.

Bake the strudels at 350 degrees for 20 minutes, brush with more butter, and reduce the oven temperature to 300 degrees. Bake for 1 hour, brushing with butter a few times, until the filling is cooked and the strudels are golden brown. Allow them to cool to room temperature before removing from the pan.

Note: The prunes and wine can be cooked a day in advance and kept, covered with plastic wrap, in the refrigerator. The lemon peel can be done a few days in advance. The apples and pears should not be added until just prior to baking.

Warm Mixed Berry Compote

Serves 6 to 8

JEREMIAH TOWER, Santa Fe Bar and Grill   This is my ideal ice-cream sundae. The warmed berries retain their own special character, and there's an incredible freshness along with the sweetness of the fruit. Tower serves it over vanilla ice cream, but I've been happier with fruit-flavored ice creams, such as Barbara Tropp's Meyer Lemon Ice Cream (page 315).

1 cup fresh strawberries
1 cup fresh blueberries
1 cup fresh raspberries
½ cup sugar
½ cup water
4 tablespoons butter
Vanilla ice cream

Wash all the berries, keeping them in separate dishes. Slice the strawberries if large.

In a 2-quart heavy saucepan, bring the sugar and water to a boil over high heat, then lower the heat to a simmer for 10 minutes. Add the strawberries and blueberries to the pan, and cook for 2 minutes, stirring gently a few times. Then add the raspberries and butter, heating just until the butter melts.

To serve, spoon onto a flat plate and place a scoop of ice cream in the center.

Orange Cheesecake with Candied Oranges

Serves 10 to 12

JAMES HALLER, The Blue Strawbery   This cheesecake is easy to make, and the intense orange flavor from the variety of ways orange is added to the batter and with candied slices makes it one of my favorite cheesecakes. It's quite rich, so a small slice is all you need, and arranging the orange slices on top makes it elegant.

1 box vanilla cookies (8 ounces)

8 tablespoons (1 stick) unsalted butter

3 packages cream cheese, softened at room temperature (8 ounces each)

6 eggs

1 cup frozen orange-juice concentrate, defrosted

½ cup Cointreau, or any light orange liqueur

¼ cup honey

4 tablespoons flour

2 tablespoons finely grated orange rind

Candied orange slices (see recipe below)

CANDIED ORANGE SLICES

2 bright seedless oranges, such as Valencia or Seville

1 cup Cointreau

1 cup sugar

Crush the cookies in a food processor fitted with a steel blade, and then mix with the melted butter. Press the crumbs to the bottom and sides of a buttered 10- or 12-inch springform pan, and refrigerate while preparing the filling.

In a large mixing bowl or a food processor fitted with a steel blade, beat the cream cheese until light and fluffy. Add the eggs, one by one, and continue to beat well until the eggs are incorporated and the mixture is light. Add the next five ingredients, and beat well.

Pour the mixture into the crumb crust, and place it in a 400-degree oven. After 15 minutes, reduce the heat to 225 degrees and bake for another 1½ hours, or until a knife inserted in the center comes out clean. Top with the orange slices and chill well, preferably overnight. Allow to sit at room temperature for 30 minutes before serving.

Slice the oranges as thin as possible, about ¼ inch, and set them aside. In a heavy 1-quart saucepan, heat the Cointreau and sugar, and boil until the volume is reduced by two-thirds and the mixture has a syrupy consistency. Add the orange slices and simmer them in the syrup over low heat until they soften, about 15 minutes. Stir gently so they do not break apart. Don't worry if at first they are not covered in syrup, since they will give off juices.

Note: The cake can be made up to 2 days in advance and kept, covered with plastic wrap, in the refrigerator.

Hazelnut Cheesecake

Serves 10

PATRICK O'CONNELL, The Inn at Little Washington   While there is no question that any cake made with cream cheese is rich, this one tastes lighter than most since there is no crust and the filling calls for no flour. The flavor of the hazelnuts complements that of the cheese, and the cake tastes like a rich, baked mousse. It's best if taken from the refrigerator at least 1 hour before serving.

1 cup hazelnuts

2 pounds cream cheese, softened at room temperature (4 eight-ounce packages)

1¾ cups sugar

4 eggs

½ teaspoon grated lemon rind

Spread the nuts on a baking sheet and toast in a 350-degree oven for 10 minutes, or until lightly browned. Rub the skins off and grind the nuts coarse in a food processor fitted with a steel blade or in a nut chopper.

In a mixer, beat the cheese until light and fluffy. Add the sugar and continue to beat. Add the eggs, one at a time, beating well after each addition. Fold in the nuts and lemon rind, and pour the batter into a buttered 10-inch springform pan.

Set the pan in a baking dish and pour 1½ inches of hot water into the dish. Bake in a 350-degree oven for 1½ hours, or until a cake tester comes out clean. Turn off the oven, leave the oven door open 2 inches, and allow the cake to sit in the oven for 1 hour. The top will be golden brown and dry.

Note: The cake can be made up to 2 days in advance and kept, tightly covered with plastic wrap, in the refrigerator.

Hazelnut Torte

Serves 10 to 12

ROBERT ROSELLINI, Rosellini's Other Place   This rich torte comes from the European buttercream tradition, and the combination of chocolate and hazelnuts flavors both the densely textured génoise layers and the rich buttercream. Rosellini further enriches the torte with a topping of pure chocolate, but I've sometimes skipped this step for the sake of time and calories without detracting from the finished product.

For the génoise:

6 eggs, at room temperature

1 cup sugar

½ cup sifted flour

½ cup cocoa

½ cup finely chopped hazelnuts

½ cup clarified butter, cooled

For the buttercream:

1⅓ cups sugar

⅔ cup water

8 egg yolks

1 pound unsalted butter, at room temperature

¼ pound semisweet chocolate, melted over hot water and cooled

½ cup sugar

⅓ cup hazelnuts, toasted for 10 minutes in a 350-degree oven

CHOCOLATE ICING

½ pound semisweet chocolate, melted over hot water and cooled

1 to 2 tablespoons tasteless vegetable oil

I n a mixer or food processor fitted with a steel blade, beat the eggs and sugar until thick and lemon-colored. Sift the flour with the cocoa and fold into the eggs, one-third at a time. Fold in the hazelnuts and butter, and pour the batter into a greased and floured 10-inch torte pan. Bake in the middle of a 350-degree oven for 30 to 35 minutes, until the cake springs back when lightly touched in the center. Loosen the edges with a knife, and unmold onto a rack. When the cake has cooled, cut it into 3 layers and set aside.

Boil the sugar and water until a soft ball forms when a bit of the syrup is dropped into a cup of ice water (238 degrees on a candy thermometer). While the syrup is boiling, beat the egg yolks with an electric mixer or in the bowl of a food processor fitted with a steel blade until they are thick and lemon-colored. Gradually add the syrup in a thin stream, and continue to beat until the mixture has cooled. Gradually add the butter, a few tablespoons at a time, and beat until thick. Fold in the chocolate, and chill in the refrigerator while preparing a praline to add to the buttercream.

In a small saucepan, heat the ½ cup sugar over medium heat until it caramelizes and turns golden brown. Be careful it does not burn. Pour onto a greased cookie sheet and chill until it hardens. Break into small pieces and grind with the toasted hazelnuts in the bowl of a food processor fitted with a steel blade until they form a fine powder. Fold into the buttercream, beating well. Chill the frosting to spreading consistency.

Fill the cake layers with the buttercream, and spread it on the sides and top of the cake, smoothing with a spatula. Decorate with a few toasted hazelnuts or chocolate icing.

Mix the chocolate with enough oil to give it a pourable consistency. Pour onto the center of the cake and allow it to drip over the sides. Garnish with nuts and chill.

Note: The torte can be made a day in advance, and kept tightly covered with plastic wrap in the refrigerator. If you put toothpicks into the top of the cake the plastic will not adhere to the buttercream topping. It should sit at room temperature for 45 minutes before serving to soften the buttercream.

Bourbon Pecan Torte

Serves 6 to 8

PATRICK O'CONNELL, The Inn at Little Washington   This torte has a wonderful combination of flavors and textures, with a layer of chocolate lining the bottom of the crust and then a cream-based filling loaded with crunchy pecans and laced with bourbon. It's a lighter version of pecan pie in some respects, and an alternative to the classic Derby pie of Kentucky.

1½ cups sugar

⅓ cup water

1 cup heavy cream

1 cup pecans

¼ cup bourbon

¼ cup melted butter

1 egg yolk

1 egg

4 ounces bittersweet chocolate, melted

1 prebaked tart shell or pie shell (9 or 10 inches)

In a small heavy-bottomed saucepan, bring the sugar and water to a boil and cook over medium heat until golden brown and caramelized. Take off the heat and add the cream little by little with a long-handled wooden spoon, turning the pot away from you since the cream will bubble furiously at first. Cook over low heat for 3 minutes, stirring to dissolve any remaining lumps of caramel. Strain the mixture through a sieve, and allow it to cool for 15 minutes.

Place the pecans on a cookie sheet and toast in a 350-degree oven for 5 to 7 minutes, or until lightly brown. Set aside.

Beat the bourbon, butter, egg yolk, and egg into the cooled caramel mixture, and whisk until smooth. Stir in the pecans.

Spread the melted chocolate in the bottom of the pie shell, and pour the filling over it. Bake at 400 degrees in the center of a preheated oven for 15 minutes, then reduce the heat to 350 degrees and continue to bake for an additional 15 minutes. Serve at room temperature.

Sweet-Potato Pecan Pie

Serves 6 to 8

PAUL PRUDHOMME, K-Paul's Louisiana Kitchen   The flaky crust holds a creamy sweet-potato filling, and the pecans and their syrup topping it add yet another texture to this delicious pie. The sweet potato holds a place in Cajun cooking as well as the cooking of other areas of the South, and this recipe is one of my favorites to end any hearty dinner. The combination of tastes tempting the palate is glorious. While I find it needs no augmentation, Prudhomme serves it with a dollop of crème chantilly.

Dough:

3 tablespoons unsalted butter, at room temperature

2 tablespoons sugar

¼ teaspoon salt

½ large egg, beaten until frothy (reserve other half for filling)

2 tablespoons milk

1 cup flour

Filling:

2 or 3 large sweet potatoes, for 1 cup pulp

¼ cup packed light-brown sugar

2 tablespoons sugar

½ egg (reserved from dough)

1 tablespoon heavy cream

1 tablespoon unsalted butter, at room temperature

1 tablespoon vanilla extract

¼ teaspoon salt

¼ teaspoon ground cinnamon

⅛ teaspoon ground allspice

⅛ teaspoon ground nutmeg

Pecan pie syrup:

¾ cup sugar

¾ cup dark corn syrup

2 eggs

1½ tablespoons unsalted butter, melted

2 teaspoons vanilla extract

Pinch of salt

Pinch of ground cinnamon

¾ cup pecan pieces or halves

For the dough: Place the softened butter, sugar, and salt in the bowl of an electric mixer or a food processor fitted with a steel blade. Beat until light and fluffy, then add the egg and beat another 30 seconds. Add the milk and beat for an additional minute. Then add the flour and beat until just blended, since overmixing will result in a tough dough. Shape the dough into a ball, dust it with flour, and wrap it in plastic. Refrigerate for at least 1 hour, and then roll the dough into a 12-inch circle on a lightly floured surface. Place the dough in a greased and floured 8-inch round cake pan, press firmly in place, trim the edges, and refrigerate 15 minutes.

For the sweet-potato filling: Bake the sweet potatoes in a 400-degree oven for 45 minutes to 1 hour, or until very soft. Peel them when cool enough to handle. There should be 1 cup of pulp. Combine all the filling ingredients, and beat until smooth with a mixer or in the bowl of a food processor fitted with a steel blade. Set aside.

For the syrup: Combine all ingredients except the pecans and beat until the syrup is opaque, about 1 minute. Stir in the pecans.

To assemble: Spoon the filling into the pie shell and pour the syrup on top. Bake at 325 degrees for 1 hour and 45 minutes, or until a cake tester inserted in the center comes out clean.

Note: The pie is best the day it is made, and if it is served within 24 hours, Prudhomme says it need not be refrigerated.

Ginger Spice Cake with Orange Curd

Serves 10 to 12

BRADLEY OGDEN, The Campton Place Hotel If you have fond memories from childhood of gingerbread, you'll love this cake as much as I do. It's a highly spiced gingerbread, with a slight undertaste of orange that ties to the sauce, also light since it contains no flour. While you can cut the cake in the kitchen and serve it with a band of sauce on top of each piece, what I do is play on its old-fashioned nature and dust the top of the whole cake with powdered sugar over a paper pattern, and pass the sauce separately.

GINGER SPICE CAKE

1 cup dark molasses

½ cup (1 stick) unsalted butter

½ cup dark-brown sugar, packed

2¾ cups cake flour

1 tablespoon ground ginger

½ teaspoon ground cinnamon

½ teaspoon ground nutmeg

½ teaspoon ground cloves

1 teaspoon salt

1 teaspoon baking soda

1 cup buttermilk

¼ cup orange juice, freshly squeezed

2 eggs, slightly beaten

ORANGE CURD

2 oranges

1 cup sugar

4 tablespoons unsalted butter

2 egg yolks

2 eggs

In a small heavy saucepan, mix the molasses, butter, and brown sugar, and heat slowly, stirring occasionally, until the butter is melted and the mixture is smooth. Set aside to cool. Sift the dry ingredients together and set them aside in a large mixing bowl.

When the mixture is cool, stir it into the dry ingredients and beat well. Then beat in the buttermilk, orange juice, and eggs.

Butter and flour a 10-inch round cake pan with high sides, at least 2 inches, or the cake can be baked in a buttered and floured rectangular baking pan, 9 by 12 inches.

Bake at 350 degrees in the middle of the preheated oven for 35 to 40 minutes, or until a cake tester inserted in the center comes out clean. Cool in the pan on a rack and then remove the cake. Store tightly covered, and serve with Orange Curd, either on top or passed separately.

With a zester, vegetable peeler, or sharp knife, remove the orange zest from the oranges, being careful not to cut into the white pith, and cut the zest into a fine julienne. Then juice the oranges (you should have about ¾ cup of juice), and set the juice aside.

In a bowl, beat the sugar and butter until light and fluffy. Add the egg yolks, eggs, and orange juice, beating well. This can also be done in a food processor fitted with a steel blade.

Place the mixture in the top of a double boiler over simmering water, or in a small heavy saucepan. Heat slowly, stirring constantly, until the butter melts and the curd thickens. Be careful not to let the mixture come to a boil, or the eggs will curdle.

Place a few dabs of butter on the surface of the sauce so a skin will not form, and cool the sauce to room temperature. Refrigerate the sauce, if not to be served immediately.

Note: Both the cake and Orange Curd can be made a day in advance. The cake should be kept tightly covered with plastic wrap at room temperature, and the sauce should be refrigerated, with wax paper pressed directly onto the surface so no skin will form.

Crème Brulée Tart

Serves 6

JONATHAN WAXMAN, Jams   The creamy crème brulée, topped with its crunchy caramelized brown-sugar crust, is given a dramatic presentation in this puff-pastry shell. I use frozen puff pastry right from the supermarket, or many bakeries now sell it by the pound. What I like about preparing crème brulée this way is that it becomes a more complex dessert rather than a dressed-up custard, and it looks so attractive coming to the table.

2½ cups heavy cream

1 piece of vanilla bean, split (1 inch), or 1 teaspoon vanilla extract

6 egg yolks

½ cup granulated sugar

¼ pound puff pastry

½ cup dark-brown sugar

In a 1-quart saucepan, bring the cream and vanilla bean or extract to a boil. Turn off the heat and allow the vanilla bean to steep for 10 minutes.

In a mixing bowl, combine the egg yolks and sugar, and beat until thick and lemon-colored. Slowly add the warm cream mixture, straining out the vanilla bean if used. Pour the mixture into a buttered 6-cup soufflé dish, and set it in a baking pan, pouring hot water halfway up the sides. Bake in a 375-degree oven for 30 to 45 minutes, or until the top is brown and a knife inserted in the center comes out clean.

Roll out the puff pastry to ¼-inch thickness and place in a 9-inch false-bottom tart pan. Press the dough into place and bake in a 375-degree oven until golden brown, about 30 minutes.

Unmold the crème brulée into the shell by inverting the soufflé dish, and carefully spread to smooth and even the filling. Sift the brown sugar evenly over the top and place the tart in a broiler, about 6 inches from the heat, until the sugar is caramelized and bubbling. Carefully remove the tart from the pan and serve immediately.

Note: The pastry shell can be prepared up to 6 hours in advance and kept at room temperature, and the custard can be made a day in advance and refrigerated; bring it to room temperature before unmolding. The final assembly and browning should be done at the last minute.

INDEX

Breast of Duck with Savory
Olive Tart, 275
Brioches, 292–293
broccoli, angel-hair pasta with
goat cheese and, 201
broccoli, with fried corncakes
and duck breasts in Pinot
Noir sauce, 276–277
broccoli rabe, *see* Rabes
broiled foods, 210
Broiled Salmon with Sorrel,
217
Fresh Broiled Cod with
Eggplant Caviar, 212–213
Rockfish with Escargots, 213
Rockfish with Prawns, 214
Brook Trout Pan-Fried with
Black Walnuts, 269
Budweiser Beer Ice, 311
buffalo, charred, chili corn sauce
for, 223
Burgundy sauerkraut, roast pork
with cabbage, potatoes and,
234
Burros, Marian, 114
butter, to make, 297
butter cream, chocolate, 327
butter cream, hazelnut, 347
Buttered Scallions, 221
butters, flavored, 297
Curried Pear Butter, 297
Orange Beurre Blanc, shrimp
in tequila with, 138
Sweet Curry Butter, 297
tomato, crabcakes with, 135

cabbage:
Ladies', grilled rib steak with,
220–221
lobster sausage with, 130–131
roast pork with potatoes,
Burgundy sauerkraut and,
234
Caiyo, Robert, 32
California, food in:
pizzas, 193
salads, 176
Campton Place Hotel, San
Francisco, 55–57
candied lemon peel, loin of veal
roasted with garlic and, 242
candied oranges, orange
cheesecake with, 345
candy, pumpkin, 306
Cape Scallops with Garlic and
Herbs, 262
Caplan, Frieda, 118
Caramel Ice Cream, 316

caramel-pumpkin ice cream,
316–317
cassis, pears poached in red wine
and, 330
caviar:
Caviar Beggar's Purses, 125
fried plantains and, 126
golden, pizza with smoked
salmon and, 209
oysters with, 142
Terrine of America's Three
Smoked Fish, 126–127
Chambrette, Ferdinand, 106
Champagne sabayon, Comice
pear with, 331
chanterelles, wild, lamb pasta
with, 205
Charley's 517, Houston, Texas,
21–23
cheese:
with crabmeat and tomatoes
on corn capellini, 200–201
goat, angel-hair pasta with
broccoli and, 201
Goat-Cheese Salad with
Arugula and Radicchio, 183
Grilled Sonoma Goat Cheese
in Vine Leaves, 157
Raclette Gratin with Radicchio
Salad, 181
sautéed, and asparagus with
grapes and green
peppercorns, 184
and spinach breadsticks, 292
wines with, 122
cheesecake:
hazelnut, 346
orange, with candied oranges,
345
with Smoked Salmon, 128
chefs:
and advance preparation, 119
American, 11
chervil, foie de canard with
endive and, 146
chestnuts, roasted, grilled
bluefish fillet with fennel
and, 211
Chicago, Ill., Jackie's, 17–19
chicken:
boning of, 254
Breast of Chicken in Lemon
Sauce, 274
Chicken Breast with Coconut,
249
Chicken Breast with Sweet
Garlic Sauce and Garlic
Flan, 271

chicken *(cont'd)*
Chinese Noodle Soup with
Toasted Almonds and
Deep-Fried Ginger, 171
green-chili, 144
grilled, with garlic and Italian
parsley, 227
grilled, salad of, 191
Grilled Chinese Chicken
Wings with Orange Peel
and Garlic, 151
medallions of, Boston lettuce
custard with prosciutto,
sweetbreads and, 252–253
Sauté, 272
and Seafood Jambalaya,
250–251
Stir-Fry with Raisins and
Sambuca Mayonnaise, 273
warm, and papaya salad, 190
wine with, 122
Child, Julia, 10, 92
chili, cornbread with, 296
Chili Corn Sauce for Charred
Buffalo, 223
chilies, *see* jalapeno chilies
China Moon, San Francisco,
99–102
Chinese Crab, 258
Chinese Duck with Endive and
Lime Juice, 243
Chinese eggplant, grilled, with
spicy Szechwan peanut
sauce, 156–157
Chinese greens, stir-fried with
wild rice, 299
Chinese Noodle Soup with
Toasted Almonds and
Deep-Fried Ginger, 171
Chinois on Main, Santa Monica,
73–75
chive cream sauce, rack of lamb
with, 231
chocolate:
bittersweet, pâté with Grand
Marnier sauce, 322–323
consumption of, 320
devil's food cake, 328
terrine, with two sauces, 321
white, *see* white chocolate
Chocolate Ice Cream with
Brandied Raisins, 319
chocolate ice cream, with
dark-chocolate sauce, 31
chocolate icing, for hazelnut
torte, 347
Chocolate Marquise Torte,
327